ANTARCTIC SCIENCE

For over 200 hundred years ships have been crucial for Antarctic exploration and science. Here the British ship RRS Bransfield *sails along the Antarctic Peninsula.*

ANTARCTIC SCIENCE

Edited by

DWH Walton

with contributions by
CSM Doake, JR Dudeney,
I Everson, R M Laws FRS
and DWH Walton,
British Antarctic Survey, Cambridge,
and with an introduction by
Sir Vivian Fuchs FRS

*The right of the
University of Cambridge
to print and sell
all manner of books
was granted by
Henry VIII in 1534.
The University has printed
and published continuously
since 1584.*

CAMBRIDGE UNIVERSITY PRESS
Cambridge
London   New York   New Rochelle
Melbourne   Sydney

Published by the Press Syndicate of the University of Cambridge
The Pitt Building, Trumpington Street, Cambridge CB2 1RP
32 East 57th Street, New York, NY 10022, USA
10 Stamford Road, Oakleigh, Melbourne 3166, Australia

First published 1987

Printed in Great Britain by W.S. Cowell Ltd, Ipswich

Library of Congress cataloguing in publication data

Antarctic science.
Bibliography
Includes index
1. Antarctic regions – Discovery and exploration.
I. Walton, D.W.H. II. Doake, C.S.M.
G860.A555 1986 919.8'904 86–6154

British Library cataloguing in publication data

Antarctic science.
1. Antarctic regions
I. Walton, D.W.H.   II. Doake, C.S.M.
998'.9   G860

ISBN 0 521 26233 X

Contents

*Vehicles, plastered with drift snow, contrast sharply with the
natural beauty of an Antarctic sunset.*

Preface

Antarctica is both a continent and an ocean. The continent, comprising almost 10% of the land surface of the globe, is inextricably linked to the vast extent of the Southern Ocean surrounding it. Remote from all centres of population and with no indigenous people it has only spasmodically attracted public attention. Explorers and scientists recognised its value as early as the eighteenth century, although any sustained degree of major international interest in the area is largely a twentieth-century phenomenon.

The present upsurge of public interest is linked to expectations that rich and untapped resources exist in the region. These riches are both living – in the form of krill and fish – and mineral – in the form of oil, gas and metallic ores. Many of the present economic assumptions concerning these are based on little or no data but make convincing political statements. Why then, after more than 25 years of research, are the data necessary for considered and accurate judgements lacking? Have any substantial contributions to science been made by research in Antarctica?

This book is an attempt to put Antarctic science in a more general perspective. The authors have considered the breadth of studies in their respective subjects and chosen from amongst them those that appear to have been the most important scientific developments. The choice is necessarily subjective yet the material to choose from is truly international. Within the framework of the Antarctic Treaty, the last 25 years have seen a growth in the range and complexity of science that would gladden the hearts of all those early Antarctic scientists. A major feature of this has been the exceptional degree of international collaboration in programmes and a willingness to help others. This has transcended the political difficulties that have characterised world history during the period.

Since the Antarctic Treaty was ratified in 1961, Antarctica has been a continent for science and international accord. With the approach of 1991, when the terms of the Antarctic Treaty may be reviewed, it is appropriate that we assess scientific progress so far and suggest profitable lines for future research to follow. Antarctic science shows great vigour and great promise. The next 25 years seem likely to be even more productive than the last.

D.W.H. Walton
June 1986

*Edmund Hillary, Vivian Fuchs and Admiral George Dufek
meeting outside Amundsen – Scott Station at the South Pole
during the Trans-Antarctic Expedition, which made the first
overland crossing of the continent (a journey of 2,158 miles
in 99 days).*

Introduction

Throughout the ages Man's curiosity, sometimes reinforced by religious zeal or commercial ambition, has led him to probe the unknown regions of the world. Such ventures tended to be inspired by adventurers; only when they had reported the discovery of new lands and peoples did governments take an interest. It is therefore scarcely surprising that the vast, barren and inhospitable Antarctic continent remained largely unexplored until the first years of this century.

The early sporadic essays provided no scientific continuity; indeed science was a very minor objective for some of them. Lieutenant Adrien de Gerlache, a Belgian naval officer, led the first party ever to winter within the Antarctic Circle – albeit involuntarily – when his ship, the *Belgica* was trapped in the ice in 1898. De Gerlache was sympathetic to scientists, but they were not encouraged to linger over their work. However, landings were made along the coast when possible, and their geologist gave a delightful account of the occasion when the Leader himself rowed them ashore:

A few strokes of the oars brought us to the beach amid cries of "Hurry up Arctowski!" I gave a hammer to Tellesen with orders to chip here and there down by the shore, while I hurriedly climbed the moraine, picking up specimens as I ran, took the direction with my compass, glanced to the left and right, and hurried down again full speed to get a look at the rock in situ. Meanwhile Cook had taken a photograph of the place from the ship – and that is the way geological surveys have to be carried out in the Antarctic!

The first attempt at any cohesive long-term planning came with the establishment of the Discovery Committee by the British Colonial Office in 1923. Under its auspices a regular scientific programme (Discovery Investigations) was mounted from two ships – RRS *Discovery* (and, later *Discovery II*) and RRS *William Scoresby*, commencing in 1925. The work was almost entirely confined to oceanography and marine biology and was mainly in connection with the whaling industry, which is perhaps not surprising since the money came from the taxes levied on the whaling companies operating from South Georgia. The scientific results published in thirty-seven large volumes of *Discovery Reports* testify to the immense amount of work which was accomplished; but the outbreak of World War II temporarily put an end to such field work.

In 1908 British Letters Patent (amended in 1917) had consolidated the earlier territorial claims of British explorers as Dependencies of the Falkland Islands. These covered all territories between latitudes 50° and 58°S and longitudes 20° and 50°W, and south of latitude 58°S in longitudes 20°–80°W. No other nation challenged or even commented on this at the time.

In 1925 the Argentine Government formulated claims to the South Orkney Islands, two years later extending these to include South Georgia. By 1938 they were claiming the whole of the area designated by the British as the Falkland Islands Dependencies. The outbreak of war perhaps encouraged them to believe that British preoccupation in Europe would leave them free to move into Antarctica, for on 8 February 1942 the Argentine vessel *Primero de Mayo* sailed to Deception and other islands, and their Government declared the region south of latitude 60°00′S and bounded by longitude 25°00′W and 68°34′W to be Argentine Territory. This was formally reported to the British Government seven days later.

The British reaction was to despatch HMS *Carnarvon Castle* to Deception Island, where all Argentine marks of sovereignty were obliterated, a Crown Property notice erected and the Union Jack hoisted. The British notice was removed by the Argentines in a second visit of the *Primero de Mayo* two months later – in March 1943. At about that time Britain decided to mount a small military force, under the direction of the Admiralty, which was code-named 'Operation Tabarin'. This party occupied Deception Island (which has one of the most important natural harbours in the Southern Ocean) and another site on the mainland, thus making it possible to report on the activities of Argentine vessels, and indeed any German commerce raiders which might use or take refuge in the area.

Prominent among those advising the Colonial Office on Antarctic matters were James Wordie, a member of Shackleton's ill-fated *Endurance* expedition of 1914–1916, Dr Brian Roberts, biologist with the British Graham Land Expedition, 1934–1937, and Dr Neil Mackintosh, Director of Discovery Investigations. They all recognized that the bases to be occupied for political and military reasons could provide platforms for science, and the Government was persuaded that suitably qualified personnel serving in the Forces should be seconded to TABARIN.

Such was the origin of the modern British Antarctic Survey, for since the first parties wintered in 1944 there has been no break in the continuity of the scientific studies which they began. At the end of the war the name was changed to the Falkland Islands Dependencies Survey (FIDS), and in 1962 the organisation finally became known as the British Antarctic Survey (BAS).

The appropriate men having been recruited, at first only a minimum amount of materials and equipment was provided, and there was no coherent scientific planning. We were in a reconnaissance stage when priority had to be given to exploration and mapping. No one knew what

research opportunities there were at the various sites chosen for the small stations, which by 1957 numbered fourteen, but useful work was done whenever there was an opportunity. Political considerations and practical capabilities dominated planning until the late 1940s. When, after the War but still in its aftermath, I first sailed south to Stonington Island in 1947 in overall command of ten bases, I received no guiding directive about a general scientific programme. We had virtually a blank cheque to devise and carry out whatever seemed to be a good idea in the field.

There were, however, a few 'set pieces' which had already been established. At Deception Island, Port Lockroy and the Argentine Islands (now re-named Faraday), they were already required to maintain 3-hourly surface meteorological observations. At Signy Island (South Orkney Islands) the Base Leader, Dick Laws (now Director of BAS), had his own specific planned study of the elephant seals, while at Admiralty Bay, King George Island (South Shetland Islands), Eric Platt was free to undertake what geological work he could. At Hope Bay two surveyors were committed to extending earlier topographical surveys over the northern tip of the Antarctic Peninsula, but only one geologist was sent there to travel with the mapping parties and do anything he could wherever they found exposed rock.

At Stonington things were more complicated because we had a much larger complement – eleven men – which included two surveyors, two geologists, a budding biologist intent on studying Emperor Penguins, and a pilot and aircraft mechanic to fly and maintain a small de Havilland Hornet Moth aircraft, which we hoped would greatly increase the range of our field activities.

The crated plane was carried on the upper deck of the *John Biscoe* and on checking our stores in mid-ocean we discovered that no skis had been packed – without them the plane could not land at Stonington. A hasty message home elicited a promise that they would be flown out to meet the ship in Montevideo. However, they never arrived and we continued south, having arranged that HMS *Snipe* would pick them up later and take them to Stonington. When they finally arrived at Deception and the crate was opened, the contents were found to be two lengths of stove pipe for one of the huts. In those days the logistics provision was sometimes as unpredictable as the scientific programmes!

This had many repercussions and when, in the following summer, the ice did not go out of Marguerite Bay it was impossible for a ship to relieve Stonington. Had we had the aircraft the five second-year men in my party could have been flown north to open water, whereas they now faced a third consecutive Antarctic winter.

Surveying and geology were the principal objectives of field work undertaken from British bases prior to IGY.

The British station at Halley Bay, built by the Royal Society in 1956 for the International Geophysical Year (IGY).

I had also hoped to extend the scientific effort by more field work. Stonington and Hope Bay were the recognized travelling bases and were provided with field equipment and dog teams, but at the latter station there was only one geologist. 'Jumbo' Nicholls at the Argentine Islands was keen that his men should be able to travel to the nearby mainland but they had no tents and no sledging rations. Eric Platt at Admiralty Bay had tents but no sleeping bags. It had been my intention to supply most of the stations, including Signy, with balanced field equipment from our extensive stocks at Stonington. In the event, Platt, who had managed to get through his 'medical' at home without disclosing a known heart condition and was determined to accomplish at least some limited geology, set off on a walk of 20 miles around the base in one day, only to collapse and die within a few miles of home. It was to be another ten years – 1960 – before the Survey was provided with aircraft.

Until 1954, when plans were made for an International Geophysical Year (IGY) in 1957/58, facilities for scientists remained primitive indeed. Meteorology was confined to surface observations, geologists went into the field with nothing more than a hammer and a notebook, and biologists were provided with alcohol, formalin and some bottles. They could do little more than collect and observe. The IGY provided a much-needed boost to Antarctic

science and all the FIDS bases contributed to a wide range of IGY programmes in addition to continuing their normal routines. However, the main British contributions were from a geophysical observatory set up by the Royal Society at Halley Bay, and the FIDS Argentine Islands station (Faraday) which had been expanded as a second observatory. At the end of the IGY, Halley Bay (now known as 'Halley') was handed over to FIDS. In 1959 dog teams and travelling equipment, including tractors, were sent there and it was at last possible for field work to be extended to distant inland ranges, such as the Shackleton Range, some 400 miles further south.

Although, prior to the IGY, useful work had been done in the Antarctic by individual expeditions or nations, or by their combined effort in specific areas (for example, the Norwegian–British–Swedish Expedition to Dronning Maud Land in 1949–1952), much had to await more widespread cooperation. Most geophysical research required a whole network of stations, coordinated observations and data centres, and the value of other projects would obviously be greatly enhanced by the pooling of information from the whole continent.

In spite of the 'cold war' in Europe and the continuing existence of conflicting territorial claims in the Antarctic, the IGY proved a great success. Not only were the scientific results extremely valuable, but the spirit of cooperation which the IGY engendered had so tempered the long-standing rivalries that the twelve participant nations were able to agree terms for an Antarctic Treaty. This was drawn up and signed in 1959 and ratified in 1961.

Thus, not only was work in the Antarctic facilitated but, as the United Kingdom had entered into international commitments, first for the IGY and then for the Antarctic Treaty, the future of FIDS/BAS was assured. Long-term planning of scientific programmes therefore became possible.

As Director of BAS until 1973 I participated in these developments. The value of Antarctica for many disciplines had become apparent. With secure funding not only were we able to undertake increasingly sophisticated programmes but, with the coordination afforded by SCAR, the scope for international collaboration steadily increased.

This book, in highlighting the international achievements since the IGY, shows that Antarctic science is no longer a backwater but an important area of research in many disciplines. Thus Antarctica has become a continent for science and also plays a significant role in international relations.

V.E. Fuchs

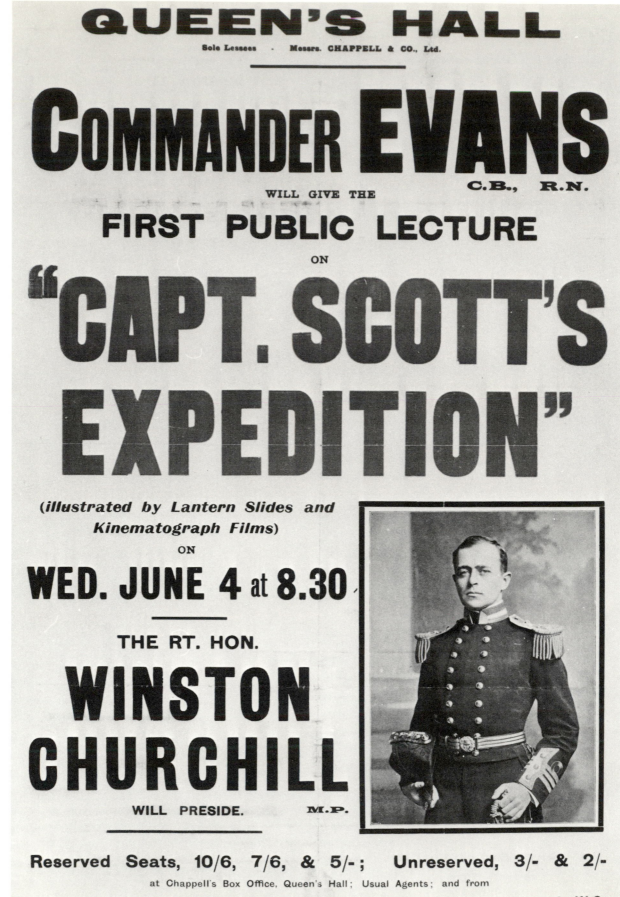

QUEEN'S HALL

Sole Lessees - Messrs. CHAPPELL & CO., Ltd.

COMMANDER EVANS

C.B., R.N.

WILL GIVE THE

FIRST PUBLIC LECTURE

ON

"CAPT. SCOTT'S EXPEDITION"

(*illustrated by Lantern Slides and Kinematograph Films*)

ON

WED. JUNE 4 at 8.30

THE RT. HON.

WINSTON CHURCHILL

WILL PRESIDE.   M.P.

Reserved Seats, 10/6, 7/6, & 5/-;   Unreserved, 3/- & 2/-

at Chappell's Box Office, Queen's Hall; Usual Agents; and from

THE LECTURE AGENCY, Ltd. (Gerald Christy), The Outer Temple, Strand, W.C.

Part·I
Geography, politics and science

Chapter·1
Exploration in search of new lands

Early explorations

Captain James Cook, one of the earliest visitors to Antarctica, had a rather low opinion of it. 'I make bold to declare', he said, 'that the world will derive no benefit from it'. But he was wrong then and his prophecy remains wrong now in 1986, although for different reasons. In the intervening period, the Antarctic has proved not only productive for man but also increasingly important to his continued well-being on the Earth – all this in ways that Cook could scarcely have been expected to foresee.

The history of man's interest in Antarctica is episodic. The lack of an indigenous population and its distance from major centres of civilization have ensured that it has attracted public attention only spasmodically over much of the past 200 years.

Originally a place of myth and fable, the hypothetical Antarctic continent was needed by Elizabethan geographers, such as Mercator, to balance the land masses of the northern hemisphere on the newly designed globes. The gigantic mass of *Terra Australis* dominated these earlier maps of the world and excited speculation about the population and resources of such a large area.

Hope springs eternally in the thoughts of empire builders and it was with thoughts of conquest, trade and colonisation that the Europeans set out to discover the riches of Antarctica. Despite evidence of icebergs and desolate islands, the Frenchman Charles de Brosses and the Englishman Alexander Dalrymple were both busy in the mid-eighteenth century championing a continent larger than Asia, filled with people and awash with produce of all kinds.

In search of this illusion Yves-Joseph de Kerguelen-Tremarec set sail in 1772. Returning to France with glowing reports of a land he had not properly investigated, he was sent back, to what he had called 'South France', to establish trade with the natives. Alas, his discovery turned out to be the islands of Kerguelen or 'Land of Desolation' as he then renamed it.

Dalrymple's influence encouraged a British expedition to these southern latitudes. James Cook was chosen to lead it and his careful investigation and reporting finally disposed of the dream of a rich, temperate and inhabited continent. Sailing in 1772, he spent 3 years on his circumnavigation. His attempts to penetrate the pack ice led him as far south as 71°10'S but he never claimed to have seen the continent itself.

His detailed account of the voyage and the whales and seals he saw stimulated a massive shift south of American and British sealers who had by then laid waste the northern populations of seals. Beginning in 1784 on the subantarctic islands, the sealers moved steadily southwards, stripping each breeding ground of all Fur Seals. By 1830, the Fur Seals were almost extinct.

Other than fur for making slippers, little of value was gained from this slaughter. Sealing captains were secretive about their activities so that no new charts of the southern islands resulted. With very few exceptions, no scientists were able to travel on the sealing vessels, so that man's knowledge of Antarctica was not greatly increased.

The discovery of Antarctica is claimed by three nations. Britain's Edward Bransfield is believed to have sighted the Antarctic Peninsula in February 1820. The Russian

The earliest Antarctic explorer was James Cook, on his ship HMS Resolution. *His reports disproved the myth of a rich and temperate* Terra Australis.

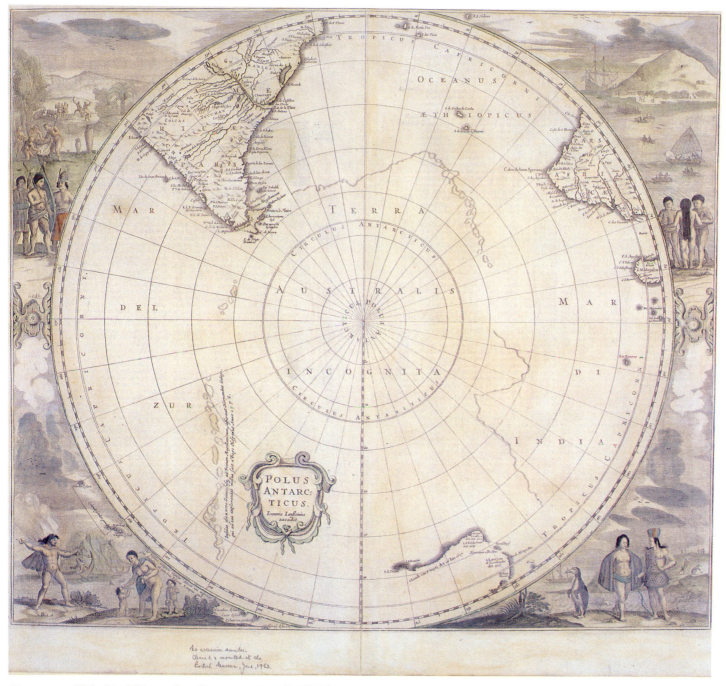

This map, published in 1650, was based on one prepared in 1641 by Henricus Hondius. The polar continent is delineated partly by island chains and partly by an 'inspired' line.

The systematic butchery of Fur Seals on the subantarctic and maritime Antarctic islands between 1786 and 1835.

Thaddeus von Bellingshausen, sent by Czar Alexander I to find staging posts for an expansion of trade, is a second likely contender in January or February 1820, although Bellingshausen himself never claimed to have seen the continent. The Americans, meanwhile, have championed Nathaniel Palmer, a sealing captain from Stonington, Connecticut, for a sighting in November 1820. Palmer's subsequent fame owes much to the publicity organised by Edmund Fanning when Palmer returned to the USA. All of these claims rely on historical assessments of what was likely to have been visible from positions given in a ship's log. Who was the first to discover the continent from amongst these claimants, however, is of little significance scientifically, especially since, in early 1821, Captain John Davis of the sealer *Huron*, went ashore on the Antarctic Peninsula and left a documented account of this landing. His log for 7 February 1821 concludes 'strong gales at ENE with cloudy unpleasant weather attended with snow and a heavy sea concluded to make the best of our way for the ship. I think this Southern Land to be a continent.' If the landing really did take place, and there seems little reason to doubt this, Davis was the first to set foot on the continent by 74 years.

The most significant voyages of the early nineteenth century were those of Bellingshausen, Wilkes, Dumont d'Urville and James Clark Ross. All were scientifically oriented and, in retrospect, scientifically important.

Bellingshausen was instructed to expand on Cook's southern explorations, circumnavigating the continent over two seasons. He discovered Peter I Island and Alexander Island, charted around South Georgia, South Sandwich Islands and South Shetland Islands and penetrated the pack ice to 69°53'S. His discoveries were however of insignificant interest to Russia and it was 10 years before his narrative and charts were even published.

The United States Exploring Expedition led by Charles Wilkes was successful despite itself. Badly organised, poorly equipped and with rotten ships, Wilkes still managed to follow the Antarctic coast for nearly 2400 km. On his return, he was court-martialled by the United States Navy for his conduct as Commander, whilst the Royal Geographical Society awarded him a gold medal for his achievements! Congress was niggardly in voting funds for the writing-up of the scientific data and much of great importance was lost.

The French expedition, at the same time, was led by a man of culture, Jules Sebastien Cesar Dumont d'Urville. Claiming a piece of the continent for France he named it Adélie Land after his wife. The scientific work was published in 32 volumes between 1842 and 1851 and Dumont d'Urville was accorded considerable recognition, both in France and elsewhere for his voyage, which had taken 3 years and 2 months. Of the 183 men who had set sail, only 130 returned to France. His natural history specimens numbered thousands, largely of species then unknown to science. Believing that the South Magnetic Pole was at 66°S 146°E from calculations by Gauss, he was suprised to find on arriving at this point that the pole was hundreds of miles away on the continent. Charles Wilkes reached the same conclusion.

Best prepared and most successful of all was the British expedition. James Clark Ross had already had 18 years' experience in the Arctic and his ships and crew showed this. Picking officers and men with experience in ice, he had his ships, *Erebus* and *Terror* reinforced and double sheathed in copper. His instructions from the Admiralty concentrated specifically on magnetic measurements. Hearing that Wilkes and Dumont d'Urville had preceded

Thaddeus von Bellingshausen led the first Russian
expedition to Antarctica aboard two ships, Vostok *and* Mirny.

him in the area nearest the South Magnetic Pole, he headed further east. Eventually reaching 77°S he discovered the Transantarctic Mountains and the great barrier of ice forming the Ross Ice Shelf. He also found two volcanoes, naming them after his ships. Although this was a naval expedition Ross managed to include four biological scientists in his complement – Robert M'Cormick, Joseph Hooker, John Robertson and David Lyall – signing them on as surgeons and their assistants. The plant collections made by Hooker (later to become Director of Kew Gardens and a major force in nineteenth-century botany) were to prove of enormous importance in the development of southern hemisphere botany.

These nineteenth century explorers and scientists, together with those on the *Challenger* expedition, provided the initial data on which was based the scientific plans of the early twentieth century expeditions. Their pioneering voyages and the quality of the scientific reports produced show them to be important milestones in man's scientific progress.

In step with the growth of science in human history has been a corresponding, and an often scientifically essential, increase in technological capabilities. The achievements of any historical period should be viewed in the context of capabilities at that time. Modern science in Antarctica is only possible because of the complex and sophisticated logistical support that is now provided. The challenge for the late twentieth-century man in Antarctica is not one of great physical hardship but of intellectual challenge. Although our knowledge of Antarctica has greatly increased, its environment remains just as hostile and unforgiving to the unlucky and the unprepared.

Two subjects characterise the close relationship between the development of science and logistics. Even now in 1986 ships are still the dominant form of transport to Antarctica for personnel and cargo. The evolution in their design has been critical for Antarctic exploration. Crucial for the success of any expedition is the health of its participants. To what extent have ill health, accidents and deaths held back progress in Antarctica?

The earliest explorers of Antarctic waters after James Cook were the sealers, venturing south in small wooden vessels. Weddell's ships Jane *and* Beaufoy *were typical of these.*

Charles Wilkes, the leader of the United States Exploring Expedition, and his ship Vincennes.

The French Antarctic expedition, led by Dumont d'Urville, landed on an iceberg from the two ships Astrolabe *and* Zélée.

Antarctic ships

It is difficult in the late twentieth century to appreciate just how small the ships used by the early explorers really were. Some expedition leaders were unable to choose their ships – as Cook had done – often having manifestly unsuitable craft forced upon them. Wilkes, for example, had to take two pilot boats amongst his flotilla, none of which was sheathed against ice. Dumont d'Urville and Ross both had their ships copper sheathed, whilst Ross even added watertight bulkheads and strengthening timbers. Bellingshausen's second ship, *Mirnyi*, was of unsheathed pinewood with its interior sealed in tar-soaked canvas.

All the ships were cramped by modern standards and it is remarkable how many men were carried in them. Weddell's brig *Jane* was only 150 tons and carried twenty-two men, whilst Dumont d'Urville's ship *Astrolabe* was a converted lighter of 380 tons carrying seventeen officers and eighty-five men. Some ships, such as the *Sea Gull*, were lost at sea with all hands.

The upsurge of interest in Antarctic exploration at the end of the nineteenth century initially used a well proven ship type, the whalers and sealers of the Arctic. New ships were built for some expeditions. For instance, *Discovery* was built for the National Antarctic Expedition. Its design owed much to the design of the *Fram*, built in 1893 for Nansen. The *Fram*, designed by the Scottish ship designer Colin Archer and built in Norway, set new standards for expedition ships destined to work in polar ice. The ship had heavy, leakproof bulkheads, the deck and bulkheads were thickly insulated, the wooden hull was barrel-shaped to ride up under ice pressure, and the propeller and rudder were housed in wells to avoid ice damage.

Increasing commercial activity from 1920 onwards in the icy waters north of Scandinavia and the Soviet Union stimulated further developments both in ice-strengthened ships and in icebreakers. These developments ensured that

Erebus and Terror *in the Ross Sea in 1841. Mt Erebus is in the background.*

A new type of ice-strengthened cargo ship is now in use. MV Icebird uses containerized units, which can be easily changed from cargo to accommodation, to fulfil a variety of tasks.

after World War II Antarctic activities could recommence with modern ships specifically designed for working in ice. Ice-strengthened cargo vessels were chartered by several countries from Lauritzen Lines in Denmark, whilst the Soviet Union and the USA both deployed icebreakers originally built for northern ice. The US icebreakers were the *Wind* class whilst the Soviet Union built several *Moskva* class, one of which, the *Lenin* became the world's first nuclear-powered icebreaker. Argentina built the *General San Martin* and Japan the *Fuji*. Whilst *Fuji* and the *Wind* class had displacements of less than 9000 tons, the Soviet ships displaced 15 000 tons or more.

Conditions on board expedition vessels steadily improved and a growing trend to use the ships for oceanographic studies as well as logistic work has resulted in greatly increased sophistication. At present the most advanced polar expedition ship is the German *Polarstern* with a carrying capacity of 40 scientists, a variety of well-equipped laboratories and two helicopters. With two variable pitch propellors giving a maximum speed of 15.5 knots she can maintain 5 knots through ice up to 1 m thick. Fully equipped with winches, sonar, radar and satellite navigation she can perform virtually any oceanographic, surveying or logistic task likely to be required by an Antarctic expedition.

(Above) *Ice-strengthened cargo ships from the Arctic are ideal in many respects for Antarctic logistic support. Several nations have chartered* Dan *ships from Lauritzen Lines for this purpose.*

(Below) *At present the most sophisticated polar research and logistic vessel is* MV Polarstern, *operated by the Alfred Wegener Institute in the Federal Republic of Germany.*

Disease, accidents and deaths

Despite James Lind having proved the value of lemon juice in preventing scurvy as early as 1753, the disease was rife on many of the Royal Navy ships. Its compulsory inclusion in the diet throughout the British fleet in 1803 virtually eliminated the disease. Ross had little difficulty with the disease during his expedition but, in 1860, the substitution of West Indian limes for Mediterranean lemons reduced the vitamin C content by 75%, allowing scurvy to reappear. Since at that time the vitamins had not been isolated as active agents, the fall in effectiveness of lime juice as a preventative and curative agent for scurvy was inexplicable. By the end of the nineteenth-century confusion reigned on the causes of scurvy.

On Scott's first expedition, the provisions list was drawn up by Dr Koettlitz, a veteran of the Jackson–Harmsworth Arctic Expedition. The basic rations were low in vitamin C and the lime juice available was not issued regularly. The initial attempts to use fresh seal meat, a good source of the vitamin, were frustrated first by Scott and then by the cook. Scurvy appeared quickly in the sledging parties whose dried rations contained no vitamin C at all. Only the reorganization of the diet by Armitage at last produced sufficient of the vitamin to maintain health in most of the party.

Shackleton improved the diet in his 1907–1909 expedition. Regular use of fresh seal and penguin meat, together with high-quality dried milk, meant that no cases of scurvy developed. Further improvements in the range of foods taken were shown on Scott's second expedition but since the idea of scurvy as a deficiency disease had still not been fully grasped, scurvy again reappeared in some of the sledge parties. Remarkably, the polar party, even after a vitamin C-free diet for 21 weeks, did not apparently show any signs of advanced scurvy but died of starvation, weakness and frostbite. After World War I all expeditions had adequate diets and scurvy did not reappear. Other problems remained, however. Frostbite, snow blindness and hypothermia can occur nowadays to the unprepared or the unwary, although better clothing and organisation have made their incidence much less frequent than on earlier expeditions.

During the twentieth century the health of men during Antarctic expeditions has been investigated in increasing detail. Until very recently there has been a paucity of published medical statistics but enough general accounts to allow some broad conclusions to be drawn. The men selected for Antarctic work are atypical since expedition leaders have generally demanded a higher state of fitness than is found in the general population. This, coupled with the bias in favour of young men and the lack of epidemics of disease in Antarctica should generally result in a low incidence of medical problems.

E. Ekelof published probably the first summary of medical problems encountered on an Antarctic expedition in his scientific paper on medical aspects of the Swedish Expedition. Cook had earlier written of the problems

Sledging rations (for one man-day) on R.F. Scott's first expedition (below) *contrasts very markedly with both the amounts and variety of food in a modern sledging box (for 20 man-days).*

encountered during the Belgian Expedition, whilst J.B. Charcot's narrative of his two French expeditions also contains comments on medical treatments. The commonest medical difficulties in recent times seem generally to be fractures and dislocations, dental problems, and skin problems. In only a few cases have the patients been incapacitated for long periods. Despite the isolation of Antarctic stations, mental illness appears to be rare. It is true that, especially during winter, there is often increased social strains amongst small groups. The development of 'Big-eye' or 'FID stare', where individuals go into a temporary trance-like state, has been reported for most Antarctic stations. However, mental breakdown or the development of a serious mental illness appears to be much less frequent than in the general national populations. It would seem, therefore, that medical problems during the last 50 years of Antarctic research have had only a minimal effect on the achievement of major scientific objectives.

Indeed deaths on Antarctic expeditions have been surprisingly few, considering the inadequate food on early expeditions and the generally hostile climate. Between 1898 and 1922, 489 men overwintered in Antarctica and there were 17 deaths. Whilst there has always been some deaths from diseases unrelated to living in Antarctica, the major cause of death between 1904 and the present is some type of fatal accident. Motorised vehicles and aircraft account for over 75% of the fatal accidents, with fatalities in the DC10 crash on Mt Erebus dwarfing all the fatal accidents over the decades of polar exploration. There appear to be no close correlations between either occupation or age and death. Between 1904 and 1964 the average number of deaths on Antarctic bases from all causes was 0.65 per year. Based on an estimated total population of c 7700 men during this period, the overall mortality rate was 5.36 per thousand, very low indeed compared to general population levels. Inclusion of personnel on summer expeditions for 1951–1964 (c 47 000 men) shows an even lower mortality rate of only 0.73 per thousand. Antarctica seems to be a remarkably safe place to live!

Over 250 people died in the DC10 crash on Mt Erebus in 1979, the first major fatal accident associated with Antarctic tourism.

Chapter·2
The early twentieth century

The 'Heroic Age'

The explosion of international interest in Antarctica between 1895 and 1915 increased scientific knowledge about the continent by several orders of magnitude. The attainment of this was only possible by the extraordinary courage, dedication and perseverance of these early explorers and scientists. Some died and many suffered in pursuit of their objectives. Not for nothing has this been called the 'Heroic Age' of exploration in Antarctica. There are many published accounts of this period, both from contemporary writers and from later historians. Nevertheless, it is useful to look again at some of the major expeditions and their achievements, in order to set the later Antarctic work in a proper context.

Although both the Dundee Whaling Expedition of 1892/93 and the expedition led by H.J. Bull in 1894/95 both made some scientific observations and collections, the first important expedition was that led by Adrien de Gerlache de Gomery in 1897. Supported by the Belgian Government, he sailed in a small Norwegian sealer renamed *Belgica*. His rather cosmopolitan crew included the Norwegian Roald Amundsen as second mate, the American Frederick Cook as doctor, a Polish meteorologist (Henryk Arctowski), and a Rumanian naturalist (Emil Racovitza). De Gerlache, although a naval officer, was interested in science and frequent, if short, landings were made along the western side of the Antarctic Peninsula. The ship froze in during March and the expedition, trapped for 347 days in the Bellingshausen Sea, became the first to overwinter intentionally in Antarctica. One man died, two went mad and some of the remainder suffered from lethargy and depression during the long winter. The leader, lacking polar experience, was clearly unprepared for this and it was left to Cook to try and keep the party's spirits up.

Whilst *Belgica* was frozen in, another expedition, led by Norwegian-born Carsten Borchgrevink, was leaving England for the Ross Sea. Borchgrevink had been ashore 3 years previously at Cape Adare and had decided to return and overwinter on land. His ship, the *Southern Cross*, carried three scientists – Nicolai Hanson (zoologist), Hugh Evans (assistant zoologist) and Louis Bernacchi (physicist) – and Dr Herlof Klovstad as the expedition doctor. During the winter Hanson died of an intestinal disease, depressing everyone's spirits. Unable to penetrate far inland from Cape Adare, the party sailed further south the following summer along the Ross Ice Shelf. Borchgrevink and two companions sledged inland to 78°50′S, using dog teams for the first time in Antarctica. Charts of the Ross Sea area made by Captain Colbeck were to prove very useful to the next visitors to this region.

In 1901 the first fruits appeared of the Sixth International Geographic Congress on Antarctica. Sir Clements Markham, President of the Royal Geographical Society, had urged that the assault on Antarctica should be not only international but also coordinated. The German, Swedish and British expeditions of 1901 reflected this planning. In July 1901 Markham had examined the routes by which future exploration of the continent should be pursued. Seven routes were identified and each expedition persuaded to follow a different route. Erich von Drygalski, a professor of geography, led the German expedition with five other scientists and a ship, the *Gauss*, built especially for polar work. They were the first to explore the Indian Ocean sector of Antarctica, lying between the continental discoveries of Kemp and Balleny. Locked in the ice for winter, they made valuable magnetic and astronomical observations. In spring they sledged to the coast (named Kaiser Wilhelm Land) and discovered an extinct volcano (Gaussberg). Drygalski used a captive balloon to rise 1500 feet up to see into the crater, a technique also employed by R.F. Scott on his expedition.

The Swedish expedition had a much more exciting time. Led by the geologist Otto Nordenskjöld, and with C.A. Larsen as captain of *Antarctic*, they sailed into the Weddell Sea to explore the east coast of the Antarctic Peninsula. The first year went according to plan, with Nordenskjold and five companions overwintering on Snow Hill Island. The following summer, however, the pack ice did not melt sufficiently for the *Antarctic* to reach

C.E. Borchgrevink, leader of the British Antarctic Expedition 1898–1900. His was the first party to overwinter on land in Antarctica.

The first expedition deliberately to overwinter in Antarctica was led by the Belgian Adrien de Gerlache de Gomery, aboard the Belgica.

The first photograph of a Leopard Seal, taken on board the
Balaena *in 1892 during the Dundee Whaling Expedition.*

the party. Three men were landed at Paulet Island to make their way on foot to Nordenskjold's hut but open water blocked their way and they were forced to remain isolated on Paulet Island for 9 months. Meanwhile the ship, caught by the ice midway between Snow Hill and Paulet Island, had sunk, leaving her crew marooned as a third party. These three parties then had to spend a second winter in Antarctica, two living in makeshift accommodation and subsisting on penguin meat and seal blubber. Only one man died (of tuberculosis) and by the most extraordinary coincidence, the three groups were reunited and rescued by the first Argentine ship to venture into Antarctic waters.

The third expedition, led by R.F. Scott, wintered on board *Discovery*, moored to the ice edge in McMurdo Sound. With six scientists on board and a strong scientific programme, much was accomplished, and geographical exploration was not neglected. Scott, Shackleton and Wilson sledged south to 82°17′S, within sight of the Trans-antarctic Mountains. A combination of scurvy, illness and snow blindness, together with the death of all nineteen dogs, meant that the three men only just survived the journey. Just as important was the journey by Armitage, leading the first party ever to reach the polar plateau.

Overlapping in time with Scott's, Drygalski's and Nordenskjold's expeditions were those to the Weddell Sea and South Orkney Islands led by W.S. Bruce, and to the west coast of the Peninsula led by J.B. Charcot. Bruce had conceived the idea of the Scottish Antarctic Expedition after visiting the Antarctic with the Dundee Whaling

Expedition. His plans were entirely scientific and his expedition was very successful, given its limited comple-ment and private financing. Jean-Baptiste Charcot's first expedition aboard the *Français* (1903–1905) was originally conceived mainly as a rescue for Nordenskjold and his men. Finding this already accomplished, Charcot stayed on to explore and chart. The emphasis in this expedition and in Charcot's second expedition (1909–1910) was on surveying, but glaciological, geological and biological observations were also made. In typical French fashion the expeditions were well supplied with wines! Charcot was innovative, using electric lights (the second expedition to do so in Antarctica), a De Dion–Benton motor boat and yellow-glass goggles which proved 100% effective against snow blindness.

Ernest Shackleton's expedition had a clear geographical object – to reach the South Pole. However, Shackleton appreciated the value of science and took with him several talented scientists. Mawson, David and Priestley were all to make their mark on Antarctic geology and glaciology on this and other expeditions. Although Shackleton failed to reach the geographic pole by only 180 km, another party led by David did attain the South Magnetic Pole. Priestley's work in South Victoria Land also greatly improved the topographical and geological maps of the area.

Raymond Priestley was soon back again in the same area with Scott's second (*Terra Nova*) expedition. This time no new major geographical discoveries were made, although excellent studies in biology, meteorology, geology and glaciology were carried out. Amundsen's expedition, at the same time, did discover the extension to the Dronning Maud Mountains and pioneered a new route to the plateau, but made no significant scientific studies. These two expeditions ended the quest for the South Pole. Amundsen reached it 33 days before Scott, returning safely to his base camp. All of Scott's pole party died on their return journey.

The second expedition led by Shackleton aimed at crossing the continent from the Weddell Sea to the Ross Sea. His ship, the *Endurance*, was crushed in ice and he and his men embarked on a hazardous trip, first to Elephant Island in the South Shetland Islands. Later Shackleton and five companions sailed to South Georgia in a lifeboat, crossed the unmapped centre of the island and finally, at the fourth attempt, rescued all the remaining men on Elephant Island. The expedition was a failure in all its main objectives but provided one of the most remarkable stories of leadership in polar history.

Douglas Mawson too was unable to stay away from Antarctica. The avowed aims of the Australasian Antarctic Expedition were all scientific and a great deal was accomplished. Topographical surveys were undertaken by four parties whilst a range of geological and biological work was completed. Especially significant were the meteorological data, establishing Cape Denison as one of the windiest places in the world. Mawson was lucky not to die when his sledge party was struck by disaster. Ninnis was killed, falling into a crevasse with a sledge containing most of the food. On the return journey Mertz died of vitamin A poisoning due to eating dog livers, leaving Mawson, in a very weakened condition, to cover the final 80 miles back to base on his own.

Three final expeditions from the 'Heroic Age' need to be mentioned. All were unsuccessful to some extent. A German expedition led by Wilhelm Filchner in 1911 was intended to determine if the Antarctic was one piece of land. After the near loss of their base hut, their ship

Every detail of each sledging journey was meticulously recorded on Scott's expeditions, as in this page from Edward Wilson's notebooks.

(Right)
The first Australasian Antarctic Expedition, led by Douglas Mawson, suffered from the same cramped conditions as the earlier expeditions.

Sketch by Edward Wilson of three men inside a pyramid tent.

Deutschland was trapped by the Weddell Sea ice for nearly 9 months. Science and exploration was thus limited to an area now called the Filchner Ice Shelf. Also in 1911, a Japanese expedition aboard the *Kainan Maru*, led by Nobu Shirase, arrived in the Bay of Whales where they met Amundsen's expedition. Shirase had intended to attempt to reach the pole but, on learning that Amundsen and Scott had already left for there, he abandoned this idea. After a month of limited travel and exploration including a sledge journey 257 km inland, the expedition returned to Japan. Finally, Shackleton's last expedition aboard the *Quest*. Failing to get money from the Canadian Government for an expedition to the Beaufort Sea, Shackleton proposed instead to map 3200 km of the Antarctic coastline and make extensive meteorological and geological investigations in the Weddell Sea sector. His death from heart failure at South Georgia on the way south should have aborted these plans, but Frank Wild assumed command and some useful scientific work was completed before the return to Britain.

The land rush

In the period between the two World Wars, Antarctic exploration took on a new slant. Most of the expeditions were still privately funded but overt government interest in territorial claims was now being expressed by several countries. In 1908 and 1917, Britain had issued a formal claim to Antarctic territory and islands around the Antarctic Peninsula. British title to what is now the Ross Dependency was formally claimed in 1923 and Australian Antarctic Territory was proclaimed in 1933. These claims, especially those in the South Atlantic area, were to provide ample scope for escalating disagreement at a later period. France formally annexed Adélie Land in 1924 while, just before World War II, Norway formally claimed Dronning Maud Land. The war awakened Argentine and Chilean interests in Antarctica and both countries laid claim to the Antarctic Peninsula and Weddell Sea, their claims overlapping both with each other and with that of the British. At this stage the USA put forward no territorial claims and has ever since officially reserved its position on the sovereignty of Antarctica. The Soviet Union has had a similar policy since the International Geophysical Year (IGY).

The effect of this diplomatic interest in territorial extension on the pursuit of Antarctic science was initially quite minimal, but when R.E. Byrd began his series of American expeditions it assumed a greater significance. The most important post-War advance in Antarctic exploration was the increased dependence on the aeroplane. Flying was dangerous but aerial reconnaissance allowed the survey of 4000 square miles in an hour – previously a whole season's work using dog teams. Scientific parties could be flown inland to remote localities for sampling and stations established on the inland ice could be partly

Bacterial and fungal isolates from soil collected on the Danco Coast during J. B. Charcot's first expedition. This was one of the first microbiological investigations of Antarctic material.

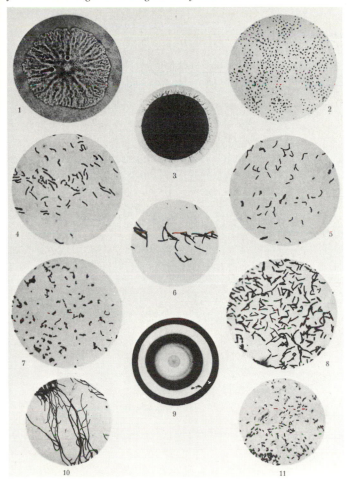

The track chart of the Scotia, *1902–1904, shows how far south the expedition sailed in the Weddell Sea. On expeditions such as this, every opportunity was taken to visit Atlantic islands en route.*

supplied by air. On his first expedition in 1928 Byrd, in a dramatic gesture, flew over the South Pole. Over 1600 aerial photographs were taken, covering an area of about 150 000 square miles, and during these flights the Rockefeller and the Ford Mountains were discovered. The expedition clearly demonstrated that planes could be flown successfully over long distances in Antarctica and could land in the field to lay depots or to put in field parties. Byrd exploited this development even further during his second expedition.

Other expeditions also used aircraft. Sir Hubert Wilkins had made the first flight in Antarctica in 1928 from his base at Deception Island. Although he failed to fly across the continent he did obtain some remarkable aerial photographs of the peninsula area. A more significant use of aerial exploration was that by the Norwegian whaling expeditions, under the direction of Lars Christensen. To supplement coastal surveys by the whaling fleets between

20° and 45°E, inland surveys were carried out by air in 1929/30, 1930/31, 1933/34, 1934/35 and 1935/36. These various Norwegian activities discovered over 2000 miles of coast and mapped about 80 000 km^2 from the air.

The trans-continental flight by Lincoln Ellsworth and Herbert Hollick-Kenyon from the Antarctic Peninsula to the Ross Ice Shelf in 1935 discovered the Sentinel Range and the Hollick-Kenyon Plateau. Ellsworth claimed the area between 80° and 120°W for the USA but the US Government took no action to support this. Another more determined attempt at aerial support for territorial claims was made during the German expedition of 1938/39. Although the *Schwabenland*, under the command of Alfred Ritscher, was only there for 3 weeks, 350000 km^2 were photographed and thousands of aluminium darts engraved with the German swastika were dropped at regular intervals throughout the region.

Sovereignty claims to parts of Antarctica were an important determinant of Antarctic activities prior to the Treaty. Their principal effect was to determine the position and number of stations maintained by each nation but international tensions created by the claims did lead to the deployment of warships.

Photo reconnaissance, beginning in 1928 with Wilkins and Byrd, led to the rapid photography of large areas of Antarctica which had not been explored overland. Much of the early photography was inadequate for cartographic purposes but did allow the identification of many major features.

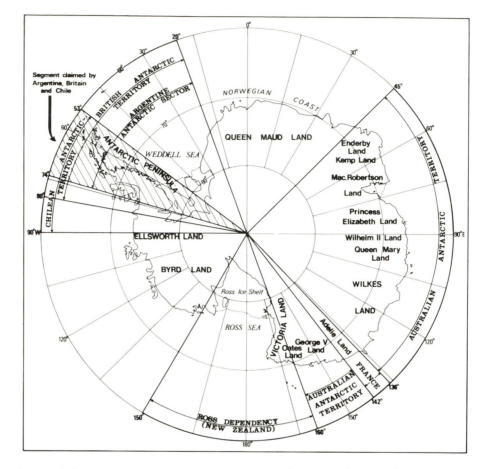

The 'Heroic Age' expeditions were undertaken at a time when nineteenth-century values and social structures lingered on. Social stratification was most marked in Scott's expeditions where a clear distinction was maintained between officers and other ranks. In retrospect this was not the most efficient way to have organized an Antarctic expedition but the military mind is slow to change and similar social structures can be found in later expeditions with a dominant military presence.

In these early expeditions there was plenty of suffering. Aside from those who died, many men suffered from scurvy, frost bite and exposure. There were also deeds of great bravery, dedication and fortitude, and the growth of an international camaraderie of Antarctic men with a common experience.

Expeditions were mainly privately funded and were frequently in debt on their return. Expedition members were often involved in months of public lectures to raise money to meet the bills. Those who were natural speakers, like Ernest Shackleton, could attract large crowds. Today, when Antarctic expeditions are funded by governments, they are usually required to explain their activities to the public in justification of their expenditure of public funds. Eighty years ago public relations was just as important as today.

The general public interest in Antarctica had diminished after the attainment of the South Pole and the disruptive effects of World War I. Geographical exploration could kindle some official support and skilful public relations, as employed by Byrd, was able to stir national interest – but only for a limited duration. Apart from the whaling industry, Antarctica was still considered to have no value to man.

Apart from Byrd's expeditions there were other privately organized ones between the World Wars but these were all small and had strong scientific objectives. Especially noteworthy for its scientific programme was the British Graham Land Expedition. For sheer tenacity under difficult circumstances it would be difficult to find a better example than Bagshawe and Lester who spent a year, by choice, living beneath an upturned boat to collect meteorological and zoological information.

The indicators of the future direction of Antarctic organisation and support can now be seen as the German *Schwabenland* Expedition and the US Antarctic Service Expedition. Whilst the former was organized and wholly funded directly by the German Government to carry out territorial claims, the latter was still partly based on private financing. The major difference this time was that Byrd was no longer in sole charge but responsible to an

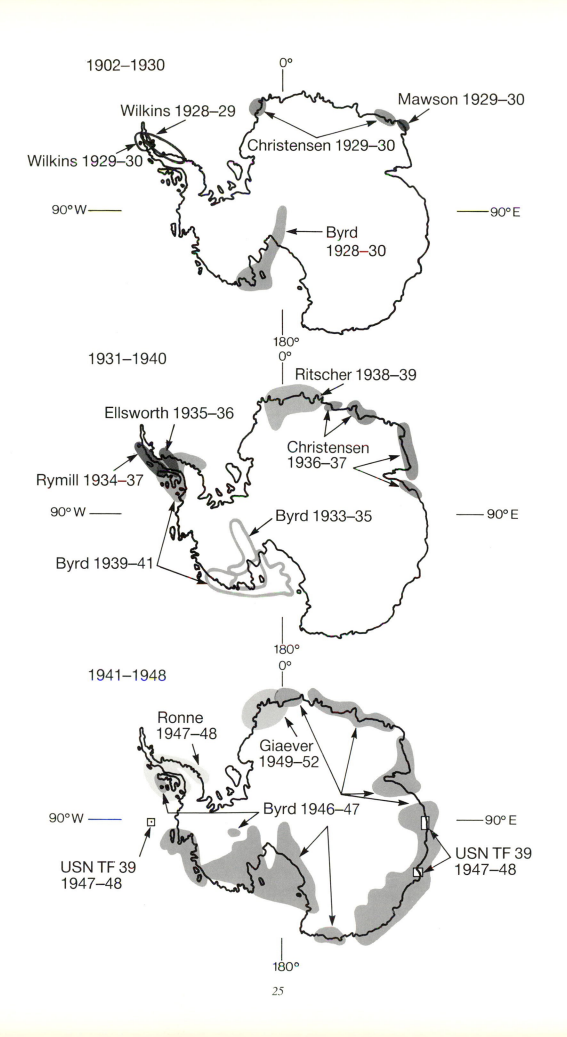

1902–1930

Wilkins 1928–29
Wilkins 1929–30
0°
Christensen 1929–30
Mawson 1929–30
90° W
90° E
Byrd 1928–30
180°

1931–1940

Ritscher 1938–39
0°
Ellsworth 1935–36
Christensen 1936–37
Rymill 1934–37
90° W
Byrd 1933–35
90° E
Byrd 1939–41
180°

1941–1948

0°
Ronne 1947–48
Giaever 1949–52
90° W
Byrd 1946–47
90° E
USN TF 39 1947–48
USN TF 39 1947–48
180°

The use of aircraft marked a major step forward in Antarctic exploration. On 28 November 1929 the Floyd Bennett *(here being dug out of winter snow) became the first aircraft to reach the South Pole.*

interdepartmental committee in Washington. The era of the Antarctic explorer as a private individual was virtually over – salaried government employees were about to take his place.

The development of whaling

Commerce came to Antarctica after the publication of Cook's account of his circumnavigation in 1777. Sealers from the USA and Britain descended like locusts and quickly reduced Fur Seals almost to extinction. The commercial value of new sealing grounds was considerable, so few captains were willing to divulge anything of importance about their voyages. James Weddell was an exception and it is largely from his account (and that of Edmund Fanning) that we know anything about the details of this period. Although Weddell and other sealing captains employed by the Enderby Brothers contributed something to our general knowledge of sea and ice conditions in the Weddell Sea, these early commercial ventures added very little scientific information on the region. For that, a more substantial industry was necessary and that began in 1904.

C.A. Larsen had seen for himself the potential for whaling in the Scotia Sea area during his three voyages to the Antarctic. In 1903 he had discovered an ideal site for a whaling station at South Georgia and in November 1904 he arrived back at the island to establish the first Antarctic whaling station, funded by Argentine capital. From this small beginning grew an international multimillion pound industry centred, for many years, around the shore stations established on South Georgia.

The whaling activities stimulated several significant moves on the part of the authorities. The Governor of the Falkland Islands, who was also responsible for South Georgia, issued the first 'Ordinance to regulate the whale fishery of the Colony of the Falkland Islands' in 1906. Although primarily intended to lay down the rules for commercial exploitation, it also allowed the Governor to control the industry and can be considered the first legal instrument in a conservation policy.

The extension of whaling to the South Orkney Islands and South Shetland Islands prompted the British Government to establish and define the 'Dependencies of the Falkland Islands' by proclamation in 1908; this definition also contained a territorial claim to the Antarctic Peninsula. They even continued to use the Norwegian whalers to annex further territory for the British crown. For instance in 1910 a Norwegian whaling expedition called at Heard Island to allow a British subject to claim it formally for Britain!

Initially Antarctic whaling was very wasteful, with only the blubber oil being extracted and the remainder of the carcass being thrown away. This came to the attention of a Norwegian, J.A. Mørch, who wrote an article in 1908 for the magazine *Scientific American* in the course of which he stated that the British Government should not issue whaling licences to any company without agreement to utilize the whole carcass. The present situation, he maintained, was a scandalous waste of raw material. In fact

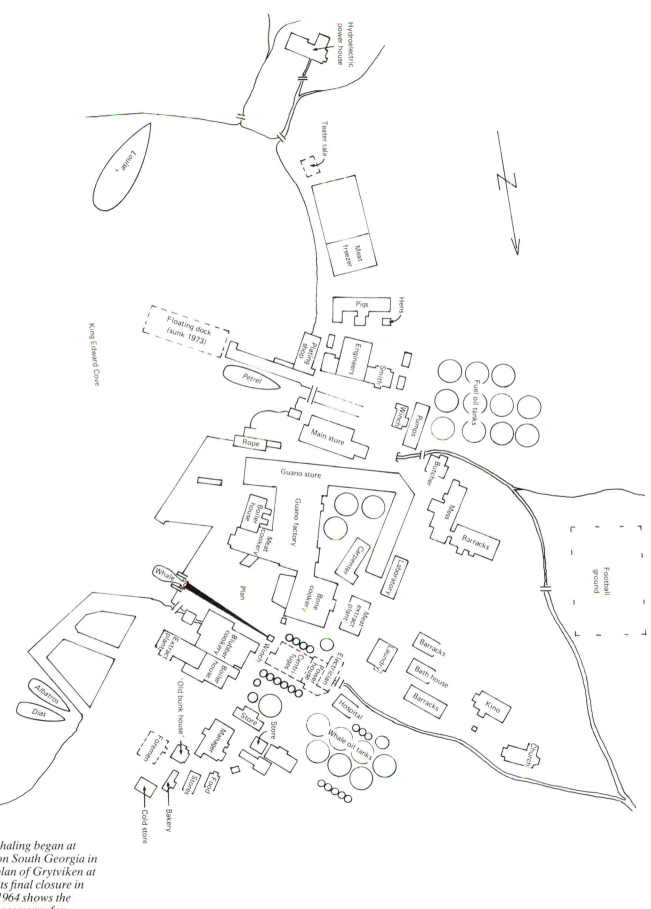

Hydroelectric power house

'Louise'

Teater sala

Meat freezer

King Edward Cove

Floating dock (sunk 1973)

Pigs

Hens

Plating shop

Engineers

Smithy

Petrel

Winch

Pumps

Fuel oil tanks

Butcher

Main store

Rope

Guano store

Mess

Barracks

Boiler house

Meat cookery

Guano factory

Carpenter

Bone cookery

Laboratory

Meat extract plant

Football ground

Whale

Plan

Extract plant

Blubber cookery house

Boiler house

'Old bunk house'

Winch

Centri-fuges

Electrician power house

Laundry

Barracks

Bath house

Barracks

Kino

Albatros

Dias

Foremen

Manager

Store

Store

Hospital

Whale oil tanks

Church

Stores

Food

Bakery

Cold store

Antarctic whaling began at Grytviken on South Georgia in 1904. The plan of Grytviken at the time of its final closure in December 1964 shows the complexity necessary for complete utilisation of the whole carcass.

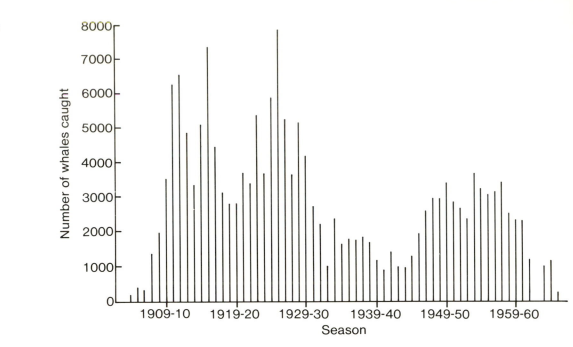

Annual catch of all whale species at South Georgia between 1904 and 1965.

The first legal control on Antarctic whaling was established when the Governor of the Falkland Islands issued an ordinance in 1906.

THE FALKLAND ISLANDS GAZETTE.   109

A BILL

ENTITLED

An Ordinance

To regulate the Whale Fishery of the Colony of the Falkland Islands.

BE IT ENACTED by the Governor of the Colony of the Falkland Islands with the advice and consent of the Legislative Council thereof as follows :—

1. It shall not be lawful for any person to kill, take, or hunt, or attempt to kill or take any whale in Colonial Waters unless he shall have first been duly licensed, and shall have entered into a bond to the Colonial Government, with one sufficient surety, in the sum of one hundred pounds—   *Unlawful to take whales without a license.*

    (*a*) to pay into the Colonial Treasury the royalties specified in the Schedule to this Ordinance ; and

    (*b*) to render to the Government an accurate account of the number and description of whales taken by him under his license.

2. (1.) The Colonial Secretary, or such other officer as the Governor may appoint for the purpose, may grant Whaling Licenses to such persons as may apply for them, for such periods, and on such terms and conditions, as may be approved by the Governor.   *Granting of Whaling Licenses.*

    (2.) There shall be paid into the Colonial Treasury for and in respect of each Whaling License granted under this Ordinance the sum of twenty-five pounds : provided that a Whaling License under this Ordinance, may, with the approval of the Secretary of State, be granted to any person without payment of the sum of twenty-five pounds as aforesaid, and without such person being required to enter into the bond specified in section 1 of this Ordinance.

3. The Governor in Council may from time to time make regulations—   *The Governor in Council may make regulations*

    (*a*) for fixing the terms and conditions on which Whaling Licenses may be granted ;

    (*b*) for regulating the number of Whaling Licenses to be granted in any year ;

    (*c*) for defining the limits within which any holder of a Whaling License shall be allowed to take whales ;

    (*d*) for regulating the number of whales to be taken in any year by any holder of a Whaling License ; and

    (*e*) for disposing by sale or otherwise of any whales, whale-oil, or whale-bone forfeited under the provisions of this Ordinance ; and

    (*f*) generally for carrying out the provisions of this Ordinance, and the intent and object thereof.

And the Governor in Council may impose penalties not exceeding ten pounds for the breach of such regulations.

Britain introduced this requirement on all licences issued from 1 October 1909.

Mørch had other ideas too. He wrote to the British Museum (Natural History) in London in June and July 1910 in support of his contention that no definite assertions could be made about the relations between catching and whale stocks without some direct scientific investigation. He suggested three ideas which were to have far-reaching effects. The first was that every whale catcher should record in a logbook every whale killed, with details of place, species, sex, if pregnant, occurrence of plankton in the water and weather data. On the basis of the information, his second suggestion was that charts of whale distribution and frequency with time could be prepared. This seems to be the first record of these two ideas. Risting used the logbook principle for his International Whaling Statistics begun in 1930 whilst C.H. Townsend hit upon the chart idea in 1915 for his analysis of old American whaling records. The third idea was to set aside some part of whaling receipts to fund scientific investigations relating to whale stocks.

Discovery investigations

The Director of the Museum had passed Mørch's memoranda on to the Colonial Office in 1911 and, in 1912, was able to confirm that his information from South Georgia supported all of Mørch's original assertions. As a result of this, Major G.E.H. Barrett-Hamilton was sent to Leith Harbour in South Georgia in 1913 to study whaling practices. He died on the island in January 1914 but his paper was used as the scientific report on South Georgia whaling at the 'Interdepartmental Committee on Whaling and the Protection of Whales', established in 1914. This

The RRS Discovery *(together with the smaller* RRS William
Scoresby) *provided the marine scientists with a robust and
dedicated sampling platform for all Antarctic waters.*

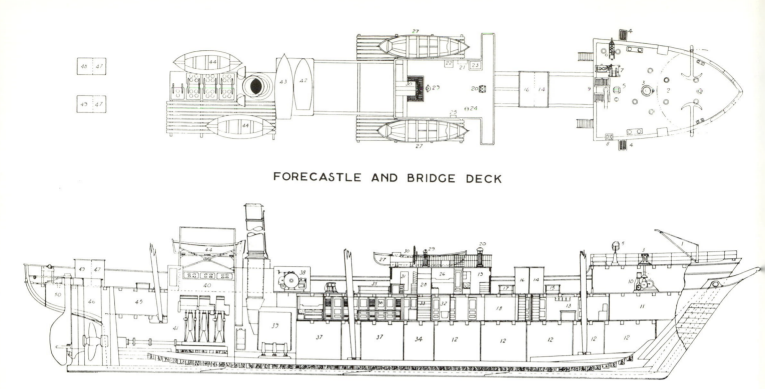

FORECASTLE AND BRIDGE DECK

PROFILE

R.R.S. 'DISCOVERY'

Profile and plan of Forecastle and Bridge Deck

1. Anchor davit
2. Deck lights and mushroom ventilators
3. Capstan
4. Sounding platform
5. Searchlight
6. Lucas sounding machine
7. Deep-water hydrological machine
8. Pedestal for small harpoon gun
9. Galley skylight
10. Windlass
11. Chain locker
12. Stores
13. Galley and kitchen
14. Galley companion
15. Skylight to kitchen
16. Crew-space companion
17. Skylight to crew space
18. Quarters of crew and petty officers
19. Chart house
20. Standard compass
21. Flag locker
22. Wireless accumulator box
23. Chart table
24. Engine-room telegraph
25. Laryngaphone to engine room
26. Deck cabin
27. Whaler
28. Wardroom entrance
29. Steering compass
30. Steam and hand steering gear
31. Deck laboratory
32. Bathroom
33. Wardroom companion
34. Freshwater tank
35. Wardroom skylight
36. Wardroom
37. Main bunker
38. Winch house and winch
39. Main boiler
40. Engine-room casing and skylight
41. Engine room
42. Norwegian pram
43. Dinghy
44. Lifeboat
45. Sail locker
46. Propeller well
47. Officers' water-closet
48. Armoury
49. Lamp locker
50. Rudder well

RRS Discovery *was fitted out for marine biology and oceanography.*

The Marine Biological Station at South Georgia was especially built for the Discovery Investigations. A substantial building, it provided both living and laboratory accommodation. It is still in use today as workshops and store rooms.

Committee asked for Norwegian cooperation in gathering data but their work was interrupted by the outbreak of war.

A committee was established in 1917 under the name of the 'Interdepartmental Committee on Research and Development in the Dependencies of the Falkland Islands'. It included as major objectives consideration of actions needed to preserve and develop the whaling industry and of what scientific investigations were most needed in the Dependencies. Its report, published in 1920, contained thirty-six recommendations, seventeen of which concerned whaling. Of particular significance were those recommending detailed scientific studies on whale biology, an expansion of statistical data for whales caught, carcass utilisation, and licence terms. The Committee suggested that research vessels should be acquired and the scientific staff paid out of an additional tax on whaling revenue. Thus, all of Mørch's original ideas were endorsed. The formation of the 'Discovery Committee' to organize the scientific work was a remarkable vindication of his foresight.

The 'Discovery Investigations', beginning in 1925 with a shore station at South Georgia and the first scientific cruise of *RRS Discovery*, have proved to be the most important Antarctic marine science studies up until modern times. The shore laboratory remained open for 6 years whilst cruises of *RRS Discovery* and *RRS William Scoresby* continued until 1939. A final cruise took place in 1950/51. The cruises covered all seasons and all parts of the Southern Ocean. The scientists, led initially by Stanley Kemp, turned their attention to many fields beyond whale biology. Birds and seals were an early interest, whilst the investigation of the marine food chains culminating in whales provided a wealth of new specimens and data on virtually all marine groups. The whale-catcher logbooks, together with data from *Discovery* cruises and from biological observations on dead whales during processing, produced the first detailed charts of species' distributions, both for predators and prey.

All this work was costly but a tax on each barrel of whale oil produced more than adequate funds. In 1923 the tax produced £300 000 (1985 equivalent £4.2 million) and by 1929 almost £600 000 (1985 equivalent £9 million). Most of this money came from Norwegian enterprises, a point not overlooked by either the whaling companies or the Norwegian Government.

The whaling companies supported other research, often unconnected with whaling. They granted transport facilities to scientific expeditions to the Antarctic and Subantarctic. The weather reports from catchers and factory ships allowed the study of Southern Ocean meteorology to develop. As already mentioned, some whaling expeditions were also concerned with exploration and discovery of continental coasts, whilst their captains built up a practical store of knowledge concerning Antarctic ice, never since equalled.

Whaling is an exploitative primary industry and, despite the scientific research and its recommendations, drove itself into extinction by a combination of greed and politics. Despite this it has left us greatly enriched in our understanding of Antarctic marine biology but at a great cost in terms of the world's largest mammals.

Chapter·3
Antarctic science comes of age

Inception of the Polar Year

In 1875 the German Arctic explorer Lt. Karl Weyprecht, then serving in the Austro-Hungarian Navy, first put forward his idea of an international collaboration to take detailed and synchronised measurements of meteorology, magnetism, aurorae and ice at both poles. Although he did not live to see the plan put into action, an enhanced version of it became the International Polar Year of 1882–1883. Ten countries established Arctic stations, together with three in the southern hemisphere, the most southerly of which was on South Georgia. Despite difficulties the results of these studies proved very useful, especially the magnetics data which provided a new insight into the global magnetic field.

The First Polar Year coincided with a sunspot minimum. In 1927 the German polar scientist Johannes Georgi proposed a Second Polar Year for 1932–1933, 50 years after the first and again coinciding with minimum activity on the sun. Much greater international interest was apparent and forty-four nations took part. Increased planning and the involvement of several international bodies ensured a great improvement in organization. Again the emphasis was on meteorology, magnetism and the aurorae. 'International Days' for simultaneous observations were declared and a range of new techniques – auroral cameras, radiosondes, La Cour magnetometers – was introduced. The observing routine adopted then was later to provide a framework, extended to even greater effect, for the next international polar investigations.

World War II disrupted the publication of data from the Second Polar Year. Irreplaceable records were lost during the turmoil, as was much of the momentum needed to write up the now archival information. By 1951 work had ceased on the data and a final bibliography was published.

It was possibly this final activity of the Second Polar Year which inspired the discussion in Maryland on the evening of 5 April 1950. A group of senior geophysicists was gathered at the home of James van Allen to talk to Professor Sydney Chapman from Imperial College, London. Discussion of scientific advances since the Second Polar Year culminated in a suggestion that a new 'Polar Year' would be justified after only 25 years. This time the activities would be concentrated at a solar maximum, as this was expected to make several phenomena easier to measure.

An approach by Chapman and Lloyd Berkner to the next meeting of the Commission on the Ionosphere was received enthusiastically and the proposal was passed on to the International Council of Scientific Unions (ICSU). ICSU was a federation of thirteen international specialist scientific unions, together with representatives of forty-five national academies of science. ICSU was, and is, a non-governmental body and operates in parallel to UNESCO but without the bureaucracy normally associated with international bodies.

The ICSU Executive Board accepted the proposal in 1951 and set up a special committee, Comité Spéciale de l'Année Géophysique Internationale (CSAGI), to plan

The German station at Royal Bay, South Georgia, for the International Polar Year 1882–83.

the scientific programme and invite participation. The meteorologists and magneticians protested that, for their scientific requirements, the scope should be widened beyond the polar regions. Chapman proposed the new name of 'International Geophysical Year' (IGY) as the tempo of activity began to increase.

By May 1954 over twenty nations had agreed to participate but it was not until October 1954 that the Soviet Union finally agreed to take part. It was at this point that Antarctica was selected as an area of special attention. It represented, in the report of CSAGI,

a region of almost unparalleled interest to the fields of geophysics and geography alike. In geophysics, Antarctica has many significant, unexplored aspects: for example, the influence of this huge ice mass on global weather; the influence of the ice mass on atmospheric and oceanographic dynamics; the nature and extent of Aurora Australis, for, although the Aurora Borealis has received considerable attention in recent years, the detailed characteristics of Antarctic aurorae remain largely unknown; the possibility of conducting original ionospheric experiments northward from the South Polar Plateau during the long total-night season to determine the physical characteristics of the ionosphere during prolonged absence of sunlight. These and similar scientific considerations lead the CSAGI to recognize that Antarctica represents a most significant portion of the earth for intensive study during the International Geophysical Year.

Karl Weyprecht, the moving force behind the First International Polar Year.

IGY and its organization

The first CSAGI Antarctic Conference, held in Paris in July 1955, merits a significant place in Antarctic history. Its primary role was to decide the distribution of stations and provide coordination for both scientific and logistic objectives. This, in retrospect, provided the basis for much of the present geographical location of research stations, as well as providing the framework that was later developed into the Antarctic Treaty.

Despite the expectation of difficulties in reconciling Soviet and American plans for IGY the spirit of cooperation overcame all. The tone had been set at the first meeting – IGY was about science, not politics, and politics would not be allowed to intrude. The USA agreed to establish the station at the South Pole whilst the Soviet Union undertook the equally difficult task of placing stations at the Pole of Inaccessibility and the South Geomagnetic Pole. Even the UK, Argentina and Chile managed to agree on station positions in what was then actively disputed territory in the Weddell Sea sector and Antarctic Peninsula.

The enthusiasm for collaboration swept through the meeting. A US proposal to establish an international meteorological bureau at Little America to collect all Antarctic data was accepted. The idea matured and eventually the 'Antarctic Weather Central' was staffed by specialists from seven nations.

The difficulties of coordinated radio transmissions were raised at this first conference but it was not until the third conference in the summer of 1956 that the complex plan of nodal links was actually accepted. The same meeting adopted plans for World Data Centres to archive the expected scientific output from the many nations. Cooperative plans for research in meteorology, geo-magnetism, aurorae, ionospherics, cosmic rays, solar activities, glaciology, seismology and gravimetry were also accepted. The proposal by the Soviets for a map of the whole continent was agreed. But, since mapping did not fall within the remit of IGY, it was left to individual countries to carry out whatever survey work they wished without any formal attempt at coordination.

The second CSAGI conference in September 1955 had added an important additional research area to the major physical ones. It had been recognized that the establishment of so many Antarctic stations would provide unrivalled opportunities for biological and medical research. Thus, although these fields (together with geology) were never part of principal programmes, ancillary work was encouraged, but on an *ad hoc* basis.

The final CSAGI conference took place just before the formal start of IGY in 1957. This meeting reviewed the state of knowledge in a range of IGY science and set in motion planning for post-IGY activities. The first volume of the *Annals of the International Geophysical Year* appeared in late 1957 and the series eventually finished at volume 48 in 1967. This was, however, only a small part of the scientific papers and articles that finally resulted from the 18-month period of data collection.

Some national scientific achievements during IGY

The most dramatic tractor traverse during the IGY period was not an IGY project at all but a journey of exploration. Although conceived with important scientific objectives, the Commonwealth Trans-Antarctic Expedition also clearly harked back to the early abortive attempt by Sir Ernest Shackleton to cross the continent from the Weddell Sea to the Ross Sea. Conceived in 1949 by V.E. Fuchs as a private venture, planning was initiated before the first IGY intentions were made public. The main crossing party, led by Sir Vivian Fuchs, did seismic shots every 30 miles and gravity readings every 15 miles. The crossing took 99 days and the tractors had travelled 2180 miles to reach McMurdo Station. Various scientific papers were published on the work of the expedition of which the most significant were on geology, glaciology and meteorology.

The seismic traverses by the British, Americans and Soviets established the separate identities of Greater and Lesser Antarctica. Snow and ice cores allowed detailed investigations of accumulation rates and the meteorological investigations of all nations began to demonstrate the climatic characteristics of the Antarctic year at both coastal and inland stations. The Soviets in particular had problems in establishing and maintaining their inland bases but despite these their IGY contributions were of great significance. Their seismic profiles established important features beneath the interior ice cap and in addition they expended considerable effort on mapping the coast.

Soviet observations, especially at Mirny, covered most of the IGY disciplines. Aerial observations of Enderby Land were a particular feature of the Soviet programme whilst their inland tractor traverses provided both ground control for mapping and detailed ice-thickness data. Glaciological observations on ice movement were made at the coast and inland. The establishment of a station at Bunger Oasis allowed detailed measurement of an Antarctic 'oasis' microclimate for the first time. Soviet work in oceanography along the coastal areas of Greater Antarctica was especially noteworthy and included many sediment cores and bottom samples to link with geological studies on land.

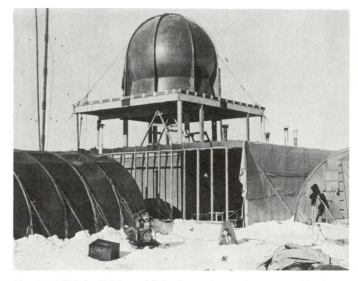

During IGY the USA established a station at the geographical South Pole. All men and equipment were flown in.

The United States programme was by far the largest in Antarctica, both in the range of observations made and in the cost. Substantial contributions were made in all the IGY disciplines with important additional work in biology and human physiology. Their collaborations with other countries were of especial importance in view of the later development of the Antarctic Treaty.

The Japanese at Syowa were dogged by misfortune with their supply ship trapped in ice and the loss of a hut and its scientific records by fire. Their station had to be closed halfway through IGY as it became impossible to relieve it. The Belgians, goaded into participation by Baron de Gerlache's son, established a station, Base Roi Baudouin, in Dronning Maud Land. They undertook a broad geophysical programme as well as some aerial survey work. The crash of their plane 400 km inland from the station tested the IGY emergency procedures, which worked well, with a Soviet aircraft rescuing the four men unhurt. The studies on radioactivity in precipitation and in rocks were more detailed than elsewhere in Antarctica.

Only limited work was carried out at the Norwegian station, and the French stations of Dumont d'Urville and Base Charcot. France concentrated its efforts on two main programmes. The major studies concerned magnetism and its relationship to atmospheric phenomena, but they also managed a 500 km journey inland from Dumont d'Urville. Seismic sounding of ice thickness in Adélie Land showed that the continental rock lay below sea level.

The major British station was the one established by the Royal Society at Halley Bay, beginning a series of

geophysical observations in 1956 which have been continued ever since. The UK had another ten operational stations on the Antarctic Peninsula, the maritime Antarctic islands and on South Georgia. All of these contributed to the IGY records to a greater or lesser extent. Indeed, limited contributions from stations in critical areas were to prove of great importance in the final synthesis of the international data.

New Zealand was already contributing to the Trans-Antarctic Expedition and it was with apparent reluctance that the Government finally agreed to support Scott Base on McMurdo Sound as a main IGY observatory. Extensive survey work in South Victoria Land was also done from the joint US/NZ station at Cape Hallett. The Australian Government had already established stations and these all showed greatly increased activities during IGY. In addition Davis Station was opened in the Vestfold Hills and a 650 km traverse inland from Mawson was achieved by tractor train. Australian measurements of cosmic rays, ionospheric characteristics and aurora at Mawson and Macquarie Island were the major parts of a large programme which also included glaciology, atmospheric ozone and geology.

A limited Chilean programme undertook studies in meteorology, seismology, auroral incidence and marine biology, whilst Argentina concentrated on meteorology and glaciology. An attempt by Argentina to establish a permanent meteorological station on Thule Island, South Sandwich Islands, was foiled by a nearby volcanic eruption.

Achievements in geophysics

The history of the physical, as contrasted with the geographical, exploration of the Antarctic is not well known, yet for this sphere of scientific investigation the Antarctic would finally prove to be supremely suitable.

The first investigations into Antarctic geophysics date back to Edmund Halley in 1700 when, aboard the *Paramour*, he made magnetic dip measurements at 52°S. His compilation of charts showing magnetic variations stimulated interest in the Admiralty and Cook, Weddell and Foster on later British expeditions, were all encouraged to make magnetic measurements as far south as possible. Bellingshausen, Dumont d'Urville and Wilkes also considered this to be of the highest scientific priority. One of the main objectives of the expedition led by James Clark Ross was to extend the contemporary knowledge of terrestrial magnetism to even higher southern latitudes than had previously been attained. Ross made magnetic observations of all three dimensions – declination, inclination and intensity – throughout his 3-year cruise, sending them back for Edward Sabine to work up and publish in the *Philosophical Transactions of the Royal Society*. Ross measured a major magnetic disturbance at Iles Kerguelen, and later noted it had also been recorded at Toronto in Canada. At the end of his Antarctic voyage physicists were able to recompute the expected position of the South Magnetic Pole much more accurately.

Most early explorers had mentioned the sightings of the spectacular displays of the aurora australis and Cook gave a detailed description of its appearance and behaviour. In sketches and paintings, several artists had tried to record it. In the nineteenth century physicists, when considering the aurora borealis, had suggested that there might be a connection between aurorae and magnetic disturbances in the Arctic. To establish the connection it was necessary to improve both auroral photography and magnetic recording. On Scott's first expedition experimental auroral photography proved a failure. He tried again on his second expedition with improved cameras and film but was still unsuccessful. The first recognizable photographs of Antarctic aurorae were probably those taken by Douglas Mawson in 1908 but these were of little value for scientific analysis since the exposure time was too long. By the time the Australasian Antarctic Expedition went south in 1911, there had been substantial film improvements and Mawson could now obtain good photographs with exposures of only 10 s rather than 10 min. Despite this, auroral studies languished for many years, awaiting the development of rugged and reliable all-sky cameras. By IGY progress had

been made and the observing network of all-sky cameras used from 1956 onwards has resulted in significant advances in the studies of Antarctic aurorae.

Any general understanding of the functioning of the upper atmosphere requires data from a wide range of physical sciences. Some investigations arose out of practical problems. Douglas Mawson, when organizing the Australasian Antarctic Expedition of 1911–1914, decided to use radio to maintain contact with Australia from the expedition's continental base at Cape Denison. This was the first use of radio from the Antarctic continent and proved to be beset by problems. He established transmitting stations at Macquarie Island and Cape Denison in 1911, together with a receiver on board the expedition ship *Aurora*. Although the Macquarie Island station worked well throughout the period, the Antarctic station failed to work until 1913. This was due to storm damage to the aerials and poor maintenance and operation of the equipment, as well as periodically difficult transmitting conditions. Later analysis of the radio logs by Charles Wright suggested that radio conditions were good during periods of low magnetic activity and that certain forms of aurorae severely affected radio wave propagation.

Unfortunately these detailed analyses were not published until 1940 and this pioneer early work was unknown to Byrd when planning his first Antarctic expedition of 1929–1931. Malcom Hansen was Byrd's chief radio engineer, responsible both for radio communications with

Little America during winter, with hoar frost sparkling on the aerial wires.

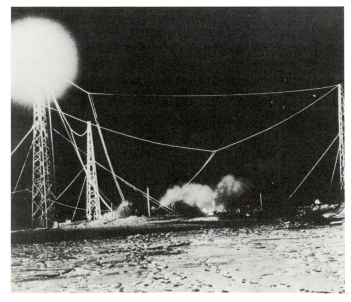

The South Magnetic Dip Pole moves about 10–15 km per year in a northwesterly direction. This pole was first reached by Mawson, David and Mackay in 1909.

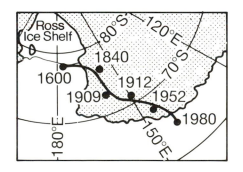

New Zealand and the USA, and for a range of upper-atmosphere physics experiments. These included the first direct radio-sounding measurements of the characteristics of the 'Heaviside Layer' in the upper atmosphere above the Antarctic. Hansen worked under astonishingly difficult conditions, operating the equipment from a small tent at −55°C with a primus stove tucked under his parka to keep him warm. His major discovery of the persistence of the F-layer during the polar night and its pronounced diurnal variation in virtual reflection heights, although mentioned in many popular accounts of the expedition, apparently remained unknown to the scientific community until IGY brought it to light. It appears to be a good example of how data published in the wrong place fails to reach the specialists that it would interest.

An even more significant case of important physical data unknown to later scientists was the work by John Dyer on very low frequency (VLF) phenomena in 1934 on the Second Byrd Antarctic Expedition. He appears to have been the first person to study VLF phenomena in the Antarctic and probably the first to measure whistlers (see Chapter 17) in either polar region. His results were never published, nor were they referred to in any accounts of the Expedition. This was unfortunate since his observations would have been of considerable use in planning the IGY whistler programme.

These scientific fields were not the only ones in which the early Byrd expeditions collected important data. Erwin Bramhall and Arthur Zuhn made significant advances in cosmic-ray work during Byrd's second expedition: in this, however, they built on earlier foundations. Simpson and Wright made the first measurements in the Antarctic on Scott's Terra Nova Expedition, using a primitive electroscope designed by Wulf. More detailed and precise

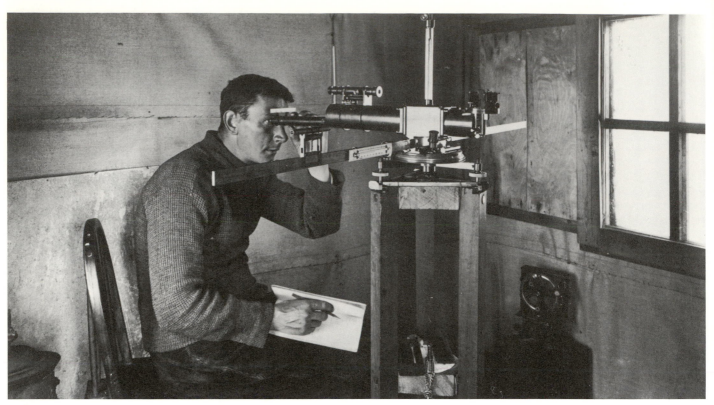

Detailed magnetic observations were made by G.C. Simpson (above) and C. S. Wright during R.F. Scott's second expedition.

Meteorological screen used on Charcot's expedition during winter.

measurements were possible on the British–Australian–New Zealand Antarctic Expedition (BANZARE) when Alec Kennedy used a Geiger–Muller electron tube counter with an amplifier. His data provided the framework for Bᵣamhall's later investigations.

The magnetic data collected by Halley, Cook and others together with these early experiments combined to demonstrate to physicists the unique characteristics of the Antarctic atmosphere which have made it an essential area for atmospheric physics and geomagnetism. It could be said that physics and meteorology, providing both the catalyst and impetus for IGY, are the true progenitors of Antarctic science as we know it today.

Exploration and Antarctic geology

An interest in the rocks of Antarctica has been shown by virtually all expeditions to visit the continent in the nineteenth century. Rock exposures are few and mainly close to the coast, an obvious attraction to any expedition seeking firm ground on which to establish a base. Yet the first hundred years of Antarctic geology (1847–1947) were restricted to limited observations on small areas, providing at best only tiny fragments of a very complex jigsaw.

Although Antarctic geology is often considered to have started with the collections made by Arctowski on the *Belgica* Expedition, significant finds were made earlier in the nineteenth century. James Eights collected fossil wood from the South Shetland Islands in 1830 but this remained unnoticed by the geological community. Important rock collections were made by Dana on Wilkes' Expedition and by Foster aboard the *Chanticleer* when it visited the South Shetland Islands in 1829. More significantly, deep-sea sampling in the Southern Ocean during the *Challenger* Expedition produced examples of continental rocks. Confirmation of the existence of a continent was needed and it was this that provided an important part of the scientific reasons for mounting the 'Heroic Age' expeditions. Initial confirmation came from the fossils discovered on Seymour Island in 1893 by C.A. Larsen and by the granite rocks sampled *in situ* by Borchgrevink at Cape Adare in 1894.

More substantial contributions were made by the geologists on several of these early expeditions. The activity was limited to two areas – the Antarctic Peninsula and the area inland from the Ross Sea. Arctowski, Wilckens and Gourdon all provided important initial data on Lesser Antarctica. Especially important were the fossil collections made by the Swedish Expedition on Seymour Island and Snow Hill Island. Here, however, Miocene and Late Cretaceous floras were identified. Fossil woods of *Nothofagus*, *Araucaria* and *Podocarpus* were found, together with several ferns and a range of shrub genera. Ammonites were the most abundant fossils followed by bivalves, fish and corals. A basic sedimentary sequence for the Peninsula region was established.

The earliest account of the general geology of the eastern side of the Peninsula was by Andersson in 1906, working from notes and specimens collected on the Swedish Expedition. It was not until nearly 50 years later that this was significantly extended by FIDS geologists, especially R.J. Adie. On the western side of the Peninsula the early collections by Gourdon on Charcot's two expeditions were initially supplemented by Fleming's investigations during the British Graham Land Expedition. Geological collections from the two United States expeditions before and after World War II improved the general knowledge of the southern section of the Peninsula. The systematic mapping begun by FIDS in the late 1940s was crucial in knitting all the data together to produce geological maps for an especially complex area.

Geology in the Ross Sea area began in earnest with the work of Hartley Ferrar in 1901–1904. He described the basement shield and an overlying sequence of sedimentary rocks for South Victoria Land, providing an excellent basis for the studies by David, Priestley, Mawson, Taylor and Debenham on the later British expeditions. By 1914 the geology of South Victoria Land was better known than anywhere else in Antarctica, whilst the geomorphological observations made by the British expeditions were the first for the continent. The Australasian expedition (1911–1914) to Wilkes Land added some further detail to what had been described of the Greater Antarctic Shield

Antarctic Geological Investigations up to IGY

Expedition Nationality	Years	Geologists	Area of mapping
American	1820–21	B. Astor	South Shetlands
British	1840–43	R. M'Cormick	Antarctic and subantarctic islands
Norwegian	1892–93	C. A. Larsen	Seymour Island
Belgian	1897–99	H. Arctowski	West Coast, Antarctic Peninsula
British	1898–1900		Cape Adare
German	1901–03	E. Philippi	Wilhelm II Coast
British	1901–04	H. T. Ferrar	Prince Albert Mountains
		O. Wilckens	
Swedish	1901–04	J. G. Andersen	Northern part of Antarctic Peninsula
		P. Dusen	
		O. Nordenskjold	
Scottish	1902–04	J. H. H. Pirie	South Orkney Islands
French	1903–05	E. Gourdon	West side, Antarctic Peninsula
British	1907–09	T. W. E. David	Prince Albert Mountains
		R. E. Priestley	
		D. Mawson	
French	1908–10	E. Gourdon	West side, Antarctic Peninsula
British	1910–13	R. E. Priestley	Prince Albert Mountains, Admiralty Range
		T. G. Taylor	
		F. Debenham	
German	1911–	F. Heim	South Georgia
British	1911–14	D. Ferguson	South Shetland Islands and Antarctic Peninsula; South Georgia
Australasian	1911–14	D. Mawson	Wilkes Land
		F. L. Stillwell	
		A. D. Watson	
		C. A. Hoadley	
British	1914–17	J. M. Wordie	South Shetlands
British	1921–22	G. V. Douglas	Weddell Sea area; South Georgia
Norwegian	1927–28	O. Holtedahl	South Georgia, South Shetlands
German	1928–29	L. Kohl-Larsen	South Georgia
American	1928–30	L. M. Gould	Rockefeller and Queen Maud Mts
American	1933–35	F. A. Wade	Queen Maud Mts and Marie Byrd Lane
		C. G. Morgan	
		Q. Blackburn	
British Graham Land	1934–37	W. L. S. Fleming	Southern part of Antarctic Peninsula
US Antarctic Service	1939–41	F. A. Wade	Southern part of Antarctic Peninsula; Esdel Ford Range,
		C. F. Passel	Rockfeller Mountains, Marie Byrd Land
		L. A. Warner	
		P. H. Knowles	
Falkland Islands Dependencies Survey	1943–57	A. F. Trendall	Systematic mapping of Antarctic Peninsula and Islands
		V. E. Fuchs	
		R. J. Adie	
		D. H. Matthews	
		J. A. Exley	
		H. G. Wright	
		A. W. Reece	
		E. Platt	
		G. Hattersley-Smith	
		M. B. Bayly	
		W. N. Croft	
		W. R. Flett	
		D. Jardine	
		P. R. Hooper	
		A. J. Standring	
		R. Stoneley	
		M. C. Green	
		J. R. F. Joyce	
		D. H. Maling	
American (Ronne)	1947–48	R. L. Nichols	Southern part of Antarctic Peninsula
		R. Dodson	
Argentine	1947–57	J. Olsacher	South Shetland Islands
		I. R. Cordini	
Norwegian–British–Swedish	1949–52	A. W. Reece	Princess Martha Coast
		E. F. Roots	
French	1949–57	P. Vincent	Kerguelen, Adélie Land
		G. Heurtebize	
		E. Aubert de la Rue	
Australian National Antarctic Research	1954–57	B. Stinear	Prince Charles Mountains, MacRobertson Land, Heard Island
		A. J. Lambeth	

by Drygalski's expedition (1901–1903). Further data on Greater Antarctica were collected during BANZARE and the Norwegian–British–Swedish Expedition but much less was known about this area before the IGY than about the western part of the continent.

Prior to IGY geological data had established that Antarctica consisted of two distinct land masses, an idea first put forward by Nordenskjold in 1913. Greater Antarctica was considered to be a shield area with a basement complex of mainly Precambrian schists and gneisses overlain by Palaeozoic and Mesozoic sediments. Lesser Antarctica on the other hand appeared to be composed of greatly folded Mesozoic and Tertiary sediments fairly similar to the Andes. The major question facing geologists in the 1950s concerned the structural relationships between Lesser and Greater Antarctica.

At that period, plate tectonic theory had not been formulated but questions concerning the relationship of Antarctica to the other southern continents were being posed. The fossils of plants and animals found on both sides of Antarctica clearly indicated that the climatic

history of the continent had included much more favourable periods than at present. A paper published in 1904 by A.G. Nathorst, on fossils from the Hope Bay area, had concluded that a subtropical environment had once been enjoyed there. This created a scientific sensation at the time but more widespread collecting of fossils from warm-water and over thirty species of cycads and conifer showed that Nathorst's suggestion was well founded.

To explain these clear indications of earlier climates, to relate the scattered geological data for the two geological provinces and to take into account biogeographical evidence for connections, for example between South America and Australia, proved difficult. Prior to IGY three theories were current. The first was that the oceans between Antarctica and the other southern continents had once been land and had now subsided. By 1950 this was thought to be unlikely. The second hypothesis proposed land bridges along island areas and submarine ridges together with some degree of movement over the earth's crust. This provided no adequate explanation of the climatic changes. Finally, the continental drift theory, proposed by

Geotectonic map of Antarctica as envisaged by Fairbridge in 1949.

Coal seams discovered in the Transantarctic Mountains during IGY.

Wegener and developed by du Toit, offered the most promise for the future but needed more data to substantiate it. As R.W. Fairbridge put it in 1952,

In Antarctica we see geologically a "normal" continent whose past history is closely comparable with other continents; its great coast-to-coast glaciation of today makes it unique, and in the solution of this riddle may lie the key to many fundamental problems in the evolution of our planet.

During IGY the major geological work was carried out by expeditions from New Zealand, USA, UK, the Soviet Union and Australia. Some limited collecting was done by Japan, Belgium, Argentina, France, Norway and South Africa.

The development of glaciology

Glaciology is a diverse discipline covering subjects as far apart as the mass balance of ice sheets, the physical properties of ice and the reconstruction of past climates and atmospheres. Present glaciological studies in the Antarctic cover all these fields and more. Many research subjects have developed only fairly recently, for instance glacio-chemical studies of pollution and oxygen isotope ratios for climatic temperature trends.

All the early Antarctic expeditions made lengthy qualitative comments on icebergs and ice shelves in their narratives. The first scientific observations on glaciers appear to be those made by Moseley on the *Challenger*, comparing the positions and effects of glaciers on Iles Kerguelen and Heard Island.

Henryk Arctowski on the *Belgica* Expedition was probably the first Antarctic scientist who could be called a glaciologist. He studied the glaciers along the western coast of the Antarctic Peninsula, drawing attention to evidence of ice recession and suggesting that the ice sheet formerly covered the whole continent.

Over the following 15 years all the major expeditions carried out some glaciological studies. In most instances these were secondary to geological observations and were carried out by geologists. Nevertheless these 'amateur' glaciologists made major contributions. Scott's second expedition was the first Antarctic expedition with a scientific programme of glaciological research, resulting in an outstanding monograph by Wright and Priestley on glaciology in Victoria Land.

The general mechanisation of field travel was of great significance to glaciological research. Planned aerial survey operations, mainly pioneered by Byrd, rapidly extended general knowledge of the interior of the continent and allowed glaciologists to look much further inland than previously. The first seismic soundings to determine ice thickness were made by T.C. Poulter on Byrd's Second Expedition whilst snow-pit sampling was introduced by F.A. Wade in 1940/41.

After World War II more information on glaciers and ice shelves was collected by F. Ronne's expedition and the activities of FIDS surveyors in the Antarctic Peninsula region. This was all descriptive material, however, with little detailed investigation of processes. The first and most significant expedition in this respect was the Norwegian–British–Swedish Expedition in 1949–1952. During this period several glaciologists (Robin, Schytt, Swithinbank) devoted themselves to a carefully planned investigation of both the ice shelves and the inland ice sheet in Dronning Maud Land. Studies in a 13 m snow pit and of an ice core 100 m deep provided a detailed account of the transformation from firn to ice at temperatures continually below freezing, as well as establishing annual accumulation rates over many years from snow stratification. Eighty seismic shots on an inland traverse established that the ice sheet was at least 2400 m thick, whilst the study of the 'hinge' zone between the floating ice sheet and the inland ice was novel. Work by the meteorologists,

Antarctic Geological Investigations up to IGY

Expedition	Years	Glaciologists
Belgian	1897–99	H. Arctowski
German	1901–03	E. Philippi
British National	1901–04	H. T. Ferrar
Scottish	1902–04	J. H. H. Pirie
French	1903–05	E. Gourdon
British	1907–09	R. E. Priestley
		D. Mawson
British (*Terra Nova*)	1910–13	C. S. Wright
		R. E. Priestley
Australasian	1911–14	D. Mawson
Byrd	1928–30	L. M. Gould
Byrd	1933–35	T. Poulter
		F. A. Wade
British Graham Land	1934–37	W. L. S. Fleming
US Antarctic Service	1939–41	F. A. Wade
		P. H. Knowles
Falkland Islands Dependencies Survey	1943–57	D. Mason
		G. Hattersley-Smith
		A. W. Reece
Ronne Antarctic Research	1947–48	R. L. Nichols
Norwegian–British–Swedish	1949–52	C. W. M. Swithinbank
		V. Schytt
		G. de Q. Robin
French	1949–55	F. Loewe

especially on radiation balance, and by the surveyors all added to a better understanding of the glaciological data.

The pre-IGY expeditions had provided descriptions of ice sheets, ice shelves and glaciers for a number of isolated localities. In only a few instances had quantitative measurements of processes been attempted and virtually nothing was known of the vast proportion of the inland ice sheet. The establishment of permanent stations by the British, French and Australians had allowed some continuity of measurements to be attempted but, overall, the data base for Antarctic glaciology was scanty.

The major questions for IGY were therefore concerned with measurements of ice thickness to allow calculation of the volume of ice, of accumulation and loss to calculate mass balance, of ice cores to determine climatic fluctuations, and of micrometeorology to assess the thermal regime. The IGY inland journeys by the Americans, Soviets and the Trans-Antarctic Expedition produced much new information on ice thickness and bedrock topography. The ice cores drilled at Byrd Station in 1958 (308 m) and at Little America in 1959 (256 m) opened up new fields for glaciological research which are still expanding today. The data from IGY enabled, for the first time, the preparation of generalised diagrams for the whole continent showing snow accumulation rates, the general direction of movement of the ice sheet and crude estimates of mass and heat balances.

The Dry Valleys in Victoria Land, discovered during the expeditions led by Scott and Shackleton, have proved a centre for a wide range of scientific studies since 1956.

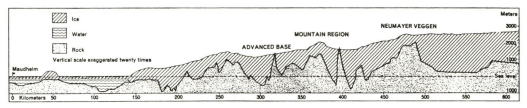

Profile of the ice surface and of the bedrock surface as determined by the seismic group.

Drilling of the ice sheet during and after IGY produced the first extensive historical records of annual snow accumulation.

(Below) Exploration of the inland ice by the Norwegian–British–Swedish Expedition produced the first detailed profile of under-ice topography.

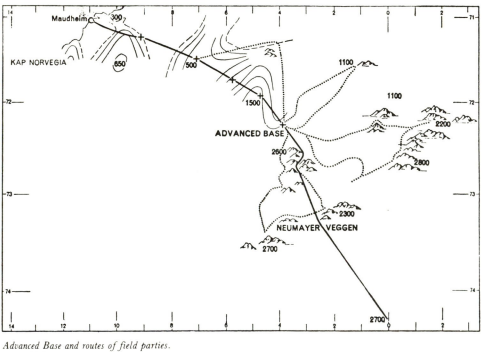

Advanced Base and routes of field parties.
.... Sledging routes
——— Route of seismic group

*Depth sounding of the ice-sheet
by seismic shots.*

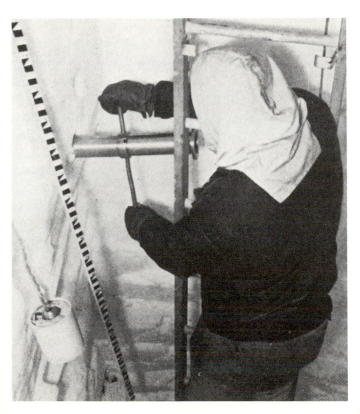

*Snow samples being taken in a pit at West Base during the US
Antarctic Service Expedition. The snow sampler kit was made of
steel and brass.*

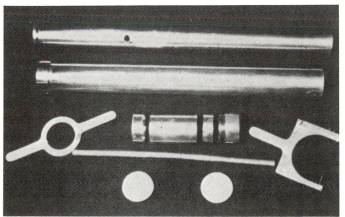

Biology – an overlooked field

The earliest investigations in Antarctic biology can be attributed to the naturalists J.R. and G. Forster who accompanied Captain James Cook on his circumnavigation of 1772–1775. Their Antarctic material was largely overshadowed by the importance of the exciting collections made in Australasia. Nevertheless, their work can now be seen as setting Antarctic biology off on the right footing.

During the nineteenth century several well-known experts made biological contributions, all mainly in the marine field. Indeed, it is clear historically that virtually all the major early advances in Antarctic biology were concerned with the Southern Ocean rather than with the land. The biological exploration of the Southern Ocean falls into three historical periods. The earliest expeditions began the cataloguing and descriptive phase. Extensive collections of animals and plants were made and preserved for later description by taxonomic specialists in each group.

The earliest scientific collections of Antarctic marine animals were those made by the American James Eights, who visited the Antarctic Peninsula (in 1829–1831) with Captains Pendleton and Palmer. Eights' reports on the natural history of the South Shetland Islands, published in 1833, and the beautifully illustrated account of the ten-legged sea spider *Decolopoda australis* apparently remained unknown to other Antarctic scientists until the twentieth century.

An equally unfortunate fate overtook another American in this field, T.R. Peale, a naturalist with the United States Exploring Expedition led by Charles Wilkes. Not only did Peale lose most of his specimens in a shipwreck but the problems surrounding the publication of the scientific results of the expedition effectively negated any contribution he might have hoped to make to Antarctic biology. One of the other scientists of this expedition, James Dana, did however leave his mark by providing the first description and illustration of krill, *Euphausia superba*.

The *Challenger* Expedition (1872–1874) led by Charles Wyville Thomson epitomises this period, producing an extensive and valuable set of expedition reports published over a long period. The main concern of the scientists was to describe the morphology of the organisms, to name and and classify them and, if possible, to draw some conclusions about their geographical distribution.

Wyville Thomson and his colleagues set new standards in the sheer range and variety of material with which they dealt. They were, however, continuing in an earlier tradition, well established for other parts of the world, and particularly well developed during the whole of the nineteenth century – the period of rapid colonial expansion and exploration for Britain.

The *Challenger* collections had been preceded by others, much less voluminous and wide ranging, but significant in their time. On James Clark Ross's expedition

The laboratory aboard HMS Challenger.

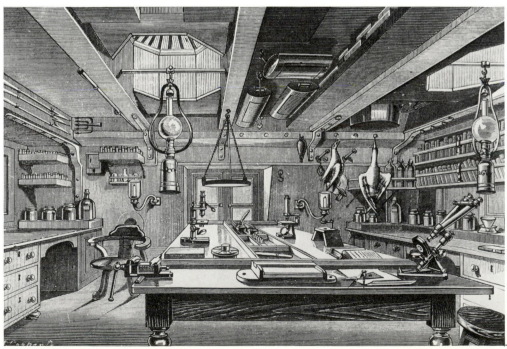

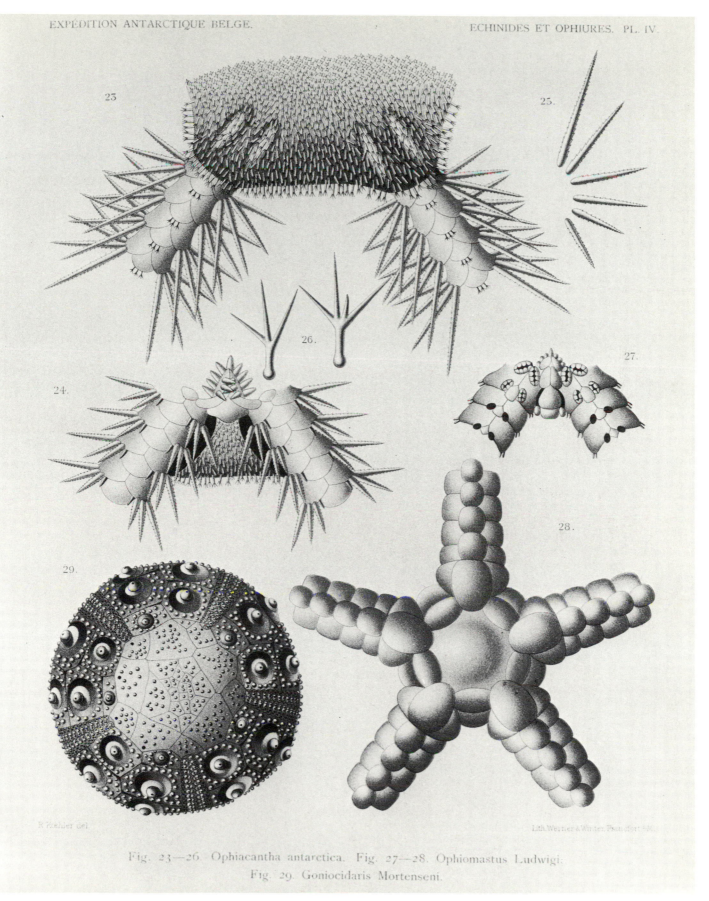

R. Koehler del.   Lith. Werner & Winter, Frankfort ªM.

Fig. 23—26 Ophiacantha antarctica. Fig. 27—28. Ophiomastus Ludwigi.
Fig. 29. Goniocidaris Mortenseni.

The Belgica *expedition made major biological collections of marine organisms.*

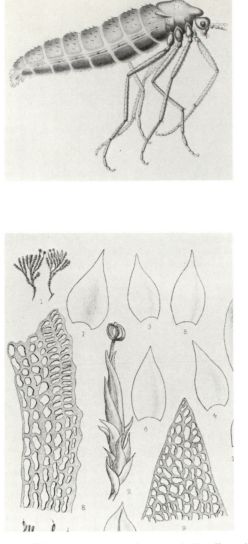

The Belgian expedition discovered the largest native land animal on the Antarctic continent – a wingless fly Belgica antarctica.

A new species of Antarctic moss Andreaea gainii *collected by Gain during Charcot's Second French Antarctic Expedition 1908–10.*

(1839–1843), marine collections had been made by M'Cormick and Robertson whose collection of fishes was the first described from the Antarctic region. The fish collection (including a substantial number of specimens held by Ross as a private collection) was originally very large but many specimens were badly damaged during the long period of storage in spirit. Despite this, 234 species were later recognised, of which no fewer than 145 were new. Deep dredging was initiated on this expedition.

An even larger collection of fishes was made on Wilkes' expedition but lack of money and support ensured that Louis Agassiz never completed his descriptions. In the end many of the specimens and the labels were lost in storage and even the original manuscript by Agassiz disappeared. Even earlier than this the French Expedition of 1837–1840 led by Dumont d'Urville, had brought back coelenterates and crustaceans, but these were of relatively little significance on their own.

This early period of biological collection had led to a number of important conclusions. Ross had established that abyssal depths separated the Antarctic continent from its northern neighbours and that marine life existed to great depths. J.D. Hooker laid the foundation for botanical work both in the Southern Ocean and on the subantarctic islands. The expeditions led by Ross, Wilkes, Dumont d'Urville and Wyville Thomson provided the

Observations on whale behaviour made by Emil Racovitzai during the Belgian Antarctic Expedition. An active collector of all biological material, Racovitzai was also a good biologist making many new observations on Antarctic natural history.

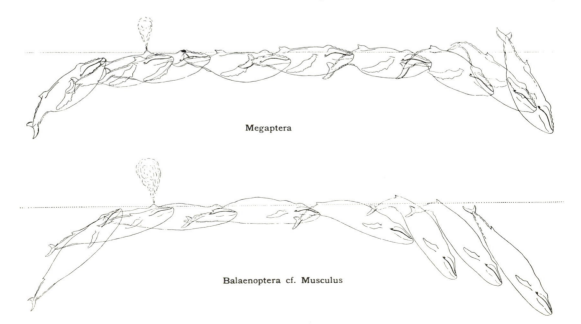

Megaptera

Balaenoptera cf. Musculus

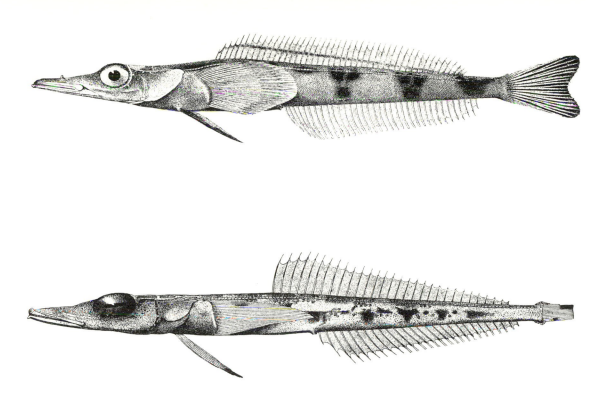

Two new species of Antarctic fish collected by the Belgian Antarctic Expedition. Both the leader, De Gerlache, and the biologist, Racovitzai, are commemorated by the generic names Gerlachea (above) *and* Racovitzaia (below).

basic oceanographic data for the Southern Ocean and their marine collections provided the foundations for characterising the unique flora and fauna.

By the end of the nineteenth century a range of basic information was available but had been gathered unevenly, both in taxonomic and geographic terms. The German Expedition aboard *Gauss* (1901–1903) contributed much new information on the plankton and benthos as did the earlier *Valdivia* Expedition (1898–1899). R.F. Scott's two expeditions carried out marine biology and oceanography both on board their ships and through the sea ice, from their base camps. Other major expeditions of this period, led by Bruce, Mawson, Charcot, De Gerlache and Nordenskjold, all made major contributions to our knowledge of the marine system.

Without doubt the greatest single historical contribution to southern-hemisphere marine biology has come from the fourteen years of cruises by the ships of the Discovery Committee. Between 1925 and 1939 nearly the whole of the Southern Ocean was sampled for its benthos and pelagic fauna whilst water sampling enormously increased our knowledge of oceanography in these turbulent waters. The final cruise took place in 1950–1951. The original collections of benthos and pelagic fauna were so large that, for some groups, material still remains to be examined in detail. A shore laboratory was maintained for 6 years on South Georgia where work concentrated mainly on the biology of whales. A special series, *Discovery Reports*, was established to publish the findings of the Discovery Investigations. Volume 1 was published in 1929 and the series continues today with volume 38 in preparation.

These later volumes are not necessarily based on the pre-War Discovery collections but add to the principal original objectives of the Investigations an understanding of the marine ecosystem especially in the context of whales. The significance of these studies was fully appreciated in 1946 when the establishment of the International Whaling Commission put the control of whaling on an international basis and the conservation of whales onto a scientific basis.

Important pre-War work in biology was undertaken on land, during the British Graham Land Expedition, by B.B. Roberts on birds and G.C.L. Bertram on Weddell and Crabeater seals. Biological studies were conducted on both the Second Byrd Antarctic Expedition (1933–1935) and the US Antarctic Service Expedition (1939–1941). A.A. Lindsey studied Weddell and Crabeater seals in the Bay of Whales during the first expedition whilst P.A. Siple collected vegetation, cultured bacteria, observed birds and investigated human physiology during both expeditions.

During Byrd's second expedition J.E. Perkins collected numerous bird and seal specimens from around the Bay of Whales. A visit inland to the Fosdick Mountains produced a good collection of mosses and lichens. The bulk of bird skins and skeletons collected by C. Eklund at East Base had to be abandoned at the emergency evacuation of the base. Further bacteriological studies were made to supplement those made in 1934. This expedition also made collections of inshore marine life which considerably extended the biogeographical data for several species.

The distribution of krill in the Southern Ocean, plotted in 1962 by J W S Marr from Discovery Investigations data.

Ship tracks for the Discovery Investigations. Virtually all of the Southern Ocean was visited and some areas were subjected to repeated study to record seasonal changes.

By 1945 the major biological achievements in Antarctica were almost all observational. The bulk of the published material was taxonomic or biogeographical and it was clear from the species distribution maps that collections were most unevenly spaced. The few areas that had received detailed investigation were all marine. The general biology of many whale species, several seals and a few birds (mainly penguins) had been established. Plankton had also been the subject of some intensive studies as had the general oceanography of the Southern Ocean. Many of the rarer species and all the common species had by now been collected and described.

There were however major areas with little data. On land the collections of plants and animals were very limited. Oceanic squid and the abyssal bottom fauna were largely unstudied, and the life cycles of very few animals were known. The concept of food chains had been developed but they were unquantified and oversimplified. Few measurements of population size had been attempted for any species.

After World War II the establishment of permanent

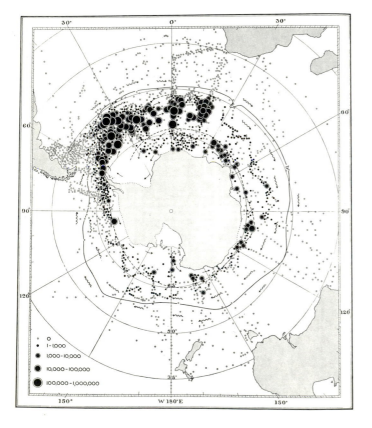

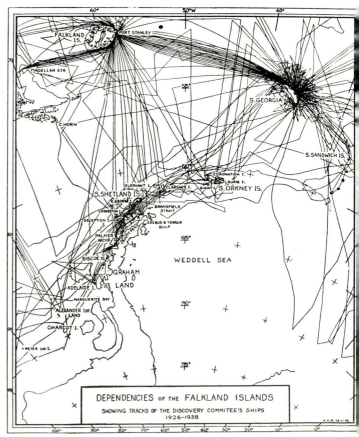

stations, together with the continuation of national expeditions of limited duration, allowed some further biological progress before IGY, but progress was slow. There were some important and detailed studies by R.M. Laws on seals, W.J.L. Sladen and B. Stonehouse on penguins, I.M. Lamb on lichens, C.J.F. Skottsberg on marine algae, and J.M. Sieburth on bacteria. Oceanic cruises by *Brategg* and *Discovery II* added further data on marine biology, which confirmed that the pattern of vertical water circulation in the Southern Ocean was circumpolar, although with localised distortions.

The beginning of IGY saw Antarctic biology at the end of a major phase. Widespread collecting of material had outrun taxonomic assessment for many groups. Life cycle studies on selected species had just begun but little ecological research had even been planned. Observation rather than experimentation still reigned supreme.

IGY helped to increase the pressure for an increase in biological science for the future, not in any structured way but as a concomitant of the increased scientific interest in the continent. There was no overall plan, as for the IGY

The British Graham Land Expedition concentrated its biological research on birds and seals. Note the great length of legs in this X-ray photograph of a Wilson's Storm Petrel.

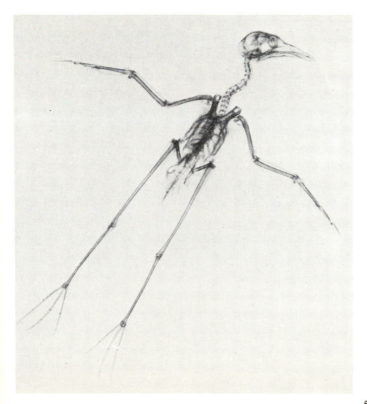

geophysical work, and the expansion that followed was uneven both in effort and objectives. The foundations of these programmes are to be found both in earlier Antarctic studies, for instance the life cycle of Antarctic birds and marine mammals, and also in studies elsewhere in the world, for instance physiological research on marine organisms. Many biological programmes were undertaken as part-time efforts by scientists principally occupied on physical measurements or employed as medical officers on the stations. Indeed, some significant studies in human biology, especially on the physiological responses to stress, were carried out both before and during IGY. Nevertheless, the sum total of these efforts, both amateur and professional, together with the example of IGY achievements in the physical sciences, provided the basis for the massive expansion in biological research during the 1960s.

Logistic developments

Any advancement in science is generally dependent on both human insight and technical support. Indeed, in modern Antarctic science a high degree of technical sophistication is essential for many of the experiments. The history of scientific investigation in Antarctica shows clearly the importance of matching the techniques of a developing science to an enhancement in logistics to provide the essential support. The costs and complexity of both grow, in step, together with the supporting bureaucracy!

During the early phase of exploration all the observational data were novel and largely collected close to coastal sites. The expeditions on *Belgica* and *Southern Cross* had proved that man could survive winter in the Antarctic. The remarkable efforts made by the scientists on expeditions between 1901 and 1915 added enormously to the information available but the time and effort necessary to travel and survive inhibited any large-scale scientific developments.

The importance of the internal combustion engine to geographical exploration was realised as early as 1907 by Ernest Shackleton. Scott tried tractors in 1910 but all these attempts were generally unsuccessful. Douglas Mawson had greater plans, intending in 1912 to try an aircraft in Antarctica but, alas, the plane crashed whilst still in Australia. Later attempts to use motorised transport became steadily more successful and here Byrd pioneered the way.

By 1940 the reliability of tractors and aircraft was such that expeditions were planned around their use. Man now

Sketch by Edward Wilson of the stone hut constructed at Cape Crozier to house three men.

The hut at Waterboat Point on the Antarctic Peninsula in which T. W. Bagshawe and M. C. Lester spent a year recording meteorological and biological data.

The living area in the main hut of the British Graham Land Expedition. As with all expeditions space was at a premium.

LC-130 ski-equipped Hercules aeroplanes have proved ideal for both Antarctic logistics support and aerial survey work. This US Navy plane flies a regular shuttle service for cargo and personnel between Christchurch, New Zealand, and Williams Field in McMurdo Sound.

Flight routes for the Swedish Air Force group with the Norwegian–British– Swedish Expedition in 1949–1952.

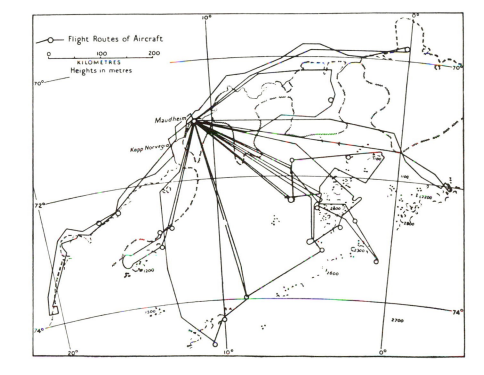

had the ability not only to mount oversnow traverses by tractor train but also to reconnoitre the way ahead by aircraft. Field camps could be set up inland and adequately supported. The capacity of the new transport systems to move considerable amounts of supplies introduced changes not only in scientific capabilities but also in other aspects of logistic support. Food became a minor component of the total weight moved, giving great flexibility to the supplies officer to make the menus more attractive and interesting. Time considerations, especially when using aircraft, became much more important because of the limited duration of range and available flying time.

These features of transport developments were fully exploited by the Norwegian–British–Swedish Expedition in 1949–1952, providing a useful fund of experience to add to that of the British and Australians in the logistical planning for IGY. During the IGY huge numbers of ships, aircraft and tractors were deployed by all nations in an attempt to collect the necessary scientific data during the observing period. The use of large ski-equipped long-range cargo aircraft by the USA opened up a new era in transport to and from Antarctica. For the first time men could regularly visit the continent for a very short period, providing new and more attractive research opportunities for busy senior scientists who would not have been able to fit a long visit to the Antarctic into their schedules. The increasing use of helicopters, especially for field parties in Victoria Land, meant that no locality was any longer inaccessible.

In few spheres of human endeavour are the demands upon a supply organization as onerous as in Antarctica. To ensure both survival and scientific activities, supply procedures need to be as near foolproof as possible. Polar history is full of the hardships caused by failures of organization and inadequate logistic experience. Only when an experienced team is available to provide logistic support do these problems become less dominant. IGY marked the initiation of this phase for many nations.

(Left) *A photograph of the coast in MacRobertson Land was taken during the US Operation Highjump. It was used by Phillip Law to choose Horseshoe Harbour as the site of the first Australian station (Mawson) on the continent.*

(Right) *The effect of IGY on Antarctic activities is shown in the number and distribution of stations established before (●) and during (○) IGY.*

The period of preparation for IGY was too short to allow for much innovation but the problems encountered provided the stimulus for many later logistic developments. Some nations, notably the UK, Argentina, France, Chile and Australia, were already deeply involved in Antarctica before IGY and were able to mount their activities using experienced teams. Others, such as the Soviet Union, looked to their current Arctic activities or, as in the case of the USA, to an earlier period of Antarctic activities for experienced personnel.

During the IGY fifty Antarctic stations were operating, with forty-seven of them operational throughout the winter. The establishment of the inland stations high on the Antarctic plateau was a major achievement. Temperatures proved to be even lower than expected and considerable difficulties were experienced in operating vehicles at temperatures down to −68°C. The cost of establishing and maintaining these inland stations was high – estimated by the USA at around one million US dollars per man for Amundsen–Scott base in 1957. The period of major field activity (July 1957 – December 1958) saw the population of Antarctica rise to over 5000 as international expenditure on Antarctic science reached several hundred million US dollars.

The design of the stations built during IGY varied considerably. British and Norwegian expeditions used conventional timber-framed buildings, whilst the French used prefabricated pressed steel huts. Australian, American and Soviet huts on rock sites showed striking similarity in construction. All used prefabricated aluminium or plywood insulated panels, clamped together to produce flat-roofed box-like buildings.

A major technological advance produced by IGY was the development of reliable and extensive telecommunications both between Antarctic stations and with the outside world. The need for immediate transmission of meteorological data to forecasting centres, the administration of large stations and the extensive use of aircraft all required high-power transmitters and major aerial arrays, as well as reliable 24-hour power. An elaborate network of 'mother' and 'daughter' stations was organized to channel data efficiently. The availability of regular contacts between many national stations did much to improve collaboration between the scientists involved and set up a new standard in the provision of communications required for future stations.

The development of this took place under especially difficult conditions for radio communications. Magnetic storms were common, causing frequent 'black-outs'. The difficulties of earthing equipment on either rock or snow exacerbated the static electricity problems caused by drift snow blowing across aerials. Extensive tests on radio

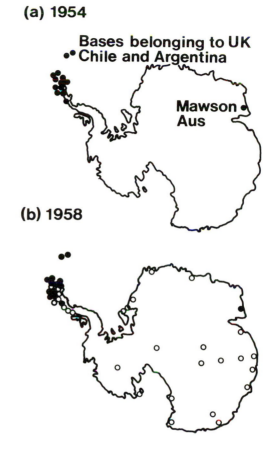

(a) 1954

Bases belonging to UK Chile and Argentina

Mawson Aus

(b) 1958

equipment before shipment to the Antarctic proved of little use in combating the special conditions. In many cases it was the *ad hoc* developments by individual radio operators that ensured effective communications. The practical lessons learnt were of considerable use in the development of permanent and complex transmitting stations after IGY.

Prior to the IGY clothing for Antarctic expeditions had been generally made to measure since the numbers on any one expedition were usually small. The large numbers involved in IGY operations necessitated mass production and, in keeping with the times, a range of synthetic materials was tried in place of natural fibres. Of the few innovations in design evident, only the 'thermal boot' developed by the USA and the extensive use of zip fasteners seemed of long-term significance.

The sheer scale of IGY focused logistic planning and development in a way never before seen. Without this necessity many of these developments could have taken decades to arrive. In logistic terms IGY was a watershed. Before it, Antarctic exploration and science was mainly conducted by private or semi-private expeditions. The size and international scope of the new endeavours required government funding and organization. The backbone of support for continuous long-term scientific activity was forming.

Clothing on R.F. Scott's expedition, sketched by Edward Wilson.

Modern Antarctic clothing.

Chapter·4
Science and Antarctic politics

The success of IGY

In the light of the political discord between the USA and the Soviet Union in the 1950s – the 'cold war' period – it is remarkable that IGY ever took place. That it did must be attributed to the exclusion of politicians from the planning meetings at which the scientists managed to achieve and honour agreements which would have been unattainable in the political arena. The extraordinary success of IGY must have been due in great part to its limitations. It did not try to tackle all scientific problems but confined itself to those disciplines concerned with the earth and the forces that affect it. Clear priorities were established in the planning phase, with the highest priority always being given to questions requiring data from multiple simultaneous observations at many points on the globe. This is reflected in part by the subject areas of the IGY Annals – ten volumes are devoted to aurorae and airglow, nine to the ionosphere, but only one each for glaciology, oceanography and meteorology.

Analysis of the magnetic and gravity data, together with some seismological information, established clearly for the first time that Greater Antarctica was indeed a continental shield whilst Lesser Antarctica was an archipelago. Gravity readings showed the continental rock and ice to be in isostatic equilibrium (Chapter 12) whilst the ice depth records allowed the first realistic assessment of the effect on world sea levels of the melting of the ice cap. Ionospheric studies had demonstrated the unusual nature of the ionosphere above the continent, whilst the regular meteorological data gave an initial insight into the effects of continental weather on southern hemisphere climatic patterns. Considerable progress had been made in a variety of glaciological fields whilst many more of the limited outcrops of rock had been given a preliminary geological examination. IGY on a global scale had been even more successful, partly because most other sites used did not face as many formidable logistic difficulties as those in the Antarctic.

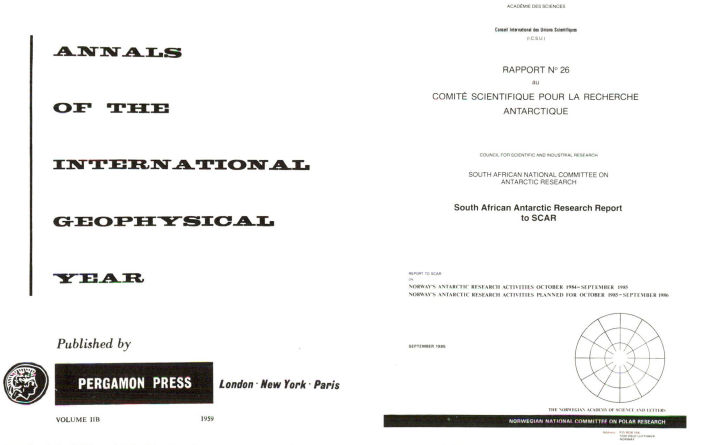

Annals of the IGY, published in 48 volumes, contain a primary record of the international achievements. Many more scientific papers and general articles were published elsewhere.

Every year each SCAR national committee prepares a report on the achievements of the last Antarctic season and the plans for the next one.

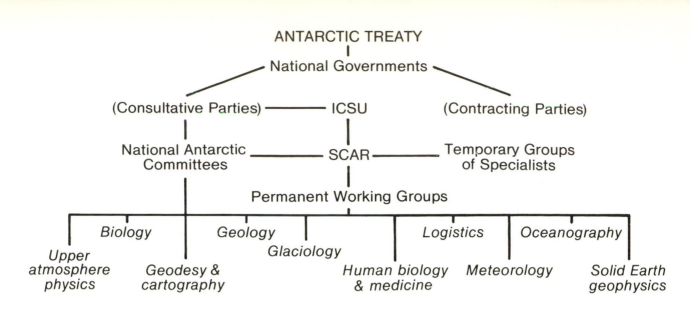

ANTARCTIC TREATY

National Governments

(Consultative Parties) ——— ICSU ——— (Contracting Parties)

National Antarctic Committees ——— SCAR ——— Temporary Groups of Specialists

Permanent Working Groups

Biology   Geology   Logistics   Oceanography

Upper atmosphere physics   Geodesy & cartography   Glaciology   Human biology & medicine   Meteorology   Solid Earth geophysics

The relationships between the various SCAR committees which provide an active and non-political forum for the discussion of Antarctic science.

Questions had already been asked before the official start of IGY about its continuation after 1958. The USA was in favour, as were the British, but other members of CSAGI were doubtful. At the CSAGI Assembly in Moscow in July 1958 the Soviet Union proposed to extend IGY on several grounds, one of the most significant of which was the limited return achieved by them on the massive investment in Antarctica. This agreed with the earlier American proposals made in 1957 and clearly had a powerful effect on the uncommitted nations. A further year of IGY activity, called the Year of International Geophysical Cooperation, was important in keeping the scientific impetus in Antarctica and underpinning the early period of SCAR, the Special (now Scientific) Committee on Antarctic Research. This had been formed in 1957 by ICSU as a result of the USA initiative and was clearly the most suitable body to act as the coordinator of the post-IGY programmes. Besides one delegate from each of the nations active in Antarctica, the Committee also included representatives from ICSU scientific unions and from other international scientific bodies such as the World Meteorological Organisation. An important outcome of the IGY and an example of the international development of SCAR was the major contribution made by 35 Antarctic stations to data collection during the International Year of the Quiet Sun (1964–65).

Antarctic Treaty negotiations and the formation of SCAR

The success of the international exchanges, of data pooling and of programme coordination exemplified by the Antarctic studies in IGY reopened the question of a permanent international solution to the persistent political problems caused by territorial claims. On 2 May 1958, the US Government circulated a note to the eleven other nations at work in Antarctica, proposing a treaty that would set the continent aside for scientific use only.

Similar suggestions had been made before but now the climate of opinion was different. Sixty secret meetings to establish a common basis of agreement preceeded the formal Treaty conference in Washington on 15 October 1959. Although the Soviet Union was generally at odds with most of the other countries, eventually most difficulties were resolved. Despite all this preparatory work the conference lasted six and a half weeks instead of the expected two weeks. Finally, on 1 December 1959, the Treaty was signed; after ratification by the member states, it finally came into force on 23 June 1961.

The Treaty is unique in the field of international affairs. Surprisingly concise (see Appendix 1), it managed to resolve the then existing problems and yet allow sufficient flexibility to cope with unformulated future difficulties. It guarantees freedom of scientific research and exchange of data, forbids nuclear explosions and the disposal of radioactive waste, prohibits all military activities and opens all installations to international inspection. Although there is provision for a review of its Articles 30 years after it came into force, there is no termination date for the Treaty.

The Treaty was preceeded by the formation of SCAR and indeed SCAR is regarded as the source of all scientific data required by the Consultative Parties (full Treaty members) for the biennial Treaty meetings. It is from the Specialist Working Groups set up by SCAR that the extensions of Treaty provisions to protection of the environment (Agreed Measures for the Conservation of Antarctic Fauna and Flora; Convention for the Conservation of Antarctic Seals; Convention on the Conservation of Antarctic Marine Living Resources) have come. SCAR has a permanent secretariat, at present at the Scott Polar Research Institute at Cambridge, and is financed by a levy on all national organizations in proportion to their Antarctic activity. The budget is extremely small and in no way reflects the total cost of administering all the SCAR activities. The very considerable influence of SCAR must be attributed to the scientific distinction of its membership internationally, and to their authority within their national scientific communities. Since SCAR is a subcommittee of

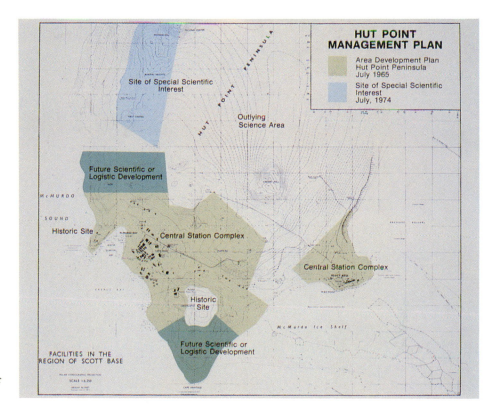

Competition for suitable station sites can interfere with scientific research. The production of agreed land-use management plans is likely to be essential for both scientific and conservation reasons.

ICSU, membership is not limited to countries which have acceded to the Treaty. Likewise, Treaty signatories are not necessarily members of SCAR, although in practice all Consultative Parties need to be in order to work most effectively. At present, the German Democratic Republic is a member of SCAR but not a Consultative Party, whilst China and Uruguay, both recently accepted as Consultative Parties, have yet to join SCAR.

Despite the provisions in the Treaty for full and free exchange of all scientific information, the biennial Treaty meetings at government level are held in considerable secrecy. The Consultative Parties have always avoided forming any permanent secretariat, arrangements for each meeting being left in the hands of whichever government has offered to host a particular meeting. SCAR, however, publishes a full report each year as a supplement to the journal *Polar Record*. Its major activity is the coordination of national scientific activities and the provision of specialist information to Treaty meetings via member governments. The Antarctic Treaty nowhere mentions SCAR, and the SCAR Constitution and Standing Resolutions barely refer to the Treaty. SCAR is a planning and coordination organization operating on a shoestring; yet the Consultative Parties have increasingly seemed to regard it as their scientific secretariat, requesting actions and activities from it which have severely strained its resources. Despite this, its contribution to scientific progress on a broad front can be seen in the number and range of international symposia it has promoted during the last 26 years (see Appendix 2).

National organization of Antarctic research

The way in which Antarctic research is organized differs considerably between countries. A major difference is whether organization is highly centralised, integrating logistics and science, or whether it is dispersed between different agencies. A second important feature is whether those who determine policy and administer programmes are actively involved in research.

All nations use a National Antarctic Committee of some type to report to SCAR on their present and future activities, but the way in which projects are selected and supported is surprisingly varied. In all cases there appears to be a mixture of government and university scientists, and the diverse and costly nature of Antarctic logistic support always ensures that a variety of other official bodies is involved. An example of the degree of complexity is shown by the structure of Antarctic research in the United Kingdom. Nearly all logistic support and the majority of scientists come from one government-supported institute, the British Antarctic Survey (BAS). This is a centralised system, yet there are also university scientists using BAS logistics and limited Antarctic support from the Ministry of Defence. Political interest is expressed via the Department of Education and Science, the High Commissioner for British Antarctic Territories and an informal link to the Foreign Office. Scientific control rests with the Natural Environment Research Council and a subcommittee of the Royal Society.

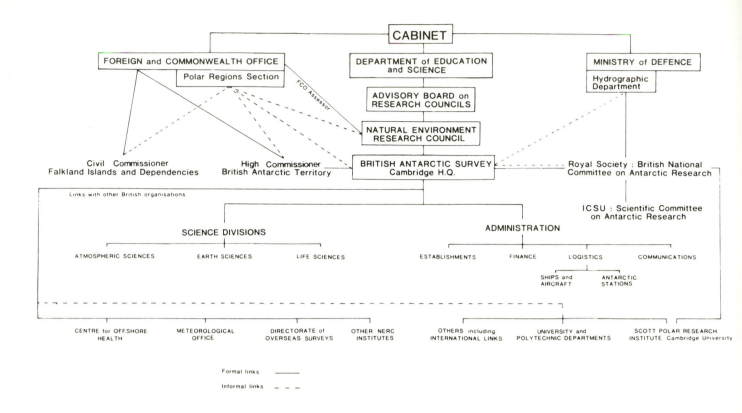

The organization of polar research in the United Kingdom.

Some other countries also run a mainly institute-based integrated science and logistics system. The Soviet Union controls all its Antarctic activities through the Arctic and Antarctic Research Institute which coordinates science and logistics. Many scientists work for the Institute but others are seconded from the wide range of Government departments. A similar system exists in Japan. In Argentina and Chile the Armed Forces supply all the logistics whilst scientific programmes only are the responsibility of the research institutes.

However, in the USA responsibilities are dispersed. Scientists come mainly from the universities, logistics are provided by the US Navy and US Coastguard whilst a commercial company is contracted to run the bases. Funding for all activities is from a central budget controlled by the Division of Polar Programs in the National Science Foundation (NSF). Although there are polar centres within the US universities, they are not permanently supported as such by the NSF.

By contrast the South Africans use the Department of Transport to provide all logistics. Although many of their scientific projects originate with individual university scientists, they are now increasingly attempting to concentrate particular subject areas in selected university centres. The Council for Scientific and Industrial Research coordinates the scientific activities.

Australia organizes its efforts through a central institute, its Antarctic Division in Tasmania. Although a core of permanent and contract scientists is employed there, many university scientists are also involved in Antarctic programmes. Meanwhile, New Zealand supplies all its logistics through the Antarctic Division of the Department of Scientific and Industrial Research (using RNZAF and US Navy aircraft), but relies on other government institutes and the universities to provide all of the scientists. New Zealand scientific programmes are all vetted by the Ross Dependency Research Committee, comprised of both university and government scientists with Antarctic experience.

The German Democratic Republic is organized in a more unusual way to support its Antarctic activities. Having first become involved in Antarctica during IGY as participants on a Soviet station, it was not until 1981 that GDR joined SCAR. The scientific and logistic organization is carried out by the Central Institute for Physics of the Earth in the Academy of Sciences, but transport is still provided by the Soviet Antarctic Expeditions.

France also has an unusual organization. All the Antarctic and subantarctic territories are gathered as an autonomous unit – Territoire des Terres Australes et Antarctiques Françaises (TAAF) – under the Ministry for Overseas Territories. The administrator of TAAF is responsible for implementing any scientific programmes sent to him by Comité National Français des Recherches Antarctiques (CNFRA). Logistic support is organized by TAAF.

The Soviet station Bellingshausen also provides research facilities for scientists from the German Democratic Republic.

(Right) *Assistance for the British ship* RRS John Biscoe *from US icebreakers* USS Edisto *and* USCGS North Wind *in the Penola Strait.*

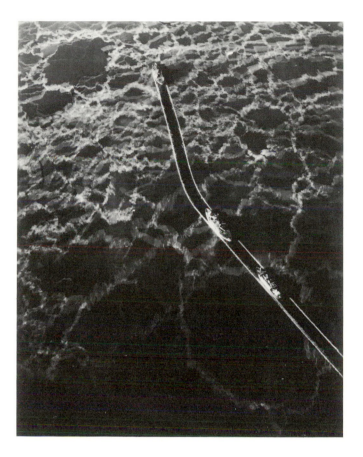

The newest active nations in the Antarctic have been able to study the advantages of each of these systems before formalising their own. In the Federal Republic of Germany, the Alfred Wegener Institute for Polar Research was established in 1980 and plays a major role in organizing all logistic support for polar work. However, the Institute for Sea Fisheries and the Institute of Polar Ecology are both closely concerned with the biological studies, whilst a wide range of government institutes and university departments is involved in providing scientists for atmospheric and earth science programmes.

Poland, on the other hand, coordinates all its scientific programmes through the Polish Academy of Sciences, whilst relying on the Polish Navy or the Soviet Union to provide logistic transport. India uses the Defence Department to provide aircraft, with the Department of Ocean Development acting as the logistics and scientific organizer. Ships are chartered as necessary from Norway or Finland. China supplies its scientific staff principally from the Academy of Sciences and the Academy of Fisheries Science, with the National Bureau of Oceanography

organizing logistic support. They are however considering the establishment of a polar research institute which may well take over many of these roles.

It is not always easy for those outside Antarctic circles to discover what activities are at present being planned and how they might become involved in a particular scientific programme. Appendix 3 provides addresses for the Consultative Parties from which further information may be obtained.

The way in which each nation organizes its Antarctic science is subject to continual change, as is all scientific effort within any national framework. Although it is relatively easy to document the apparent organizational structures used by the Treaty countries it is much less obvious where the control and initiation of scientific programmes lies. It seems likely that the British system does not accord with the Australian, nor the American with the Soviet. Politics plays a major part in Antarctic affairs and it must be expected that political considerations will inevitably intrude, in some countries, in the selection of which scientific activities to support. On purely scientific

grounds, the evidence of the past 20 years suggests that in some cases a great deal of money has been spent in some programmes supporting poor scientific objectives, or activities which are poorly coordinated and apparently represent no planned or systematic effort to fill in clear gaps in our knowledge. Considerable improvements are possible here but political and academic pressures may make them impossible to carry through.

Developments during the Treaty period

Throughout the 1960s the Treaty appears to have worked without any major disagreements ruffling the surface. It was, and still is, open to all nations for accession and although no progress had been made with the question of resource exploitation, this did not seem to be unduly pressing. During the 1970s various developments began to alter this cosy scenario.

The growing strength of the Third World countries at the United Nations and their suspicious view of the activities of the major industrial powers made the Treaty and the Consultative Parties an obvious target. As early as 1956 India had suggested United Nations trusteeship for the whole of Antarctica but this had received little support. The Treaty was increasingly seen as an elitist concept, deliberately drawn and managed to discriminate against the majority of countries. Political speculation on the extent of Antarctic living and mineral resources fed those

flames, leading to suggestions that the Antarctic be declared a 'global common' with any profits from its exploitation being shared amongst all nations. This view is not at present acceptable to the Consultative Parties. The issue has now however widened considerably and, at the behest of non-Treaty nations, appears regularly on the United Nations agenda.

Within the framework of the Treaty a great deal of international collaboration has taken place between national research groups. Some of the most significant have resulted in major coordinated programmes spread over many years. The Dry Valley Drilling Programme, although principally involving the USA, New Zealand and Japan, has provided field opportunities and samples to scientists of many nationalities. At present BIOMASS (Biological Investigation of Marine Antarctic Systems and Stocks) requires a high degree of collaboration and coordination between nations to investigate the marine living resources of the Southern Ocean. There are very many other examples, including aerial radio-echo sounding of ice, deep drilling of marine sediment cores and meteorite research.

Of equal importance have been developments in the interpretation and application of the Treaty. The importance of conservation was recognized many years ago. Agreement on specific protection from damage or disruption for some Antarctic organisms was achieved at an early stage. A later development has been the designation of specific areas as protected sites. These fall into two categories: sites of special scientific interest (SSSI), and

Rubbish dumps are a prominent feature of many Antarctic stations. The Treaty nations, with the assistance of SCAR, have agreed a code of conduct to ensure that toxic materials are not left in Antarctica and that as much rubbish as possible is removed.

Helicopters have made access possible to many areas of great scientific interest. Most Antarctic nations now use some degree of helicopter support. This helicopter is delivering supplies to a remote field party in the Dry Valleys.

The Antarctic Treaty allows nations to designate historical monuments in Antarctica which are worthy of preservation. These may be as large as Shackleton's hut at Cape Royds (seen here) or as small as a commemorative sign.

those which must remain undisturbed, specially protected areas (SPA). The Consultative Parties have also shown increasing concern about the control of environmental damage. SCAR have been asked to produce a code of practice to minimise disturbance and control pollution.

One of the unresolved problems in the application of any environmental code of practice in Antarctica is that of interpretation. Previous experience suggests that each nation is likely to implement its provisions and to weight its importance in a different way. This will not be for political reasons in most instances, simply a reflection of the very diverse cultural backgrounds of the Treaty nations.

A second problem, and no less significant, is the one of effective policing of any agreed code. If any one nation refuses to implement conservation provisions adequately at a practical level in Antarctica what, if anything, can be done about it? The growing concentration of stations on King George Island makes it likely to be the first area in which a critical test will arise of the ability of the Treaty countries to grapple successfully with this problem. The increasing number of areas subject to some degree of pro-

tection from development and disruption will inevitably reduce the availability of sites for new scientific stations. What practical steps can be taken if a non-Treaty country establishes a base for mineral extraction in a protected area? Some of these questions are being addressed in the current negotiations for a mineral regime within the Treaty framework and the policies decided upon are likely to have a most significant effect on the future of Antarctic conservation.

At present research stations are the major foci of environmental damage. The vast amounts of packaging material used every year for transporting the food, equipment, fuel and building materials necessary to support the research has ensured that sawdust and polystyrene granules have been widely dispersed around the stations. Many of the buildings are of wood and its abrasion by wind-driven ice particles has resulted in the dispersion of wood fibres for considerable distances downwind. The sewage effluent poses some difficult problems. Poor disposal techniques have produced unwanted enrichment of habitats in nutrient-poor areas and has introduced new bacteria to Antarctica. The increased sophistication of Antarctic science now

Tourists have been visiting Antarctica for many years. Where they are well briefed and carefully guided the overall effect is a gain in public knowledge and concern for the continent, with little direct effect in the field.

requires careful consideration to be given to disposal of laboratory waste, which may contain a wide range of toxic organic and inorganic chemicals. All Treaty nations need to make much greater educational efforts to increase awareness amongst their scientific and support staff of the environmental consequences of their actions.

Tourists, although now a regular feature of some Antarctic environments, need careful briefing and shepherding so that damage is minimised. At the moment tourism is on a small scale and unlikely to grow rapidly because of the costs involved. There have been incidents which have seriously strained essential logistic support and disrupted research programmes. The most tragic of these was the DC10 air crash on Mt Erebus, in which all the passengers and crew died on impact. Whoever was to blame, the crash raises the question of how such tourist activities should be controlled in an area with no international air traffic control and virtually no navigational aids. Tourist ships have also run aground and needed assistance. The number of private yachts and aeroplanes visiting Antarctica has greatly increased. These often need

assistance, generally in the form of fuel or food. Research stations are not equipped to meet this need and the Consultative Parties have now agreed to provide no further assistance to non-governmental expeditions.

Despite this, Treaty countries may continue to provide humanitarian assistance to any party that requires it, as the USA did in 1986 for the 'Footsteps of Scott' expedition. That particular expedition demonstrated clearly that even if a private group makes what it regards as sufficient logistic provision for its field parties to be independent of the scientific stations, it is not able to afford adequate back-up to cope with the unexpected. Operating safely in Antarctica is very expensive and it seems unlikely that non-governmental organizations will ever be able to afford the level of support deemed essential by the Treaty nations.

Antarctica needs conservation in advance of exploitation to ensure its future. The recent initiative bringing SCAR and IUCN together for joint discussions on this topic must be a good omen for the future.

*Summer snow falls are only one of the difficulties encountered by
Adélie Penguins during their breeding cycle.*

Part·II
Life in a cold environment

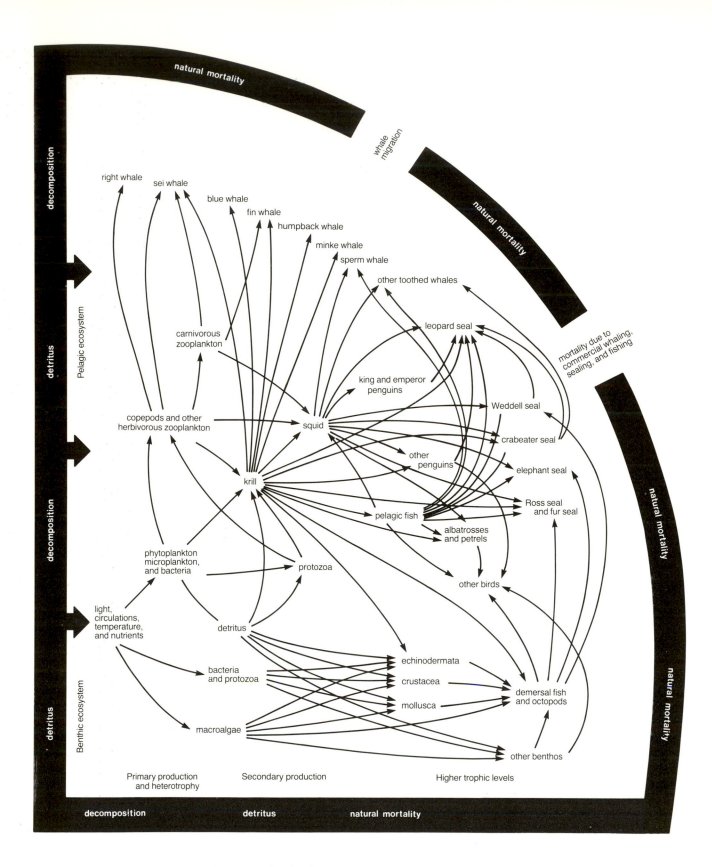

All life in the Antarctic is linked within a great food web. Primary production by phytoplankton and microplankton supports bacteria, protozoans and zooplankton. Other key groups in the food web are copepods, carnivorous zooplankton, some crustaceans, squid and fish. Together with krill, these organisms directly or indirectly form the food base for the more conspicuous birds, seals and whales.

Chapter·5
Biogeography and ecological niches

Ecological environments

On the apparently inhospitable land of Antarctica and in the cold seas surrounding it, some plants and animals not only survive but actually thrive. Unlike the Arctic, species diversity in Antarctic terrestrial communities is low. In the marine ecosystem the reverse is true; not only are there many species but often large numbers of a single species can be found in Antarctica. What then, are the key variables that control living processes and how unfavourable or favourable are they to life in the Antarctic?

Assuming that light, oxygen, carbon dioxide, water and nutrients are the basic essentials for any ecosystem in Antarctica, two other factors – temperature and shelter – appear to play a prime role. Temperature affects organisms directly by altering the rate at which reactions occur. As temperature declines, reactions slow down until eventually freezing occurs. Thus not only do temperatures slow or stop vital processes, at sub-zero levels they may produce lethal effects by ice formation. Equally important in terms of habitat favourability are the characteristics of the temperature regime – stability, rates of change, and extremes.

The concept of 'shelter' must be related both to the type of organism and to its activities. For organisms which are attached permanently to a substrate this needs to be a compromise between the ambient temperature, light level, carbon dioxide, oxygen and nutrients/food on the one hand and the optimal conditions for growth, development and reproduction on the other. Clearly, mobile organisms have an advantage here in that they can migrate to locations where conditions are most favourable for a particular phase of their life history.

Both the biological requirements of the organism and the environment in a habitat vary with time. Two major time scales need to be considered, the annual and the daily (diel). If the effect of cloud cover is excluded then it is safe to assume that incident light levels at a given point on the earth's surface vary with time of day and season in a predictable way. The key variables here are latitude and date. The higher the latitude, the greater the day length in summer. Day length is however only part of the requirement, since it is not only duration of illumination but quality of radiation that is important for the plants. Due to the absorption of light in the atmosphere, the amount of energy reaching the earth's surface will be dependent on the sun's elevation. Thus, day length can vary from 24 h darkness to 24 h daylight south of the Antarctic Circle, an extreme example of marked seasonality in terms of energy content of light reaching the earth's surface, and especially significant in polar latitudes.

Nearly all of the Antarctic continent is covered to a very great depth by ice and snow; exposed rock surfaces account for less than 2% of the surface. The enormous amount of frozen water present in the continent is effectively unavailable to living organisms. Thawing only occurs when the air is warm or in situations where the snow is dirty and absorbs, rather than reflects, radiation. When ice is in contact with exposed rock, heating of the rock by reflected radiation also causes localised melting. Where glaciers are retreating, the water is not always released in streams. At high altitudes sublimation becomes important and in that situation no free water is released. The significance of this can be seen in the Dry Valleys of South Victoria Land which are characterised by their aridity.

In spite of the generally low air temperature of the region many lakes are present. During the winter, both the lakes and much of the sea are covered in ice which, generally, melts in summer. The ice forms a physical barrier that reduces the amount of light entering the water and also prevents direct contact between air and water. This reduction is greatest in winter when the ice, with its accumulated snow cover, is thickest.

The ice barrier is a very important feature, since it affects both wind-induced turbulence and gaseous exchange. In ice-free lakes the wind blows the surface water downwind, causing deeper water to come to the surface and, because lakes are generally shallow, the water column becomes more or less totally mixed. The oceanic situation is quite different in that the geographical boundaries are effectively limitless, hence there is much less of a 'turnover' effect but more of a wind-induced current – the West

Distribution of land and water areas in the southern hemisphere by 5° zones. Most of the earth's surface between 50 and 65°S is covered by the Southern Ocean and much of that is covered by pack ice in winter.

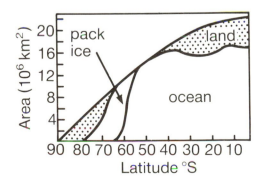

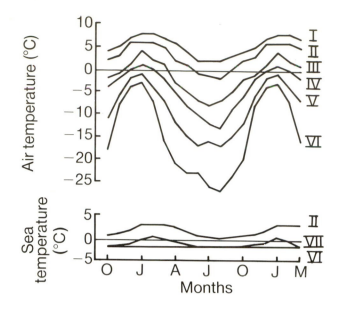

I   Kerguelen
II   South Georgia
III Deception Is
IV   Adelaide Is
V   Dumont D'Urville
VI   McMurdo Sound
VII Signy Is

Mean monthly air temperature at six Antarctic localities compared with the mean monthly sea temperature at three localities. Air temperatures fluctuate far more than water temperatures. The amplitude of the fluctuation is greatest for air temperature and least for sea temperature, the further south the observations.

Many Antarctic lakes are unusual in that they have a dense growth of mosses on the lake floor.

Wind Drift. This wind-induced circulation still operates in the pack-ice zone, although it should be remembered that the wind itself will be affected by whether it is blowing over ice or open water. Where fast ice occurs it is clearly impossible for the wind to influence the water movement in either lake or open ocean and under these conditions vertical mixing is reduced and the water column becomes stable.

In lakes, since fresh water has a maximum density at 4°C, the temperature will increase steadily with depth in non-saline lakes (Antarctic lakes are generally too shallow for a persistent thermocline to be established). In the ocean the lack of turbulence leads to a significant degree of stratification during the winter. An important consequence of the reduced turbulence under ice is that suspended matter tends to sink, leaving the water very clear.

A detailed discussion of the processes of ice formation is beyond the scope of this chapter, but one particular aspect does have especial biological significance. Under certain circumstances, in shallow water, the sea can be at its freezing point at the sea bed. Anchor ice then forms on any 'freezing nuclei', such as rocks, plants or even animals, that are present. Since ice is less dense than sea water, as the patch of anchor ice grows its buoyancy increases until

it eventually wrenches whatever it is attached to away from the sea bed.

Some Antarctic lakes contain highly saline water. Many of these were formed by continual evaporation over long periods of time, resulting in a steady increase in the concentration of salts in the lakes. This is the origin of many of the lakes in the Dry Valleys of South Victoria Land. Other saline lakes are formed from the isolation of pockets of sea water by movement of the land closing the connection with the open sea. The salinity of all these lakes is often very high, sometimes several times that of normal sea water, and such lakes thus form another unique and extreme habitat for living organisms.

Generally, no animals and only a few plants and bacteria are present in these highly saline lakes. By contrast, fresh-water lakes typically contain a diverse algal flora, some living freely as single cells or strings of cells in the open water whilst others form mats on the lake floor. Mosses are also found on the beds of some lakes, often forming a dense and thick covering. Bacteria are present within the water column as well as on the lake floor. The fauna is often very limited. Copepods of several species are common as are rotifers, tardigrades, ostracods and a fairy shrimp (anostracan).

An important habitat is at the interface between land

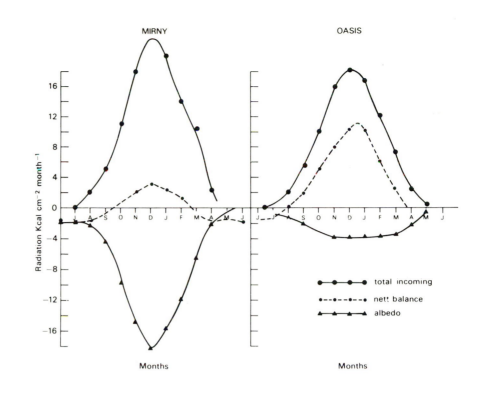

MIRNY OASIS

Radiation Kcal cm^{-2} month^{-1}

total incoming
nett balance
albedo

Months   Months

A comparison of the radiation balance over snow at Mirny Station and snow-free ground at the Bunger Oasis.

Snow and ice reduce the amount of light which can enter the water: (a) the thickness of sea ice and snow at a site in the South Orkney Islands; (b) the proportion of light that penetrated through the snow into the water below.

and water. In lakes this habitat is restricted to a very narrow band because the water level remains more or less constant for long periods. In the sea tidal movement produces a much wider band. In both situations the continual grinding and abrading by floating ice requires that organisms living in that region are either able to withstand significant physical abrasion or are restricted to sheltered crevices.

The two dominant habitats on land are rock and snow. Marked differences in their reflection of radiation (albedo) means that there are enormous differences in the radiation balance. Most solar energy is reflected by white snow whilst dark-coloured rock faces reflect little. Thus where there is a marked diel light regime there is likely to be a very great variation in the surface temperature of rock faces. Similar in this respect is the situation in moss banks, which, being generally dark in colour, also tend to absorb solar radiation. In still air on a sunny day, therefore, a moss bank, with warm air trapped in its interstices, will be warmer than a rock face, which in turn will be much warmer than a snow surface.

The snow which accumulates over the winter period affects the underlying plant habitats in several ways. It acts as a filter, reducing the amount and spectral quality of light reaching the plants, and as a barrier that restricts air circulation. When the snow layer is shallow, infra-red heating of the air entrapped beneath the snow can produce a 'greenhouse effect', especially in spring. The snow also acts as a thermal insulation, protecting the underlying habitat from very rapid changes in temperature.

On land the most conspicuous plants are the mosses and lichens, although many algae are also present. Fungi

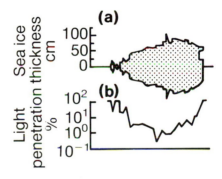

(a)

Sea ice thickness cm

(b)

Light penetration %

occur widely in both organic and inorganic soils. The majority are filamentous species although a few basidiomycetes (toadstools) are known. Bacteria are also present but the fungi appear to be largely responsible for the decomposition of dead material. Within the 60°S boundary only two species of flowering plants are present and they are restricted to favourable habitats in the Maritime Antarctic. The flora of the subantarctic islands is much more diverse but still very impoverished when compared to similar latitudes in the northern hemisphere.

There are no naturally occurring terrestrial mammals, although reindeer, cats, rabbits, rats and mice have all been introduced to some subantarctic islands. The characteristic species of the Antarctic terrestrial fauna are small insects, mainly Collembola (springtails), and mites, all of which are small and live within moss banks or under stones. In the Subantarctic a range of beetles, flies and spiders is also found.

73

This photograph, taken through the window of an aircraft, is of the Bunger Hills, one of the largest areas of exposed rock in Wilkes Land. Although a station was established there during IGY it was difficult to maintain and the area has been visited very rarely. It is typical of many of the oasis areas. Ecological diversity is very limited in all of the oases which must constitute some of the most hostile areas on Earth for colonisation and survival.

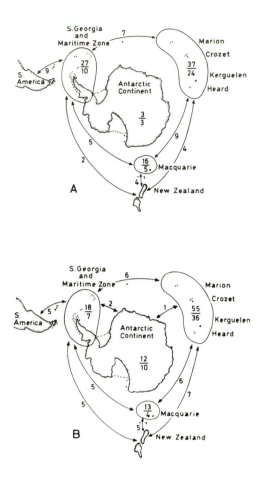

Biogeography

Biogeography has a long scientific history in Antarctica. Only now, however, when adequate collections have been made, can sound explanations be proposed for the origin and dispersal of the flora and fauna. As early as 1851 J.D. Hooker had suggested that the present southern flora was derived from a former great land mass now fragmented, a theory only recently acceptable to geologists. Present tectonic reconstructions of the break-up of the super-continent Gondwana are providing a time scale for Antarctic biogeography and a non-biological explanation for the similarities between the floras of New Zealand, Tasmania and southern South America. Some plant geographers believe that Antarctica may have been a major evolutionary centre for many genera in the southern hemisphere. Synthesis of biological and geological data should help to clarify this.

The Antarctic continent and the subantarctic islands are separated from the other major land masses by the wide expanses of the Southern Ocean. This forms an effective barrier restricting colonisation of the region by new species. Some species that are present are considered to be direct descendants of those that were present when the continent and its subantarctic islands were formed. There are almost certainly many species that could exist in the Antarctic but which have not colonised the region because they have not been carried there. Indeed, transplant experiments from South Georgia to Signy Island have established this.

Isolation is also evident in animals which have colonised the coastal marine habitats but in this case it is seen not in the lack of species diversity, although some groups such as crabs and shrimps are rare, but in their reproductive strategies. Species living in shallow coastal habitats and separated by hundreds of miles of deep ocean from adjacent islands tend to produce eggs and larvae which live on the sea bed, since planktonic eggs and larvae are likely to be lost in the open ocean.

The pelagic environment contains examples from all the main planktonic groups, varying in size from the smallest bacterium to the largest jellyfish. This is not surprising since, although the water is cold, there is continuity between the Southern Ocean and the Atlantic, Indian and Pacific Oceans to the north.

The dominant surface currents are towards the west (East Wind Drift) close to the continent and to the east and north (West Wind Drift) further offshore. Some way north the West Wind Drift sinks below the subantarctic surface water at the Polar Front. Beneath the surface layer of the West Wind Drift is a thick layer of slightly

Distribution of species and subspecies of cryptostigmatid mites (A) and Collembola (B) in different areas of the Antarctic. The proportion of total species recorded to the number of endemic species is indicated for each area. The numbers of species common to two areas are shown by figures and arrows.

warmer water moving southwards, the warm deep water. This is recognizable well north, even as far as the equator. Between the East and West Wind Drifts are upwelling zones from the warm deep water which supply nutrients to the surface water. The release of nutrients at the surface promotes high localised primary production during the summer months when the sun's elevation is greatest and the ice cover minimal. Feeding on this primary production is a diverse assemblage of zooplankters, many of which also occur well north of the Polar Front. One of the dominant species is krill (*Euphausia superba*) and this in turn forms the staple food of some whales, seals, birds, fish and squid.

The Southern Ocean is therefore highly productive locally and contains many species that also occur well to the north. The environment is relatively stable with little variation of temperature, although there is marked seasonality in ice cover and light. By contrast, on land, the sparse flora and fauna are restricted to a few rock exposures and the coasts of the land mass, while climatic fluctuations are extreme.

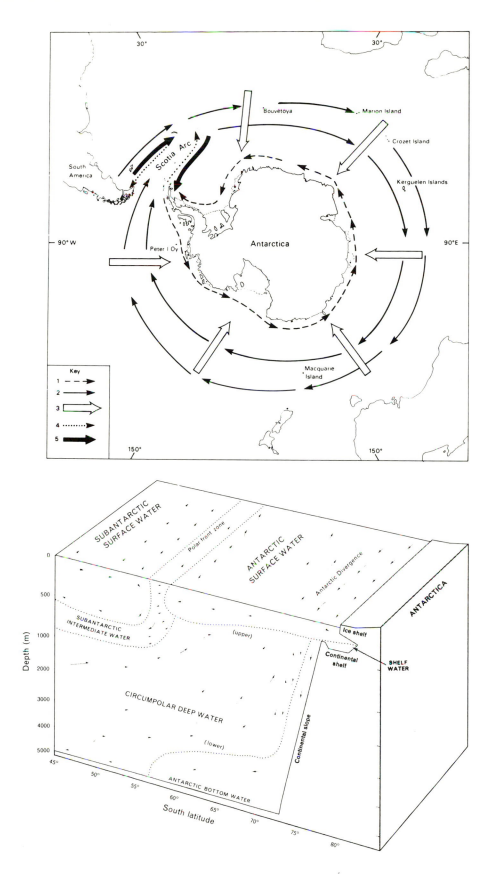

Origins and dispersal of the Antarctic marine fauna: (1) dispersal by East Wind Drift; (2) dispersal by West Wind Drift; (3) migration of deepwater groups; (4) migration north on Scotia arc; and (5) migration south on Scotia arc.

Generalised representation of the currents and water masses in the Southern Ocean.

Chapter·6
Ecological adaptations

Living patterns

The seasonal nature of the temperature regime on land and the light regime generally imposes upon the habitat, and thus the organism, a series of environmental patterns. These patterns differ in periodicity, amplitude, synchrony and regularity, and call for a variety of different adaptations. To understand these adaptations it is necessary to look for environmental variation in the major habitats identified in Chapter 5 and then to consider how the organism takes advantage of favourable conditions and protects itself in adverse situations.

For two dominant ecological variables, light and temperature, for the most part, day-to-day variation tends to be irregular, whilst seasonal variation is more regular and therefore predictable. Adaptations must somehow take account of the regular seasonal patterns whilst being able to take advantage of temporary favourable conditions when they occur.

Either the whole organism, or groups of organisms, can be expected to show adaptations to the environment and it is in this context that biological characteristics of the species will be considered. The markedly seasonal light regime has considerable influence on photosynthesis and thus on primary production. This is therefore a convenient starting point from which to consider living patterns.

Primary production

Primary production is dependent on the presence of sunlight, carbon dioxide, nutrient salts and water, whilst the rate is controlled by the levels of these factors and by the ambient temperature.

Let us consider first the oceanic environment. During winter, incident light at the surface is very low; in addition sea ice with its snow cover means that very little light gets into the sea. The sea ice, by acting as a barrier between the wind and sea, eliminates turbulence and thus vertical mixing. This causes negatively buoyant cells to sink, whilst nutrients, released by decomposition deep down, are not brought to the surface. With the arrival of spring and summer the sea ice breaks up, exposing the water to light. The effect is dramatic. Within days a phytoplankton bloom develops as a result of rapid multiplication of resting spores brought to the surface and also released from the now fragmenting ice layer. At Signy Island, the sharp rise in the amount of phytoplankton occurred within the same 10-day period in each of three successive seasons.

As the summer progressed, a combination of increased turbulence, taking cells out of the euphotic zone for longer periods, and, possibly, nutrient limitation caused a decline in the phytoplankton. This study was in a coastal region in which productivity was almost certainly very much higher than in the open ocean, due to turbulence regenerating nutrients from the sea bed. No analogous studies have been made anywhere in the open ocean.

In the pelagic environment just described, ice is both a barrier to light and also a substrate on which algae can grow. During the winter, and until the ice breaks up, a brown algal scum develops on the underside of the ice and it is from these and the other algae actually growing in the interstices of the ice that the planktonic bloom develops. Ironically the layer of ice-associated algae further reduces the amount of light penetrating into the water, ensuring that even though incident radiation reaching the ice surface is increasing in spring this is not so for light actually entering the water.

A generalised picture probably applies of marked seasonal pulses on, for a given locality, a more or less regular date, with light as the main controlling factor. Temperature does, however, have some effect, particularly on the balance between photosynthesis and respiration. Photosynthesis, the conversion of carbon dioxide and water to carbohydrates, is the direct opposite of respiration, the process by which energy is released within the cells. To a great extent both processes are enzyme-controlled and thus vary with temperature. The initial stage of photosynthesis is a photochemical dissociation of water which is little affected by temperature, whereas the subsequent processes are by chemical reactions and are temperature-dependent. Lowering the temperature will therefore reduce respiration more than photosynthesis. Even though the seasonal temperature range in the sea is quite limited, it is sufficient to cause major differences in the balance between photosynthesis and respiration. It is much more important in fresh-water and terrestrial habitats where daily and seasonal temperature variations are very much greater.

In fresh-water lakes there are enormous differences in production between even geographically adjacent lakes. For example, in Sombre Lake on Signy Island very little seasonal variation was detectable, while in Heywood Lake a clearly marked cycle was present. At the latter site during winter, with ice 1 m thick, and snow 0.5 m thick, only about 0.01% (0.002 W m^{-2}) of the incident light entered the water. Few algal cells were present in the water and radiocarbon uptake was immeasurably low. With the onset of spring, the increased solar energy caused the snow to melt so that the light level entering the water rose to 2 W m^{-2}. This produced an immediate and

In the very dry bare areas of Victoria Land plants need protection to survive. Some plants live within the sandstone rock, growing between the mineral grains. These endolithic plants grow in layers. In this section the black layer is a lichen, with a white powdery layer of fungus below, followed by a green band of algae.

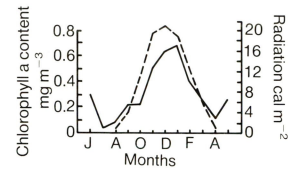

The peak in primary production (shown here as chlorophyll concentration) occurs later than the peak in solar radiation in Antarctic waters.

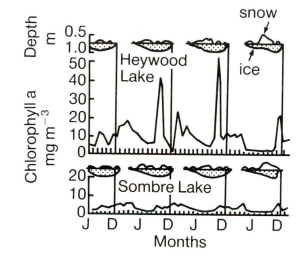

Mean chlorophyll a concentrations, from mid-1978 to 1981, are related to the depth of snow and ice cover and its duration on these Signy Island lakes.

dramatic increase in the dominant blue-green algae, their populations doubling every 6 to 7.5 days. The rapid increase was thought to be assisted by the release of spores from shallow water. As the summer progressed and the ice melted, the density of plant cells in the water reduced the light level and this, with nutrient depletion and the formation of new ice in autumn, brought the biomass and production down to the winter level. The open water of fresh-water lakes is thus very similar to the coastal marine environment, with brief pulses of production occuring at more or less regular times of the year. On the lake bottom, mosses and blue-green algae are well adapted to low light levels with light compensation points (at which photosynthesis exactly balances respiration) as low as 0.12 W m^{-2}. The deep-water mosses have much larger leaves and longer stems than the terrestrial forms, enabling them to make the best use of available light. In all except June, July and August photosynthesis exceeds respiration, but the growth rate is slow and annual production is low. This low light compensation point is not an adaptation in the strict sense but is due to the differential response to temperature by photosynthesis and reproduction. There is as yet no good evidence to support the suggestion that some of the algae show an increased enzyme concentration as a form of cold adaptation.

In the terrestrial environment there is a greater diversity of plant orders present. The coastal zone is generally dominated by the mosses whilst bare ground further inland is more often colonised by lichens. Since the mosses themselves form the habitat for many of the micro-organisms and arthropods considered later, one of the common Maritime Antarctic moss communities will be described as an example. *Polytrichum alpestre* occurs from the Falkland Islands to the Antarctic Peninsula and has been intensively studied over much of its range. It forms compact and often extensive stands underlain, in some areas, by up to 2 m of moss peat. During the winter the thick accumulation of snow prevents light reaching the plants and thus causes a cessation of growth. As soon as the snow melts in the spring, photosynthesis begins and continues through to March. Thus once again there is a seasonal cycle triggered by the spring thaw. Although widespread, moss species do not appear to form the main food of many insect species, which tend to eat algae and fungi growing amongst the moss stems in preference to moss leaves.

From the limited measurements made so far on photosynthesis in Antarctic plants, it appears that lichens and mosses are able to continue photosynthesis at sub-zero temperatures, down to $-10°C$ for *Polytrichum* and even below that for *Usnea* lichens. For moss photosynthesis, light levels seem not to be limiting and up to 30% of the annual growth can occur under snow. Water is, however, very important. On moistening, mosses from dry habitats on boulders and in fellfield areas recover their photosynthetic ability much more rapidly than those from wet

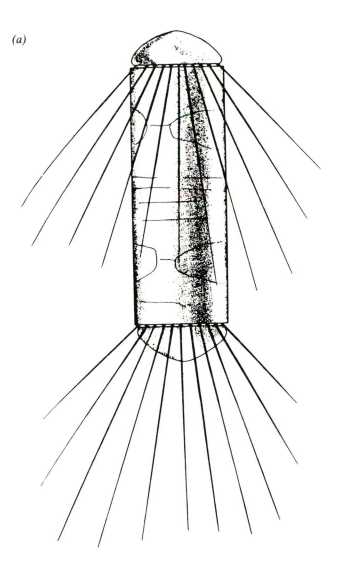

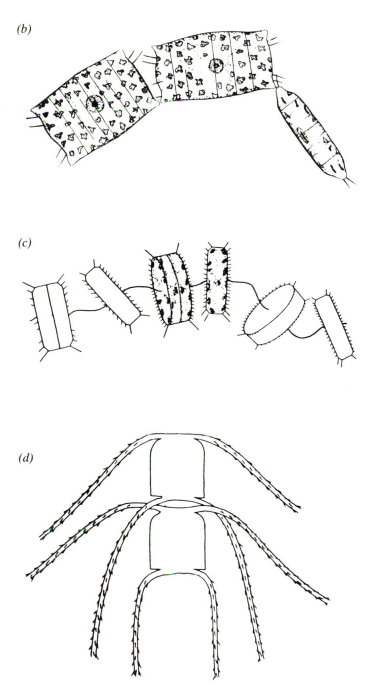

Diatoms such as these are common in the Southern Ocean and contribute greatly to the primary production. Recent research has shown that even smaller organisms, the micro- or picoplankton, may contribute as much if not more. (a) Corethron criophilum. *(b)* Odontella weissflogii. *(c)* Thalassiosira gravida. *(d)* Chaetoceros criophilum.

sites. Rapid recovery of metabolic activity on rewetting is also a feature of Antarctic lichens. The ability to survive very low temperatures, and to rapidly re-establish photosynthesis at low temperatures as soon as liquid water is available is of critical importance in responding to the selective pressures operating on all would-be colonists of the terrestrial Antarctic environment.

The green alga *Prasiola*, which is quite widespread at Signy Island, grows very rapidly between December and March, during which time the dry weight of its thalli can double every 2 weeks. Presumably light limitation due to snow cover and low temperatures stops production in winter. Microalgal spores carried by the wind develop in the snow. Evidence for this can be clearly seen as a

reddish-brown stain on snow slopes in spring. By enhancing the absorption of solar radiation, the ice algae increase the rate of snow melt and accentuate the rapid change from winter to summer production rates.

Thus on land, as in the aquatic habitats, there is a peak of production during the summer with very little activity in the winter. Plant material is, however, available all year round on land and in some lakes in the form of mosses and algae. Although primary production by mosses is low it is still more than the herbivores are able or willing to eat. The low temperatures slow down microbial decomposition of the excess organic matter which can accumulate steadily unless removed by physical processes.

Secondary production

The regular pulses of primary production seen in the marine environment are obviously likely to impose a similar cycle on the herbivores. There are several excellent examples of this; e.g. the copepods *Calanoides acutus* and *Rhincalanus gigas* feed extensively during the productive summer months. Both these species build up large lipid stores to help them survive the winter period when food is scarce. Lipids are commonly used by zooplankters for food storage and they have the added advantage that they provide additional buoyancy so that the animal needs to expend less energy to prevent itself sinking. Not all herbivorous zooplankters lay down lipid stores. Two very important exceptions are krill (*Euphausia superba*) and the salp *Salpa thomsoni*; it is not all clear how they live through the winter. The same is probably true of the salp *Salpa thompsoni*. During summer the two species take advantage of favourable conditions in different ways, krill by growing rapidly and salps by budding.

Sudden periods of plenty followed by famine require the aquatic herbivores to respond rapidly to changing circumstances if they are to make full use of the available food. Rapid multiplication either by asexual budding, as in the case of salps, or by short generation time, as with some copepods, are two such responses. The suddenness with which the change occurs means that, due to time lags in responses, much of the initial pulse of algal production is uneaten and a large proportion just sinks towards the bottom. In other oceans this produces layers as deep as 1000 m that decompose under bacterial action to release nutrients to the environment. The same is probably true of the Southern Ocean. Later on in the season grazing by the herbivores prevents much remaining uneaten.

In the deep ocean nearly all decomposition occurs in the water column but in shallow coastal water and in lakes much of this material reaches the bottom. Much is consumed by the diverse variety of benthic filter-feeders, while the remainder accumulates as detritus on the sea or

*Plankton haul containing many krill larvae which can be recognized by their orange bodies, and copepods (*Calanoides acutus*).*

Towards the end of winter patches of snow may become streaked with red as populations of snow algae are concentrated near the surface.

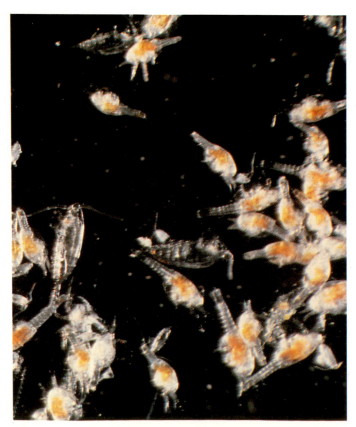

lake bed. Like the pelagic system, therefore, the benthic system receives its energy input in pulses but because decomposition is quite slow the energy release takes place over a long period. It is this detrital component that allows the much-reduced population of the copepod *Pseudoboeckella* to exist over winter, feeding on the algal mat on the lake floor. It may also explain how the large population of krill exists throughout the winter in the sea. The steady rain of detritus also provides food directly for the wide diversity of benthic filter-feeders. For them the slow decomposition rates act as a buffer so that the clearly marked pulses of food characteristic of the pelagic system become very blurred. This, in part, accounts for the high biomass of Antarctic benthic detritus- and filter-feeding invertebrates.

On land the mite *Alaskozetes* feeds only during the summer months. As autumn approaches and the temperature falls regularly below zero, feeding stops, not because of lack of food but because any food present in the gut could form freezing nuclei. Thus the greater temperature range on land, rather than the availability of food, controls the feeding cycle of this species. There is little information on other species but since the collembolan *Cryptopygus antarcticus* seems able to grow in most months of the year, even though prone to freezing, it must have some adaptation in addition to supercooling (see Chapter 7). This could be through a more rapid digestive process that clears food quickly, thus eliminating freezing nuclei.

Pulses of primary production coming at more or less clearly defined seasons have induced several adaptations. The limited aquatic productivity, for example, under ice and on the fringes of lakes is grazed continuously. Animals restricted to open water either rely on food reserves established during the preceeding summer or else over-winter as eggs. On land the overriding constraint is that of preventing freezing which in turn, means that, even when food is available, they cannot always feed.

Growth

The clearly defined seasonal pattern in the availability of food to the detritus- and plant-feeders will have a profound influence on their reproductive strategies and their growth rates. Furthermore, since carnivorous species, both vertebrate and invertebrate, are dependent on the herbivores, they will in turn be influenced by the same patterns. The patterns may be somewhat diluted by time lags in responses, an extreme example being the isopod *Glyptonotus*, which breeds throughout the year.

The important factors in considering growth are the

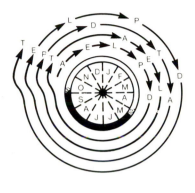

Possible life cycle of the mite Alaskozetes antarcticus *on Signy Island. E–egg, L–larva, P–protonymph, D–deuteronymph, T–tritonymph, A–adult. Shading on the inner ring indicates snow cover.*

A postulated life cycle for the marine copepod Calanoides acutus. *The productive summer season allows a complete generation to grow up during the summer but during the winter very little growth takes place due to the lack of food. I–VI are different instars in the life cycle; at any one time different numbers of these are present.*

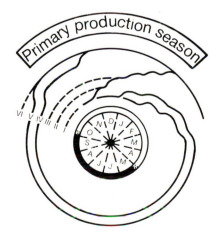

time taken for an animal to reach sexual maturity and the rate of change of size with age. The two are clearly related for a given species and will therefore be considered together. Since growth is dependent on the assimilation of food whose availability has already been shown to be seasonal, growth rate cannot be expected to be constant. Slow annual growth rates with a marked seasonal pattern are therefore likely to characterise Antarctic animals.

The marine environment has the greatest diversity of species. Since good data exist for many marine groups these will therefore be considered first to allow comparisons to be made with fresh-water and terrestrial species.

There is currently no method for determining the age of individual zooplankters. The only methods for determining growth are either lengthy laboratory observations on individuals (in which case there is no guarantee that the laboratory conditions represent realistically those in the field), or following the size frequency distribution of animals resulting from a single spawning. Laboratory experiments on krill have indicated an impossibly slow growth rate and, although techniques are continuing to improve, the results cannot yet be used to give an unequivocal statement on growth. Examination of the size frequency distribution of cohorts presents different problems. Krill size frequency distributions typically have a peak around 30–45 mm length and another at around 50–60 mm. Initially it was assumed that this indicated a 2-year life span. This has been questioned and there is now increasing evidence to suggest that the larger grouping is actually composed of several year classes which cannot be separated on the basis of size alone.

To determine how many year classes are contained in the second-year peak it is necessary to know the age of individual krill. This has been achieved in many animal and plant species by counting 'annual' growth rings in hard structures; unfortunately, this approach is impossible with crustaceans since they moult their hard exoskeletons at regular intervals. Recent research on laboratory insect populations has shown that the concentration of the pigment lipofuchsin is a good indicator of metabolic age. The same technique has been applied to krill with varying success. The main problems are associated analysis of preserved with samples; formalin, a commonly used fixative, causes massive increases in fluorescence at the same frequency as lipofuchsin. In addition it is not known at what rate the lipofuscin accumulates so that, whilst peaks in concentration undoubtedly occur, these have not been linked to the true age of the animals in the population. Research is currently in progress to resolve these difficulties and, since the biochemical assay methods are very expensive, also to determine a morphometric dimension that can be related to age. Whilst the actual age of individual krill

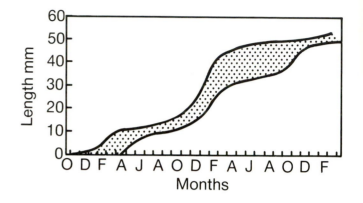

Generalised picture of growth in krill. Although growth virtually ceases above about 50 mm length, it is now believed that, having reached that size, the krill can live for a further 3 years or more.

cannot be ascertained, there is good information on growth patterns throughout the year. Based purely on the size frequency distributions it is clear that growth is most rapid during the summer and virtually ceases in winter – as would be expected for a herbivore.

A similar pattern of summer-only growth is found in *Euphausia triacantha*. It grows to a smaller ultimate size, and the year classes can be more easily determined from size frequency distributions. *Calanoides acutus*, a copepod, likewise has a period of fast growth during the summer and no growth in winter. Most individuals in the winter population are immature and will reach sexual maturity coincident with the spring phytoplankton bloom. Even though growth during the summer is rapid enough for a complete generation to be completed before the autumn, it is much slower than for an equivalent temperate species.

All of the species discussed so far can overwinter as either immature or mature individuals, rather than as eggs, and this means that there is a continuous supply of food for the carnivorous species. It is no surprise therefore that arrow worms (e.g. *Sagitta*) and amphipods (e.g. *Themisto*) are both present during the winter and, in the former case, do show significant growth, probably due to the presence of copepods as food. In the case of the zooplankton then, growth tends to be slow, probably as a result of food availability since the ultimate sizes reached are no different to those in other oceans.

In the benthic invertebrates there is good information available for both crustaceans and molluscs. Growth patterns in the shells of bivalve molluscs have provided confirmation that growth rates do tend to be slow. For

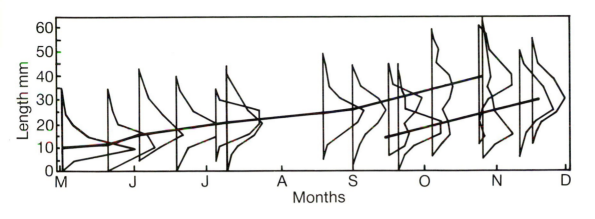

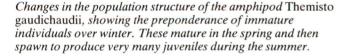

Growth of the arrow worm Sagitta gazella *can be followed in changes in the size frequency distribution. The mean trend is shown by the solid line. This species appears to grow through the winter, presumably because it continues to feed on other zooplankters such as copepods.*

Changes in the population structure of the amphipod Themisto gaudichaudii, *showing the preponderance of immature individuals over winter. These mature in the spring and then spawn to produce very many juveniles during the summer.*

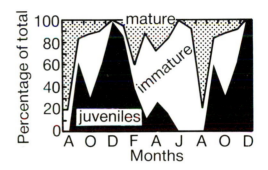

example, *Yoldia* at Signy Island may take 20 years to grow to 2 cm in length. Similar slow growth rates have been described for other species. Even the faster-growing species, such as the scallop *Adamussium*, grow more slowly than similar species from temperate waters; but since in this case growth was estimated on an annual, rather than a seasonal, basis, its slowness may be a reflection of a short primary production. The bivalve *Lissarca miliaris* does have a strong seasonal growth pattern which would tend to confirm this. A similar picture is true of the many crustacean species studied, although in these cases, in spite of a slow growth rate, many species grow to a large size. Thus for this group as well, an extended life span is normal.

The other major benthic group for which adequate information is available is the fish. In general, where fish are feeding predominantly on benthic invertebrates, growth rates tend to be slow, with the result that sexual maturity is reached only after 7 or 8 years. Growth is faster for those species that feed pelagically on krill, such as the icefish *Champsocephalus gunnari* and the marbled notothenia *Notothenia rossii*. Seasonal growth is very difficult to measure in all fish species, but since distinct seasonal layers are present in otoliths and opercular bones, it seems likely to be the case. Another indicator of seasonal variation in size is a condition factor – the ratio between weight and length. This is at a peak during the summer months and, following spawning in the autumn, remains low until the following spring; this would indicate that growth is minimal during the winter.

The thermally stable conditions in the marine habitats are not as pronounced in many fresh-water bodies and are generally absent from all land habitats, with the result that temperature, as well as food availability, plays a significant part in controlling growth rate. In the fresh-water lakes the copepod *Pseudoboeckella* is able to grow throughout the year although the growth rate is fastest in summer, particularly in the smaller pools where the temperature can get relatively high. The anostracan *Branchinecta* over-winters as an egg, giving it the most extreme seasonal pattern; since the generation time is completed within the summer season, the growth rate at that time is quite rapid.

On land the situation is even more severe due to the low temperatures in winter. If food particles act as freezing nuclei in the insect gut, winter survival requires that feeding must cease, even though food might be available. Only limited amounts of energy can be channelled to growth, even during the summer, so that growth is slow; nonetheless, providing the animals survive the winter, they can live for several years.

In all three major environments there is a clearly defined pattern of seasonal growth which is more or less dependent on the primary production season and this is further accentuated by the frequent sub-zero temperatures on land.

The remaining groups of animals – the birds, seals and whales – are all homeotherms, a condition which requires a different set of adaptations. The establishment of a stable thermal environment within the animal means that,

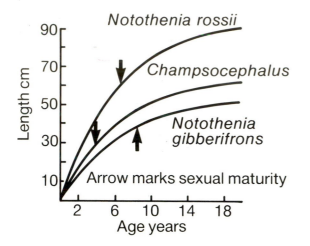

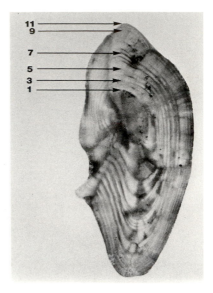

Growth curves for three species of Antarctic fish. There is typically a steady increase in length over a number of years. The arrows show the point of sexual maturity for each fish. Microscopic examination of the otoliths (ear stones) of fish reveals annual growth rings which are used to determine age.

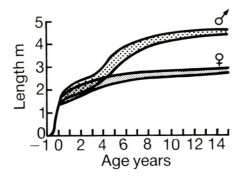

(Left) The growth patterns for Elephant Seals at South Georgia and Macquarie Island show marked differences between the sexes. Initially growth is very rapid. After about 3 years the males, as is typical of harem-breeding species, continue to grow. The photograph shows a family group; the largest seal is the bull, there are several cows and a few small black pups.

Whales, like the seals, have very rapid initial growth in the first 2 years of life. The growth curves are very similar for all four species shown here.

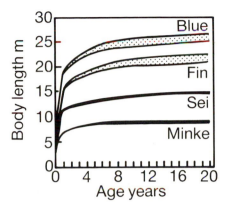

Growth curves for three species of seal. Growth is very rapid over the first year of life of non-harem-forming species of seal. Size then remains more or less constant for the rest of the seal's life and there is only a small difference in length between the sexes. The photograph shows a Weddell Seal cow with her pup.

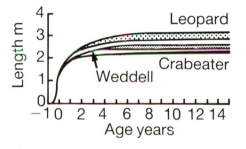

for the most part, metabolic processes become independent of external temperature changes, so that temperature itself has no direct effect on growth. It can, however, affect it indirectly by varying the amount of energy the animal must utilise in order to maintain its body temperature. Two types of adaptation are important in this respect. First, adaptations to minimise, or at least control, heat loss; these are discussed in Chapter 7. Secondly, those adaptations aimed at gaining the optimum size as rapidly as possible; these are related to feeding rates and conversion efficiencies.

The baleen whales have very rapid growth rates. Blue, Fin and Sei Whales all grow to about 75% of their maximum length and 40% of their maximum weight in their first year. Calves are large when born and growth is particularly rapid in the months following birth. In the 7 months up to weaning Blue and Fin Whales increase their weight by five or six times. Growth is greatest in the main body of the calf and only later does the head end increase in length to the proportions of the adult. As puberty is reached growth slows down but continues at a decreasing rate until physical maturity is reached. The rapid growth rate prior to weaning causes a great drain on the food reserves of the mother, with the result that her blubber content falls to a very low level. Since weaning is not complete until the whales are feeding in the Southern Ocean, the blubber layer at this time would be barely sufficient for thermal insulation in a stationary animal. Swimming generates a considerable amount of heat, however, and it seems unlikely that the blubber layer in a healthy whale is ever reduced to a critical level in terms of heat balance in the animal. This illustrates the dual role of blubber as both thermal insulation and an energy store.

Seals, in common with the whales, are relatively large at birth and also have their most rapid growth during the first year. All species have attained 80% of their maximum possible length by the end of their second year. In common with the whales the seals show a marked seasonal variation in total weight due to the varying quantity of blubber, as for example during lactation or annual moult.

For the mammals, therefore, growth in length is very rapid during the first 2 years of life, whereas growth in terms of weight fluctuates seasonally due to the imposed rhythms of feeding, breeding and migration. The most rapid growth occurs during the period when the young animal is small and therefore most vulnerable to cold stress. The pup or calf very efficiently utilises the highly nutritious milk produced by the mother, which in turn means that the mother's reserves of energy are rapidly depleted. Thus, in all except harem-forming seals, the females are larger than the males, in order to accommodate the necessary fat reserves.

Growth in birds is, characteristically, complete within a few months of the chicks fledging. Since this is a world-wide phenomenon it cannot be related to temperature. The reason is that size, and in particular length, is an important factor in determining the type of flight typical of a particular species. As flight patterns do not change markedly with age the newly fledged chick tends to fly in the same manner as its parents and hence it will be of approximately the same size. Within this framework there is considerable variation in weight due to the energy requirements for egg production, incubation and chick feeding. Studies on bird growth have therefore been restricted to the chick phase.

In general the larger the bird, the larger the eggs it lays. However, relative to their weight, smaller birds lay proportionately larger eggs than large birds. There are inevitably exceptions to this generalisation. Penguins and diving petrels lay small eggs for their weight probably because the elimination of flying for the former and the reduction of flight in the latter has meant that their weight relative to length is much greater than for other groups. Incubation time increases with egg size as also does chick size at hatching, but since the smaller birds tend to lay proportionately larger eggs their chicks are also proportionately larger. Unlike the mammals, where food is readily available as milk when required, chicks receive food at regular, although frequently widely spaced, intervals, with the result that growth is in the form of a series of steps. Meal sizes are typically between 10% and 20% of the adult weight and are thus easily monitored by continuously recording chick weights. This method has been used with considerable success on the albatrosses at Bird Island and has contributed greatly to our understanding of the inter-relationships between them and their principal prey.

The homeotherms therefore, unlike the poikilotherms, have very fast growth rates over the critical period before they are of a size that is unlikely to suffer cold stress. Whilst large size is an advantage to the homeotherm, beyond a certain point further increases in size confer no additional advantages in thermal stabilisation. The Minke Whale, smallest of the Southern Ocean baleen whales, tends to remain in the Southern Ocean. Thus for the whales, increased size which allows faster sustained swimming is possibly an adaptation to a migratory habit and not strictly to low temperatures. The direct effects of the low Antarctic temperature on homeotherms are therefore small, the main moderating influences coming through availability and quality of food; these are considered later.

Reproductive strategies

The environmental features of low temperature and seasonally available food clearly affect the pattern of growth of the organism. Likewise they affect the strategies employed in optimising the utilisation of energy for the formation of gametes. This is often considered in terms of 'r' and 'K' strategies. These are considered as two extremes; the r strategy involves selection so as to maximise the rate of population increase, while K selection involves maximising competitive ability in an environment where food is limiting. The theory suggests that when the environment is homogeneous, or when temporal variations in climate and resource availability are predictable, K strategies will be favoured. The characteristics of a poikilotherm K strategist are: slow growth, deferred maturity, greater longevity, low fecundity and the production of large yolky eggs. The opposite characterises the r strategist. Few species can be considered totally r or totally K, the majority exhibiting characteristics of both strategies so that there is a continuum between the two extremes.

The Antarctic marine environment, with its characteristic bursts of high summer primary production followed by winters of low food availability, would thus seem to favour the K strategy. Is this borne out in practice?

Earlier discussion has shown that growth rates tend to be slow, maturity tends to be deferred and longevity is increased relative to temperate species. That leaves characteristics related to the reproductive cycle. Several strategies are distinguishable in benthic poikilotherms. Probably the most extreme case is that of many fish, where ovarian production continues throughout the year but the production of ripe eggs takes over 2 years. Sexually mature female *Notothenia neglecta* normally have two sizes of yolky eggs in their ovaries, small ones in their first year of development and large ones, up to 3 mm in diameter in the months leading up to spawning, which have been developing for over 2 years. Although first described for *N. neglecta* at Signy Island, this pattern has now been confirmed in a wide variety of Antarctic fish. Spawning tends to be in the winter and the large yolky eggs develop slowly to hatch in the spring so that by the time the yolk-sac reserves are fully used the post-larva is quite large and able to feed on copepod larvae in the plankton. Bottom-living or demersal fish, being restricted to the shelf region, were for a long time thought to produce demersal eggs. It was assumed that the less time the eggs and larvae spent in the plankton, the more likely they were to remain in a favourable locality. Recent net hauls around South Georgia have shown that the eggs, for part of the time at least, are at the surface and are therefore drifting freely in the ocean, permitting wide dispersal of eggs and larvae.

Using an artificial nest, built over a balance, and data logging equipment, chick growth can be measured accurately without disturbing the bird. In the computer plot of weight data for a Grey-headed Albatross chick in February, the chick's weight increases greatly each time it is fed by a parent, and then slowly declines as it metabolises its food. The arrow marks the onset of rain and shows how sensitive the automatic weighing equipment in the artificial nest can be.

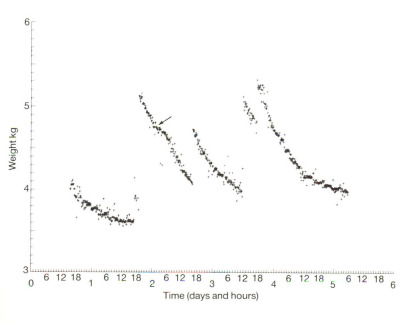

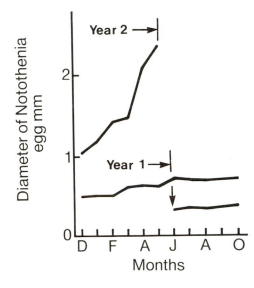

Size of eggs contained within the ovary of Nothothenia neglecta. *Yolk deposition starts at the arrow and continues for 2 years. Spawning is annual so that, in a mature ovary, two year-classes of yolky eggs are always present.*

Of the invertebrate groups the most intensively studied is the Crustacea. Comparisons of the shrimps *Chorismus antarcticus* and *Notocrangon antarcticus* have shown that their brood size was smaller, egg size larger and larvae more advanced on hatching than in directly comparable species from temperate waters. Energetically this could be achieved by simply diverting the same amount of energy from a large number of small eggs to a small number of proportionately larger eggs, but this is not the case since, in terms of annual reproductive output (RO – measured as grams fresh weight of eggs per grams fresh weight of female shrimp), the Antarctic species have much lower values than the temperate ones. There is a further energetic requirement in that the species referred to above all 'brood' their eggs. Brooding lasts for 9 or 10 months in both Antarctic species but for only 2–4 months in the temperate ones. Carrying a brood around for that period of time must require a significant increase in energy expenditure. Whether the difference between the two energy requirements of the two types is balanced by their respective broods is unknown.

A similar situation has been found for several other crustacean species, but it is by no means universal as there are exceptions. The isopod *Glyptonotus antarcticus* does not have a defined spawning season but appears to breed at all times of the year. Being a scavenger there is probably some food available all year round, although it does have slow growth rate, low fecundity and large egg size.

The dominant crustacean groups of the benthos are the Isopoda and Amphipoda, two groups which characteristically brood their young throughout their range. Elsewhere in the world other crustacean groups, such as the Decapoda and Cirripedia, achieve at least equal dominance. The brooding habit of Amphipoda and Isopoda is a pre-adaptation to colonisation of polar regions and this may explain the success of these groups in the Antarctic. Such an imbalance is not evident in the other dominant benthic phyla. The Mollusca, Annelida and Echinodermata are much more evenly represented but a much larger proportion of the species undergo non-pelagic development than those from lower latitudes. All the species of mollusc for which data are available, *Philine gibba*, *Laevilacunaria antarctica*, *Lissarca miliaris* and *Kidderia bicolor*, produce large eggs; both eggs and larvae are non-pelagic. Slow development of eggs and sperm are also characteristic of these species. The limpet *Nacella concinna* is an exception, producing many small eggs which hatch into planktotrophic larvae.

The echinoderm *Odontaster validus* produces demersal larvae and has very slow gametogenesis, the ova taking up to 3 years to develop fully, while those of the polychaete worm *Scoloplos marginatus* take a full 2 years to develop. This is coupled with a 6-month period for egg development and larval metamorphosis and a 3.5-year period from hatching to full sexual maturity.

As expected from the continuous low temperature and more or less predictable seasonal pulses of primary production, the vast majority of examples cited from the benthos can be considered *K* strategists. In the pelagic environment, there is very little information concerning the zooplankton apart from krill. Relative to other euphausiids, krill spawn large eggs (0.7 mm diameter) but there is some disagreement as to how many are produced per season. Initially it was thought that the spawning season was related to latitude and, by implication, to the start of the production season, but more recent research has shown that spawning proceeds more or less continuously throughout much of the summer. This does not involve a steady depletion of the ovary throughout the breeding season but rather a continuous production process and, at the end of the spawning season, the ovary reverts to more or less its pre-spawning condition. This has two consequences: first, ovarian maturation takes place quite rapidly, and, secondly, it is impossible to determine fecundity just from an examination of the ovary. In contrast to the benthic invertebrates where there is a strong tendency towards a *K* strategy, krill, at least as far

Summaries of the two reproductive strategies of Antarctic marine invertebrates.

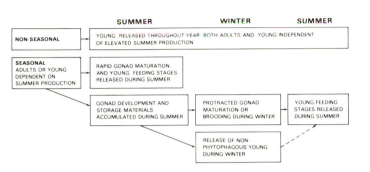

Species of the lichen genus Usnea *are important constituents of the fellfield communities. Often growing in very exposed sites, they are subjected to very wide seasonal variations in temperature and moisture availability.*

as egg production is concerned, are more *r* than *K* strategists. Their slow overall growth rate is, however, a further *K* adaptation. Detailed information on other species is very limited but tends to indicate that in general the zooplankters do not tend to be nearly as *K*-adapted as the benthic invertebrates.

On land the oribatid mite *Alaskozetes* oviposits on several occasions after reaching maturity and can also breed in successive seasons. Superficially this would seem to be contrary to expectation. But food is available more or less continually throughout the summer and only unavailable when the habitat is frozen and the animals cannot feed. The springtail *Cryptopygus antarcticus*, like *Alaskozetes*, appears to lay eggs throughout the summer, so that all life history stages are likely to be present at any one time. Egg production by individual females is very limited as batches are generally less than fourteen eggs. Thus for these terrestrial invertebrates there are two conflicting approaches. Growth and development are slow, a typical *K* strategy, but breeding is more or less continuous whilst the animals are active, features typical of an *r* strategy.

Plants have adopted a very conservative approach to reproduction, relying almost entirely on asexual or vegetative reproduction. Individuals appear to be long-lived and growth is generally slow, for both lichens and mosses.

Poikilotherms have very little control over where they might be present in the Antarctic. Terrestrial, fresh-water and benthic species are limited by habitat, whilst the marine planktonic species are carried on the prevailing currents. Homeotherms, being much larger and more able to migrate over great distances, can arrange their breeding cycles to take greater advantage of favourable conditions wherever and whenever they occur. Thus the Blue and Fin Whales only migrate into the Southern Ocean for about 100 days in summer to feed; calves are born in warmer waters to the north. Others, such as the Antarctic Tern and Wilson's Storm Petrel, breed in the Antarctic during the productive summer months but migrate northwards, in the case of the former as far as the Arctic Circle, in the austral winter.

All the seal species breed annually. Crabeater, Ross and Leopard Seals, even when breeding on the pack ice, are not social animals. From about mid-October onwards the female Crabeater Seals haul out onto the ice to pup. The pups grow very rapidly on the very nutritious milk produced but, by the time the pup is weaned at 4 weeks the female has lost about 50% of her initial weight. Mating occurs soon after weaning, giving a gestation period of about 11 months. The cycle for the Leopard Seal is thought to be similar but occurs a month later in the year. By contrast the Weddell Seal hauls out onto the fast ice close inshore to pup; the timings of pupping, weaning and gestation are essentially similar to those of the Crabeater Seal.

The remaining species of seal breed on land, often in quite large groups or harems. In September the bull Elephant Seals arrive on the beaches from their pelagic winter feeding grounds, to be followed a few days later by the females. The pups are born, one per cow, about 8 days after the females haul out. The cows must remain on land for the full 3-week interval until the pups are weaned, so all the milk they produce is at the expense of their blubber reserves. The dominant bulls, 'beachmasters' as they are known, do not leave the beaches at this time but live off their blubber reserves. They expend considerable energy in ritual display and aggression to keep the less-dominant bulls away. The cows are mated by the 'beachmasters' just before weaning so that the gestation period is just over 11 months. The energy requirement of the 'beachmasters' is so great that they cannot hold territory for more than a couple of seasons before dying or giving way to younger bulls. After weaning the pups remain on the beaches for several weeks. They live on the extensive blubber reserves that they have accumulated before they leave for the pelagic feeding grounds in early January. The cows, following a period of intensive feeding to make good their

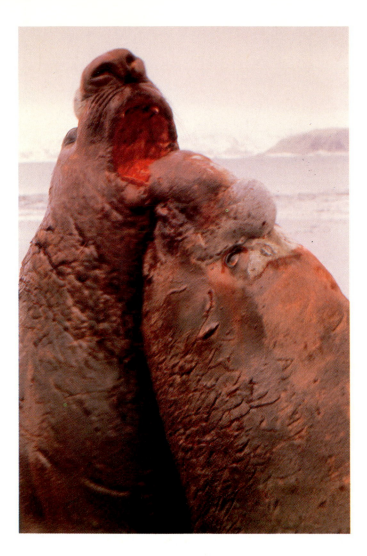

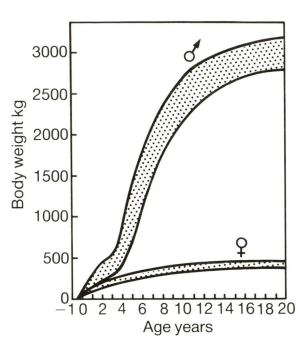

(Left) *Elephant Seal bulls fighting to establish dominance on a breeding beach.*

Growth curves, for South Georgia and Macquarie Island populations, demonstrate the enormous difference in size (sexual dimorphism) between male and female Elephant Seals.

blubber reserves reduced during lactation, return to land in January for a period of several weeks to moult. Once again they fast but without the added load of feeding pups their reduction in weight is not so drastic. The annual feeding pattern for the Elephant Seal may therefore be considered as one of winter feeding prior to the breeding season, a period of fasting during breeding when they live off their blubber reserves, another bout of intensive feeding, and then fasting during moulting until the winter feeding period begins again.

The other land-breeding species is the Fur Seal, which has established large colonies on rock or shingle beaches with easy access to the sea. The bulls are first to arrive in late October and they are followed 2 or 3 weeks later by the cows. The pups are born 2 or 3 days after the cows haul out and the cows are mated again just over a week later. In these respects the pattern is very similar to the Elephant Seal. However, after mating the bulls leave the cows to suckle the pups for about 3.5 months. This different pattern of suckling is necessary because of the Fur Seal's very limited blubber. It cannot therefore rely on internal food stores to produce milk but has to make regular feeding trips of 3–6 days for each period of 2–5 days spent suckling the pups. Pup development is therefore dependent on the availability of food (largely krill), immediately

following birth, rather than during the preceding winter as in the case of the Elephant Seal. During this period their foraging range is limited and local availability of food is therefore vital to them.

For birds the breeding pattern is more variable. At South Georgia most species of albatross and petrel lay eggs in October or November, with fledging occuring between February and April. Fledging time is a function of size so that the larger species, producing larger eggs, tend to take the longest. In general breeding seasons are synchronised so that the chicks fledge at around the time of maximum food abundance. Many of the smaller petrels nest in burrows and, since these are not clear of snow until well into the summer, particularly in the more southerly locations, the timing of the thaw controls the start of the breeding season. Sudden heavy falls of snow during fledging can block the burrows and may be a cause of significant chick mortality.

Large birds which have large chicks have an energetic price to pay for the extended fledging period. In two species at South Georgia, the King Penguin and Wandering Albatross, the time from laying to fledging is about 11 months, leaving the adults no time in which to build up their strength in order to breed again in the season in which the chicks fledge. Even though the remaining species

*An Emperor Penguin incubates its single egg tucked under a flap
of skin and resting on its feet. The newly hatched chick can be kept
warm in a similar fashion.*

Weight changes during the breeding season in adult Macaroni Penguins showing the effects of rearing chicks on the adult's food reserves. (Below) *The Macaroni Penguin is the most abundant species on South Georgia.*

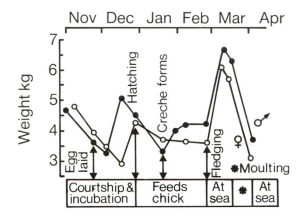

are able to fledge their chicks during the summer, this does not mean that they are capable of breeding in successive years. If they successfully rear a chick in one summer, both Grey-headed and Light-mantled Sooty Albatrosses will not breed in the next because it takes too long to get back into breeding condition.

The most amazing of all bird breeding cycles must be that of the Emperor Penguin. Living in very high latitudes it has only a very short summer season. This is clearly too brief a period for the largest of all Antarctic birds to fledge a chick. Eggs are therefore laid at the end of the summer when the adults are in their peak condition. The chicks hatch and are fed throughout the cold winter months and finally fledge at about midsummer. This leaves the adults just long enough, if conditions are favourable, to come into breeding condition before the onset of winter. Such a strategy requires that the chick is raised during winter when it is smallest and most vulnerable to cold stress. Heat loss is considerably reduced by the huddling together both by the chicks and adults, an interesting behavioural adaptation in this extreme environment. The parents must travel great distances across the sea ice to get to the feeding grounds, leaving the chicks in a creche supervised by only a few adults. Parental visits are therefore at widely spaced intervals. In the early stages of growth, the chick does receive food in the form of a milky secretion from the stomach wall, regurgitated by the adults when required. Later, the chicks are fed on more solid food caught by the parents at sea.

Thus, in terms of strategies, the homeotherms must be thought of as more K than r strategists since their reproduction and growth are very closely linked to the summer production season. The same is true of the poikilotherms which, while few exhibit all K characteristics, show a distinct tendency in that direction.

94

Bird behaviour has been a major feature of ornithological research in Antarctica. Adélie penguins, seen here copulating, have been studied in detail. Courtship and breeding behaviour are now well documented for this species.

Emperor Penguin chicks soon become too large to be incubated on their parents' feet. They then form creches, a form of social organization which frees more adult birds for feeding and allows the chicks to huddle together to keep warm.

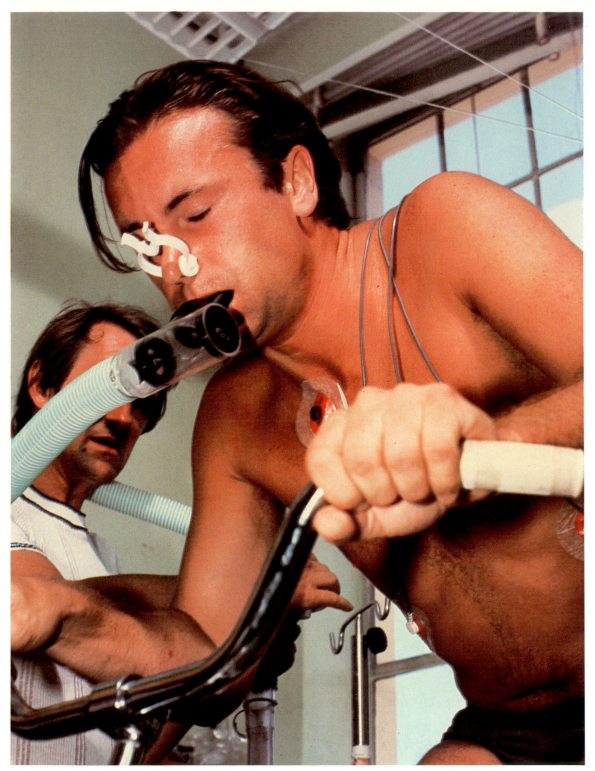

A wide range of medical experiments and investigations have been conducted by doctors in Antarctica. Psychiatric problems experienced by small groups of men have been investigated at several stations, as have those concerned with increased susceptibility to infection after living in such a clean environment. More recently studies have been concentrated on metabolism and physiology. The International Biomedical Expedition in 1980–81 was especially concerned with assessing whether men can become acclimatised to cold. Doctors from five countries took part in field experiments and laboratory tests. The photograph shows a doctor being tested for physical fitness after periods of exposure to severe Antarctic weather.

Chapter·7
Physiological adaptations

Freezing resistance

For most Antarctic environments temperature is often at or below the freezing point of water for considerable periods of time. Avoidance of freezing is thus likely to be an important consideration for living organisms. The equilibrium freezing point of an aqueous solution is dependent on the ionic concentration of the solute. For example, fresh water, which by definition contains very low salt concentrations, freezes at or just below 0°C. Sea water, with its much higher salt concentration, freezes at around −1.8°C. Animal body fluids are aqueous solutions and hence their freezing points will be below zero.

In fresh water, providing the lake does not freeze solid, the minimum temperature that can be reached is only very slightly below 0°C. The ionic concentration of the body fluid of fresh-water organisms is much higher than that of the surrounding water so that there is no likelihood of the organism freezing. Thus although the animals live in an environment close to freezing they themselves are unlikely to suffer that fate.

Turning to the marine environment the body fluids of most invertebrates are either hyperosmotic or isosmotic with sea water. Providing the sea remains unfrozen they will also. For many polar species of fish the temperature of the sea water in which they live is up to one degree below the equilibrium freezing point of their body fluids. Some adaptation is clearly needed to take account of this small but very important discrepancy. There are two possible approaches to the problem: the fish can either make an 'antifreeze' or else it can become 'supercooled'.

Supercooling, the phenomenon whereby solutions remain liquid at temperatures below their freezing point, only occurs when no ice crystals or other 'freezing nuclei' are present. Contact with ice causes immediate freezing, so for this mechanism to be effective the fish must live in an environment in which it will not come into contact with ice. A small number of species do avoid freezing in this manner by living permanently in deeper water away from ice. It is, however, the shallow-water coastal zone that is the most productive and to live there some other adaptation is needed.

The alternative approach of producing an antifreeze has also been followed. The difference that needs to be compensated for is up to one Celsius degree. About half the disparity is made up by an increase in the sodium and chloride ion concentrations. The remainder of the compensation is due to the presence of macromolecular antifreezes in the body fluids. These antifreezes tend to be either glycoproteins or peptides, only one type being found in a particular species. A typical example is that

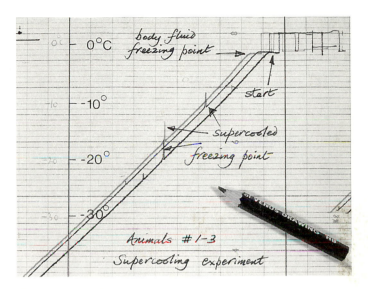

Recorder traces from an experiment to determine the super cooling points of three Antarctic terrestrial invertebrates. When the animal freezes there is a release of heat during ice formation and this appears as a spike on the trace.

found in *Pagothenia borchgrevinki*, a species commonly living in amongst the ice, whose antifreeze glycoproteins consist of a repeating sequence of the tripeptide alanine–alanine–threonine, with the disaccharide galactose–N-acetylgalactosamine attached to each threonine residue. Being a repeated sequence it is theoretically possible for the glycoprotein chains to be a wide variety of different lengths. This apparently only occurs to a limited extent since only eight size fractions are present, the smallest having a molecular weight of 2600 and the largest of 33 700. The glycoprotein antifreeze is only present in low concentrations in the blood and thus makes only a small contribution to the osmotic strength. Consequently, the antifreeze has little effect on the equilibrium freezing point. The mechanism by which this thermal hysteresis is achieved is therefore not by lowering the freezing point. Precisely how they do function is not clear, although it seems very likely that growing ice nuclei become bound to the glycoprotein. Thermal agitation then breaks up the ice nucleus, freeing the antifreeze molecule for further action. Thus so long as there is antifreeze circulating in the blood the fish is protected from freezing. This is not without cost since energy must be used to produce the antifreeze but the energy needed is not great since the molecule is not denatured by its action of preventing freezing. As the antifreeze molecules are relatively small, some adaptation is necessary to prevent their being lost with the normal excretory products via the kidney. Nototheniid kidneys are aglomerular to prevent such losses, so that urine production must be by secretion rather than by the more energy-demanding process of filtration. The blood is not the only body fluid. Cerebrospinal fluid, the aqueous humor of the eye and fluid in the hind gut lumen all contain similar antifreeze substances as, like the blood, they are all potential sites for freezing.

In the terrestrial environment the problem is of much greater magnitude. Whereas the fish has only to make good a deficit of about one degree, the terrestrial organisms may need to compensate for differences as great as 50 or 60 degrees. The glycoproteins produced by the fish would afford little protection under these circumstances, although similar thermal hysteresis proteins occur in temperate and some Arctic insect species. These have more hydrophilic amino acids and a much lower alanine content than those of fish. Two different physiological strategies have evolved in response to low winter temperatures. Animals are either 'freezing-tolerant', in which case they have evolved mechanisms to minimise damage to cells and tissues during the freezing process, or they are 'freezing-susceptible', in which case they avoid freezing, which is always lethal. Of the two strategies, freezing-tolerance tends to be the exception in the Antarctic having only been demonstrated in one species, the midge *Belgica*

antarctica and then only in the larval stage. During the summer they can withstand temperatures down to −15°C, even though their mean supercooling point is only −5.7°C. Freezing-tolerant species often use nucleators in their body fluids to ensure freezing at a relatively high sub-zero temperature, e.g. −10°C.

Behavioural strategies may also be of survival value. The animals tend to cluster in large numbers beneath rocks. This gives them protection against rapid changes in temperature since the thermal capacity of the rock will maintain a more stable microenvironment. Water may stay liquid for longer periods beneath the rock than in much of the surrounding soil matrix and algal films are frequently found around the buried edges of boulders.

Freezing-susceptible implies that the animal either avoids freezing conditions (a behavioural response) or else has a mechanism for lowering its own body fluid freezing point. In general the main supercooling agent is glycerol or a polyhydric alcohol (polyol). The amount that is present is dependent on the temperatures to which the animals have been exposed and thus it might be expected that glycerol production would be related to season. Experimental studies on the oribatid mite *Alaskozetes antarcticus*, simulating seasons by adjusting the photoperiod, did not affect glycerol production. The main

The antifreeze molecules are absorbed onto the face of the crystal at the step. These bound molecules then force water molecules (shown as cubes) to join the ice lattice between the absorbed molecules, resulting in growth in the form of areas having a high radius of curvature. For ice to grow in this way the freezing point must be lowered.

Basic repeating structural unit of glycopeptide antifreezes isolated from the blood of Antarctic fish. The polypeptide backbone is made up of only two amino acids, alanine and threonine, in the sequence alany–threonine. Every threonine is joined to a disaccharide of galactose and N–acetylgalactosamine.

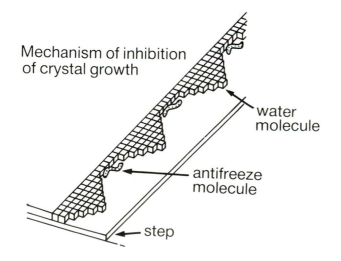

Mechanism of inhibition of crystal growth

water molecule

antifreeze molecule

step

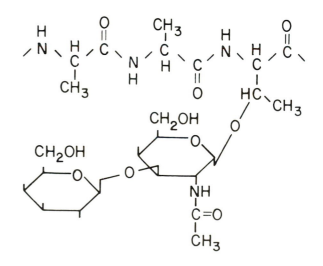

factors stimulating glycerol synthesis were found to be low temperature acclimation, suppressed feeding and desiccation. Glycerol synthesis increases in two phases during the autumn: first, during a period of about a month when ground surface temperature fluctuates little from 0°C – the animals continue to feed at this time; and secondly, as the mean daily temperature falls to −10°C in early winter – feeding is simultaneously reduced for most, but not all of the population.

Consequently there are two groups in the population, one with good low-temperature protection to about −25°C, the other protected only to about −10°C. In cold winters only the lowest temperature-adapted group will survive but in mild winters all will survive. Having expended less energy in glycerol production, the less cold-adapted group may be more able to take advantage of favourable growth conditions in spring.

Many of the polyols found in terrestrial arthropods appear to be identical to those present in their food. Evidence so far suggests that the polyols are synthesised *de novo* by the animal and are not absorbed unchanged from the food.

A reduction in feeding activity could be a result of several factors, for example lack of available food or a general slowing down of enzyme controlled systems. Both may apply but must be remembered that food particles themselves form potential freezing nuclei and that their very presence in the gut could prompt freezing in spite of the action of the glycerol. The freezing protection afforded by glycerol is largely through increasing the osmotic concentration and thus lowering the freezing point of the fluid.

In answer to the simple question 'How do Antarctic animals avoid freezing?', five mechanisms have now been identified: (1) production of polyhydric alcohols to facilitate 'super-cooling', e.g. the mite *Alaskozetes*; (2) formation of glycoprotein antifreeze to eliminate ice crystals as they begin to form, e.g. shallow-water fish; (3) tolerance of freezing – only demonstrated in the midge *Belgica* but may be more widespread; (4) supercooling without production of any special compounds, e.g. deep-water fish; and (5) for some species no adaptation is necessary since although they live close to the lower thermal limit ambient temperatures rarely if ever go below it, e.g. marine and fresh-water invertebrates.

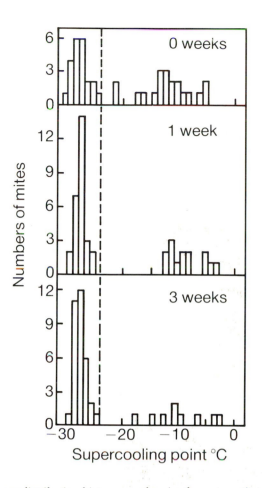

Frequency distribution histograms showing how starvation for up to 3 weeks increases the number of adult Alaskozetes antarcticus which can supercool to below −25°C.

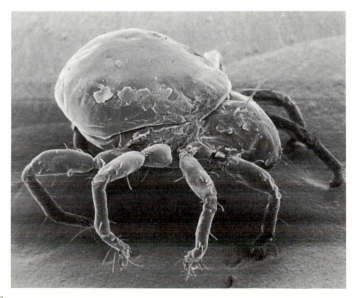

A female mite Alaskozetes antarcticus *magnified 320 times. It lives under rocks and lichens, and in amongst penguin guano and algae. Only 1 mm long, it is one of the largest Antarctic terrestrial invertebrates.*

Temperature and enzyme activity

Rates of chemical reactions are greatly affected by temperature. Providing the reactants remain in the same physical state, increasing the temperature speeds up a reaction while decreasing the temperature slows it down. Rates of biochemical reactions are further affected by enzymes which are themselves affected by, and are also sensitive to, temperature. The living organism contains a vast number of interacting enzyme-controlled reactions, proceeding sequentially and simultaneously, all of which will be affected by temperature. Enzymes do have optimal operating temperatures which generally reflect the temperature of their environment. Polar enzyme systems can therefore be expected to operate most effectively at low temperatures.

The direct effect of temperature on reaction rates alone leads to the immediate conclusion that at polar temperatures everything will proceed slowly. For the animal this means that digestion and assimilation will be slow, likewise the formation of new tissue (growth) and the replacement and servicing of old tissues (maintenance). Formation of gametes will be slow, as will the release of energy for movement. On the other hand if enzyme systems are low-temperature-adapted then these rates should be the same everywhere; any differences being due to substrate (food) availability. Looked at in this way there are several categories within which the effects of changes in reaction rate can be studied and perhaps provide an answer to the question 'Does everything slow down and if so, why?'

A major difficulty is the limited data available, making ideal comparisons difficult to find. At present a series of drastic compromises must be initially accepted in order to make generalisations about how organisms function in the Antarctic.

Growth has been studied for a variety of species and is therefore a reasonable starting point. In the marine environment growth tends to be slow, with only a few species growing as rapidly as directly equivalent temperate species and the majority growing more slowly. This is true for crustaceans, molluscs and fish, the three groups for which reliable data are available. The conclusion is further reinforced by considering generation times, which are generally protracted, indicating that growth to maturity is slow. In the terrestrial environment there is no direct information but since generation times for small invertebrates tend to be at least a year it indicates that growth is slow. For many species feeding, and therefore growth, are only possible for a short period during the summer. The metabolic process associated with growth may therefore proceed rapidly even though the mean annual rate of growth is low.

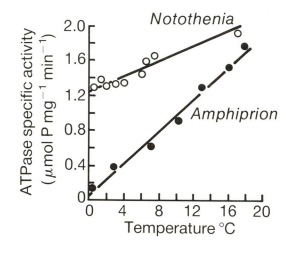

*The effect of temperature on the activity of the enzyme ATPase extracted from the white muscle of an Antarctic fish (*Notothenia*) and a tropical fish (*Amphiprion*) showing the much greater enzyme activity of the Antarctic species at lower temperatures.*

The tendency of Antarctic fish and invertebrates to produce large yolky eggs superficially suggests that much energy is needed for the process. However, although eggs tend to be large, few are produced, so that the amount of assimilated energy used in the production of eggs is no higher than in temperate species. However the final rapid maturation takes place during the summer, suggesting that food availability rather than enzyme efficiency is the limiting factor.

Movement as a result of muscle contraction is another enzyme-dependent process which may be affected in two important ways: first, the power of the muscle contraction might be affected; and secondly, the rate of contraction may be reduced. Deficiencies in power can be made good by increasing the amounts of contractile material. There is no evidence that the muscles of Antarctic poikilotherms are unduly large, although it is not easy to make valid comparisons since the same mode of life must be assumed. Changes in rates of contraction should be recognisable. In the marine environment many of the major predators are homeothermic and hence their activity will be more or less independent of the environmental temperature. Any tendency on the part of the prey to slow down will make it more vulnerable, and this in turn will provide a strong selection pressure leading to the evolution of faster acting muscles or else to improved concealment. While it is wrong to consider speed of contraction purely as an enzyme-controlled process, the enzymes involved have been studied intensively and it is probably safe to assume that they give an indication as to the selection pressures applied to the other factors.

Simplistically, muscle contraction may be considered as being brought about by interdigitated movement of the muscle proteins actin and myosin. This process occurs as a result of hydrolysis of the energy-rich substance adenosine triphosphate (ATP), this process being catalysed by the enzyme myosine ATPase, an enzyme which can be assayed *in vitro* with reasonable facility.

Comparisons have been made of the activity of myosin ATPase of polar, temperate and tropical fish at a wide range of temperatures. Although these data show that there is the expected general relation between temperature and activity for all species, these enzyme activity–temperature curves do not coincide. At around 20°C the specific activity of myosin ATPase of the tropical fish *Amphiprion* is similar to that of the Antarctic species *Notothenia rossii*. At around 0°C the situation is quite different, with the activity of the *Notothenia* enzyme being much greater than that of the *Amphiprion* enzyme. This is a clear indication of significant adaptation in the muscle, but is that the end of the story? The next question is not just 'How has the Antarctic fish muscle adapted?', but 'Why doesn't the tropical fish make use of the same high-activity enzyme as the Antarctic fish?'.

Closer examination of the enzymes yields a clue. Considerable difficulties are encountered in the assay simply because *Notothenia* myosin ATPase is very difficult to extract. The main problem is that it is very unstable, and this instability is brought about by the much more open structure of the enzyme molecule. In the case of the tropical fish a more compact and rigid structure is needed to give the molecule thermal stability at the higher environmental temperature. The *Notothenia* myosin ATPase is therefore only practical in situations where there is a very limited range of environmental temperature – such as are found in the Southern Ocean. It would be intriguing to find out whether this adaptation is typical of other enzyme systems, such as those affecting general metabolism and growth, in the fish and also whether similar adaptations are present in marine invertebrates. Similar adaptations are to be expected although none of the necessary experiments have been undertaken. On land the much wider thermal amplitude might mitigate against the evolution of such a narrow-temperature range system in terrestrial invertebrates, but once again no experiments have been undertaken. This is an exciting area for research that hopefully will receive attention in the near future.

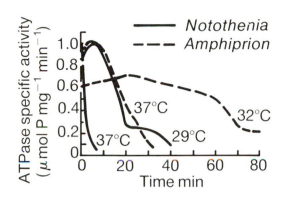

Thermal inactivation of fish white muscle ATPase. Although the Antarctic fish (Notothenia) *enzyme is more active than that of the tropical species* (Amphiprion) *it is very unstable when the temperature is raised.*

Metabolic cold adaptation

The final category for consideration of enzyme activity is that of basal metabolism or maintenance. In the most generalised terms growth is slow, reproductive effort reduced and activity slightly increased. The net effect of this should be that for the same annual energy intake a larger proportion will be required for maintenance in the polar organism, the difference often being referred to as 'metabolic cold adaptation'. That then is the theory. In practice that is what happens in some instances – but not all! Before looking in detail at specific examples it is necessary first to examine the rationale behind the theory of metabolic cold adaptation. This states that a cold-adapted species uses relatively more energy on basal metabolism than an unadapted one – not a very good adaptation considering that to maintain the species selection is likely to favour diverting energy to reproduction and growth. A better adaptation could be a lowered basal metabolism.

In the marine environment early measurements of oxygen uptake rates by fish showed they had a metabolic rate significantly higher than would be expected by extrapolation of rates for temperate and tropical fish to polar temperatures. This was taken as evidence for metabolic cold adaptation until it was noticed that basal metabolism declined steadily with time to a low level which, if measurements were made after 24 h, indicated 'no adaptation'. Although the same technique had been used for temperate and polar fish the latter took several times as long to become 'metabolically quiet'. So, in reality, fish

Representation of the effects of cold-adapted metabolism and polar-adapted metabolism in relation to the total annual energy intake of a temperate water benthic invertebrate.

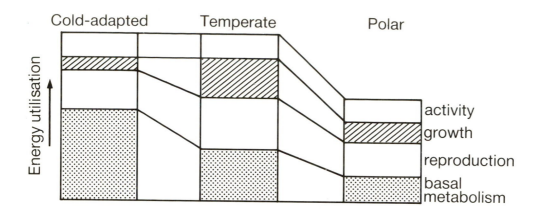

Comparison of oxygen consumption rates for Alaskozetes *and temperate species of cryptostigmatid mites, showing a marked elevation of metabolic rate or* cold adaption *on the part of the Antarctic species.*

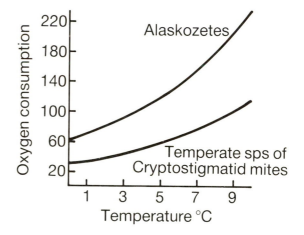

Relationship between metabolic rate (oxygen consumption) and temperature in four species of Antarctic isopod compared with temperate water species, showing that there is no elevation of metabolic rate (cold adaption) for the Antarctic species.

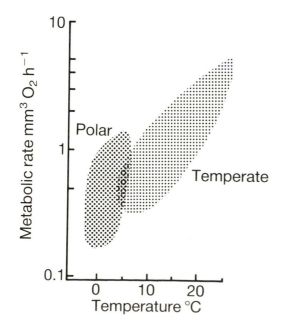

The relation between oxygen consumption rate and size indicates that in spite of its lack of haemoglobin the icefish still utilises just as much oxygen as a red-blooded Antarctic fish.

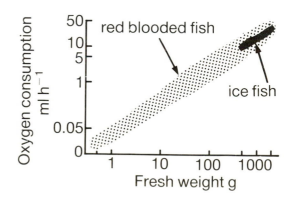

are not 'cold-adapted' and neither are marine invertebrates. This is what might be expected, but it is not the end of the story.

Turning to the terrestrial environment we find a different picture in that metabolic rate appears to be elevated in some Antarctic species but not in others. In these cases it cannot be attributed to an artefact of technique. Many of these studies have been made during, or subsequent to, the reversal of opinions with regard to fish. The time/stress artefact was known and taken into account and yet even so the measured metabolic rates remain elevated in the arthropod *Alaskozetes*. This elevated metabolic rate must be regarded as real, but since it indicates a less-efficient utilisation of resources cannot itself offer any advantage to the animal. However, resistance to freezing can only be provided at some metabolic cost. There may also be adaptations to the muscle systems analagous to those seen in the fish. No experiments have been undertaken to test this but it is to be expected that the elevation in metabolic rate is caused by the needs of such specific systems. Respiratory data for other Antarctic arthropods – *Cryptopygus antarcticus, Belgica antarctica, Ixodes uriae* – show no metabolic cold adaptation. There is obviously no general development of this physiological adaptation amongst Antarctic terrestrial invertebrates.

White-blooded fish

Some organisms possess features which, superficially at least, appear to be not just useless but positively disadvantageous. The white blood of the channichthyid fish (colloquially known as icefish because of their white gills) is one such adaptation.

The vast majority of vertebrates have in their blood a red pigment, haemoglobin, whose main function is to transport oxygen around the body. It is therefore reasonable to assume that it, or an analogous compound, is essential. Examination of icefish blood indicates that it contains no haemoglobin although a few rudimentary red blood cells (erythrocytes) have been found in larval fish.

In evolutionary terms this indicates that icefish have 'lost' haemoglobin rather than having never had it. Other species of Antarctic fish have been found to have reduced haemoglobin and erythrocyte numbers by comparison with temperate-water fish, which suggests that there is some advantage in reducing haemoglobin and that the icefish are an extreme example.

The first question that needs to be answered is whether icefish require as much oxygen as other fish. An extreme case would be if they required no oxygen at all but made use of some other metabolic pathway to release energy. In

An icefish (Champsocephalus aceratus) *rests on the sea bed.*

an earlier section some of the problems in measuring oxygen uptake rates of polar fish were outlined. In spite of these difficulties in measurement, it is clear that oxygen uptake rates for icefish and red-blooded fish are essentially the same, indicating that the normal aerobic metabolic processes operate.

How then is the oxygen extracted from the water? The major site for gaseous exchange in fish is normally the gills, although in some species significant transfer can take place through the skin. Icefish do not possess scales and it has been suggested that cutaneous respiration may be a significant process. Experiments have shown that oxygen uptake through the skin only accounts for about 3% of the total. Furthermore, as the fish grows larger the absorptive area of the gills increases by a much greater proportion than the skin. The larger the fish, therefore, the lower the proportion of the required oxygen that is absorbed through the skin. All the blood pumped from the heart goes directly to the gills, where gaseous exchange can take place, but only a small proportion goes to the skin. It seems that the adaptation is not associated with absorption through the skin.

Are there any adaptations associated with the gills? Estimates of the absorptive area of the gills have been made, which indicate that the absorptive area per unit body weight is not significantly different for icefish and red-blooded Antarctic fish. What is different is the increased diameter of the blood vessels in the gills, which almost certainly reduces the vascular resistance to blood flow.

Before continuing discussion of the size of blood vessels it is worth considering the way in which oxygen is carried in the blood. In red-blooded fish this is largely by the haemoglobin system, although some oxygen is carried in physical solution in the plasma. In common with many other processes, oxygen transport by haemoglobin becomes less efficient as the temperature is lowered. Although there is a significant level of thermal adaptation in Antarctic fish haemoglobin this does not fully compensate for the difference. Even taking this and the solubility of oxygen in plasma into account, the oxygen-carrying capacity of red-blooded fish is about ten times that of the icefish. Clearly, since icefish and red-blooded fish extract oxygen from the water at roughly similar rates, the former will need to pump blood at a very much faster rate. Knowing the oxygen uptake rate, the oxygen in the blood being pumped to and from the gills and the oxygen-carrying capacity of the blood, the gill blood flow (cardiac output) can be calculated.

Several estimates have been made of cardiac output and all indicate that the icefish heart needs to pump several times as much blood as that of a red-blooded fish

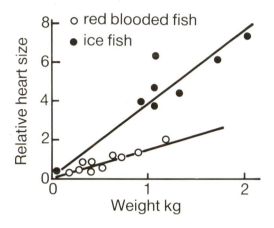

To extract sufficient oxygen from the water the icefish needs to pump much more blood around its body than a red-blooded fish and this requires a much larger heart.

of the same size. Pumping blood at a faster rate can be achieved by increasing the heart rate or stroke volume (or both). Experiments have shown that the resting heart rate is essentially the same for all species, indicating that the compensation must be by increasing the stroke volume and this indicates that an abnormally large heart is required.

Fish hearts contain two chambers, a thin-walled collecting chamber, the atrium, and a very muscular thick-walled pumping chamber, the ventricle. Assuming that ventricle weight is a reasonable index of heart size, the icefish have been shown to have hearts approximately three times the size of those in comparably sized red-blooded fish. Using the product of ventricle weight and resting heart rate to give a measure of resting cardiac output it has been estimated that an icefish pumps three to four times as much blood as a red-blooded Antarctic fish. Since the blood oxygen capacity is only about one-tenth that in red-blooded fish, the actual amount of oxygen transported is much less in the icefish, still leaving them oxygen-deficient.

Further investigations have shown that icefish utilise a very high proportion of the oxygen in their blood when at rest in comparison to red-blooded fish. This difference may increase diffusion by ensuring a high blood-to-tissue oxygen partial pressure gradient; this is less important for red-blooded fish because of other features associated with haemoglobin which facilitate oxygen release in conditions of high carbon dioxide concentration.

An increased heart size in icefish necessarily requires a large blood volume in order to maintain a sufficient reservoir for the heart to pump. Eight to ten per cent of the body volume is in fact blood – a much higher proportion than in a typical bony fish. Although from the point of view of oxygen transport the lack of haemoglobin can be considered disadvantageous, the greatly reduced number of corpuscles in the blood does mean that the viscosity is reduced. Estimating viscosity is not easy either *in vitro*, because of the presence of cellular components in the blood, or *in vivo*, because of the flexibility of the vessels. Experiments do suggest, though, an approximately two-fold reduction in blood viscosity for the icefish.

Having determined that there is a lessened resistance to flow of blood in icefish blood vessels, further consideration of the actual size of the vessels is necessary. Resistance to

flow varies as the fourth power of the radius of the blood vessel. The average diameter of an icefish capillary is about 17 μm while for other red-blooded fish the diameter is 10 μm; this would provide an approximately eight-fold difference in flow resistance. Thus the energy costs per unit volume of blood pumped must be much lower for the icefish but, due to its lower oxygen capacity, it must pump a much larger volume of blood.

The icefish circulatory system can therefore be described as one of large volume operating at low pressure and, because of the physical constraints of solubility of gases in liquids, the blood to tissue oxygen partial pressure gradient must be much higher than for red-blooded fish. The pumping system presumably has some significant advantages for icefish over red-blooded fish, particularly in terms of energy. However, the low oxygen capacity of the

A scientist dissects an icefish. Extreme anaemia is obvious from the white colour of the liver. The large orange structure in the body cavity is the ovary, full of large yolky eggs.

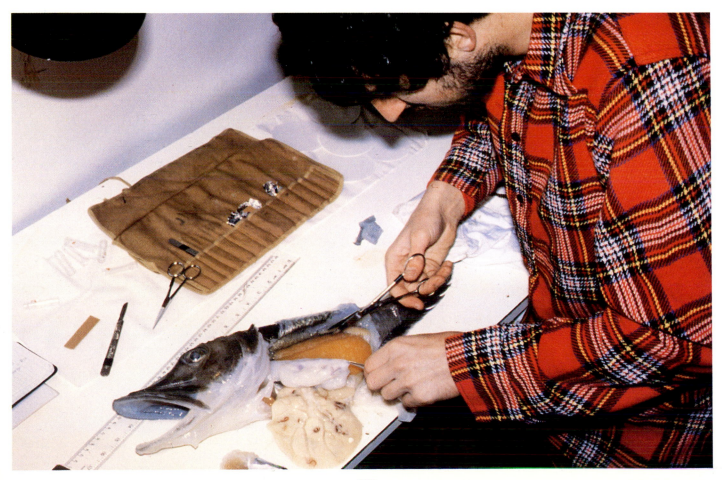

Fur seal fitted with an instrument package to monitor the time, duration and depth of each dive. The data from such instruments have proved invaluable in determining the patterns of seal activity whilst at sea.

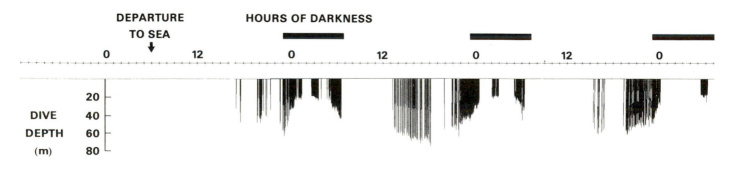

blood does mean that the fish are intolerant of low ambient oxygen tensions. Cold waters, such as those of the Southern Ocean, can hold quite large amounts of oxygen and generally are at quite high percentage saturation. Under normal conditions, therefore, the low resistance to hypoxia of the icefish is probably no physiological disadvantage. It does, however, indicate why the group is virtually restricted to the Southern Ocean.

Thermoregulation

The discussion so far has been centred on creatures whose body temperature follows closely that of their environment. In aquatic situations this means that the temperature is more or less constant around freezing. Clearly there are likely to be advantages to a creature that has a constant and higher temperature for its enzyme reactions. Such adaptations do not come cheaply. An obvious problem is that raising the temperature above the ambient requires the utilisation of energy – in effect adding to the cost of basal metabolism. A second consideration is that having expended energy in raising the temperature there are advantages in minimising heat loss; thermal insulation is the key here and, ideally, should be associated with behavioural adaptations such as avoidance of extremely low temperatures.

There are four groups of homeothermic animals in the Antarctic: whales, seals, penguins and flying birds (principally petrels and albatrosses), and all have well-adapted thermal insulation systems. Blubber, a subcutaneous layer of fat, is a characteristic of the mammals. Indeed, oil derived from the processing of blubber was one of the principal products of the whaling and sealing industries. The blubber layer itself is frequently quite thick, up to about 12 cm in the case of a bull Elephant Seal or 20 cm in a Blue Whale. Whilst insulation will never totally prevent heat loss, once the insulating layer is of a thickness that minimises heat loss, increasing it will only add to the animal's bulk without markedly improving its thermal energy conversion.

If there is little to be gained by increasing blubber thickness beyond a certain, unspecified, level, the blubber, as a proportion of the animal's total weight, should decline with increasing size. The opposite is in fact the case as the table shows.

What is even more surprising is that the smallest species (Minke Whale) lives all year round in the Antarctic zone, whereas the others migrate into the area during the summer. The answer to this paradox probably lies in the seasonal feeding cycle of the species. The Minke Whale has food available all year round in the form of krill,

whereas the Blue Whale only experiences good feeding conditions when in the Southern Ocean during the summer. The latter species uses the blubber as a food reserve to see it through the season spent in warmer waters which are less favourable for feeding.

The relatively thinner blubber layer of the Minke Whale is thus adequate for thermal insulation, whilst the increased blubber content of the larger whales serves both as a food reserve and to improve the animal's hydrodynamic shape.

Heat loss is controlled by the thickness of the insulating layer and is also a function of the surface area of the location through which heat is being lost. Put simply this means that to minimise heat loss, surface area needs to be minimised. It is simple mathematically to prove that the body shape that optimises this condition is a sphere. Spherical whales and seals are obviously ridiculous; however their smoothly contoured shapes do have advantages both hydrodynamically and in terms of thermal conservation.

Another approach to minimising surface area is by increasing size, since volume increases as the cube of the length whereas surface area increases only as the square of the length. In this context large size can be considered an adaptation to thermal conservation and this in turn poses a problem since all animals must start off small before they grow large. A rapid early growth rate is therefore important.

Whilst blubber is the only thermal insulation of whales and phocid seals this is not true of the Fur Seal and birds; they have a protective external layer of fur or feathers, respectively. The coat of a Fur Seal is amongst the densest found on any mammal, and the animal's thermal insulation comes largely from their fur and not from blubber. The fur acts as an insulating layer by trapping air in a very dense and fine underlayer, which contains up to 40 000 fibres per square centimetre. This air layer must however be formed when the seal is out of water; that in itself is no great problem. In the water, however, there are potential hazards. At the surface the air layer will be subject to normal atmospheric pressure and the layer will function as effectively as on land. On diving, the air layer will be subjected additionally to the pressure of the water and this pressure increases very rapidly with depth. At 10 m the pressure relative to the surface will have doubled and this will halve the thickness of the air layer and consequently its insulating efficiency. For each additional 10 m the air layer will again be halved, further decreasing effectiveness. Thus, any Fur Seals making deep dives severely limit the time they spend at depths at which their fur no longer insulates effectively.

Similar in function to the dense fine-hair layer of the fur

(Right) Flensers removing the blubber layer from a whale. Blubber acts as both insulation and food reserve for the whale.

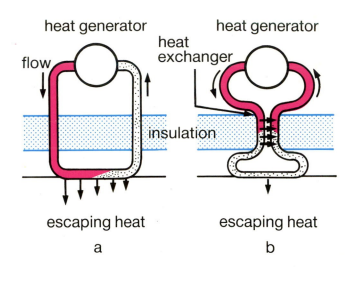

The principle of the countercurrent heat exchanger. (a) Simple system with no countercurrent. Warm liquid (blood) flowing from the heat generator (the body core) will lose heat to the exterior (the sea). (b) Countercurrent system. The flow and return pipes (arteries and veins) run in close contact with each other. The coldest liquid (venous blood) entering the insulation (blubber) is warmed by extracting heat from the hot outflowing liquid (arterial blood). Because the directions of flow are opposite (countercurrent), the maximum temperature gradient is maintained between the two flows over the distance they are in contact and thus the maximum amount of heat is exchanged.

seals are the down feathers of birds. Like fur the down operates by entrapping a layer of air close to the body; exactly the same problems in terms of diving are therefore present.

Blubber, fur and feathers are all good adaptations to keeping heat in by forming a continuous insulating layer. No animal can function as a closed system, however; all need to breathe and also to take in food. Furthermore, because of its thickness, the insulating layer could, if continuous over the whole body, compromise the animal's aerodynamic and/or hydrodynamic shape.

Even though the environmental temperature may be low, there will be occasions when excess metabolic heat needs to be dissipated in order to maintain a stable internal temperature. As a consequence of this a variety of features have evolved in order to minimise, or control, heat loss.

Breathing brings cold air into the lungs. Heat is then lost when this warmed air is exhaled. An obvious adaptation here is a heat exchanger which recovers the heat from the exhaled air. Such a mechanism is present in the nasal passages of penguins and seals, and in the case of Adelie and Gentoo Penguins it is estimated that 83% of the heat added to the cold inhaled air is recovered. Heat exchangers are also found in the blood circulation system of penguins, seals and whales. These operate by cooling the arterial blood, using the returning venous blood, before it reaches the extremities. The muscles thus supplied

receive oxygen, essential for muscular action, without causing excessive heat loss.

These adaptations have been considered purely from the point of view of minimising heat loss. Maintaining a stable temperature means that although conserving heat is of paramount importance any excess, as for example following muscular exertion, may require some heat to be dissipated. Such adaptations cannot be constant in their action but need to be under rigorous control.

The degree and manner in which this control is achieved differs between the major groups. Phocid seals and whales are almost totally enveloped in a layer of blubber and it has been assumed that the insulating qualities of such a layer are purely dependent on its thickness. Were blubber just a layer of inert fat this would be true, but it is not! Many blood vessels extend into the blubber layer and since these will be carrying warm blood from the core of the animal this will be cooled by the surrounding water. Temperature control can thus be achieved by increasing the amount of blood flowing to the blubber layer when the animal is warm and decreasing blood flow when it is cold.

Birds and fur seals can achieve some control when out of water by adjusting the thickness of the air layer next to the skin or the rate at which it is changed. When swimming this option is clearly not available since the insulating layer is surrounded by water. Water pressure will reduce the thickness of the layer so that heat loss could be

increased by the animal diving; although there is no evidence to support this idea. A much more reliable system than that is required. An alternative form of control is present in the flippers where, in addition to the counter-current heat exchanger system described for the whales and phocids, there is also a heat dissipation system similar to that present in blubber. Penguins are able to cool off during periods of activity by increasing the blood flow to the flippers.

The future

Adaptations to the Antarctic environment are clearly present at the physiological and biochemical levels. The examples quoted are not exhaustive and none is at that point where it is safe to say that a particular line of research is finished. There is still much that can be done in the study of mechanisms and processes within the living organism. Hopefully some, at least, of these topics, will be tackled in the near future. We still do not fully understand how antifreezes operate, neither is it clear what the over-riding control mechanisms are for enzyme systems. Much of the research so far has concentrated on only a few species and this may have led to unwarranted generalis-ations. The data on fish physiology is more detailed than that available for any other Antarctic group and since fish live in a buffered habitat, when compared with Antarctic

terrestrial organisms, the adaptive pressures on them might be considered much less than those acting on an orobatid mite. The Antarctic offers not only interesting basic problems in physiology but, for species inhabiting a steep environmental gradient, fascinating prospects for comparative physiology.

Only two flowering plants – the grass Deschampsia antarctica *and the cushion plant* Colobanthus quitensis *– are native to Antarctica. Photosynthesis is highest at low temperatures for both species.*

Antarctic terrestrial communities are largely composed of bare rock and mineral soil sorted by frost action. The vegetation is composed of mosses, lichens and algae. The sorted patch in the photograph has a well developed cover of vegetation around it.

Antarctic Krill Euphausia superba *– a species at the hub of the Southern Ocean food web.*

Chapter·8
Antarctic food webs

The concept of a food web is really quite simple. It developed from the food chain, an oft-quoted example of which is that from phytoplankton through krill to whales. Clearly, because other herbivores are present, that is not the only path for the energy contained within the phytoplankton to follow. Branching paths, ramifying in many directions to form a web, are the norm. Expressed in these terms the food web is just a qualitative description of the system.

Such a description gives no information as to the relative importance of the components. Two ways of assessing this importance are in terms of the amount of each component, the biomass, and the rate of change, the production. One important application of such information is in assessing the effects of man's exploitation of living resources but, while exploitation can be seen as being an obvious justification for such studies, it is not the only one. Understanding the structure and functioning of ecosystems is a complicated process because it requires that a complex web of interactions is described in terms of its components. Clearly the fewer the components the easier the job so that the more amenable systems to study are the simplest. The Antarctic terrestrial and fresh-water systems are some of the least complex anywhere in the world and this makes them particularly interesting to study.

The dominant transfers between the Antarctic terrestrial, fresh-water and marine systems are simple. Transfers from the sea to the land come in the form of sea spray and aerosols being blown onshore and also, in coastal regions, from faeces from resting and breeding birds and seals. The same transfers apply to the fresh-water systems.

In a typical Antarctic fresh-water lake, nutrients are released by the action of bacteria in the lake sediments and to a lesser extent in the plankton. These are utilised by the primary producers – mosses, benthic algae (some of which are epiphytic on the mosses) and phytoplankton. Feeding on this plant material are a few species of herbivores, while at the top of the food chain is a carnivorous copepod. The main external interactions are associated with the interchange of atmospheric gases, in particular oxygen and carbon dioxide. Ice, with its associated snow cover, imposes a pronounced seasonality on the lake by attenuating light and reducing turbulence. Research on Signy Island lakes has shown that variations in the abundance of both herbivores and decomposers are directly related to the availability of their food. Algal production is therefore the key to the quantitative functioning of the system. Apart from a brief period each year these systems are essentially sealed. Only when inputs of meltwater enter the lakes and gaseous interchange occurs at the lake

Signy Island has sixteen freshwater lakes, covering the complete nutrient range from eutrophic to oligotrophic. Integrated studies on the lake systems are now being extended to include the catchment areas.

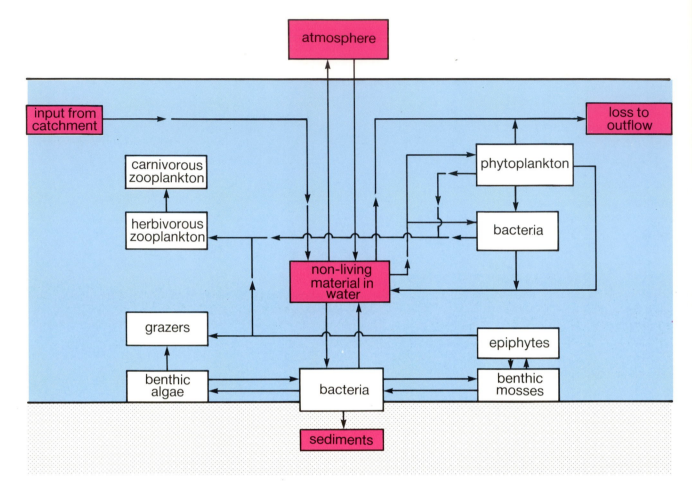

The simple food web characteristic of many non-saline Antarctic lakes.

surface is the system open. This simplicity, coupled with the very short food chains typical of these systems, makes Antarctic fresh-water lakes particularly suitable for ecosystem studies. A great deal of progress has already been made, particularly in the fields of nutrient flux and biogeochemical cycling, and it seems very likely that in the near future we will be able to model various interactive processes in what are some of the few naturally 'simple' ecosystems of the world.

Neither maritime nor terrestrial environments can be quite so easily delimited as the lakes, making the problems of quantifying the interactions within them that much more difficult. However intensive studies at Marion Island and Signy Island have indicated the main pathways of energy.

In maritime Antarctic and subantarctic habitats, minerals are derived from three major sources. Frost action accompanied by chemical and biological weathering causes minerals to be released from rocks and soils. This process is slow and most of the soluble nutrients released in this way are probably carried directly to the sea in the meltwater runoff. A second source is aerial deposition in

rain, snow and marine-derived aerosols. In the coastal zones sea spray from the surrounding ocean is a particularly important source of a range of nutrients. The third source of nutrients (especially nitrogen and phosphorus) is from the faeces of birds and seals which come to land to breed and moult.

Much of the terrestrial plant biomass in the coastal zone is composed of mosses. Although many species are present their structure is such that they can be categorised into three broad groups. Moss turf and moss carpet communities are both composed almost entirely of mosses and usually form almost continuous ground cover. Fellfield communities, on the other hand, are a mixture of cushion mosses and lichens with a great deal of uncolonised bare ground.

A typical moss turf is composed of species whose stems are structurally quite rigid and upright, and are held together by the intertwining of stem hairs. The tips of the stems are all that is visible when the turf is viewed from above. Between the stems are spaces and these allow air circulation within the turf and ensure rapid drainage. Growth is upwards, leaving underneath an accumulation of peat which decomposes very slowly due to the low temperature and lack of available water. Moss carpets are quite different – they are composed of species whose fronds have little rigidity so that they grow in a tangled mat. The lack of rigidity means that the fronds lie close on each other. Meltwater cannot easily drain out of these dense tangles so that during the summer moss carpets are wet; below the surface layer the conditions are anaerobic, and only a thin layer of peat ever forms. In the fellfield communities, much more widespread than either turves or carpets, ice formation in the soil produces frequent disruption of the plant associations and the formation of patterned ground features. This community is far more unstable than either of the other two.

The turf and carpet communities have been studied intensively at Signy Island. The moss turves have a much higher level of arthropod activity than carpets because the Acari and Collembola make use of the interstices between the fronds as a habitat. These primary consumers are not, however, feeding on the mosses but on the microalgae, dead organic matter and micro-organisms. The bulk of the moss production is uneaten and is slowly recycled by fungal and bacterial decomposition. Freeze–thaw cycles during the spring rupture cell membranes, causing the release of nutrients. These, particularly soluble carbohydrates and amino acids, along with the meltwater, contribute to the initially rapid microbial production. As the season progresses the nutrients become depleted and productivity declines.

The fellfield community, widespread in various forms throughout snow-free coastal areas of Antarctica, offers opportunities for the investigation of ecological processes. The communities are in severe microenvironments, generally with frequent freeze–thaw cycles in summer (which disrupt soil structure), thin snow cover in winter (resulting in low minimum temperatures at ground level) and high winds (producing dessication). The Fellfield Ecology Research Programme of BAS is using fellfield sites to assess the importance of water and substrate type in colonisation and survival by a range of organisms from bacteria to mosses.

The outline described above is that of a 'typical' coastal habitat and is only representative of a small proportion of the Antarctic continent. It must always be remembered that the bulk of the continent is ice, snow or bare rock, free of all except microscopic life.

At a first glance it is easy to conclude that marine mammals and birds contribute greatly to the supply of nutrients to the land. Large breeding colonies of birds and seals are commonly present and the resultant faecal production might be expected to add significantly to the available nitrate and phosphate. However, levels of nutri-

Moss turf, formed principally of Polytrichum *species, is found on subantarctic and Antarctic islands. It can accumulate a layer of peat over 2 m deep and thousands of years old.*

A moss carpet on Signy Island. The rapid growth of the Fur Seal population is having severely detrimental effects on this terrestrial community which is quickly fragmented by seal activity and killed by seal faeces.

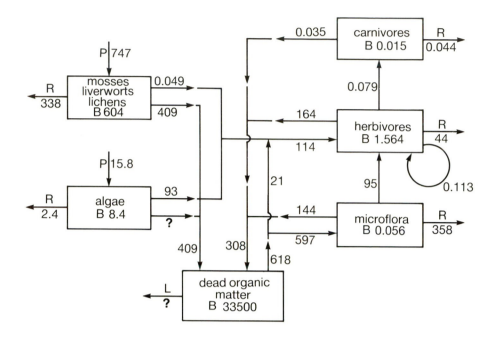

Food web for a moss turf community on Signy Island. All figures are g dry weight $m^{-2} yr^{-1}$. P – production; B – biomass; R – respiration. The dead organic matter dominates this system with the total biomass of all consumers being almost insignificant.

Antarctic soils are subject to frequent disruption by ice formation during freeze–thaw cycles. Here, needles of ice formed overnight have raised up a cap of soil. This frost-stirring of the soil makes it a very unstable habitat for colonisation by plants and animals.

ents are often so high as to be toxic for most organisms, and much of the guano deposited is washed off directly into the sea, enriching the benthic rather than the terrestrial ecosystem. Trampling by the large numbers of birds and seals present in the denser colonies prevents immediate plant growth, except for algae. However, if these sites are abandoned they are rapidly colonised by plants. Studies at Marion Island have shown that abandoned seal wallows soon develop a luxuriant growth of grasses. Also, where the density of breeding birds is lower, as for example in albatross colonies, the manuring in the vicinity of nests enhances local plant growth.

By comparison with the simplicity of the terrestrial and fresh-water communities, the marine community is highly complex. The continuity of the ocean between localities increases the chances of immigrants landing up at suitable sites. A more significant reason, though, is the protection from wide temperature fluctuations afforded by the huge thermal mass of the sea. The period available for evolution in the marine ecosystem has been much longer than in the terrestrial ecosystem, where major ice advances have

Vanda Station, by Lake Vanda in south Victoria Land, is the only permanent research station in the Dry Valleys. Free of snow, very dry and cold, these valleys are amongst the most severe environments on earth. The lakes that they contain are saline, almost permanently frozen and in some cases almost sterile. Here the ecosystem is at its most simple.

caused massive species extinctions. In spite of its greater complexity a thorough understanding of the marine ecosystem has become of paramount importance, especially now that man has become the top predator in the food chain. 'Overfishing' of whales and seals in the early years and more recent depradations of fish stocks has given considerable cause for concern, lest the same fate should befall the krill.

The bulk of primary production is by the phytoplankton and for many years this was considered to be dominated by diatoms. Whilst these might be the most conspicuous group, due to their size and general robust structure, there is increasing evidence that other groups, particularly those forming the very small picoplankton (less than 2mm), may be more important. Problems in estimating pelagic primary productivity mean that no current estimate is available for the whole Southern Ocean, although every indication points to the figure being over 10 000 million tonnes wet weight per year. Relative to the area this figure is not large and there is now increasing evidence that the Southern

Ocean is no more productive than other oceans of the world.

In common with other oceans, productivity is greatest in coastal regions. Much sinks to the sea bed and is broken down by bacteria and other micro-organisms so that the nutrients are quickly released to the environment. But not everything is immediately broken down. Some is eaten by brittle stars, gastropod molluscs and other detritus feeders. It is this rain of particulate matter reaching the sea bed that is responsible for the high biomass of benthic organisms.

In open water, phytoplankton is consumed by three dominant groups – krill, salps and copepods. Although all are present over most of the Southern Ocean they rarely occur in great abundance together. All three occur in regions of high phytoplankton productivity, but these are not necessarily regions of high phytoplankton biomass. Grazing will reduce the biomass but the digestive processes will recycle nutrients in the faeces, maintaining high phytoplankton productivity. It is not at all clear what proportion

(Left) *Crabeater Seals, accompanied by a diver, swimming under sea ice.*

The Southern Ocean is rich in species.
(a) Euphausia superba
(b) Decolopodium antarcticum
(c) Atola *sp.*
(d) Nacella concinna
(e) Utricinopsis *sp.*

(a)

(b)

(c)

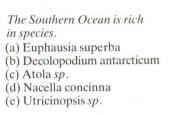

(d)

(e)

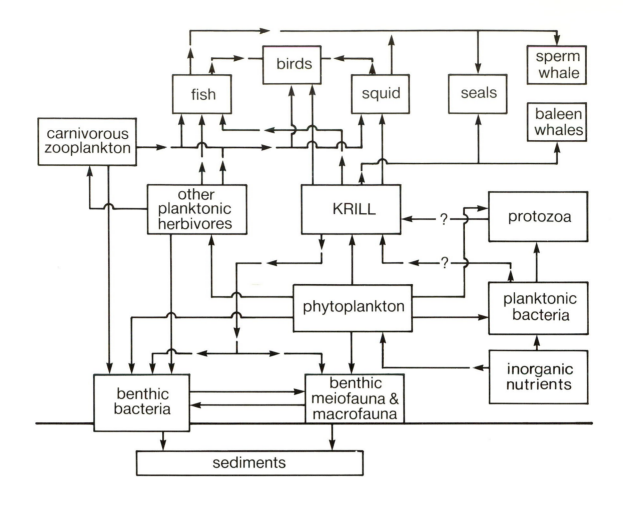

Diagrammatic food web for the Southern Ocean. The lack of quantitative data and the question marks on many of the connections show how little is known about this ecosystem.

of the phytoplankton production is eaten by planktonic species and how much reaches the sea bed. Significant amounts must follow both pathways since production in the pelagic and benthic parts of the system is quite high. If the amount sinking to the sea bed in the shelf zone is high, it is only to be expected that in productive regions over deep water much particulate matter must sink and be decomposed in the water column. Nutrients released this way would be recycled by the general water circulation. No figures are available to indicate the extent of either of these and this must be seen as being a major gap in our knowledge at the first and second levels in the food web.

The next level in the food web involves those species feeding directly on the zooplankton and, for simplicity, we shall be concerned purely with consumers of krill. There are many species that are totally or partially dependent on krill for food. At the turn of the century the largest consumers of krill were undoubtedly the great whales which between them ate over 150 million tonnes each year. To put this in proportion the total world fish catch is currently about 70 million tonnes. Overfishing during the earlier part of this century has meant that the whales currently have much less impact on the krill stocks, although the current estimate of the amount of krill eaten

by whales is still 40 million tonnes per year. The two largest whales, the Blue and Fin Whale only enter the Southern Ocean to feed for about 4 months during the summer; the rest of the year they spend in warmer waters to the north eating very little. The disparity in size between predator and prey, Blue Whales growing to 30 m in length and krill only to about 6 cm, means that to eat sufficient food the whales must take advantage of the swarming behaviour of krill. Krill commonly occur in dense swarms, sometimes of considerable size which often contain several hundred tonnes. Those krill that are present in a swarm are likely to be eaten and there can be no selection for just the large animals. The whales are therefore feeding by taking in relatively few mouthfuls to eat the enormous amount of krill which they need. The krill consumption is very high, a Blue Whale consuming between 3.5 and 5 times its own body weight per year.

The much-reduced present population of whales now eats 100 million tonnes of krill less per year than they did originally. What happens to extra krill? Is it a surplus that could be harvested and what would be the effects of a substantial krill fishery? Whilst the whales were declining more krill became available to other consumers and the populations of these in turn have been increasing – or at

The main components of the diet of species of albatross and penguin. Supplies of fish and squid are more predictable than those of krill. Krill is more nutritious and allows a faster growth rate. Thus in poor krill years there is high mortality among Black-browed Albatross and Macaroni Penguin chicks.

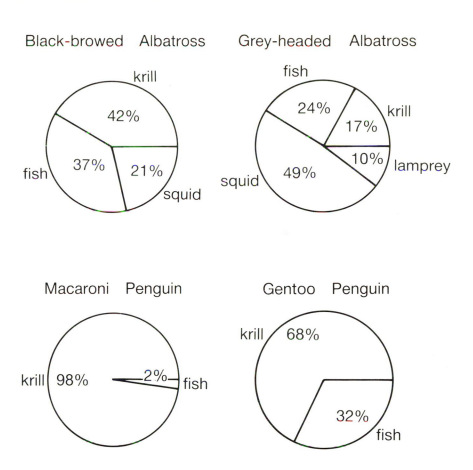

least that is what we assume to have happened. In order to substantiate changes of that sort estimates of population size for the major predators, now and before whaling began, are needed and they are not known. The Minke Whale is one of the smallest baleen whales and it was therefore not the target for fishing in the early years. It is one of the species that may have increased in numbers in recent years, possibly in response to the reduced predation pressure on krill consequent on the decline of the Blue and Fin Whales. Even though there is currently no whaling for Blue and Fin Whales, so that their numbers can increase, some scientists believe that the Minke Whale population has been increasing at a much faster rate. This suggests that in situations where food does not limit population increase, the smaller Minke Whale can achieve a faster reproductive rate. When there was more competition for food, as for example before the start of commercial whaling, the larger whales had the advantage.

It is not only the baleen whales that feed directly on krill. The largest present-day consumer of krill is almost certainly the Crabeater Seal, a species of the pack-ice zone all around the continent. It is difficult to estimate how many Crabeater Seals are present in the Southern Ocean because at any one time an unknown proportion will be underwater and not countable. Thus, even though reasonable estimates are available for the amount of krill eaten by an individual seal in a year, it is not known with any accuracy how much is eaten by the whole population. In spite of this it is clear that the figure is large, probably well over 100 million tonnes.

The third species of seal that feeds extensively on krill is the Fur Seal. These were reduced by the fur trade to the point of near extinction by 1850, following a period of very heavy and totally uncontrolled exploitation. Even during the 1930s they were still very rare but during the past 20 years they have increased dramatically, particularly at South Georgia where the population is now fast approaching a million. Fur Seals probably feed by searching for krill swarms and unlike the whales, they do not appear to eat krill at random but rather pick out the larger individuals.

Similar food selectivity is shown by Adelie, Macaroni and Chinstrap Penguins. These are all major consumers of krill over much of the Southern Ocean although, like the seals, their precise numbers are unknown and as a result it is not possible to specify accurately how much they take. It almost certainly amounts to several tens of millions of tonnes. Like the Fur Seal most species do not dive very

(Above) *Defending their breeding territories is a high-energy requirement for the bull Fur Seals and causes many to die. Their remains are rapidly eaten by scavenging Giant Petrels.*

(Below) *Many penguins are attacked by Leopard and Fur Seals when in the water. This Adelie Penguin, although badly mauled in an attack, has managed to escape onto land and survives – for the moment.*

Crabeater Seals do not eat crabs but krill which they filter from the water through their teeth. The cheek teeth in both upper and lower jaws have a series of points which, when the mouth is closed, form a very effective sieve.

deep in search of their food. However the King Penguin is the exception, with dives as deep as 240 m being recorded in pursuit of its main food source of squid.

Generally the flying birds are restricted to feeding at the surface and many feed at night when the krill come up to the surface. From the opposite direction fish, such as *Notothenia rossii* and *Champsocephalus gunnari*, migrate up from the sea bed to feed on krill swarms. The importance of fish and squid as consumers of krill is again not clear since information on their numbers and the significance of krill in their diet is lacking.

Both fish and squid figure in the diet of many vertebrates, such as King and Emperor Penguins, albatrosses and petrels, Weddell and Elephant Seals, and Sperm Whales. The quantity of krill taken indirectly in this manner is even more difficult to assess than the direct consumption discussed first, and hence an overall budget for krill in the ecosystem is currently impossible to determine. The quality of the data that are available fall far short of what is required in order to be able to predict what would be the effects of changes resulting from harvesting.

Todarodes, a common species of Antarctic squid. Squid are eaten in great quantity by very many predators in the Southern Ocean. Surprisingly little is known about their biology.

Antarctic Fur Seal.

Chapter·9

Exploitation of Antarctic fisheries

The history of exploitation

The harvesting of living resources in the Southern Ocean goes back almost two centuries. Soon after the discovery of South Georgia by Captain Cook, hunters arrived in search of Fur Seal skins. During the period 1801–1822 over 1 200 000 skins were taken from that island alone, with the result that the population was reduced to a very low level. In 1819 the South Shetlands were discovered and this opened up many new sites, although the industry only lasted for about two seasons since by that time the sealers had become so efficient at their job that stocks were rapidly depleted. Over 250 000 skins were taken in the second season (1820/21) there and since many dead or dying seals were reportedly lost the total number killed must have been enormous. So few Fur Seals remained that the populations were very slow to regenerate. Sealing expeditions to South Georgia in the 1870s could find only 1450, 600 and 110 seals in three successive seasons. Ever since then there has been no commercial catch of Fur Seal, but by this time the population size must have been so drastically reduced that any increase in number would be very slow. By the 1930s the population at South Georgia numbered no more than a few hundred but since then, particularly in the 1960s and 1970s, there has been an extremely rapid increase in numbers. It is tempting to attribute an expansion rate of 17% per annum, far faster than normal for a natural mammal population, to a super-abundance of krill engendered by reduced krill predation by the whales. This may be true but there is no way of confirming it without reliable and consistent indices of krill abundance throughout this century.

Fur Seal was not the only seal species to be exploited. Elephant Seals, because the oil that can be extracted from their blubber is of a higher grade than that from whales, have also been taken. Running in conjunction with the whaling industry, the Elephant Seal 'fishery' was under much closer scrutiny and control. This did not prevent a steady decline in numbers between the 1930s and 1952. In fisheries, numbers of animals are almost never censused directly, rather, an indicator of abundance – the catch per unit of effort (CPUE) – is used. When the animals are plentiful they can be caught relatively easily whilst when they become rare a much greater effort is required to catch an individual. The CPUE therefore declines as the population size decreases. For Elephant Seals a convenient unit of 'effort' is the catcher's day's work (CDW). During the 1930s the CPUE was just over 38 seals per CDW but by 1952 this had declined to 27 per CDW. This, along with other ecological indications such as the size structure of the population, indicated that closer control was needed over the industry. Accordingly in 1952 a revised total

catch figure of 6000 animals was introduced. The allowable catch was distributed in proportion to the abundance of seals around the island. This, with the establishment of a minimum size, allowed the population to increase rapidly so that the catch rate was nearly 35 per CDW by the 1955–1958 four-year accounting period.

South Georgia is not the only site at which harvesting of Elephant Seals has taken place, although it is the only site at which resource management has been implemented. Macquarie Island also supported quite a large industry, although the situation there is somewhat different because of less association with the whaling industry and because of differences in the social structure of the species at the breeding sites. King Penguins have also been taken at several sites to provide oil, but while this probably had some significant local impact the practice was probably not widespread, since seals, which would also be available locally, would provide far more oil and would thus be more profitable.

By far the largest 'fishing' operation in the Southern Ocean this century has been whaling. Initially the operation was shore-based and this imposed a form of natural control

There has been a dramatic increase in numbers of the South Georgia Fur Seal following its near extinction last century. The increase has probably been accelerated by more krill becoming available as a result of the decline of the great whales.

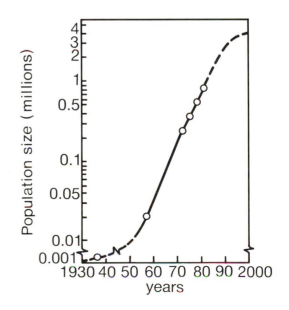

125

Elephant Seals lie in very large groups, during the breeding season, on the beaches of the subantarctic islands. They were harvested under licence on an annual basis at South Georgia until 1965. The kill was restricted to males only and was controlled both by a quota limit and by a rotation of sealing areas.

Antarctic whale catches showing the sequence of harvesting starting with the Humpback and progressing successively through the Blue, Fin, Sei and Minke whales.

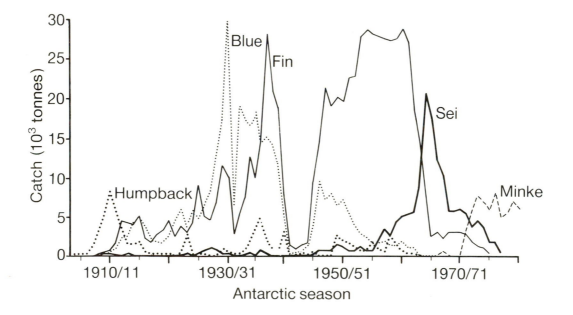

Krill may be a major food resource of the future. Catches at
present are treated in various ways.
(Right) *Krill protein following removal of the exoskeleton
during processing trials on the West German research vessel
Walther Herwig.*
(Above) *Frozen cooked krill.*
(Below) *The Japanese have tried hard to market krill products in
a variety of forms.*

on the level of exploitation by restricting activities to within a relatively small radius of selected sheltered bays. With the introduction of the large floating factories with stern slipways in 1925, the situation changed very rapidly. Operations could then be made independent of land stations and this had two major effects. First, the whalers were able to go anywhere in search of the whales, rather than waiting for them to enter the fishing grounds. Secondly, the size of the industry was no longer controlled by the availability of licences and leases. The fleet therefore expanded to a point where the total population was susceptible to capture rather than the small proportion of it that came within range of shore stations. The result of this is well known – the industry expanded and, initially, the catch increased. Being the largest and also containing the largest amount of oil, the Blue Whale was the first species to be taken in great quantity. From a peak catch of around 30 000 in 1930/31, the catch declined to less than 10 000 when whaling recommenced following World War II. As the Blue Whale declined, attention turned to the Fin Whales and they formed the bulk of the catches until the early 1960s by which time the stocks could no longer sustain the fishing pressure. Attention then turned to Sei and, more recently, Minke Whales, the latter being the only baleen whale species currently exploited.

The decline in the stocks of great whales was due entirely to overfishing. Management proved inadequate for two important reasons. First, because in the early years the mathematical models on which fishery management decisions are now based had not been developed, so that while it was clear that overfishing was possible and might happen, no advice was available to indicate what harvesting levels could be sustainable or what would be the effect of different harvesting strategies. Secondly, by the time it became clear that there was an overfishing problem the industry had become overcapitalised and operators were then in the position of trying to realise the maximum from their investment before the industry collapsed. Neither situation is in the least bit satisfactory but it is clear that the establishment of the International Whaling Commission (IWC) immediately after World War II steadied the decline, even though the advice came too late to allow maintenance of the larger whales at reasonable stock levels. The Antarctic Treaty nations did not want to see the same thing recurring when other resources were considered for exploitation, hence, even though there are currently no plans to harvest seals, there is a Convention for the Conservation of Antarctic Seals (CCAS), which came into force in 1972. At that time much was known about seal population dynamics although not necessarily enough to provide a good scientific basis for management should exploitation recommence. This

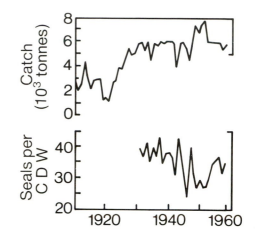

convention has therefore been a stimulus to ecological research.

CCAS was agreed at a time when seals were under no threat, however, the presence of an expanding fishery for krill and finfish caused concern amongst the Treaty nations and from their desire to protect these resources came the Convention for the Conservation of Antarctic Marine Living Resources (CCAMLR). Whilst krill and finfish are its current primary concerns, because of its intention to manage on an ecosystem basis it has much wider interests.

The first exploratory fishing expeditions in search of krill were made in the early 1960s by the Japanese and the Soviets. From these small beginnings the fishery took some time to get established, for several important reasons. First, the remoteness of the fishing grounds from major port facilities put enormous logistic constraints on the fleets. However the two main fishing nations are also the main whaling nations and therefore well versed in operating on the high seas. Secondly, krill was a new resource for which the industry needed to develop new catching and processing technology as well as to establish new markets.

The swarming habit of krill was the principal feature of its ecology that was used in developing new fishing techniques. Swarms were known to occur in the top 100 m of the water and in particular at the surface. With the expectation of finding surface swarms quite commonly, side trawls were developed. These were fished at the surface alongside the vessel. The intention was that they would be left fishing more or less continuously, the cod end being continuously pumped. In theory this would produce a continuous supply of fresh krill in good condition.

Trends in the annual catch and catch per unit of effort in the South Georgia Elephant Seal industry. The coastline was divided into zones, one of which was not exploited in rotation each year. The graph of four year means thus gives a smoother representation of changes in abundance than the more widely fluctuating annual figure.

(Right) The cod end of a commercial midwater trawl for krill coming on board. The fine mesh is necessary to retain the krill in the net.

(Below) Krill swarms can be detected using high frequency echosounders. These echocharts show the difference in krill behaviour observed by day and night. Small, compact and dense swarms were present by day but these dispersed into a large low-density layer at night.

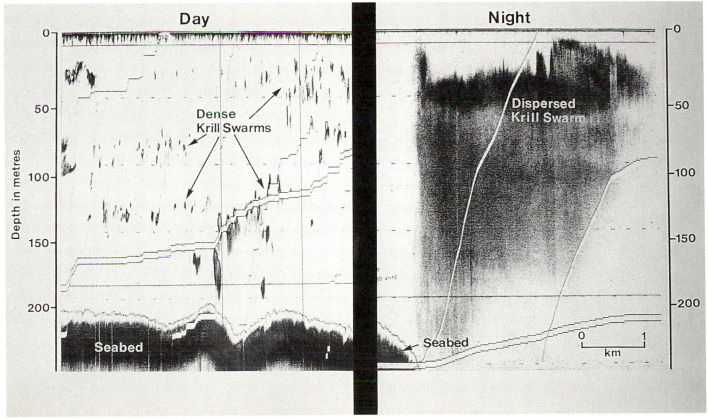

The whole of the whale carcass had to be utilised by whaling companies operating from South Georgia. This encouraged the development both of new methods of processing and of new markets. The equipment illustrated is an experimental hydraulic press for extracting oil from blubber, and was installed at Grytviken shortly before whaling ceased.

*The whaling fountain at Sandefjord, a monument to an industry
now deemed cruel and unnecesary.*

ATLANTIC OCEAN SECTOR

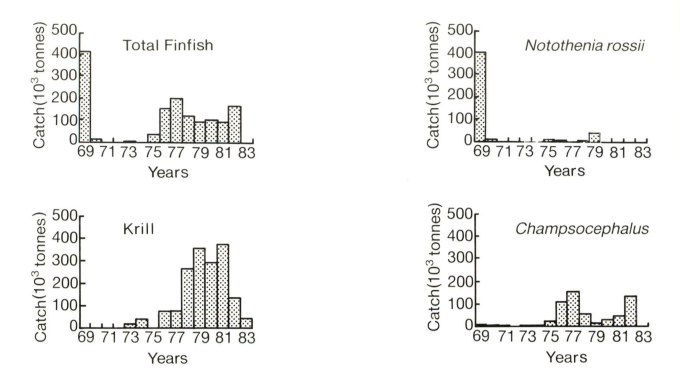

Fish and krill catches for two major sectors of the Southern Ocean.

INDIAN OCEAN SECTOR

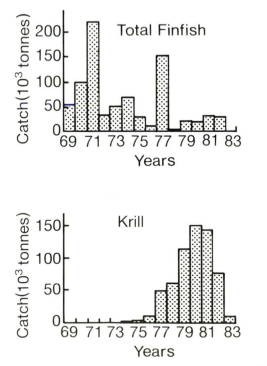

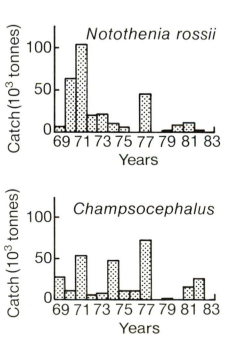

Soviet stern trawler entering Cumberland Bay, South Georgia.
The Soviet Union has been by far the largest fishing nation
operating in the Southern Ocean.

Notothenia *awaiting filleting on board a trawler.*

Unfortunately operating such gear in the exposed waters of the Southern Ocean imposed too many difficulties and the experiments were discontinued. Two modifications to existant types of net were also tried. Fine-mesh purse seines were tried but without much success. The most consistently successful type of net has undoubtedly been the midwater trawl Several modifications have been made to the design based on that developed for pelagic fish. Unlike fish, krill are not shepherded into the net by the coarse mesh in the wings and this has been dispensed with, leaving nearly all of the net made of fine mesh material. The effective mouth area of a krill trawl would be about 200 m^2. Krill swarms are readily detected on echo sounders so that fishing boats can maintain catch rates of 10–20 tonnes a haul or a 100 tonnes a day.

The main problems in getting the fishery established have been associated with processing krill. Initially krill paste and krill cheese products were produced in the Soviet Union but these do not seem to have gained widespread popularity. More recently much effort has gone into 'peeling' krill but although quite successful their processing rate is too slow for them to be economically viable.

Krill have also been converted to krill meal for feeding to pigs but in competition with other types of fish meal krill is very expensive. Furthermore krill contain large amounts of fluoride in their exoskeletons; this is removed by peeling but is retained in the fishmeal process.

Against this background it is easy to understand the trends in annual catch rates. The exploratory and experimental phase continued throughout the 1960s with a total annual catch of less than 1000 tonnes each year. During the 1970s there was a steady increase leading to peak figures of 424 000 tonnes in 1979/80 and 528 000 tonnes in 1981/82. Since then there has been a steady decline in the total reported catch to 229 000 tonnes in 1982/83 and 128 000 tonnes in 1983/84. This low annual catch is likely to be repeated for the next two or three seasons at least, while efforts continue to develop new products and markets.

Large-scale fishing for finfish began in the late 1960s around South Georgia. Precise figures concerning the build-up in the fishery are not available, since at that time there was no requirement on the part of the fishing nations to report catches from that area. Every indication is that the total annual catch increased with enormous rapidity from a few hundred tonnes in the 1967/68 season to 90 000 tonnes in 1968/69 and then to a peak of 400 000 tonnes in 1969/70. Nearly all of the catch at this stage was *Notothenia rossii*, with only about 1% of the icefish *Champsocephalus gunnari*. The following season the Soviet fleet moved to Kerguelen and caught about 212 000 tonnes of *N. rossii* in

that year and then just over 100 000 tonnes in 1971/72. The catches at both sites remained at a low level for the next few seasons but then there was an increase in the catch rates at South Georgia beginning in 1975/76 when the catch was 11 000 tonnes of *N. rossii* and then in 1979/80 when the catch was 25 000 tonnes. By this time several nations were fishing in the Southwest Atlantic although the Soviet Union was catching by far the largest amount. Not only was the stock depleted by the very large catches between 1969 and 1971, but the relatively small catches taken since then have been sufficient to cause further declines. The reason for this is not hard to find. *Notothenia rossii*, since it produces relatively small numbers of large yolky eggs, is dependent on a relatively large spawning population to maintain the stock. The enormous reduction in the spawning stock as a result of fishing means that there has also been a large reduction in total egg production and consequentially also of young fish.

During this period fishing also extended to the South Orkney and South Shetland Islands with the fleets concentrating more on *Champsocephalus gunnari* as the target species. There are conflicting views concerning the reasons for this change. On the one hand it is alleged by the Soviet Union that the change is in response to 'customer preference', whilst on the other hand there is an increasing body of evidence to indicate that *N. rossii* was being heavily overfished. The damage has been so great that the only way to ensure that the species can increase is to ban totally all fishing for it, whether in a directed fishery or whether the fish are caught incidentally when fishing for other species (by-catch). The intensity of fishing has been such that even species that have never been the subject of a directed fishery, such as *Notothenia gibberifrons*, are now showing the effects of overfishing.

With this background to the fishery the formation of CCAMLR is very timely, but how effective has it been in its first few years and how effective is it likely to be in the future? Thus far it has managed to get agreement that *N. rossii* around South Georgia and Kerguelen is in need of strong conservation measures. At South Georgia since the evidence indicates that the lowest possible by-catch should be aimed at, a very difficult situation to achieve, the only realistic strategy is to close the fishery until the stocks have been rebuilt. Such a firm, but nonetheless justifiable, course of action has not been taken by CCAMLR because one of its procedural methods is to reach agreement by consensus rather than by majority and the fishing nations have opposed such action. This is a very serious situation when it is considered that the indications of overfishing are clear and yet the most appropriate action is not being taken.

A Leopard Seal lies amongst Chinstrap Penguins, its normal prey. Any major changes in the Southern Ocean fish or krill stocks are likely to have a significant effect on both these species.

BIOMASS, *Biological Investigations of Marine Antarctic Systems and Stocks, has been an important organisation in identifying, initiating and coordinating research in the Southern Ocean over the past decade.*

A Fur Seal arriving ashore with a nototheniid fish in its mouth highlights one of the complex interspecific interactions that make up the Southern Ocean ecosystem.

Chinstrap penguins, searching for a quiet place to stand and moult, ironically choose the deck of a trawler, a potential competitor for krill.

Conservation

No conservation measures are currently in force for krill because the fishery is small with respect to all estimates of annual production. Management strategies for krill will need to be formulated on a different basis to those for fish, because krill are at the hub of the Southern Ocean food web and any overfishing on them will very definitely have a great effect not only on the krill but also on whales, seals, birds, fish and squid.

Traditionally fishery commissions have taken a single species approach to management. Each species is managed in isolation with little or no regard to the implications for other resources. CCAMLR was a major departure from this approach in that, for the first time, management would be on an ecosystem basis so that harvesting levels would take into account the effect not only on the target but also on the dependent species. To be effective it is essential in the first instance to describe the interactions present in the food web. This first stage is reasonably well documented. However, quantifying these interactions is more difficult and the figures quoted in Chapter 8 indicate how woefully inadequate is the current data base.

This has been realised for quite some time by the scientific community. In the mid 1970s a multidisciplinary programme named Biological Investigations of Marine Antarctic Systems and Stocks (BIOMASS) was organized. Its purpose was to provide this vital background information in the event that large-scale krill fishing operations might begin. The resultant major increase in research dealing with these interactions means that the figures quoted above are presented with more confidence than would have been sensible a decade ago. Their inadequacies, outlined above, show that although progress is being made there is still a long way to go. BIOMASS has achieved a great deal in the wider scientific community as well as providing information that the much younger CCAMLR is able to put to immediate use.

CCAMLR, with its objectives clearly set on the political objective of gaining international agreement on the wise use of resources, is dependent on altruistic science advice. This will only come from a thorough understanding of processes within the Southern Ocean. This does not mean that studies in other Antarctic environments are any less important but, on the contrary, highlights the need for further study within the simpler ecosystems on land and in fresh water. Furthermore, a thorough understanding of the processes involved will only come from a knowledge of processes within the organism. Enormous advances have been made over the past decade which have only served to highlight our limited understanding of the system. There is much that needs to be done in biochemistry, physiology and ecology.

Exploitation is not only about fisheries. Mineral resources, although currently not taken, could be extracted with the ever present danger of catastrophic, if localised, damage from oil spills or quarrying. Now is the time to begin monitoring baseline levels of potential pollutants against the time that exploitation commences.

A further current use of resources that is likely to increase is tourism. Improved communications and transport facilities have opened up many sites to tourists. The attractions are obvious – spectacular scenery and wildlife. These are the resources of man's heritage and they require conservation just as fishery resources do. Conservation measures have been enacted through the Antarctic Treaty and the Scientific Committee for Antarctic Research (SCAR). These seek to minimise disturbance not only to bird and seal colonies, obvious foci of tourist interest, but also to such less obvious features such as plant communities. The slow growth of Antarctic mosses means that the mark of a footprint remains in a moss bank for some considerable time. The break in the surface at the edge of the footprint allows the wind to grip the surface and tear the moss bank apart, causing erosion at a rate far faster than the rate at which the moss can grow. Such an example highlights the fragility of the Antarctic and demonstrates why visitors, whether scientists or tourists, must abide by the regulations. Those who do not will contribute to the gradual degradation of the world's last great wilderness.

*The Traverse Mountains (69° 51'S, 68° 02'W) are almost buried
by the Antarctic ice cap.*

138

Part·III
Antarctic ice and rocks

Chapter·10
Sea ice and icebergs

Sea-ice communities

The extent of sea ice varies greatly with the march of the seasons. By the end of the summer, in February, about 3 million km^2 of the sea is covered. With the onset of winter darkness, the area of sea covered by ice increases until in September and October it can extend over an area of approximately 20 million km^2. The seasonal difference between the maximum and minimum sea-ice cover is therefore greater than the area of the Antarctic continent itself, which is about 14 million km^2. Both the large extent and the variability of the ice cover are important for biological, climatic and oceanographic reasons.

When the sea is covered by ice, the transfer of mass, heat and momentum between sea and atmosphere is reduced. But the sea ice does not only act as an insulating blanket, it also reduces the amount of sunlight reaching the water column. This affects photosynthesis by the marine flora and thus acts as a control on the plant biomass. When sea ice is being formed, algal cells can be incorporated from the water either by scavenging or by the formation of ice crystals. Concentrations of algae can, at least initially, be higher than in the adjacent sea and are responsible for the characteristic brown colour that often stains the ice. Although little is known of these ice-associated flora, they may make a significant contribution to the annual primary production of the Antarctic seas.

Algae can be found in three major zones in the sea ice: surface, interior and bottom. Surface communities develop when snow accumulation depresses older but still permeable snow layers below sea level, allowing sea water to infiltrate and to form a loose ice–water matrix. This type of community has been observed in coastal tide cracks. Interior communities can exist at various levels within the main ice zone, depending upon how the ice formed and what its subsequent history has been. There can be several ice-formation processes, acting at different times, at different rates and over different water columns. Other influences on algal growth are temperature, light and availability of brine and nutrients. The combination of these factors leads to a wide variety of environments, but some evidence suggests that by the end of the summer an equilibrium state can be reached in multi-year ice which has survived the seasonal melting. This ice can have constant community characteristics below a depth of about 2 m. However, there is usually a great variability in the properties of seasonal ice that is less than a year old. Analyses of sea-ice cores taken in the Weddell Sea have shown that there is often little correlation between the physical, chemical and biological properties. The lack of a pattern to the salinity profiles and to the concentrations of nutrients, chlorophyll a and phaeopigments is ascribed to

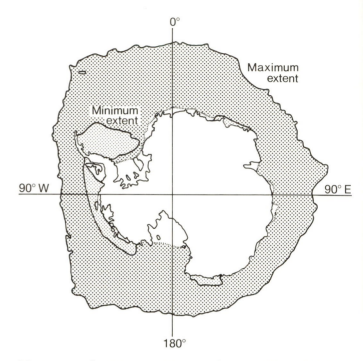

Maximum and minimum sea ice extent between 1973 and 1981. The maximum limit represents the furthest north ice has been found in this period, while the minimum limit shows areas where there is always a probability of between 80 and 100% of finding ice.

the different conditions under which the ice was first formed and then grew.

Almost three quarters of the sea ice examined in the Weddell Sea consists of frazil ice, in which biological material has been incorporated mechanically. Frazil ice is often formed in stormy conditions, when high winds and low temperatures cause turbulence in the near-surface waters. Small ice crystals, of about 1 mm, quickly coagulate into floes, growing in thickness at rates of up to several centimetres per hour. A different structure is found in congelation ice, formed slowly by heat loss through an overlying ice sheet. Larger crystals of about 1 cm grow in a characteristic columnar structure, taking several weeks to reach the thicknesses that have been observed. In contrast to frazil ice formation, congelation ice formation may exclude algal cells in the same way as it does salt, at least in the initial stages of growth. In drifting pack ice, algal concentrations are higher near the bottom of both frazil and congelation ice. In the case of congelation ice, the partly permeable columnar crystal structure allows continued cycling of nutrients from the underlying water and flushing down from the upper ice layers, giving a favourable environment for biological activity. Larger brine channels also open up in congelation ice in the summer, enhancing the

nutrient exchange. This, together with increased levels of sunlight, gives conditions suitable for encouraging the massive ice algae blooms which have been seen in sheltered waters such as McMurdo Sound. As the mechanisms for supporting nutrient exchange cannot operate in the frazil ice structure, productivity in open waters such as the Weddell Sea is lower than for the more protected near-shore environments.

Bottom communities are found in sheltered near-shore areas. A zone of brash or platelet ice, consisting of crystals not yet consolidated into the main ice mass, has often been observed to form under fast ice attached to the shore. Phytoplankton become trapped between the ice crystals as they are forming in the water column or when they float up under the pack ice. Where there is relative motion between the ice cover and the underlying sea, as in the open ocean, then this type of algal community probably does not exist.

Difficulties in gathering sea-ice samples make the estimation of annual primary production of ice-associated algae subject to large errors. Release of algae to the water column can occur continuously, as in the case of the bottom communities or in the marginal zone at the edge of the pack ice, or algae may be released in pulses when deterioration of ice reaches the stage that interior or surface communities are liberated. It is important to understand the processes by which the primary production becomes available to pelagic grazers in order to estimate the significance of the production within the ice. At present, estimates of annual primary production in ice range from 3×10^4 to 5×10^7 tonnes of organically fixed carbon,

Small ice crystals forming on the sea surface give it an oily appearance. Even a thin skin of ice damps down the small wind induced waves, allowing the sea swell to be clearly seen. The well named pancake *ice is a further stage in the development of the seasonal sea ice cover.*

equivalent to 0.007% to 12% of the annual phytoplankton production.

Sea ice and climate

As well as providing a habitat for algae, sea ice is an important factor influencing the physics of the Southern Ocean. Physical features of the environment such as temperature, light intensity, water stability and currents are thought to exert the strongest control on phytoplankton

A false colour picture of the Antarctic region imaged by the NIMBUS-5 satellite in October 1974. The continent is marked predominantly in blue, green and yellow. Sea ice appears as pink, red and brown. Note the large polynyna (open sea – grey and black) centred on the Greenwich Meridian.

cally scanning microwave radiometer (ESMR), a passive microwave instrument able to detect radiation emitted from the surface of the earth even in darkness or the presence of cloud. About 3 days of data are required to give suitable cover of the polar regions with a spatial resolution of about 30 km. More recently, a synthetic aperture radar (SAR) was flown on the SEASAT satellite in 1978. Called an active system because it transmits its own signal and receives the reflection from the ground, the SAR produced images of sea ice both through cloud and at night. With a potential resolution of around 25 m, SAR images can give the detail found in pictures taken in the visible bands from satellites such as the LANDSAT series. The penalty for the increased resolution in the SAR system is the very high amount of digital data that has to be transmitted back to earth and then processed. However, the possible commercial advantages to shipping in the Arctic, of being able to navigate using almost real-time pictures of sea-ice conditions to find leads and areas of open water, means that a number of satellites planned for the latter half of the 1980s will carry a SAR. Because satellite orbits that cover the Arctic regions will also cover the Antarctic, a wealth of information may become available for both polar areas.

Interpretation of the images from active and passive systems differs, partly because of the great difference in resolution. Passive microwave images record the intensity of naturally emitted radiance from the earth. This is usually called the brightness temperature because of its relation to physical temperature. The ratio of brightness temperature to physical temperature is the emissivity, a physical property of the emitting medium that depends on composition and structure. Thus, the ESMR images can be used to infer conditions averaged over large areas in the sea ice, the most important of which is probably the concentration. The concentration, or compactness as it is sometimes called, depends on the amount of open water within the pack. There is also a significant difference between the emissivity of ice less than a year old and that of older, or multi-year, ice, that allows a certain amount of age discrimination when describing sea-ice distribution and extent. Individual floes are too small to be seen on passive microwave images but can be identified on SAR images or those obtained from sensors in the visible or near infra-red bands. However, the presence of clouds and unresolved features such as small floes, thin ice and narrow leads can create large uncertainties when attempting to estimate ice concentrations. Airborne radars have shown that sea-ice reflectance, or backscatter, depends on the wavelength and polarisation of the transmitted radiation as well as on the age and structure of the ice.

production and are all affected by sea-ice distribution and thickness. The same factors are important for describing the role which sea ice plays in climatology and meteorology. Transfer of energy and mass between the atmosphere and the ocean is reduced by the ice cover, so that the air circulating over the Antarctic continent is colder and drier than it would be in the absence of pack ice. Atmospheric forcing of the sea ice, primarily by winds, provides a feedback mechanism which can lead to great variability in sea-ice extent, although oceanic processes also cause periodic disturbances from long-term average conditions. Sea ice will lower the temperature of the air above it; thus, the variation in position of the edge of the sea ice will enhance latitudinal temperature gradients and affect atmospheric circulation. Melting sea ice, by cooling the water, can have a profound influence on the temperature regime of the southern oceans and hence on the climate of the southern hemisphere. However, the processes controlling ice growth, deformation and decay are all interactive, so that the relation between climate and sea ice is complex and not fully understood.

Despite the climatic significance of sea ice around Antarctica it was not until the early 1970s that satellite systems were able to give complete temporal and spatial coverage. Early satellites recorded images in visible and infra-red wavebands. Obscuring cloud cover frequently prevented the sea ice from being seen. In December 1972 the NIMBUS-5 satellite was launched, carrying an electri-

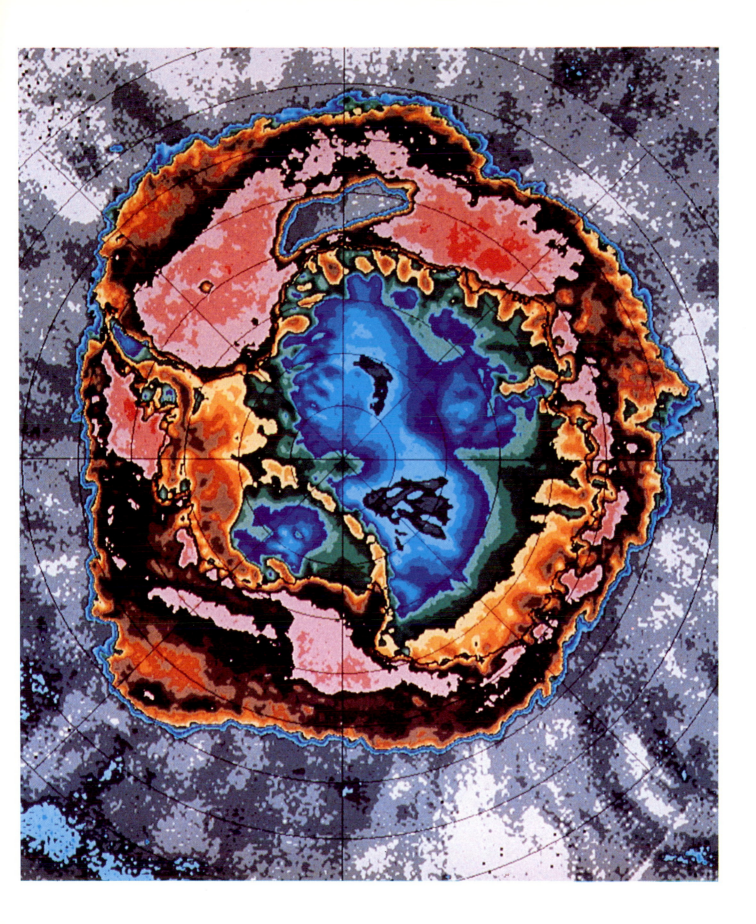

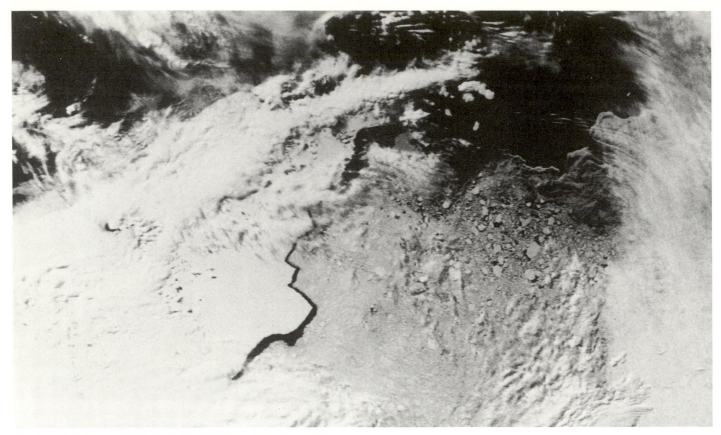

Picture taken from a NOAA satellite 1500 km above the earth's surface. The Antarctic Peninsula runs from bottom left towards the centre and is mainly cloud covered. Sea ice fills the Weddell Sea to the east.

Although sea ice occurs in many physical forms, three principal types can be distinguished on the basis of their radiometric signatures: new ice; first-year ice; and multi-year ice. The emissivity depends mainly on temperature and salinity, but density, thickness and structure can sometimes be significant. Microwave radiation emanates principally from the surface down to the optical depth (the depth to which light penetrates), a quantity determined by the salinity of the ice. For young ice, salinity is initially high and at the microwave frequencies used on the ESMR (19 GHz) the optical depth is a few centimetres. As the ice thickens, brine trapped between the crystals and platelets drains downwards by various processes such as thermal expulsion, meltwater flushing or by gravitation. The salinity depends initially on the temperature at which the ice was formed, but drainage creates characteristic salinity profiles with depth. In general, new ice has higher near-surface salinity than first-year ice, and multi-year ice has the lowest salinity. Snow cover, being non-saline, has a large optical depth and does not greatly modify radiation from underlying sea ice. New ice and first-year ice have about the same emissivities, with the slightly higher salinity of new ice causing its emissivity also to be slightly higher. In both cases, most of the radiation comes from near the ice surface. The measured brightness temperature can be increased by higher heat conduction from the ocean in

thin new ice, or by the insulating behaviour of snow on older ice allowing the ice to be warm compared to the air above it. Multi-year ice has a much lower salinity in the ice above the water line and the radiation originates mainly from ice near sea level. Emptied brine pockets in the upper layers scatter the upwards radiation and reduce the bulk emissivity. In summer, surface melting can wet the snow or ice and sometimes cause melt ponds to form. Because the emissivity of water is typically about half that of ice, brightness temperatures can be very low and for deep ponds approach those of the open ocean. Most work on sea ice has been carried out in the Arctic, where confirmatory data have been gathered on the ground to judge the accuracy of analyses of satellite data. Less ground data exist for Antarctic sea ice, but there appear to be two radiometrically distinct multi-year sea-ice types. One type is similar to that found in the Arctic, but the other, found in the Weddell Sea, is radiometrically warmer and similar to first-year ice. There does not appear to have been the drainage of brine cells in the freeboard layer above sea level that usually characterises multi-year ice.

In order to convert brightness temperature into ice concentration it is necessary to correct the observed values to allow for the ice temperature. Because it is not possible to measure this at the same time as the brightness temperature, estimates have to be made based on interpolated

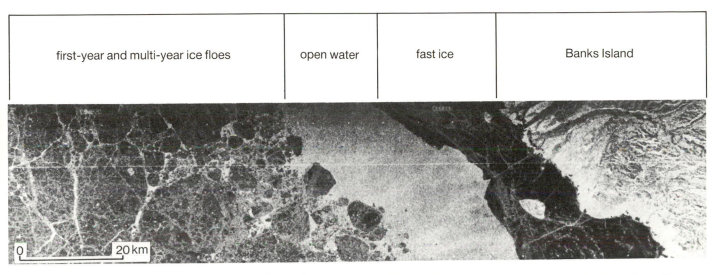

| first-year and multi-year ice floes | open water | fast ice | Banks Island |

A synthetic aperture radar (SAR) picture of sea ice in northern Canada taken from the SEASAT satellite. A mixture of first-year and multi-year floes is interspersed with ice-free leads in the left half of the picture. A zone of open water (lighter coloured) is followed by some fast ice (dark band), with Banks Island on the right.

monthly climatological air temperature data. Sea-ice concentrations for the years 1973–1976 have been derived from the ESMR data over Antarctica and examined in detail. Knowing ice extent (from the geographical limits of the ice edge) and concentration allows both the actual ice area and the amount of open water to be calculated. In the seasonal cycle, the rate of decay between October and January is much faster than the rate of growth from February to September. This asymmetry is in contrast to the more even growth and decay curves of Arctic sea ice, where maximum and minimum extents are 6 months apart, in March and September, respectively. The Ross Sea sector shows more rapid growth (March to July) than other regions in Antarctica, where maximum extent usually occurs in September.

Sea-ice concentration in summer is around 60%, increasing to 80% in winter. These values, derived from the ESMR data, agree with those shown on the US Navy–National Oceanic and Atmospheric Administration (NOAA) weekly sea-ice maps for summer. In winter, the US Navy–NOAA maps indicate a sudden increase to much higher concentrations, up to about 95%, values typical of winter ice in the Arctic Ocean where it is much more highly constrained than in the Southern Ocean. The concentrations derived from the ESMR data are considered more reliable because the techniques account for all the open water, no matter how small. Also, they show a smooth increase in mean concentration during the growth season. Near the ice edge concentrations can be low, but towards the centre of the pack concentrations often lie between 90% and 100%.

The most striking feature of the ESMR data is the large polynya, or area of open water, which persisted during the winter months from 1974 to 1976 in the eastern Weddell Sea near the Greenwich Meridian. Although smaller polynyas occur close to the coast elsewhere, the size of the Weddell Sea polynya makes it unique. No explanation for the polynya is generally accepted, but suggestions range from intensified upwelling supplying heat, to atmospheric circulation around the persistent low at 0°E. The polynya has not reappeared since 1976.

The seasonal cycle of sea-ice extent is known accurately for the period since 1973. Values from the ESMR data agree with those from the US Navy–NOAA weekly sea-ice charts for the overlapping period 1973 to 1976. For times since 1976 the most easily available data source on sea-ice conditions are the weekly sea-ice charts. These are compiled using raw data from a number of satellites and are composites of average conditions over the 7-day period. A degree of subjective interpretation is involved so there may be systematic discrepancies. However, the charts are commonly used to examine the variability in sea-ice extent

	Thickness (cm)	Salinity (‰)	Density (mgm^{-3})	Emissivity
NEW — saline ice	0.1–10	4–16		0.45–0.92
FIRST-YEAR ICE — snow (salinity=0) / saline ice	1–20	4–16	0.85	0.92
	10–200	4–5	0.92	
MULTI-YEAR ICE — snow / low salinity ice	5–50	<1	0.7	0.84
saline ice	50–500	2–4	0.8–0.9	

Variation of sea ice properties with age.

since 1973. Over the whole period 1973–1982 there is no significant trend, a decrease in extent during the mid-1970s having been reversed since then. There is a large interannual regional variability, with a decrease in sea ice in some areas being compensated by an increase in other areas. The major oceanographic anomaly, the Weddell Sea polynya, appears to coincide with a decrease of ice in that sector. Since 1977 the ice extent has surpassed its 1973 level there. An interesting modulation to the annual growth cycle suggests that there is a phase shift of 2–3 years from the Weddell Sea to the Ross Sea and then to the Bellingshausen–Amundsen Sea sector. A minimum in the amplitude of the Weddell Sea pack-ice area in 1977 was followed by a similar minimum in the Ross Sea area in 1980.

It is likely that both oceanic and atmospheric inter-actions are responsible for the complex variability pattern. Attempts to model the ice variability have met with limited success due to the restrictive assumptions that have so far been used. Advection of ice by barrier winds, formed by the impact of coastal easterlies on the Antarctic Peninsula mountain chain, seems to play an important role in creating the belt of sea ice which extends to the north east from the northern tip of the peninsula into the Weddell Sea. A similar process occurs in the Ross Sea but Cape Adare, at the northern end of the Transantarctic Mountains, extends to only 71°S compared to the latitude of 63°S reached at the northern end of the Antarctic Peninsula. In the Weddell Sea, the sea ice is forced into the circumpolar westerly winds, while in the Ross Sea the ice remains in the prevailing easterlies.

A dramatic example of how quickly the sea ice is moved by the barrier winds is given by examining the tracks of two ships that were trapped by pack ice in the early part of this century. The *Deutschland* was caught on 8 March 1912 off Coats Land. After drifting north west and then north east, she was finally released on 25 November the same year, more than 1200 km further north. A similar fate befell Shackleton's ill-fated attempt to be the first to cross the Antarctic continent. His ship, the *Endurance*, drifted from May 1915 until April 1916, from a latitude of 77°S to 62°S, ending up near the tip of the Antarctic Peninsula. The escape of Shackleton and his men from the grip of the ice onto Elephant Island, their wintering under

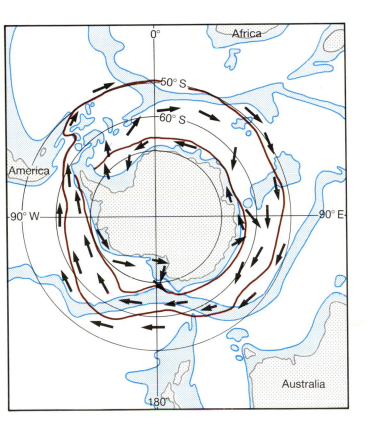

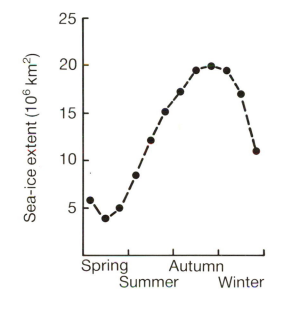

Sea surface circulation patterns. Close to shore the currents are controlled by the easterlies, while further out westerlies predominate. Sea floor areas shallower than −3000 m are shown in dark stipple.

upturned boats, the subsequent voyage by six of them in an open boat across the stormiest seas in the world to South Georgia, and the traverse of a hitherto unexplored mountain range to seek help and rescue, makes one of the most incredible stories of determination, courage and success that any traveller can tell.

The revolutionary impact that satellite data have made on sea-ice research can be judged by the impossibility of extrapolating trends of sea-ice extent backwards from 1973. In contrast to the synoptic observations that are now possible, prior to the satellite era only isolated reports from ships were available. Ice observations were made by Captain Cook during his exploration of the southern oceans between 1769 and 1775. However, records of variations in sea ice before 1890 are intermittent and, geographically, coverage is poor in several areas. Analysis of a compilation of a large number of ship-based observations suggests that there has been no significant change in sea-ice extent over the last hundred years, although a large variability is present.

Seasonal variation of sea-ice extent in 1974.

Sea-ice extent from 1973 to 1982.

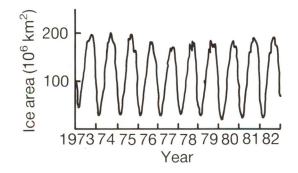

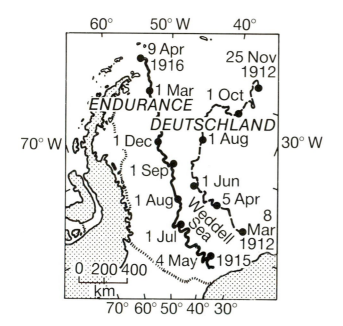

Icebergs

Records of iceberg sightings are more common than those of sea-ice extent. Icebergs often drift into lower latitudes than the extreme position of the sea-ice edge – the maximum limit reported for a floe is 26°30'S in 1894 in the South Atlantic. The density of shipping around Cape Horn and Cape of Good Hope before the Suez and Panama canals were opened ensured that good records for icebergs are available dating from about 1850. Sealers and whalers were active before then but reported little difficulty with ice until 1840. The period 1853–1858 saw many large icebergs in the shipping lanes, which were for a time diverted away from the normal Great Circle routes. In the 1890s many reports were again made of large icebergs in the shipping lanes. Another outburst of icebergs occurred in the 1920s and 1930s.

More recently, several large icebergs have been tracked using satellite pictures. One of the longest lived was Trolltunga, a former glacier tongue extending seawards from an ice shelf, Fimbulisen, near the Greenwich Meridian. This iceberg was first seen in October 1967, probably about a month after it had been calved, following a collision, from another large iceberg drifting round the coast from the Amery Ice Shelf. More than 100 km long by 50 km wide, it followed the Weddell Sea coast for 2 years, until it grounded on a shoal to the west of Berkner Island in the winter of 1969. For more than 5 years the iceberg remained stuck, changing position only slightly. Then in early 1975 it started moving again. Keeping close to the ice fronts of first Ronne Ice Shelf and then Larsen Ice Shelf, the drift track revealed the sea current gyre in the Weddell Sea. While bumping along the Larsen Ice Shelf in March 1976 it broke off a piece about 90 km by 35 km to form a new iceberg. It appears that collision between large icebergs and ice fronts may be an important calving mechanism. After passing the northern tip of the Antarctic Peninsula, the iceberg turned eastwards towards South Georgia. It eventually broke up when it crossed the Antarctic Convergence, an oceanographic boundary separating near-freezing sea surface temperatures from warmer water to the north.

By charting drift tracks of icebergs, the paths of ocean currents can be deduced. Most of the large icebergs seen over the last 15 years have circulated in the Weddell Sea gyre, but other important source areas are the Ross Sea and the Amery Ice Shelf. In nearly all cases icebergs follow easterly coastal currents before turning north into the West Wind Drift. Three major gyres around the Antarctic coastline appear to be related to submarine topography in the deep ocean basins.

A programme, begun in 1981, of systematically collect-

ing iceberg statistics from ships going to and from Antarctica has shown that mass loss from the continent may be much higher than previously thought. Since 1983/84 nearly all ships in Antarctic waters have taken part in classifying icebergs by length into four groups, with those more than 1 km long being described individually. After allowing for the area covered by observations being a small fraction of the total area where icebergs could exist, then the total mass of ice discharged annually into the sea (2.3×10^{15} kg) is several times that given by earlier estimates of iceberg calving (between 0.6×10^{15} and 1.0×10^{15} kg). The reason for this apparent disagreement may be either that the iceberg data are not representative of conditions averaged over time and area, or that the assumed half-life of 4 years is too short. Taken together with estimates of net annual accumulation of around 2×10^{15} kg and loss by melting underneath ice shelves of about 0.3×10^{15} kg, the figure suggests either that the present mass balance of Antarctica is negative (a net loss of ice) or that there are still unknown factors governing the constituent parts of the mass-balance equation. This underlines the difficulties in providing reasons why sea level has apparently risen worldwide at an average rate of around 1 mm per year over the last century.

Icebergs are not only an important part of the mass-balance equation for Antarctica, they may also be a source of economic wealth in the form of fresh water. Because icebergs are derived from snow which originally fell in the interior of the continent, meltwater from them is purer than most distilled water. In the northern hemisphere, small icebergs have been used both as a source of water (for example, Alaskan bergs were towed to San Francisco in the nineteenth century to supplement fresh water supplies there) and as a means of providing large quantities of cheap ice for refrigeration. There is currently interest in trying to use Antarctic icebergs to help solve the water shortage problems of some of the arid areas in the southern hemisphere. Calculations suggest that an iceberg about 1 km in length, if towed to say the edge of the continental shelf of southern Australia, would provide water suitable for irrigation more cheaply than sea water desalination.

An immense number of problems need to be solved before such a scheme becomes commercially viable. Despite the great number of icebergs close to the Antarctic continent waiting to be harvested, only a small proportion may be suitable for surviving a long journey across hostile seas. Although tugs could be built to move a large berg at speeds of around 1 m s^{-1} (0.5 knots), full use would have to be made of ocean currents in order to minimise the transit time in warm waters which would cause significant melting loss. Thus, the original geographical capture point of the iceberg would be crucial. Most icebergs of any

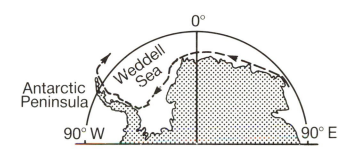

Composite drift track of icebergs around the Weddell Sea.

reasonable size are likely to contain flaws such as crevasses or rifts, which may sometimes have been filled in by snow but still exist as points of weakness that could provide focal points for fracture and disintegration when the berg is placed under stress.

Close to the coast, sea ice usually reduces deep-ocean swell to negligible amplitudes. The decay of swell has been measured by instruments placed on sea ice and can also be clearly seen on SEASAT altimeter records of sea surface level taken over Antarctic sea ice in winter. When an iceberg escapes from the protection of the ice pack, however, considerable bending stresses can be generated. In addition, as soon as the Antarctic Convergence is crossed there is an increase of several degrees in the temperature of the water. The combination of higher temperatures and stresses appears to make even large icebergs disintegrate quickly. There have been reports of icebergs, usually small, north of the Antarctic Convergence, but there is a dramatic reduction in numbers compared with areas further south. Little is yet known about how long an iceberg could survive if it were being transported, or if a sufficient mass would remain after the journey had been completed to have made it worthwhile. However, it now seems that the initial impetus behind recent interest in icebergs, that they would provide an economical source of fresh water for Middle Eastern countries, and Saudi Arabia in particular, is not soundly based. It is most unlikely that an iceberg, however well protected from the warm ocean by polythene skirts or other insulation, would manage to cross the equator crackling away in anything other than a glass of gin.

Although small icebergs are a hazard to shipping, large ones can provide shelter in a storm.

Chapter·11
Glacial and climatic history

History of the ice sheet

Ice dominates the Antarctic scene. Only 1% of the continent escapes the covering, small isolated outcrops of rock occurring mainly along the coastline and the great Transantarctic mountain range. This has been the case for at least 13 million years, probably for 20 million years, and possibly for 50 million years. Uncertainty about the history of the ice sheet extends to the present day; we still do not know by how much the volume of ice increases or decreases each year. Even if we did, we would be unlikely to know for how long the trend would continue. These basic problems form one of the major reasons for much of the glaciological research which has been carried out in the Antarctic, and which continues to be supported each year by the Treaty nations.

It has long been understood that world sea level depends on the mass balance of the Antarctic ice sheet; it is also becoming clear that currents at the bottom of the ocean basins can be driven by the cold dense waters which are formed around the Antarctic coastline by the melting of ice. These cold waters are rich in oxygen and help rejuvenate oceans in lower, warmer latitudes by mixing and upwelling. Bottom currents can be strong enough to scour the soft material on the ocean floor, causing fluctuations and gaps in the sedimentary record. A picture is emerging from the analysis of many deep-sea cores of a highly variable sedimentation rate over the last 60 million years. One explanation is that changes in the size of the Antarctic ice sheet have led to significant changes in the amount of ice floating on the sea in the form of thick ice shelves. Sea water in contact with ice at depths of up to 2000 m can be cooled to several degrees below the surface freezing point at the same salinity. During periods when there was less ice in the Antarctic and smaller, thinner ice shelves, the water would have been warmer and the intensity of the bottom currents reduced; times of ice-sheet maxima are assumed to coincide with greatest erosion on the ocean bed. From this kind of marine evidence, it is believed that the Antarctic ice sheet reached its present extent around 13 million years ago. However, it is surprising how often the major feature of a sedimentary record, which might be interpreted as the onset of Antarctic glaciation, occurs near the bottom of a core. Rarely is it possible to contrast records from an earlier, pre-glaciation age, with those from times of an assumed fully developed ice sheet. This applies also to studies of planktonic Foraminifera and Radiolaria in the sediment cores, where identification of population abundance and the discrimination of cold- and warmer-water types have led to estimates of times of ebbing and flowing of cold Antarctic waters, in response to the growth and decay of the ice sheet.

Other indicators of size of the ice sheet are the presence on the ocean floor of assumed ice-rafted debris: erratic boulders or pebbles, or quartz grains which may have been transported on sea ice or icebergs. It is often difficult to tell, however, whether a particular piece of rock originated from the continent or not, and it is not always easy to understand how ice could transport significant quantities of debris. Most of the large icebergs calving from ice shelves will be free from moraine. Melting from the underside of an ice shelf and surface accumulation of freshly fallen snow usually means that by the time the ice front is reached, the ice consists of snow collected only over the ice shelf. All rock particles will have been deposited on the sea bed underneath the ice shelf. Occasionally, small icebergs which have broken off glaciers reaching the sea in more northerly latitudes around the Antarctic Peninsula may contain basal, or other morainic, material. These icebergs seldom last for more than a few months once they start drifting about the ocean and they are unlikely to carry significant quantities of rock far away from their source. Some dust may be blown by the wind across the surface of extensive winter sea ice and be taken away from the continent. Despite all these ambiguities and uncertainties about interpreting oceanographic and marine geological data, they are still the most promising source for direct evidence about the history of the Antarctic ice sheet over the last 60 million years.

Persuasive, but also indirect, evidence of ice volume comes from interpretation of ratios of the stable oxygen

When a glacier starts floating on the sea, eroded rock melts out from the bottom and forms an unconsolidated sediment.

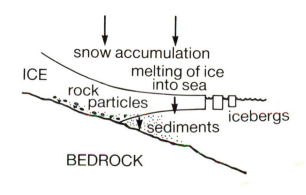

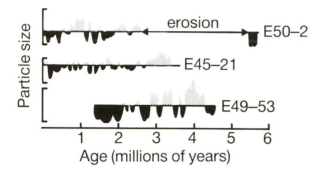

Changes in bottom water velocities can be inferred from variations in the mean particle size of silts, shown here in three deep-sea cores. Small particle sizes (shown as stipple) are taken to indicate higher water velocities.

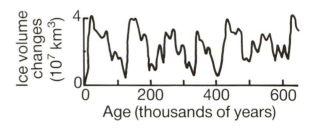

Variation of global ice volume over the last 600 000 years, deduced from $\delta^{18}O$ values in deep-sea cores.

isotopes ^{18}O and ^{16}O (see p. 156) in deep-sea cores. Snow falling over the ice sheet has a much lower proportion of the heavy ^{18}O isotope than has sea water. By assuming that the distribution of oxygen isotope ratios in the ice sheet in the past was the same as that shown in the present-day ice sheet, worldwide fluctuations in ^{18}O:^{16}O ratios in calcareous oozes and shells can be attributed to changes in ice volume in Antarctica. There is, however, an ambiguity since part of the ^{18}O variation could be due to changing ocean temperature. It appears that variations in the ^{13}C:^{12}C ratio may reflect more accurately changes in global ice volume. The evidence suggests that a gradual build-up of ice started around 50 million years ago, but no significant, continent-sized, ice sheet formed until about 25 million years ago. A sharp reduction in bottom water temperatures occurred 13 million years ago and this is thought to coincide with the first formation of large ice shelves similar to those of today. More recent variations in the ice sheet could be caused by northern hemisphere glaciations. It is possible that large parts of the ice sheet, especially Western (Lesser) Antarctica, have periodically disintegrated and reformed, in response to changing climatic conditions and sea level.

On land, geomorphological evidence of glacial history is equally vague. Most work has been carried out in the Ross Sea area of the Transantarctic Mountains. There is plenty of evidence here, and elsewhere, of higher levels of ice on nunataks (isolated peaks completely surrounded by ice) and mountain chains, but the dating of these advances is uncertain.

The generally accepted glacial history is of episodic increases in ice volume starting about 50 million years ago and reaching a full continent-sized ice sheet about 13 million years ago. This reflects the increasing isolation of the Antarctic continent as it drifted away from South America and the development of a strong circumpolar ocean current which prevented warm tropical waters bathing Antarctic shores. However, it has been shown that there is a strong correlation between periodic changes in climate, as seen for example by the northern hemisphere ice ages, and orbital variations in the movement of the earth around the sun (the Milankovitch cycles). One must therefore ask why a similar process could not have created Antarctic ice sheets as soon as sufficient land mass had gathered near the pole. The South Pole has been located within the continent for at least the last 60 million years. One reason why glaciation apparently took so long to occur could be related to the cooling of the land and surrounding ocean, and the initiation of a more vigorous atmospheric circulation. There must always have been sufficient moisture to form an ice sheet, although today central Antarctica receives less precipitation than most deserts, but only when the difference between annual snowfall and snowmelt led to a positive mass balance would glaciers grow. Considering the suddenness with which recent ice ages have waxed and waned, it seems unlikely that once mountainous regions in the Antarctic became glaciated there were not occasional ice ages there. No record of these ice ages has been found, but any evidence would be difficult to recognize and to interpret.

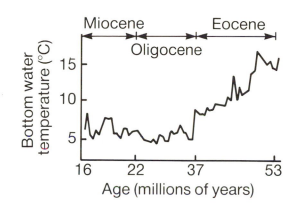

One interpretation of the δ^{18}O record from Deep Sea Drilling Project sites 277 and 279 is that there has been a gradual reduction in bottom water temperature at a sub-antarctic site from about 54 to 16 million years ago. Sudden changes, as at about 37 million years ago, may be related to specific events in the build up to Antarctic ice.

Even the presence of temperate flora fossilised in sedimentary rocks is not proof that short, sharp ice ages did not occur. Today, glaciers in New Zealand, for example, can flow past verdant forests; only 12 000 years ago much of Europe and North America which now supports a rich vegetation was covered by ice. The geological record is not only biased to preserving evidence of warm, rather than cold, climates, but it also becomes less detailed with age. Although unravelling the glacial history of Antarctica will not be easy, it may provide insight into the causes of ice ages.

Physical characteristics of the ice sheet

The Antarctic ice sheet today covers an area of about 14 million km^2, one and a half times the size of the USA. With an average thickness of 2.3 km, the ice sheet contains 90% of the world's fresh water, locked up as ice. The presence of the ice sheet makes Antarctica the highest, driest, windiest and coldest continent. The thickest ice yet found is nearly 5 km thick; the coldest temperature recorded is -89°C. Two thirds of the land on which the ice rests is above sea level and is mainly in Greater, or East, Antarctica. Lesser, or West, Antarctic bedrock is mostly below sea level, reaching depths of more than 2000 m in

places. Two large ice shelves, the Ross Ice Shelf and the Ronne/Filchner Ice Shelf, each covering an area of about 500 000 km^2, form where ice, resting on rock below sea level, thins sufficiently as it flows towards the coast for it to float in near hydrostatic equilibrium on the sea. In total, ice shelves fringe 45% of the Antarctic coastline. Almost all the snow which falls over the continent eventually travels to the coast where it either breaks off as icebergs or melts on the underside of ice shelves. Annual snow accumulation in the centre of the ice sheet can be as low as the equivalent of 2 cm of water. Over more than half the ice sheet it is less than 10 cm but increases towards the coast.

As the snow layers become more deeply buried they are slowly transformed to ice. The depth at which a particular density is reached, for example a density of 840 kg m^{-3} when the ice becomes impermeable, depends on many factors. The colder the ice, the less quickly it densifies with depth for a given accumulation rate. The layers thin in response to the weight of their overburden, causing the ice to flow in the direction of maximum surface slope in the same way as water flows in a river. Only where there is severe bedrock topography will ice at depth attempt to flow around an obstacle instead of over it. Shear stress at the boundary between the ice and bedrock acts so as to make the maximum ice velocity occur at the surface. When the temperature of the basal ice reaches its melting point a water layer can form and the ice start to slide. The effect of basal sliding on ice-sheet stability is one of the major problems of ice-sheet dynamics and has important climatic consequences.

Although possibly quite large areas at the bottom of the Antarctic ice sheet may be at the pressure melting point (temperatures down to -3°C) warmed by the geothermal heat, the surface temperature will be much lower. Snow has a very high albedo (reflectance) at the wavelengths of incoming radiation from the sun and a very high emissivity at thermal infra-red wavelengths. Therefore not only is very little of the sun's energy absorbed, but also the snow surface tends to follow the radiation temperature of the sky: for clear skies this can be very cold. Annual variations in temperature influence only the top few metres and are generally damped out by 10–20 m depth. The snow temperature at these depths is usually taken to be the mean annual air temperature. Longer-period variations in temperature propagate deeper but more slowly. It is possible that a temperature change occurring when the last northern hemisphere glaciation ended is still affecting the flow deep in the ice sheet. Deformation of ice depends on its temperature as well as the stress field. It is this interaction between temperature and velocity that poses great mathematical difficulties in analysing glacier flow.

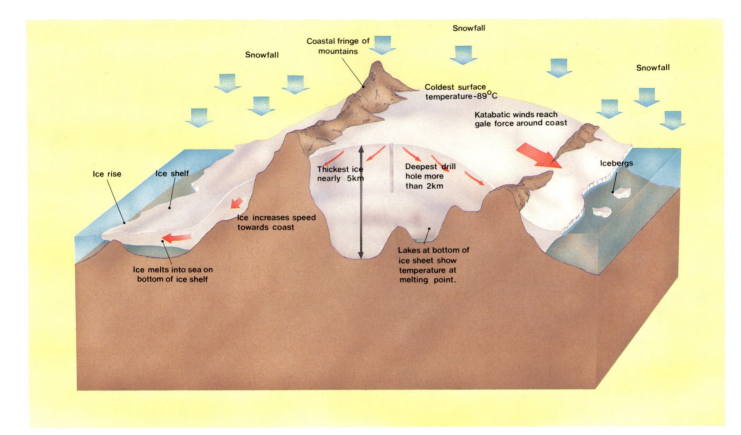

Snowfall

Coastal fringe of mountains

Snowfall

Coldest surface temperature -89°C

Katabatic winds reach gale force around coast

Snowfall

Ice rise

Ice shelf

Thickest ice nearly 5km

Deepest drill hole more than 2km

Icebergs

Ice increases speed towards coast

Ice melts into sea on bottom of ice shelf

Lakes at bottom of ice sheet show temperature at melting point.

(Above) *Schematic cross section of an ice sheet.*

(Right) *Profiles of (a) velocity and (b) temperature with depth at Byrd Station.*

(Below) *Only four drill holes at the twenty seven sites marked have exceeded 500 m in depth (shown as x) and only one of these has reached bedrock (Byrd Station).*

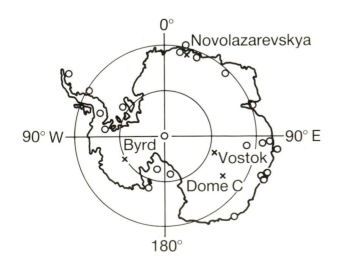

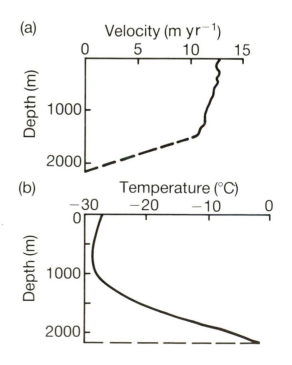

(a) Velocity (m yr⁻¹)

Depth (m)

(b) Temperature (°C)

Depth (m)

A covered pit shelters the drill but remains cold enough to prevent unwanted melting of the core.

Ice cores are usually about 10 cm in diameter. Mechanical drills can penetrate up to 1 m at a time before being withdrawn for the core to be recovered.

Drilling

Snow crystals form in the atmosphere by water vapour condensing onto minute particles which act as nuclei. Aerosols such as rock dust, volcanic ash, sea salts or industrial waste are scavenged as the snow falls. Even so, impurities in the snow are so low, of the order of 1 in 10^9 for most elements, that the ice sheet forms the cleanest natural laboratory in the world. Archived within the sedimentary strata are records of atmospheric composition at the time when the snow fell, preserved unchanged for millennia. Careful analytical techniques are needed to measure the very low concentrations of elements and ions, and a wide understanding of atmospheric and even solar physics is needed to interpret the chemical record in terms of climatic and environmental factors such as air temperature, atmospheric dust, solar activity and industrial pollution. The more sensitive methods for detecting and quantifying the amount of impurities in ice that have been developed over the last decade have reduced dramatically the amount of ice sample required for analysis. For example, a few years ago ^{14}C dating needed 1000 kg of ice to give an age accurate to 10%; nowadays, just a few kilograms will give the same accuracy.

The first significant ice core to be recovered from Antarctica was during the Norwegian–British–Swedish Antarctic Expedition in 1949–1952. A 100 m long core was

retrieved from a hole drilled by modified rock-drilling equipment on Maudheim Ice Shelf. In 1968 a drill operated by the US Cold Regions Research and Engineering Laboratory reached bedrock through 2164m of ice at Byrd Station in West Antarctica. Again, conventional drilling methods were adapted to the special conditions. It is a reflection on the cost of drilling and the time-consuming nature of analysing the core that this hole remains the only one more than 500 m deep to penetrate through the Antarctic ice sheet. Three more deep holes have been drilled since then but none has reached bedrock. At Vostok Station, near the Pole of Inaccessibility, the Soviets took from 1972 until 1983 to reach a depth of 2083 m in ice which is 3700 m thick, and they have drilled to 872 m at Komsomolskaya. Each year they continue to deepen the holes. A joint US and French team drilled to 905 m near Dome C in 1977–1978. Here the ice is 3500 m thick.

A number of holes less than 500 m deep have been drilled. Simpler drills can be used for these shallower depths, reducing both the expense and the logistic commitment to using them in the field. The sites for some of these holes have been chosen in order to investigate the recent climatic history at places where there is thick ice – such as the South Pole or Siple Station. Other drill holes have been placed on the shallower ice near the coast; for example, a series of holes has been drilled by the Australians on Law Dome. Both the Soviets and the Americans have drilled through ice shelves to study the ice and the sea underneath.

A variety of drilling techniques is used because of the intrinsic problems of drilling in ice. The ice sheet is always moving, so the drill hole is continually being bent and squeezed shut. The curvature of the hole is small near the surface and only becomes a problem if long rigid rods or drills are used near the bottom of the ice where most of the shear takes place. Wireline drills have gained in popularity because they are quicker for extracting ice core, but they may still suffer from being trapped if they have a long drill bit. Closure rate of the hole increases with temperature and depth and is usually the factor limiting how deeply a hole can penetrate before the risk of the drill being caught becomes too high. Coring drills use either mechanical cutters or a heated annulus and retrieve about 1 m of ice core each time they are raised. Hot-water drills are used when only a hole is required, either for access to the sea under an ice shelf or for studying the deformation of the hole itself. Video cameras have been lowered down holes to view the bedrock. Closure of the hole can be partially overcome by filling it with a fluid with approximately the same density as ice. However, contamination can limit the later use of the core or the hole.

Climatic records and pollution

During the 1960s techniques were perfected for measuring the ratio of the two stable isotopes of oxygen, ^{16}O and ^{18}O, which occur naturally in ice. The difference between the oxygen isotope ratio in an ice sample and in an international standard representing mean ocean water, is called the $\delta^{18}O$ value and is measured in parts per thousand. Because the vapour pressure of water molecules with the heavier oxygen isotope (^{18}O) is lower than the vapour pressure of water containing ^{16}O molecules, the $\delta^{18}O$ value of snow depends on (among other factors) the air temperature when it first condensed. Therefore, variations with depth of the $\delta^{18}O$ value reveal changes in past air temperature. Annual variations can be readily identified at sites where there is sufficient accumulation and where the temperature is low enough to prevent summer meltwater percolating through the snow and destroying the record. Longer-term changes in temperature can also be identified in deeper cores as a shift in the $\delta^{18}O$ value. Although oxygen isotope studies have formed one of the main reasons for gathering ice cores, other chemical species can give information about different climatic parameters.

In order to use the climatic record it is necessary to date the ice cores. There are three main methods, none of which can give accurate ages for deep ice. The most direct method is to identify annual layering, which can sometimes be seen in the $\delta^{18}O$ values or in concentrations of sea salts, and to count them in much the same way as tree rings. Other stratigraphic layers, such as a prominent band of volcanic ash or, for recent snow, a peak in radioactivity from β-particles, which can be identified with well-dated events such as a known volcanic eruption or nuclear test, can be used to give the age of the ice at a particular depth. The accuracy of this method is variable, but can achieve 1 year in 1000 in ideal places. The second method uses the decay of naturally occurring elements like ^{210}Pb (half-life 22 years), ^{32}Si (half-life 500 years), ^{14}C (half-life 5600 years), and ^{36}Cl (half-life 300 000 years). Absolute dates to about 5% accuracy can be achieved for up to five times the half-life of the particular nucleide. The disadvantage is that large quantities of ice are normally required to obtain sufficient radioactive material. However, there are now particle accelerators combined with mass spectrometers which require only relatively small amounts of material (a few kilograms).

The third method, and the one most commonly used for all deep holes, is to model the ice flow. Layers of annual snowfall are compressed as they are buried deeper. The amount of vertical strain (which causes the thinning of the layers) occurring at any particular depth depends on factors such as the distance from the centre of outflow, the

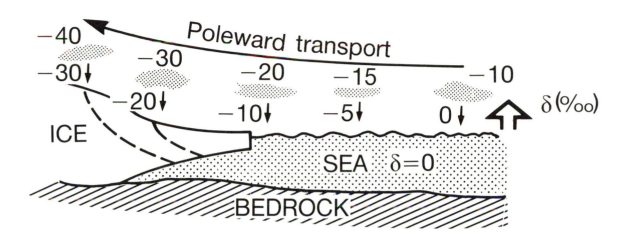

accumulation rate, the temperature, the roughness and topography of the bedrock, whether the basal ice is sliding or not, the amount of converging or diverging transverse flow, and whether the longitudinal flow is extending or compressing. Many assumptions and simplifications have to be made in order to arrive at a chronology and the greater the depth, the less accurate the age. It is unfortunate that in shallower holes the major climatic event, corresponding to the end of the last glaciation between 10 000 and 13 000 years ago, often occurs in ice within a few metres of the bottom. Near the bottom, movement of the ice over and around bedrock obstacles distorts the simple layering and may even cause overturning. This behaviour would be very difficult to detect in a record from a single hole. It is almost impossible to predict accurately the age of the oldest ice in Antarctica, but it is likely to be at least several hundred thousand years old.

The principal climatic parameter which can be interpreted from oxygen isotope data is temperature. At present there is an almost linear relation between the $\delta^{18}O$ value of the snow and the mean annual air temperature over the Antarctic continent: there is a slight bias because the atmosphere is not sampled randomly but only during snowfalls. Because the isotopic composition of water vapour in the atmosphere depends on the source area (i.e. where it evaporated from the ocean) and the subsequent path and precipitation history, it is not certain that the same relation was true in the past. There is another problem in interpreting a $\delta^{18}O$ value in terms of past temperature: when the snow was originally deposited, at a different geographical position to the drill hole, the ice surface may

Natural water has two main isotopic components, $H_2^{16}O$ and $H_2^{18}O$ with relative abundances of 99.8% and 0.2%. The heavier component, $H_2^{18}O$, has a slightly lower vapour pressure so that it evaporates less readily and condenses more easily. The $\delta^{18}O$ value is a measure of the relative isotopic concentration, becoming more negative as the heavier component is lost.

Oxygen isotope record from Byrd Station. The large change in $\delta^{18}O$ value occurring about 20 000 to 12 000 years ago corresponds to the ending of the northern hemisphere glaciation.

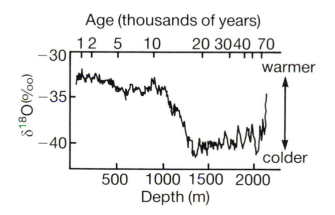

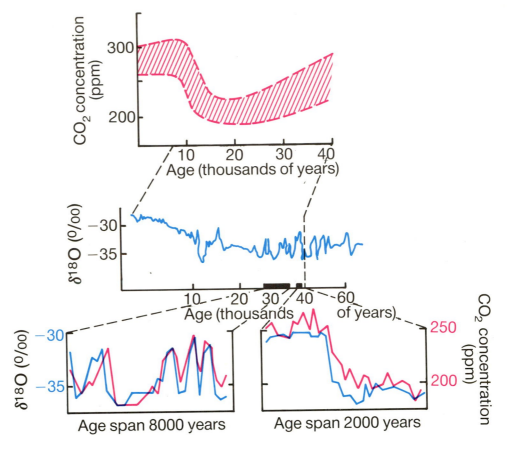

There is a striking correlation between the $\delta^{18}O$ value and CO_2 record (data from the Dye 3 site, Greenland).

have been at a different elevation and, because temperature varies with altitude, may have had a different temperature to that found today. The ambiguity between temperature and altitude is difficult to resolve. For example, the $\delta^{18}O$ value record in the Byrd core shows an abrupt decrease at a depth corresponding to a time about 12 000 years ago, when the northern hemisphere ice age ended. Two extreme interpretations can be placed on this behaviour. One is that the Antarctic ice sheet was the same size as at present but that the air temperature was several degrees (7–8°C) lower. The other possibility is that the air temperature and lapse rate were the same as now, but that the ice sheet was several hundred metres thicker. Of course, any number of intermediate combinations are also possible. This ambiguity requires other data to resolve it. A direct way of doing this is to examine the amount of gas trapped in bubbles in the ice. After snow has reached a critical density it becomes impermeable, so any remaining air

becomes compressed. Quite often cores from a few hundred metres depth shatter when the pressure from the overlying ice is removed, allowing the gas bubbles to expand. New techniques can tell from only a few grams of ice the altitude at which the snow settled. The $\delta^{18}O$ value record from ice core recovered at Dome C has been particularly well dated and goes back 32 000 years. The record shows the same trends as both the Byrd and Vostok cores. This consistency confirms that the major features are not local phenomena but represent continent-wide climatic changes.

These deep cores have also been analysed for micro-particle distributions and carbon dioxide (CO_2) concentrations. By studying the relation of other atmospheric parameters to temperature and climate, insight may be gained into the mechanism of climatic change, especially the abrupt changes over time scales of a few centuries. Given the lack of unanimity in forecasts about the climatic

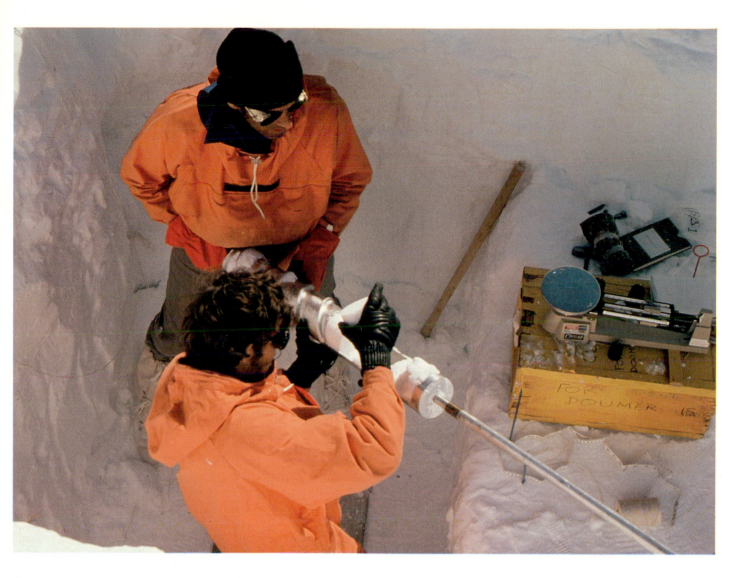

Shallow cores to about 10 m depth are usually drilled by hand.
The balance on the right is for weighing the ice cores.

effect of the contemporary rise in atmospheric CO_2, the records from polar ice cores assume a critical role. Generally reduced levels of CO_2 which persisted throughout the last ice age increased sharply as the ice age finally retreated. A 30% increase in CO_2 concentration took place in just a few thousand years between the height of the ice age and its sudden disappearance. The stable level characteristic of the 10 000 years since then has, in the last 200 years, increased by another 22%. The correlation of low CO_2 levels with ice age conditions suggests that whatever effect burning coal and oil will have, creating an ice age is not one of them. Although fossil fuels are the source of manmade atmospheric CO_2, the oceans act as a regulator and, given sufficient time, excess CO_2 in the air may dissolve in the sea.

By way of contrast, the microparticle record shows that the largest amount of dust in the atmosphere coincided with the lowest concentration of CO_2, i.e. at the time of maximum glaciation. Stratospheric dust affects climate by changing the atmospheric albedo. Analysis of the dust indicates that it was derived from the weathering of rock rather than from volcanic activity. This has been interpreted as showing that the southern hemisphere continents were more arid and that atmospheric circulation was more active then because of the increased temperature gradient between equator and pole during the ice age. Volcanic ash, found in both Byrd and Dome C cores, is likely to have a local source – Mount Takahe is 450 km from Byrd Station while Mount Erebus is 600 km from Dome C. The products of volcanic activity can also be detected by the presence of anions, such as sulphates and nitrates. Measuring continuous profiles of electrical conductivity along the core can show peaks in acidity which may sometimes correspond to individual volcanic eruptions. Ion chromatography is another new technique used to quantify anion concentrations in particular ice samples.

Changes in solar radiation at the top of the atmosphere affect the magnetic shielding against galactic cosmic rays, giving variations in the production of radioisotopes such as ^{10}Be and ^{36}Cl in the upper atmosphere. Accelerator mass spectrometry now allows accurate measurement of ^{10}Be (with a half-life of 1.5 million years) from only 1 kg of ice sample. Concentrations of ^{10}Be and CO_2 show the same trends in an ice core from Dye 3 in Greenland, and also correlate with $\delta^{18}O$ values. The major fluctuations in ^{10}Be concentrations have been considered to be caused by changes in snow precipitation rates, although there appears to be an association between ^{10}Be concentrations in recent snow and the sunspot cycle. During a period with a quiet sun (1640 to 1710), increased concentrations are found in both Greenland and Antarctic ice.

Climatic parameters such as air temperature, precipitation rate, atmospheric albedo, infra-red absorption and solar radiation can be determined from ice cores. But Man is also responsible for a host of other pollutants in the atmosphere which, although they may not cause a global climatic change, may nevertheless have severe effects on local environments. Over the last 200 years, toxic heavy metal emissions have increased dramatically; lead is causing particular concern at present. Burning oil and coal has raised acidity levels in rainfall over many of the industrial countries and their neighbours, with consequent ecological damage. Nuclear tests have released copious radioactive fallout. All of these pollutants can be detected in polar snow and ice cores. Because Antarctica is remote from the source area, concentrations measured there provide standards for comparison with other parts of the world. The change in background with time shows unequivocally Man's influence on his environment.

Hundreds of thousands of tons of lead are poured annually into the air, largely through car exhausts. However, the concentrations found in Antarctic snow are very low – of the order of one part in 10^{12}. It has been difficult to develop techniques for collecting, transporting and analysing samples so that significant contamination is avoided, but it is now possible to determine the amount of lead in only 2 g of ice. Results from Greenland and Antarctica suggest that lead concentrations may have increased by a factor of up to 200 in Greenland and by up to 40-fold in Antarctica in the last few thousand years. In the last 450 years, concentrations may have increased by a factor of three in Greenland; no recent increase has been confirmed in Antarctica.

One class of pollutants that has been of some use is the radioactive fallout from the Bikini Atoll nuclear tests by the USA in 1954 and the Soviet tests of 1960–1962. The fallout, which can be detected by relatively simple radioactive counters, has provided convenient reference horizons for dating the sedimentary snow layers.

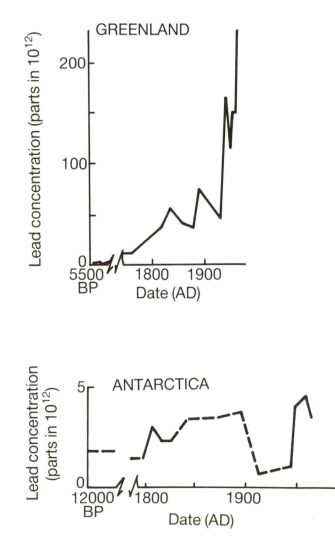

Lead concentrations have increased markedly in the northern hemisphere in the last few hundred years. No corresponding increase has been seen in Antarctic snows. Concentrations in ice several thousand years old are similar in both hemispheres.

Chapter·12

Ice dynamics and the ocean

Mass balance, sea level and dynamics

Although studying chemical impurities in ice cores can tell us about past climates, the Antarctic ice sheet not only records, but also responds to, and causes, changes in climate. It is unlikely that the ice sheet is ever in a condition of equilibrium; air and sea temperatures, snow accumulation, sea level and isostatic adjustment of the bedrock can all affect the form and flow of the ice sheet on time scales ranging up to thousands of years. As well as these external controls, there may also be flow instabilities inherent in the dynamic behaviour of large ice masses that could cause periodic surges of ice into the sea. This idea received much attention in the 1960s when it was considered as a possible mechanism for initiating ice ages; large areas of the Southern Ocean would be covered by floating ice with a high albedo, reducing the total amount of heat absorbed from the sun. Although surging of local catchment basins is still thought to be feasible, spectral analysis of $\delta^{18}O$ values in deep-sea sediment cores suggest that ice volume fluctuations are modulated by the Milankovitch cycles: the only evidence of ice sheet-induced periodicities is a 100 000 year cycle thought to be caused by the interaction between ice-sheet size and bedrock isostasy.

Mass-balance measurements have preoccupied many Antarctic glaciologists because of the impact any imbalance would have on world sea level. Records from stations all over the world have been analysed to show that there has been a rise in sea level over the last 100 years of around 15 cm. Already, some cities in coastal areas are planning their new developments inland on higher ground because of the threat of flooding within the lifetime of our grandchildren. However, not all, or none, of the rise in sea level need be due to melting of Antarctic ice. Although the volume of alpine glaciers in the rest of the world is only about 1% of the volume of the Antarctic ice sheet, there has been considerable retreat of mountain glaciers and local ice caps this century. There has also been a small net warming measured in parts of the ocean: a rise of only 0.2°C seen in the North Atlantic since the International Geophysical Year (IGY) in 1957 would be equivalent to an increase of 3 cm in the height of the water column. Total snowfall over Antarctica has been estimated at 2000 km^3 water equivalent per year. The average rise in sea level is also equivalent to adding an additional volume of 500 km^3 of water per year. So, if all the rise in sea level were due to melting of Antarctic ice, the losses each year must be 2500 km^3 per year. The independent estimates of accumulation and ablation are about the same (i.e. 2000 km^3 per year), implying that the ice sheet is approximately in equilibrium. There are, however, large errors in these estimates which may allow a small contribution to the rise in sea level.

Although there is no firm evidence for any great imbalance in the ice sheet as a whole, individual drainage basins may show different behaviour. Some may be growing while others are decaying and some may be more vulnerable than others to sudden decay. The drainage basins differ in such features as catchment area, surface altitude, bedrock elevation, basal regime, outflow constraints or latitude, all of which affect their response to changes in climate and their probability of surging. Within an individual basin, the time scale on which it would react to say a change in mean annual air temperature or accumulation, could mean that ice was thickening in one part of the basin while thinning in another part. A number of drainage basins have been examined in detail, where accumulation and velocity measurements have been made in order to calculate mass fluxes. However, errors are usually too high to be able to state definitely whether there is a net gain or loss. The ice sheet is far too large for ground traverse parties to make sufficient measurements. Not until satellite data giving ice-sheet elevations accurate to less than 1 m become available in the late 1980s will we have a standard against which changes in ice volume can be measured. The SEASAT satellite in 1978 recorded altimeter data over the coastal regions of Antarctica up to latitude 72°S. Although the radar altimeter had been designed for measuring sea surfaces rather than the steeper ice slopes, enough data were recorded to make the most accurate maps to date of surface elevations. The potential resolution of around 10 cm means that the form of the ice sheet can be studied in far greater detail than by any other method. This has great implications for studying ice flow as well as for monitoring changes in volume. One drawback with the satellite missions planned at present is that they will fly only up to latitude 82°S. The hole left unsurveyed in central Antartica includes some of the most important areas at the heads of the Ronne and Ross ice shelves, where any non-steady-state behaviour in the ice sheet is most likely to be happening. Few of the major drainage basins will be completely covered either. There are no plans for missions that will be dedicated to studying Antartica until at least the 1990s, so this gap in coverage will probably remain for some time.

The surface profile of the Antarctic ice sheet in places closely approximates to a parabola. This is the form expected if ice were a perfectly plastic material with a yield stress of 1 bar resting on a flat bed. More realistic flow laws for ice (the relation between the driving force and the resultant deformation) give profiles which in practice differ only slightly from a parabola. These theoretical curves depend only very weakly on the accumulation

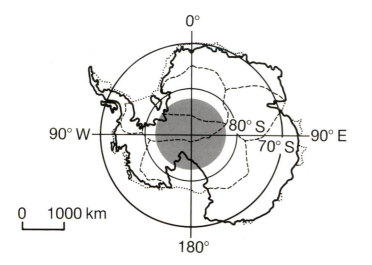

An orbit inclination of 98° means that a satellite ground track will not cover any area above 82° in latitude (shaded area), about one-fifth of the continent. Most of the major drainage basins (delineated by dashed lines) will remain only partially surveyed.

If ice were a perfectly plastic material resting on a flat bed, the surface profile would form a parabola. This is still a good approximation for more realistic cases.

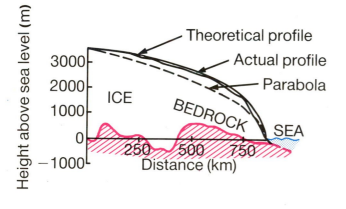

Plot of mean shear strain rate against driving stress. Note the peak in driving stress at about one bar (100 kPa).

rate, and in the case of perfect plasticity the profile is independent of accumulation. When averaged over distances of 20 times the ice thickness, the driving stress can be taken as proportional to the product of thickness multiplied by surface slope. The general pattern over the ice sheet is one of driving stress increasing towards the coast. If ice were perfectly plastic and it remained frozen to a flat bedrock, the driving stress would be constant everywhere. Therefore, comparison of observed and theoretical patterns can be used to study the physical mechanisms which operate and control the deformation of the ice sheet.

For many parts of the inland ice sheet the shearing of the ice sheet, represented by the horizontal velocity divided by the ice thickness, is approximately proportional to some power of the driving stress. However, towards the coast, the flow often tends to be channelled into outlet glaciers and ice streams which pierce fringing mountains. In these areas the simple relation breaks down because of the onset of basal sliding. As sliding velocities increase with distance along a flow line, it is found that the driving stress decreases. Simple sliding theory, which assumes that sliding velocities are controlled by the roughness, or size, of obstacles on the bed, cannot describe this behaviour. Indeed, the simple theory predicts that sliding velocities increase with driving stress and the gross form of an ice sheet sliding over its bed is almost the same as one in which ice is perfectly plastic. The factor controlling sliding velocity in ice streams is probably subglacial water pressure; not only is water produced by melting at the bottom of the ice sheet, but also the beds of ice streams are usually below sea level and probably connected hydraulically to the sea. As the land beneath the ice normally dips towards

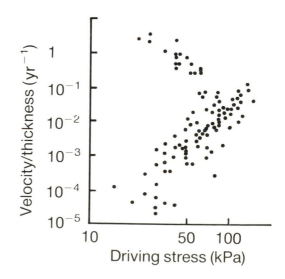

the coast, the ice streams experience a gradually increasing buoyancy force until eventually they start floating at the grounding line. Ice shelves are usually formed when several ice streams coalesce in a bay which has a suitable geometry to restrain the ice from calving and breaking out.

Most ice streams are extremely crevassed. This is a result of extending flow, the increase in velocity with distance creating a tension great enough to fracture the surface. Below a certain depth the overburden pressure is sufficient to prevent the penetration of crevasses. In theory, water-filled crevasses should extend to the bottom of the ice sheet. None has been identified, but whether this is because of inadequate supplies of surface meltwater or because of the difficulty in recognizing where this has happened is not certain. Along the side boundaries of ice streams, the heat produced by deformation and the high accumulated strain are believed to cause the ice to re-crystallise in a form which is softer and less resistant to the driving stress. This again has been difficult to verify. After an ice stream begins to float, the crevasse fields usually die away quickly because of the constraint exerted by the ice shelf into which the ice stream flows. Thick, fast-flowing ice streams slow down and gradually thin as they become incorporated into ice shelf, but will retain their individual identity until they reach the ice front and calve away as icebergs, unless bottom melting and surface accumulation have first replaced all the ice which originated over land.

Ice shelves and the ocean

Ice shelves, floating with no basal friction in hydrostatic equilibrium on the sea, thin towards the ice front under the action of the stress caused by the height of the ice above sea level. Flow rates can reach several kilometres per year and these shelves are the fastest moving parts of the ice sheet. Surface slopes are extremely small so that ice shelves appear as flat featureless plains, broken only by the occasional rift or gentle dome of an ice rise formed when the sea bed shallows and touches the bottom of the ice shelf. If the friction is great enough the forward motion stops and a local ice cap with its own isolated flow pattern builds up. The seaward extent of ice shelves often appears to be controlled by the pinning effect of ice rises, and the backward thrust from ice rises and side wall friction control the velocity and thickness distribution. The lack of basal friction means that vertical shear stresses are usually negligible; a vertical borehole would remain vertical instead of tilting forward as in a grounded glacier. This simplification makes ice shelves a good natural work site for studying deformation of ice under the low stresses and long time periods that are impossible to simulate in a laboratory, although it may be difficult to describe accurately the stress field. Theoretical models of ice-shelf behaviour are almost identical to those being used to describe the non-rigid deformation of tectonic plates. Another close analogy is between the flexure of the lithosphere at a subduction

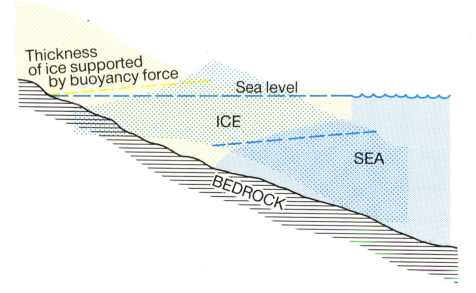

Ice resting on rock that is below sea level begins to float when its thickness equals that needed for hydrostatic equilibrium.

Thickness of ice supported by buoyancy force

Sea level

ICE

SEA

BEDROCK

David Glacier flows from the inland plateau, cutting through the Transantarctic Mountains to the Ross Sea.

As the ice shelf rises and falls with the ocean tide, a region close to the grounding line bends. The diagram shows changes in surface elevation with distance from the grounding line for hourly intervals after a time T.

Effect of an ice rise on ice-shelf extent. The dashed line shows an ice shelf in a bay with diverging sides and no ice rise. The solid line shows the ice shelf in a similar bay but with an ice rise impeding flow. The constraint allows a longer ice shelf to exist.

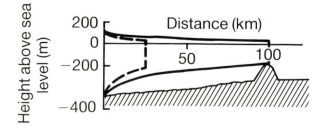

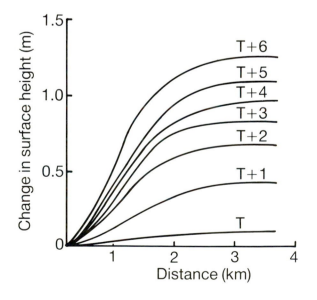

164

zone and the bending of an ice stream as it starts floating. If an example of ice subduction could be recognized, then most models of the earth's tectonics could be tested against their icy counterparts.

One region thought to react sensitively to changes in climate or ice-sheet flow pattern is that close to the grounding line. Here, a delicate balance between restraint from ice shelves and outward push from the grounded ice sheet means that any disturbance should cause the position of the grounding line to change. It is possible to locate the point at which an ice stream starts floating by measuring tidal flexing. An ice shelf rises and falls with the ocean tide but a grounded ice sheet does not; downstream from the grounding line there is a zone, a few ice thicknesses in extent, which bends with the tide. Sensitive tiltmeters can detect tidal signals of changes in surface slope which allow the position of the grounding line to be determined very accurately. Not unexpectedly, grounding lines do not appear to be simple geometrical lines but rather run sinuously across ice streams, reflecting the often complex bedrock topography and ice thickness. The concept of a single well-defined grounding line is also too simple. Rather, there is an area, probably of varying width, across which the ice gradually separates from its bed. Tidal fluctuations will cause the area to migrate periodically. Along the lateral boundaries of ice streams and ice shelves small crevasses a few millimetres wide, called strand cracks, which open and close with the tide, are diagnostic features of tidal flexing. They can often be followed for many kilometres.

If there is a significant non-elastic component of ice deformation at tidal frequencies then tidal energy will be dissipated as heat in the bending zone. Oceanic tidal records taken around the Antarctic coastline suggest that in many areas there is a lag of a few days between full

moon and the spring tide with the maximum monthly amplitude. This discrepancy, called the age of the tide, is typically found to be high in other regions of the world where dissipation of tidal energy is thought to occur. There is therefore the possibility that an appreciable part of the total tidal energy dissipated in the world is concentrated around the Antarctic coastline. As a result of this energy loss, the moon slows down in its orbit round the earth and moves further away.

Another important interaction between the ocean and ice shelf is the mass transfer. A difficult component to quantify in the mass-balance equation of Antarctica is the amount of ice melted from, or frozen onto, the bottom of ice shelves. The salinity of the sea water lowers its freezing point by nearly 2°C compared with the fresh-water ice of the ice shelves. The freezing point of both ice and sea water decreases as pressure, i.e. depth, increases. Therefore, pure ice in contact with sea water at some depth will melt until the temperature of the sea water falls to its freezing point. This equilibrium state can be determined from the phase diagram for a mixture of salt and ice and is the same phenomenon as sprinkling salt on roads to prevent icing by lowering the freezing point. Under an ice shelf, currents in the sea and the temperature through the ice shelf ensure that the mass balance is controlled by the heat exchange. In general, if the sea has already been cooled to its freezing point at a particular depth then upward movement of the water, such as a current flowing in the direction of ice thinning, will cause ice to form and to freeze onto the base of the ice shelf; downward movement, by decreasing the freezing point, will tend to melt ice. Melting of ice at the great depths found close to grounding lines of the large ice shelves can form a sea water whose temperature is colder than the surface freezing point. This very cold water, when it mixes with other components which can be warmer and more saline, helps to form the dense Antarctic Bottom Water which plays an important role in global ocean currents.

Estimates of bottom melting rates can be made from measurements of thickness and velocity and their spatial derivatives at the surface of an ice shelf. The principle of continuity of mass is used but it is not possible to separate out a non-steady-state change in ice thickness from the bottom melting rate. Other indirect methods, such as analysing and modelling temperature profiles, can help resolve the ambiguity, but it would be a major achievement to estimate actual melting rates from oceanographic parameters. There have been a number of ship cruises close to ice-shelf fronts measuring salinity and temperature profiles with depth, but the simplest water structure found so far is that under George VI Ice Shelf. Here, profiles with depth show a linear relation between temperature

Phase diagram for an ice, water and simple salt solution.

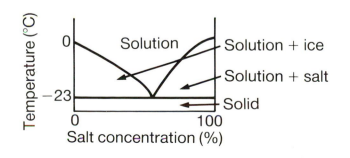

and salinity. This is the expected behaviour for a closed two-component system in which ice melts in warm sea water of fixed temperature and salinity. None of the larger ice-shelves appears to have the necessary degree of isolation from the ocean currents to allow this structure to develop. The critical parameter for calculating bottom melting, the coefficient of turbulent heat transfer, remains a quantity to be measured and not derived empirically. However, for a defined catchment area which includes an ice shelf it is possible to study the balance of conservative quantities such as mass or oxygen isotope ratio ($\delta^{18}O$), which can give an average value for bottom melting over the whole ice-shelf area. Spilling over of warm deep water onto the continental shelf under George VI Sound gives water temperatures nearly 2°C higher than those found under other ice shelves like the Ross Ice Shelf. These higher water temperatures probably explain the higher melt rates deduced for George VI Ice Shelf (2 m per year) compared with Ross Ice Shelf (0.2 m per year).

A plot of temperature against salinity for sea water at the northern end of George VI Ice Shelf shows an almost linear relation. Figures on the plot give depth in metres.

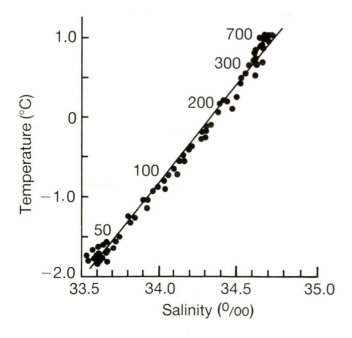

The way in which ice deformation increases with temperature means that the bottom melt rate can play an important role in controlling the behaviour of ice shelves. Usually the top surface has a net accumulation of snow at a mean temperature well below the freezing point. With basal melting, particle velocities are directed downwards, advecting cold ice towards the base. The mean temperature is colder than when basal freezing occurs, making the ice stiffer. Thus, basal melting may help to increase the stability of some ice shelves.

Radio-echo sounding

A qualitative indicator of the basal regime for an ice shelf can be obtained from radio-echo measurements. Erroneous values of aircraft height recorded while flying over the ice sheets in Greenland and Antarctica revealed that ice was transparent to low-frequency radio waves. Radar sounding of ice sheets began in the early 1960s using aircraft altimeters. Major developments in equipment and analysis of these data soon led to a revolution in polar glaciology. Ice can now be sounded rapidly and continuously from aircraft, instead of by slow spasmodic seismic and gravity traverses on the ground. As well as ice thickness, the radar records give details of internal structures such as sedimentary layering or crevasses at the bottom of ice shelves. Quantitative measurements of the strength of the bottom echo allow recognition of basal conditions. On ice shelves, strong continuous echoes are typical of areas where basal melting predominates and there is a clean, sharp boundary between ice and sea. Where there is freezing, inclusion of salt in the ice dramatically increases the absorption of radio-wave energy and gives a much weaker and intermittent echo. Thus, plotting out areas of strong and weak echoes (after allowing for temperature-dependent absorption through the bulk of the ice) indicates the nature of the bottom surface. Mapping the reflection coefficient this way does not give the bottom melting regime directly but only the integrated history along a flow line. Ice shelves to which a significant amount of saline ice has been frozen will still give a weak echo until all the saline ice has melted away.

The orientation of the individual ice crystals, called the fabric, affects the response of polycrystalline ice to the applied stress. Along boundaries of ice streams fabrics may form that favour easy flow; tidal bending across grounding lines also seems to create a strongly developed fabric. Because some mechanical and electrical properties of ice crystals are anisotropic (i.e. vary with position or direction), changes in fabric can be detected by several techniques. Seismic and ultrasonic measurements in ice cores have shown differences in compressional elastic

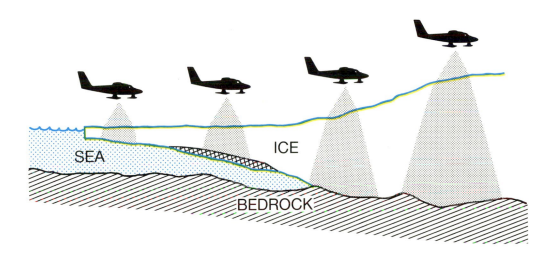

(Above) *Ice thicknesses can be measured by radar. Radio waves transmitted from aerials on the aircraft gradually lose strength as they travel through the ice. Some of the radio wave energy is reflected from the bottom of the ice and returns to the aircraft.*

(Below) *Radio echo record showing internal echoes which tend to follow the rough bedrock topography. Profile is about 250 km long and 3 km deep.*

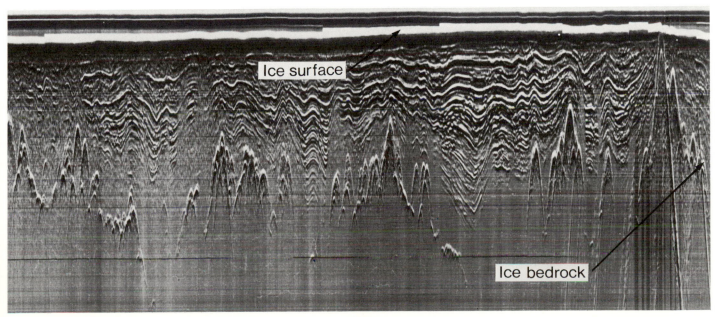

wave (P-wave) velocities that can be correlated with fabrics observed under the microscope. Ice is birefringent at optical wavelengths and radio-echo studies of polarisation behaviour suggest a slight birefringence for radio waves. An airborne method for carrying out radar polarisation surveys could reveal stress distributions in ice shelves that would help test and constrain theoretical models of ice-shelf flow.

One of the most intriguing discoveries from radio-echo sounding was the phenomenon of 'internal layering'. In many areas where the ice is cold, echoes are seen not only from the bedrock but also from inside the bulk of the ice. These internal echoes, although weak, can be continuous for distances of hundreds of kilometres. They persist in the top part of the ice sheet but usually die out before the bed is reached. Their obvious parallelism to the top surface and to each other suggests that they have a sedimentary origin, representing relic surfaces. It is still uncertain how the layer thickness or spacing depends on radio wave frequency. Attempts have been made to correlate the layers with changes in physical parameters in ice cores at the same depth, but with only partial success. In order to obtain the observed reflection coefficients for the layers, there must be a change in either the density or the conductivity of the ice. Density variations of the required magnitude occur only in the top 500 or 1000 m. Echoes from further down in the ice sheet must come from layers which have a significant conductivity contrast. There is evidence that the required conductivities could be generated by acids scavenged from the atmosphere by snowfall. Laboratory results on the magnitude of the conductivity of ice samples from deep ice cores can be explained by a model of concentrated acids confined to grain boundaries between ice crystals. Acids could be the result of volcanic activity, so that prominent layers may be associated with particular volcanic eruptions. It has been suggested that a relative lack of layers in polar ice sheets at depths that correspond to ages of around 10 000–25 000 years ago could be due either to reduced global volcanic activity or to neutralisation by salts transported by winds in a period of increased aridity and exposure of carbonates. Any increase in atmospheric acids from burning fossil fuels, such as those creating the acid rain problem at the present time over industrial areas, would only affect the upper part of the ice sheet where there are also density fluctuations. Layers close to the surface are usually obscured in airborne soundings by the surface echo and special ground-based radars have been developed to observe them. Although the layers appear to be discrete reflecting horizons on radio-echo records, they may be an artefact of the interaction between the radar pulse and a series of closely spaced annual layers of varying conductivity, and the

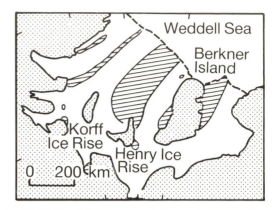

Ronne Ice Shelf. Shaded areas are where weak returns are received when radio-echo sounding, probably indicating the presence of frozen or salty ice.

Crevasses form where the ice is under tension. They are dangerous when bridged by snow, making them difficult to detect.

response of the radar receiver. A theoretical simulation of such a system gives results which look qualitatively very similar to observations.

Apart from the climatic importance of being able to interpret radio-echo layers in terms of atmospheric acidity and volcanic activity, they can also be used for investigating the flow of ice. If the layers are assumed to be former surfaces of the ice sheet then they represent isochrons, i.e. surfaces of equal age. Measurements of surface slopes, strain rates, accumulation and velocity can be checked against those necessary to reproduce observed isochronous surfaces and thereby can show if long-term changes in the state of the ice sheet have occurred. The echo-free zone in the lower part of the ice is thought to indicate the complexity of the flow close to bedrock, where there is lateral movement around obstacles and probably a degree of mixing. Theoretical models relating bedrock and surface slopes can be used to predict slopes of internal layers. Occasionally it is possible to identify echoes that have come from moraine which originally fell onto the snow suface from a scree slope near a nunatak or mountain and gradually became buried as the ice moved away. The moraine layer acts as a particle path and could be used to test flow models. A combination of internal layers as isochrons and moraine layers as particle paths would give a very complete data set for analysing ice flow.

Ice crystals from a depth of 308 m at Byrd Station, photographed between crossed polaroid filters.

Satellite images and computer modelling

Satellite images show very clearly a subdued expression of bedrock topography in the ice-sheet surface. It is possible to recognise the extension of mountain ranges buried under the ice and to pick out preferred directions of linear features. In polar regions the most useful LANDSAT and weather satellite pictures are taken with a sun angle of less than 20°. Undulations can be seen over a wide range of wavelengths from less than one to many tens of kilometres. Wavelengths are generally greatest near ice divides where velocities are small. Comparison with accurate radar altimetry on radio-echo sounding flights shows that amplitudes increase as wavelengths decrease. The size of the undulation also depends on ice thickness, but in general there is good agreement with theories which suggest that the transfer of bedrock undulations to the surface increases with wavelength. It is interesting that synthetic aperture radar (SAR) pictures from SEASAT, a satellite which flew in 1978, showed an impression of shallow sea-bed topography on the surface of the sea at certain states of the tide, a situation analogous to ice flowing over a rough bed.

An abrupt change in the surface character of the major ice streams can often be seen on satellite images. The high-amplitude, short-wavelength features give way to a much smoother surface as the ice flows towards the coast. In some cases this transition is marked by a steep surface slope which coincides with a step in the bedrock, but the significance of the connection is uncertain. It is likely that there is a change in basal flow, from shear at the bedrock to sliding. Surface slopes usually start to decrease towards the coast in this region, giving a characteristic concave-up profile as opposed to the convex-up profile expected from simple flow theory. The bedrock step may be a result of erosion controlled by basal flow regime, and there are many similarities between the subglacial topography of Antarctic ice streams and fiords in deglaciated areas such as Norway.

On ice shelves curvilinear features are seen which obviously describe flow lines. They can sometimes be traced from the grounding line for hundreds of kilometres to the ice front, as on Filchner Ice Shelf. At the grounding line, where the bedrock is often irregular, differences in lateral ice thickness can cause noticeable surface slopes. The features seen on satellite pictures may result from these surface slopes being preserved throughout the length of the ice shelf. Alternatively, the features sometimes appear to originate from extensive crevasse fields, which can also be identified on LANDSAT images, and may therefore be linked with differences in surface albedo. Whatever the explanation, they offer a means of testing present-day velocity fields against an assumed steady state. Large rifts are commonly, but unexpectedly, seen in the middle of otherwise undisturbed ice shelves; it is difficult to explain their formation without the presence of associated ice rises but in many cases none can be identified. This could be because the quality of the image is too poor to see the ice rise, or that the ice rise was an ephemeral feature and has disappeared since forming the rift. It is possible, however, that the rifts are created by unsuspected stress fields. Perhaps this is not too surprising; although relatively simple models exist for describing ice-shelf velocity and thickness profiles along a centre line, results are sensitive to the geometry of the confining bay and the boundary conditions. More complex finite-element computer models can be used to describe the whole ice shelf, but are expensive on computer time. Many valuable results have appeared from these types of large model, but there is still a need to describe the small-scale boundary conditions more exactly. Derived physical parameters, such as the hardness of the ice, show clearly the influence of bottom melting on the vertical temperature profile. For both the Ross and Ronne/Filchner ice shelves, the hardness increases towards the ice front where there is the highest melt rate and thinnest ice.

Other types of computer model are concerned with the behaviour of the whole ice sheet and its reaction to climatic variations. Simplified versions of the dynamic equations are used, parametrised to take into account the major physical processes to allow reasonably quick and efficient computation. Model ice sheets can be obtained from an initial state of a given bedrock surface and accumulation pattern. Resulting steady-state ice sheet models show a lot of similarity to real ice sheets but with discrepancies in detail and in particular areas. However, as their purpose is often to understand how polar ice sheets affect global climate so that the large general circulation models (GCMs) used by climatologists can be adjusted to be more realistic about their parametrisation of ice sheets, this is not a serious drawback. It is significant, though, that in order to achieve realistically stable ice sheets, basal sliding must be allowed for and isostatic adjustment of the bed explicitly modelled. The maximum isostatic depression of bedrock would be about a third of the ice thickness, averaged in a suitable way over area. It is the time scale for growth or decay of an ice sheet compared with the time scale for isostatic adjustment that influences the stability of model ice sheets.

Nearly all computer models use a very simplified form of the flow law, or constitutive equation, for ice, which relates the deformation to the applied stress. The flow law is allowed to be temperature-dependent but does not explicitly allow for crystal size or orientation, nor for the

Theoretical calculations of particle paths (solid lines) and isochrons (dashed lines, ages in thousands of years) showing how the old ice is concentrated near the bottom of the ice sheet.

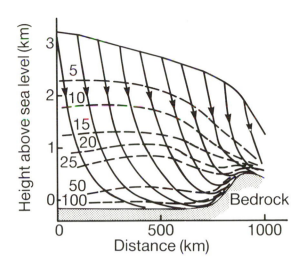

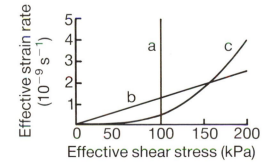

Ross Ice Shelf, showing contour of the calculated restraining force in units of MN m⁻¹. The force arises from shear stress along the margins and compression upstream of ice rises.

Relation between effective strain rate ($\dot{\varepsilon}$) and effective shear stress (τ) for various flow laws: (a) perfectly plastic material with a yield of stress of 100 kPa, (b) newtonian (linear) viscosity of 8×10^{13} kg m⁻¹s⁻¹ and (c) power law of form $\dot{\varepsilon} = A\tau^n$ where $n=3$ and $A = 5 \times 10^{-6}$ kPa⁻³s⁻¹.

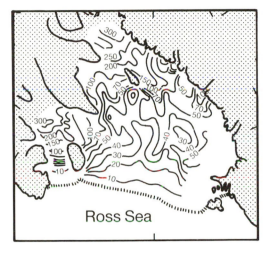

amount of impurity, either solid or soluble. Extensive laboratory measurements on both single crystal and poly-crystalline ice give a wide variation in the flow law parameters, such that strain rates can often differ by a factor of ten or more. There are relatively few values deduced from field measurements and they show equally wide variability. A careful selection of experimental results can give recommended values which agree to within a factor of two. Relevant data for polar ice sheets are very scarce. However, there is a well-defined difference in the conductivity of static (low-frequency or DC) electricity between polar ice on one hand and temperate and laboratory-grown ice on the other, which is thought to be due to the amount of acid present at grain boundaries; these acids could also be responsible for softening in polar ice. As layers of soft ice, deposited during periods of high vulcanicity or at other times of high atmospheric acidity, approach the base of the ice sheet, the flow will increase. This could be a mechanism for causing ice-sheet, and hence climatic, fluctuations on time scales determined by ice dynamics instead of by orbital periodicities.

The large size of the Antarctic ice sheet has global geophysical consequences. The mass of ice distorts the geoid (the theoretical sea-level surface, an equipotential, extended continuously through the continents) in such a way that melting of polar ice does not give a uniform rise in sea level worldwide: the dominant effect is that the gravitational attraction by the ice sheet decreases as the ice melts. This, together with compensation in the earth's crust and mantle, means that the new equipotential formed by the sea surface can lead to a fall in sea level close to Antarctica. Redistribution of water around the globe also leads to measurable changes in polar motion and the speed of rotation of the earth. At the beginning and end of ice ages, times when ice sheets are changing most rapidly in size, the magnitude of fluctuations in the speed of rotation or in flow disturbances induced in the mantle may have a measurable effect on such diverse phenomena as the generation of the earth's magnetic field or on mantle convection and plate tectonic motions.

LANDSAT picture of Ronne Ice Shelf showing curvilinear features that are assumed to correspond to flowlines. Ice is flowing towards the top of the picture.

Future trends

With the greatly increased amount of satellite-derived data that will become available by the end of the 1980s, more attention will be directed towards surface and near-surface processes. Large-scale topographic mapping of parameters such as surface elevation, snow accumulation, temperature, crystal size and orientation will become possible with accuracies not otherwise achievable. While these studies will require ground measurements to help validate the remotely sensed data, many of the scientists analysing the results will not need to set foot on the continent itself. Although many new and exciting discoveries will be made, the data can only be used as boundary conditions for the basic mathematical equations that have to be solved to answer questions about long-term changes in ice-sheet size. The exhortation of the 1960s – drill, drill, and then do more drilling – is as wise counsel now and for the foreseeable future as it was then. We know very little about conditions near and at the base of the ice sheet or of the way deformation occurs with depth. Undoubtedly there are detailed historical climatic records contained in the ice: chemical impurities, temperatures, and physical and mechanical properties of ice crystals all reflect to some degree the type of environment that existed when the snow formed and was deposited. It would be a major advance to date accurately ice from depth: the new understanding about the relation between atmospheric carbon dioxide and global temperatures arose in part because of the emphasis placed on precision and accuracy. These two words should play an increasingly important role in planning and execution of field and laboratory work. Computer modelling of ice-sheet flow shows that there can sometimes be very little difference in the final results while starting from quite different initial assumptions. Finally, it should not be forgotten that while study of the world's major ice masses is relevant to global climatology, a fairly all-embracing subject, some aspects are also relevant to more detailed and specialised areas such as molecular structure at temperatures near absolute zero, deformation of the earth's crust and mantle, and the composition of astronomical bodies.

LANDSAT picture showing Rutford Ice Stream flowing from left to right, bounded below the Ellsworth Mountains and above by Fletcher Promontory. The ice stream starts to float at a point about two-thirds of the way across the picture.

Chapter·13

Keystone to Gondwana

Introduction

About 220 million years ago the large supercontinent called Pangaea, which comprised most of the land surface on the earth, broke in two. The southern section, named Gondwana, drifted south until, at about 180–200 million years ago, it too began to split apart, the separate pieces mainly forming what are now known as South America, Africa, India, Australia and Antarctica. The similarity of the continental coastlines was one of the principal pieces of evidence which led Alfred Wegener to suggest in 1912 that the continents had previously been joined together. (An even better fit is given by the surrounding 1000 m bathymetric contour.) However, with some notable exceptions, it took the geophysical and geological community until the mid-1960s to take this idea seriously. Then, the discovery of symmetrical magnetic anomalies across the Mid-Atlantic Ridge led to the concept of sea-floor spreading and the theory of plate tectonics, which revolutionised our understanding of the earth. The basic description by Wegener of the distribution of the southern continents remains a superb graphic illustration of how Antarctica acted as, in the words of another early believer, du Toit, 'the keystone to Gondwana'. Modern techniques of measuring the remanent magnetisation in rocks can be used to determine the latitude of continents at various times in the past when those rocks crystallised. Reconstructions of these positions show, for example, that India, once tucked neatly between South Africa and Australia, moved rapidly northward and collided with the Asian plate to form the Himalayan mountain chain, a region which is still active today. Antarctica was the least mobile of all these continental plates but it continued its slow southward drift to its present position over the South Pole.

However, one of the outstanding problems when attempting reconstructions of Gondwana is to decide where Antarctica, or more precisely the Antarctic Peninsula, should fit against the other southern continents. Broad geological similarities with Antarctica and careful analysis of sea-floor spreading data allow South Africa, India and Australia to be positioned relatively accurately, but the awkward spike of the peninsula is difficult to place. Some reconstructions have placed the peninsula to the east of South America in the Atlantic Ocean, some to the west in the Pacific Ocean, and some have even superimposed parts of the two land masses. Such reconstructions are geologically unacceptable so that it is now recognized that Antarctica, as it appears today, probably does not constitute a single tectonic plate with a unique history of movement for all areas. In fact, throughout most of the Phanerozoic eon, the two major geological divisions, Greater and Lesser Antarctica have had strongly contrasting tectonic histories.

Greater, or East, Antarctica is the area bounded roughly by the longitudes 30°W and 160°E and lying mainly in the eastern hemisphere, whereas Lesser, or West Antarctica, lies entirely in the western hemisphere and includes the Antarctic Peninsula. Greater Antarctica consists very largely of a Precambrian shield, with a younger mobile belt along the Transantarctic Mountains last affected by major deformation and metamorphism about 500 million years ago. In contrast, Lesser Antarctica shows a history of tectonic activity along the margin of the Pacific Ocean through the Phanerozoic. The nature of the boundary between these two geological provinces remains one of the major problems of Antarctic geology and it is one of global significance for understanding Mesozoic and Cenozoic plate interactions.

The Transantarctic Mountains with their spectacular scenery stretch from Victoria Land on the Pacific coast to Dronning Maud Land on the Atlantic coast, intermittently breached by the ice sheet. The mountains define one boundary of the Greater Antarctic metamorphic shield and may have been gradually uplifted during the late Mesozoic and Cenozoic as a consequence of tectonic activity at the boundary between Greater and Lesser Antarctica. Other outcrops of rocks, predominantly metamorphic, are scattered around the coast of Greater Antarctica. The oldest rocks found so far are granulites in Enderby Land; these were formed more than 3100 million years ago. Granitic rocks in the Prince Charles Mountains and gneisses in the Vestfold Hills have also yielded Archaean ages. The general paucity of exposed Archaean rocks, like those which characterise other continents, is probably due to the 99% ice cover. Present-day continents have 'cores' of ancient rocks between 3000 and 4000 million years old, formed when conditions were very different to today; the crust was thinner, heat flow was higher, there was less oxygen in the atmosphere and algae were the dominant life form. A characteristic trinity of rock types (greenstones, banded ironstones and stromatolitic limestones) is common in southern Africa and Australia and other ancient shield areas but their rare occurrence in Antarctica may also be due to the ice cover. When continental fragmentation took place in the Mesozoic, breaks tended to occur in the younger, thinner (and hence weaker) belts. No Archaean rocks are exposed within 150 km of the coast in South Africa or Australia, and since much of the outcrop in Greater Antarctica is coastal, the lack of greenstones should not be surprising. The only known Antarctic member of the 'trinity' is the banded ironstone in the Prince Charles Mountains, over 500 km inland.

(a)

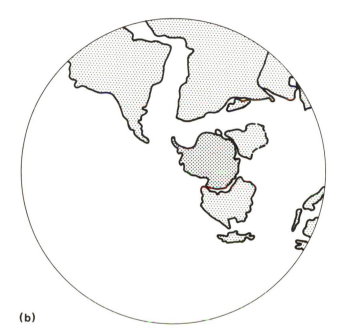

(b)

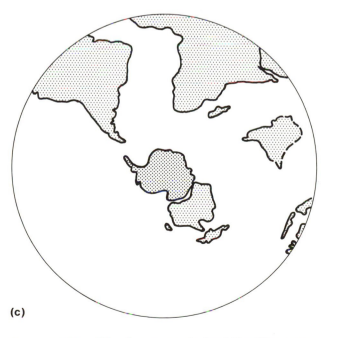

(c)

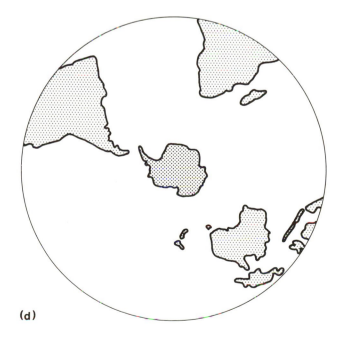

(d)

Fragmentation of Gondwana over the last 200 million years.
(a) 200 million years ago; (b) 100 million years ago; (c) 60 million
years ago; and (d) present-day continental distribution.

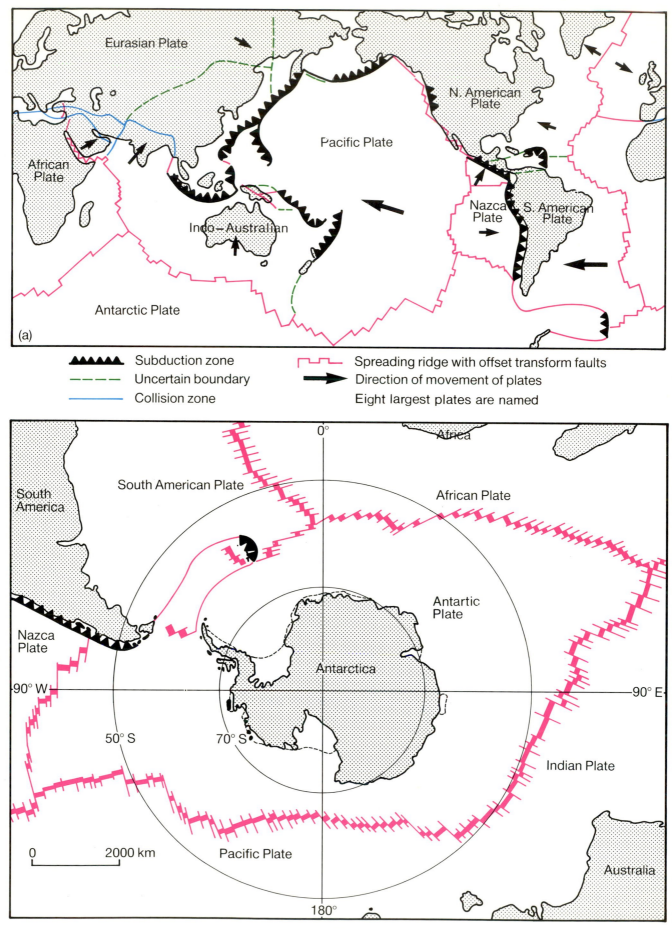

▲▲▲▲▲	Subduction zone	⌐⌐⌐	Spreading ridge with offset transform faults
– – –	Uncertain boundary	➤	Direction of movement of plates
———	Collision zone		Eight largest plates are named

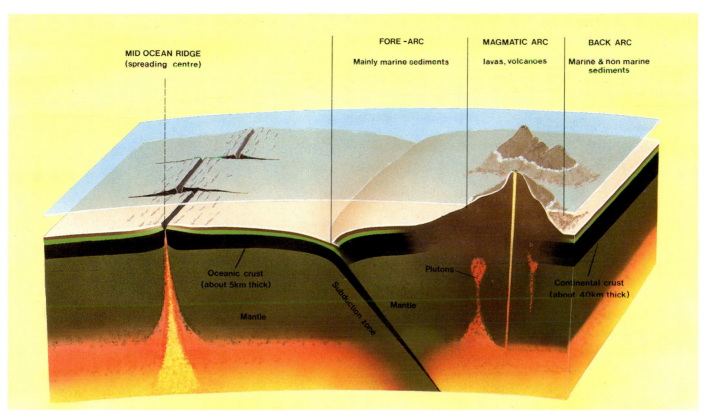

MID OCEAN RIDGE
(spreading centre)

FORE - ARC
Mainly marine sediments

MAGMATIC ARC
lavas, volcanoes

BACK ARC
Marine & non marine sediments

Oceanic crust
(about 5km thick)

Subduction zone

Mantle

Plutons

Mantle

Continental crust
(about 40km thick)

Diagrammatic impression of spreading at a mid-ocean ridge and subduction at a boundary between an oceanic and a continental plate. The subducting slab heats up as it descends, until some molten rock becomes buoyant enough to force its way through the overlying crust to form a magnetic arc. A forearc basin lies on the ocean side of the arc and a backarc basin on the continental side.

GEOLOGICAL TIME:

IGNEOUS ACTIVITY

SEDIMENTATION

GEOLOGICAL
HISTORY
OF
ANTARCTIC
PENINSULA

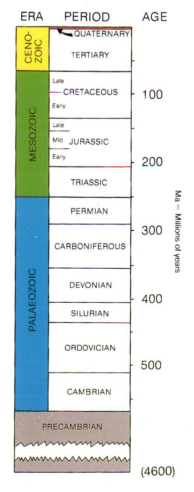

ERA	PERIOD	AGE
CENO-ZOIC	QUATERNARY	
	TERTIARY	
MESOZOIC	Late CRETACEOUS Early	100
	Late Mid JURASSIC Early	200
	TRIASSIC	
PALAEOZOIC	PERMIAN	300
	CARBONIFEROUS	
	DEVONIAN	400
	SILURIAN	
	ORDOVICIAN	500
	CAMBRIAN	
	PRECAMBRIAN	
		(4600)

Ma = Millions of years

(Left)   *The earth's outer shell consists of a number of virtually rigid plates. Movement between them causes earthquakes and volcanoes to be concentrated near their boundaries. (a) Global map of tectonic plates (eight largest are named). (b) The Antarctic Plate.*

Geological time scale.

Greater Antarctica probably has an Archaean core like other southern continents, but it lies beneath the ice cap.

Lesser Antarctica may comprise four or more discrete continental fragments, united today only by the overlying ice sheet. The major crustal fragments are the Antarctic Peninsula, Eights Coast–Thurston Island, Marie Byrd Land and the Ellsworth Mountains–Thiel Mountains ridge. The first three are separated from Greater Antarctica and the Transantarctic Mountains by the Ross Sea–Weddell Sea embayment. This region now includes the two largest ice shelves in the world and the intervening ice sheet conceals some very deep subglacial basins, possibly floored by oceanic crust.

The Antarctic Peninsula is a magmatic arc which has been active from Triassic times. Subduction of the Pacific Ocean floor beneath the margin of Gondwana gave rise to a chain of volcanoes which, together with deep-seated intrusions of granitic rocks, gradually built up an area of land. Accretion of sediment against the arc and erosion of the emerging land mass leading to deposition of sediments along its flanks, produced the geology we see in the peninsula today. Events in the Marie Byrd Land and Eights Coast–Thurston Island regions are less certain. Similar subduction processes probably occurred to a limited extent but outcrops of Palaeozoic crust are much commoner than in the Antarctic Peninsula and large areas of both regions are dominated by much younger vulcanism.

The geology of the Ellsworth Mountains–Thiel Mountains ridge is closely akin to that of the Transantarctic Mountains although the structural trend is different. Some authorities consider that there was little relative movement between the continental fragments that make up Lesser Antarctica whereas others believe that there was considerable movement and that the Ellsworth Mountains underwent a 90° rotation during lateral movement from an original position much closer to Dronning Maud Land. This latter theory does maintain a structural trend parallel to the Transantarctic Mountains and places the only known rocks in Lesser Antarctica with an age of 1000 million years (Haag Nunataks) much closer to the ancient shield of Greater Antarctica. However, critical evidence to sway the argument in favour of either theory is still being sought.

Northward of the Antarctic Peninsula, a system of largely submarine ridges and troughs loops around the Scotia Sea to join the Andean mountain chain in South America at Tierra del Fuego, with original continental fragments surfacing in the South Orkney Islands and South Georgia. Westward from Marie Byrd Land, the magmatic and deformational belt may extend through New Zealand and the western Pacific margin.

Geophysics

Because only 1% of the land area of Antarctica is exposed rock, much of the data relating to the structural and tectonic history has been gathered by geophysical methods. During the International Geophysical Year in 1957/58, a number of gravity and seismic surveys over the ice sheet were made during tractor traverses. These large ground-based operations were continued until the mid 1960s mainly by the USA and the Soviet Union and have been carried out intermittently by other countries as well since then. Aeromagnetic surveys have been carried out principally in Lesser Antarctica and the Transantarctic Mountains, with some information being gathered from the coast of Greater Antarctica. More recently, aeromagnetic surveys have been combined with radar sounding surveys of ice thickness. However, there has been relatively little increase in knowledge of the deep crustal structure of Antarctica in the last decade.

Although 99% of Antarctica is covered by ice, bedrock topography has been investigated over most of Lesser Antarctica and over more than half of Greater Antarctica by various ice sounding methods, but predominantly by airborne radar. Interpretation of the subglacial structure relies more on global analogies than on integration of geophysical data because of the lack of deep crustal studies. However, numerous features in the bedrock relief, such as extensive escarpments, basins, deep troughs, and valleys of outlet glaciers, can be recognized and interpreted as reflecting crustal structures. Bedrock depressions, bounded by steep sides and characterised by considerable depth and width, are probably major rift valleys associated with crustal stretching. Such rifts are numerous in Lesser Antarctica and around the margin of Greater Antarctica. Indeed, it has been suggested that the number of rifts and rift-like features is unparalleled on other continents. However, as most of the prominent rifts are usually occupied by large ice streams there is some uncertainty about whether they have been formed purely by erosion or that the ice, by removing the sedimentary fill, has accentuated the rift morphology. Sub-ice topography is often reflected in a subdued form on the surface of the ice sheet which can be clearly seen in satellite images. As on other continents, linear features can be identified and traced across large areas.

The basic morphology of Antarctica is well illustrated by the subglacial topography. After allowing for full isostatic recovery of the crust from the weight of the ice sheet, the subglacial contours show Greater Antarctica as a single unit and Lesser Antarctica as consisting of several major blocks separated by bedrock depressions as much as 2000 m below sea level, particularly in the Byrd Subglacial Basin. The continental shelf is anomalously

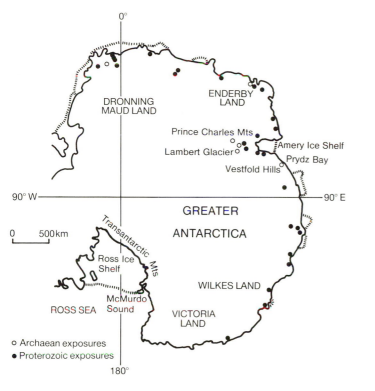

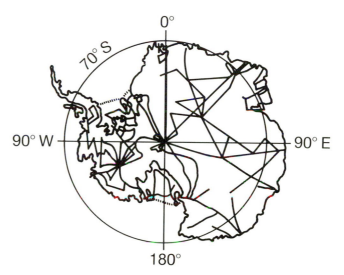

Greater Antarctic lies mainly in the eastern hemisphere and Lesser Antarctica in the western. Archaean and Proterozoic rock exposures are concentrated along the coast of Greater Antarctica; the only known Proterozoic rocks in Lesser Antarctica are found at Haag Nunataks.

Major oversnow traverses undertaken since 1957.

LANDSAT picture of an area to the west of the Ellsworth Mountains. The surface of the overlying ice sheet reflects the subglacial topography.

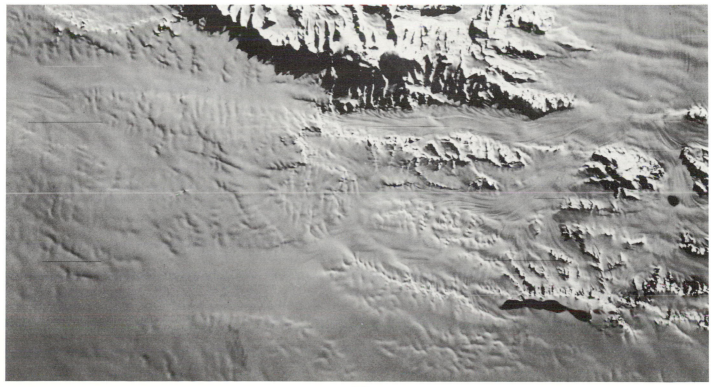

deep, averaging about 400 m below sea level compared with the worldwide average of 130 m for the other continents; this difference is often explained as the result of crustal depression by the ice load.

Gravity and seismic data show that Antarctica's major bedrock depressions are also sedimentary basins. In Lesser Antarctica, seismic velocities typical of lower crustal basement rocks occur several kilometres below the base of the ice sheet, indicating sediments up to 4 km thick. In the seas around Lesser Antarctica seismic reflection and refraction shooting have also revealed sedimentary strata exceeding 4 km in thickness. The principal basins, in the Weddell, Bellingshausen, Amundsen and Ross seas, may contain hydrocarbons, but the origin and nature of these basins must be understood before being able to judge their potential. In Greater Antarctica, the largest subglacial basin is in Wilkes Land, while the Prydz Bay–Lambert Glacier area forms a major rift system which is believed to extend inland to the Gamburtsev Mountains. Both these regions may contain considerable thicknesses of sedimentary rocks.

The crystalline basement underlying most of Greater Antarctica is best detected by shallow seismic refraction studies. High seismic velocities indicating crystalline rocks have been recorded in many areas, both beneath the sediments filling subglacial basins and also beneath the Transantarctic Mountains. The crystalline basement can also be detected by magnetic surveys, used to determine the depth to the upper boundary of magnetic bodies in the crust. This 'magnetic' surface is usually taken to be the top of the crystalline basement because sediments generally have a much lower magnetisation. Thick sedimentary basins subdue the magnetic signature, giving long wavelength anomalies with a 'magnetic' surface that subsides beneath the topographic surface. In Lesser Antarctica it has proved particularly difficult to locate crystalline basement rocks but results from the Ellsworth Mountains region indicate a similarity in the underlying crust to that in Greater Antarctica, possibly suggesting a closer relationship between the two regions in the past.

The superficial distinction between Greater and Lesser Antarctica as shown by the subglacial topography extends through the crust. The thickness of the crust has been

Distinctive colour banding of a sedimentary sequence of rocks.

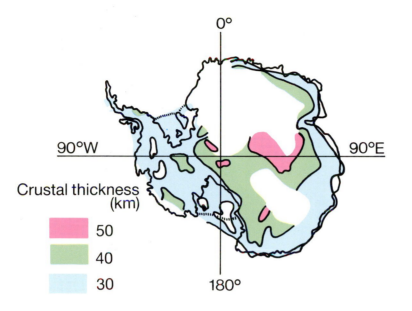

0°

90°W

90°E

180°

Crustal thickness
(km)

- 50
- 40
- 30

Crustal thickness calculated from gravity anomalies.

calculated from a few deep seismic soundings and from gravity measurements. Under the Greater Antarctic shield the mean value of the crustal thickness is about 40–45 km, typical of Archaean shields elsewhere in the world. Values exceeding 50 km occur in several places near the Transantarctic Mountains and in Dronning Maud Land, with the greatest values of up to 60 km occurring beneath the Gamburtsev Mountains. In Lesser Antarctica the thickest crust lies under the Antarctic Peninsula block, the Ellsworth Mountains and Marie Byrd Land. In these regions the crustal thickness reaches 40 km. Much lower values down to 25 km are calculated for the major rifts around the Ellsworth Mountains, along the margin of the Transantarctic Mountains and in the Lambert Glacier area in Greater Antarctica. The free-air gravity anomaly map shows a band of anomalies stretching across most of Greater Antarctica parallel and close to the Transantarctic Mountains, possibly due to very thick crust. Alternatively, the anomalies may be explained by a deeper-seated cause beneath the crust in the upper mantle. Either way, the scarp of the Transantarctic Mountains forms the most striking linear feature of the continent and represents an ancient structural suture around the edge of a Precambrian shield.

There are other respects in which Antarctica appears strange in comparison with other continents. No large earthquakes have been recorded within the Antarctic plate and the seismicity is the lowest of any continent. Only three earthquakes of magnitude greater than 4 on the Richter scale have been traced to Antarctic epicentres

and they have all been close to large outlet glaciers. It is uncertain if ice movement has been the cause or whether the earthquakes are associated with subglacial fault zones exploited by the glaciers. The total intraplate seismicity, however, is as large as other slow-moving continental plates such as Africa. The rare heat-flow measurements that have been made suggest a high flow in the McMurdo Sound area, with values similar to those found in the Basin and Range province in the USA. Unexpectedly high heat-flow values have also been found in Lutzow–Holm Bay, a marginal area of the Greater Antarctic shield and part of the continental shelf. The high heat flux in McMurdo Sound may be due to high temperatures at the crust–mantle boundary, which would be consistent with the Quaternary basaltic vulcanism in the area.

Magnetic data from the MAGSAT satellite have been used to construct a total field anomaly map over most of Antarctica. Although much of the interpretation of the map is at present uncertain, it appears that the anomalies seen in Greater Antarctica are associated with structures formed prior to the Gondwana break-up. Unfortunately, in Lesser Antarctica there is no clear correspondence between anomalies and tectonic features. Despite MAGSAT data not being able to solve the puzzle of reconstructing Gondwana, at least in Lesser Antarctica, data from polar orbiting satellites measuring gravity and magnetic fields are likely to be essential components in future attempts at synthesis. More deep seismic soundings are also required to help increase our knowledge and understanding of the Antarctic crust.

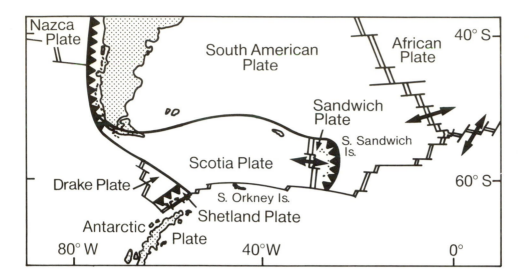

Presumed boundaries of the Scotia Plate.

Tectonic history of Lesser Antarctica

The striking mirror symmetry of the bending at the tip of South America and of the Antarctic Peninsula has intrigued minds from different disciplines for many years. It has been used as a textbook example of plastic deformation with an assumed but unexplained force punching a hole through a pre-existing straight mountain chain. Such simplicity is no longer apparent in the multitude of different models proposed by geologists and geophysicists attempting to unravel the undoubtedly complicated history of the region.

The Antarctic Peninsula has long been considered to be a southern extension of the South American Cordillera, with the relatively narrow but deep gap of the Drake Passage bridged by the Scotia Ridge. The evolution of the area, and the opening of the Drake Passage in particular, has profound consequences for climatic modelling, physical oceanography, geology and geophysics. South America was the last continent to separate from Antarctica so that the onset of a vigorous circumpolar ocean current occurred only after the breaching of this land bridge. This event modified ocean circulation worldwide and isolated Antarctica climatically which is believed to have led to the initiation of the Antarctic Ice Sheet.

The Scotia arc forms part of the boundary region between two major tectonic plates, the South American and the Antarctic plates. The Scotia Sea has been the site of intense marine geophysical investigations which have revealed the immense complexity of the region. Even now the evolution of the region is not fully understood but the analogy with a hole being punched through a mountain belt continuous from South America to the Antarctic Peninsula is a gross oversimplification. The margins of the Scotia plate show eastward movement along the north Scotia Ridge and westward movement along the south

Scotia Ridge, implying clockwise rotation of the plate. In fact there is no such wholesale rotation but the differential movements are achieved by a complex interplay of spreading centres and transcurrent faults. The most recent spreading centre has been active for the past 8 million years west of the South Sandwich Islands whereas the westward-dipping subduction zone to the east of the South Sandwich Islands' volcanic arc may have been active since Cretaceous times. This region forms one of the most active volcanic and earthquake zones around the Antarctic plate. Active vulcanism is also found today at Deception Island in Bransfield Strait, a recent extensional basin formed in response to continued subduction to the north west of the South Shetland Islands.

It is now recognized that the geological history of the Antarctic Peninsula has been dominated by igneous activity related to subduction of the crust of the Pacific Ocean floor from late Palaeozoic to late Tertiary times. The peninsula and southern South America share a similar history and have broadly comparable Pacific margin magmatic arc development. However, there must have been greater uplift in South America as the arc rocks are exposed to a deeper structural level and much of the volcanic superstructure has been eroded.

The oldest rocks in the Antarctic Peninsula that have been reliably dated are of Triassic age, although some gneisses on the east coast of Graham Land may have a Precambrian or early Palaeozoic origin. The exposed rocks are dominated by outcrops of magmatic rocks, both volcanic and plutonic, although rocks formed by accretion during subduction and sedimentary rocks resulting from erosion of the emergent arc are also present.

Reconstruction of the Scotia arc to its pre-Gondwana break-up geographical position with South America is complicated by its active and varied geological history since then. Two of the more probable models both place

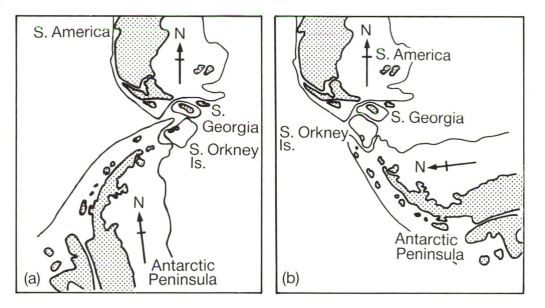

Two suggested reconstructions of South America and the Antarctic Peninsula: (a) based mainly on marine geophysical observations; and (b) based on geological evidence.

the northern tip of the Antarctic Peninsula close to the southern tip of South America, removing the oceanic crust created by sea-floor spreading in Drake Passage during the past 30 million years. In one model, where this is the only movement allowed, an eastward-pointing cusp occurs at the junction between South America and the Antarctic Peninsula. This requires acute angles of intersection of structural and intrusive trends in Mesozoic subduction complexes between South America and the platforms of South Georgia and the South Orkney Islands. Such changes do occur elsewhere along the Pacific margin, however, and perhaps the greatest doubt in this reconstruction is the relative isolation of South Georgia from the Pacific margin until the opening of Drake Passage 30 million years ago. This is inconsistent with the late Jurassic to early Cretaceous magmatic arc–marginal basin setting of the island. An alternative model has the Antarctic Peninsula rotated counterclockwise by over 90°. The trend of the peninsula then follows that of the Fuegian Andes and most of the angularity of the cusp is removed. It presents an acceptable model for the geological development of the fore-arc and arc terrains. Rotation of the peninsula to its present position may be due to opening of the Weddell Sea basin. The first model was derived from a marine geophysical standpoint and the second from a geological one. An independent way of testing these models would be by palaeomagnetism. However, the present high latitude of the Antarctic Peninsula and its small variation in latitude with time could make the resolution of the original magnetic declination difficult.

To the south of the Antarctic Peninsula, the boundary between Greater and Lesser Antarctic is represented by a broad region parallel to the trend of the Transantarctic

Mountains, lying between the Ross and Ronne ice shelves. It has geological affinities with both Greater and Lesser Antarctica and the complexity of the geology and the tectonic structure point to this area as being important for understanding the causes of the Gondwana break-up. Reconstruction in this region has proved one of the most intractable problems for the whole of Gondwana, partly because of the apparently fragmented character of the assumed microcontinental plates and partly because of the paucity of rock outcrops.

The Ellsworth Mountains are a central feature of Lesser Antarctica but for a long time their structural trend, at a large angle to the trends in the Antarctic Peninsula and the Transantarctic Mountains, has been considered anomalous. However, their broad geological similarity with other parts of the Transantarctic Mountains suggests that they have been moved from a position near the margin of the Greater Antarctic craton. If the present-day pattern of folding is compared with the relationship between the Cape fold belt and craton in South Africa, then an anticlockwise rotation of the Ellsworth block from its original position is suggested. Supporting evidence for such a rotation comes from palaeomagnetic measurements. In an extension of this model for the tectonic evolution of the area it has been suggested that the Ellsworth Mountains were originally located along the west coasts of Coats Land or Dronning Maud Land. However, recent field work, particularly new structural and palaeomagnetic data, is providing further constraints on the position of the Ellsworth Mountains and suggests that the anticlockwise rotation previously described is incorrect. In both these models some affinities are explained but other problems are raised.

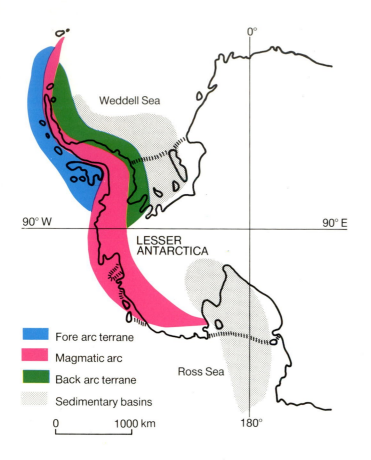

General division of Lesser Antarctica into forearc and backarc terranes during the late Mesozoic to Early Cenozoic.

Legend:
- Fore arc terrane
- Magmatic arc
- Back arc terrane
- Sedimentary basins

0   1000 km

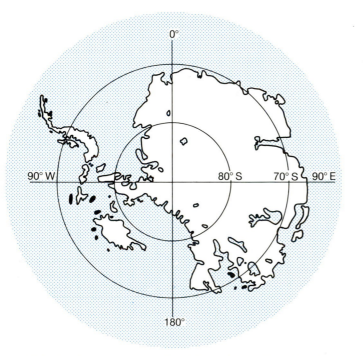

If the ice sheet were removed and the bedrock allowed to adjust isostatically, the Antarctic coastline would probably look like this.

Economic resources

The geological resources creating most interest are minerals and hydrocarbons. Although significant occurrences of economic minerals have been found in some places in Antarctica, none is considered to be commercially exploitable at current market prices. By way of contrast, there is no direct evidence of any petroleum reserves. Small traces of methane and ethane from holes drilled in the Ross Sea by the Glomar Challenger in late 1972 and early 1973, and traces of thermogenic hydrocarbons in Bransfield Strait are the only reported occurrences. Other kinds of deposits, such as sands and gravels, could only be of interest if they were close to a site of industrial development or related infrastructure. Despite this discouraging prospect, both hope and political pressure keep public attention focussed on the possibility of finding great mineral and oil wealth in Antarctica.

The justification for this hope is based largely on analogies with other continents. Predictions about the likely distribution of mineral resources are often made using the location of Antarctica in Gondwana as a guide. Precambrian rocks in the Greater Antarctic shield have affinities with those in South Africa, India and Australia, where many are rich in metallic ores. In South Africa, the Proterozoic Witwatersrand System contains gold and uranium, while chromium, nickel, copper, platinum, iron and vanadium occur in the Lower Proterozoic Bushveld complex, a layered gabbroic intrusion. Iron and manganese are found in Indian rocks of Archaean and Proterozoic age. The Australian shield contains nickel, gold and iron in Archaean rocks and iron, copper, lead, zinc and silver in Proterozoic deposits. Palaeozoic rocks in central and eastern Australia comprising the Tasman belt contain numerous, although mostly small, mineral deposits. These rocks may be correlated with the Ross belt of the Transantarctic Mountains and could be associated with the Mozambique Pan-African thermal event partly represented along the eastern side of Africa. The Andean magmatic and deformational belt extends around the Pacific margin through New Zealand, Marie Byrd Land, the Antarctic Peninsula and the Andes of South America. The northern and central Andes is one of the richest metal-producing areas in the world, but few metallic ores are found in the southern part of the Andes. In New Zealand most mineral deposits are small and consist mainly of gold, tin and copper.

Three metallogenic provinces have been recognised in Antarctica. The Greater Antarctic Iron Metallogenic Province describes the extensive occurence of iron minerals over most exposed parts of Greater Antarctica from Wilkes Land to Dronning Maud Land. The largest iron-formation deposits occur in the Prince Charles Mountains,

Volcanic eruption on Deception Island, South Shetland Islands,
in 1969.

where sequences more than 1000 m thick contain greenschist facies jaspilite beds up to 70 m thick alternating with slate, quartzite and metamorphosed gabbro and volcanic rocks. Aeromagnetic measurements suggest that the deposits extend up to 180 km under the ice, comparable in size to large deposits elsewhere in the world. However, the deposits are considered to be of lesser thickness and grade than commercial banded iron-formations in Australia.

The Transantarctic Metallogenic Province was formed in at least two metallogenic epochs, in the early Palaeozoic and in the Jurassic. Metal occurrences in the older (Ross) subprovince are small and are comparable to those of the eastern part of the Tasman fold belt. The Ferrar subprovince includes metallic minerals within the Middle Jurassic Ferrar Group of basic intrusive sheets. These occur in many places along the Transantarctic Mountains, but by far the largest body is the gabbroic Dufek intrusion in the Pensacola Mountains. The only other layered igneous complex in the world to rival its size is the enormously rich Bushveld Complex in South Africa. Although most of the Dufek intrusion is hidden beneath the ice, airborne geophysical measurements suggest that it covers an area of more than 50 000 km². There has been comparatively little field work done and only a small number of rock samples have been analysed. By analogy with similar bodies that contain economically important deposits, metals such as chromium, nickel, copper, vanadium, titanium and particularly the platinum group elements (PGE) are the ones most likely to be of interest. Although no metal concentrations of present economic significance have been found, PGE abundances in other complexes are known to be extremely variable and worthwhile deposits are usually found only by chance or by thorough prospecting. The mineralogy and chemistry of the Dufek intrusion are similar to those of other layered bodies at equivalent stratigraphical levels. Current data have been compared specifically with the Bushveld Complex in South Africa and these have been used to speculate that an equivalent to the Merensky Reef, rich in PGE, may be present about 1000 m below the lowest exposed part of the Dufek intrusion. Proof of the theory can only be obtained by drilling, which would undoubtedly have happened by now if the Dufek intrusion had been situated in a more favourable locality outside Antarctica. Even so, the vast age difference of 1900 million years between the formation of these two intrusions may render such comparisons invalid. At present, any mining house would need more than the available evidence before launching a serious venture to the Dufek intrusion. However, oversnow vehicles have pioneered a route to the coast, so that prospecting could soon be possible.

The Andean Metallogenic Province is of Mesozoic and Cenozoic age and stretches from South America through the Antarctic Peninsula and Ellsworth Land to Marie Byrd Land. Most of the reported metallic mineral shows occur in the Antarctic Peninsula and eastern Ellsworth Land and are related to the formation of alkaline igneous rocks. Occurrences containing copper and iron are the most common, but minerals containing molybdenum, lead, zinc, silver and other elements are also found. The largest occurrence is thought to be on King George Island, South Shetland Islands, and belongs to the copper subprovince but even this is far too small to be of commercial interest. Many of the rocks showing evidence of copper in the Antarctic Peninsula and Ellsworth Land appear to have been exposed by deep erosion. But Palmer Land may not be so deeply eroded and could be the best prospect for porphyry copper deposits.

The greatest likelihood of finding a commercial mineral deposit in Antarctica is thought to be in the Antarctic Peninsula or eastern Ellsworth Land, but the relative scarcity of minerals in the southern Andes compared with the central and northern Andes may extend across Drake Passage. In Greater Antarctica, analogies with Gondwana neighbours suggest that Wilkes Land may contain nickel and gold, that Dronning Maud Land may contain gold, uranium and even diamond-bearing kimberlite pipes, and that the Transantarctic Mountains may contain deposits of copper and related metals. However, because there are no exact parallels with other continents, it is more likely that any commercial deposit will be found by serendipity.

At present there are insufficient data to make reliable estimates of undiscovered hydrocarbon resources in Antarctica. Because of the harsh environment, it is likely that only supergiant fields (greater than 2 billion barrels) will be economic. It has been estimated that only a few fields of this size remain to be discovered in the world. The only practicable areas for exploitation are the continental margins which are free from a moving, grounded ice sheet. Unmetamorphosed sedimentary basins border the Weddell, Bellingshausen, Amundsen and Ross seas in Lesser Antarctica and the Amery Ice Shelf in Greater Antarctica. Marine multichannel seismic reflection studies have been carried out by a number of countries investigating the continental shelves, and the results, combined with other geophysical data, suggest that sediment thicknesses of several kilometres are usual. Drilling in the Ross Sea by the Deep Sea Drilling Project in 1972/73 revealed some methane but no economic significance was attached to the hydrocarbon potential. The largest known sources of energy are the Permian age coal measures in the Beacon strata of the Prince Charles Mountains and numerous but smaller occurrences scattered throughout the Transantarctic Mountains. However, it is unlikely that this coal will be needed for a long time.

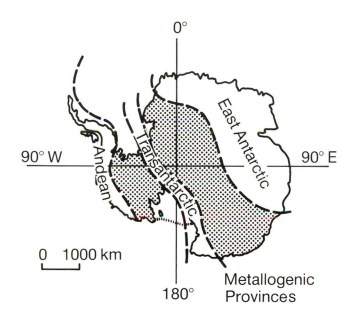

0°

East Antarctic

90° W   Andean   Transantarctic   90° E

0 1000 km

180°   Metallogenic
        Provinces

Major metallogenic provinces.

Climatic record

The existence of coal beds was taken by early explorers of Antarctica to indicate that the continent had not always been covered by ice. Fossil floras found in Mesozoic strata also suggest that the climate was at least temperate for most of this time. However, the only Mesozoic sedimentary rocks exposed in Antarctica are the Triassic strata in the Transantarctic Mountains and the Jurassic and Cretaceous rocks in the Antarctic Peninsula. None shows evidence of glacial activity, but this has not been held to rule out the possibility of limited Mesozoic glaciation. Climatic model-ling on the basis of zonal energy balance suggests that it is difficult to maintain the high latitude warmth and low temperature gradients which are usually inferred from indicators of Mesozoic climate. As an example, the late Permian to early Tertiary floras which occur at palaeo-latitudes of 65–80°S seem to indicate warm temperate conditions with frost-free winters, long growing seasons and at least some light during the winter. However, at these polar latitudes little light or solar energy would have been

available for several months each year and the growing season would have been restricted to less than 3 months. This enigma may have several possible explanations. The earth may have had a smaller axial obliquity, evening out the length of day, but this would have resulted in a rather seasonless climate and growth rings in fossil wood are strong evidence of marked seasonal growth. The palaeo-latitudes, determined by palaeomagnetic data, may be in-accurate if the magnetic and geographic poles separated during the Mesozoic. The polar climate may have been warmer, probably due to increased levels of atmospheric carbon dioxide creating a 'greenhouse' effect as suggested by other evidence, but the problem about availability of light remains. The plants may have been adapted to this special environment by a period of winter dormancy. None of these possibilities is wholly convincing by itself, although a combination of them may be sufficient to explain the apparent inconsistency between the palaeo-botanical and palaeolatitudinal evidence.

It is now generally agreed that the present ice sheet was initiated during the Tertiary period, after a prolonged interval of relative warmth since the end of glaciation in Gondwana in early Permian time. Information about the initiation and subsequent history of the Antarctic ice sheet is contained in the marine geological record of the Antarctic sea floor and of the world's oceans, as well as in the terrestrial geological record on the continent. In marine geology, interpretation of data from sediment cores de-pends upon assumptions made about the thermal structure in the southern oceans; palaeo-oceanography and palaeo-climatology are linked together. The main lines of marine evidence are the measurement of oxygen and carbon isotope composition of the calcite shells of Foraminifera, history of ice rafting, microfaunal assemblages, and sedi-mentary discontinuities. However, the piecemeal nature of the record and the need to extrapolate inferences about ocean conditions from Subantarctica or even more distant sites back to Antarctica makes interpretation difficult and has led to disagreements. There is an ambiguity in inter-preting changes in oxygen isotope ratios in ocean sedi-ments because temperature as well as isotopic dilution can affect the composition. Thus, using oxygen isotope records from deep-sea cores as indicators of global ice volume may not be as reliable as was once thought. Instead, it may be that carbon isotopes give a better record of climatic change. In Antarctica itself, the best information about Cenozoic glacial history comes from studies of landforms and glacial deposits, and from dating volcanic rocks iden-tified as having been erupted substantially subglacially. In Marie Byrd Land, glassy lavas of Oligocene age (27 million years) have been used to suggest the existence of the Lesser Antarctic ice sheet at that time; however, other

Belemnites are extinct cephalopods that were similar to squids. They are found most commonly in Jurassic and Cretaceous rocks where they are of stratigraphic value.

Geologist examining a rock face.

studies throw doubt on the size of the ice sheet that may have existed then.

Some glacial deposits found high in the Transantarctic Mountains have been shown to contain marine fossils only a few million years old. They occur too high up to have been originally deposited at sea level and then subsequently raised during a period of uplift; the required rates of lifting would be an order of magnitude greater than any so far proposed using other lines of evidence. Signs of mixing, with assemblages of microfossils of different ages varying from late Cretaceous to Pliocene occurring together, suggest that there has been considerable reworking of the sediments. One explanation is that about 4–5 million years ago the ice sheet was much smaller than now and that

there was an open seaway between Wilkes Land and the Weddell Sea, along the present-day inland flank of the Transantarctic Mountains. Subsequent growth of the ice sheet in Greater Antarctica could have picked up sediments in the basal layers of the ice and transported them towards and then over the Transantarctic Mountains. The sediments might eventually have been redeposited during a period of retreat or because of basal melting. If this account is accepted, it implies that variations in sea level previously thought to have been caused by fluctuations in the ice sheets in the northern hemisphere or Lesser Antarctica may instead be due to changes in size of the ice sheet over Greater Antarctica. There is still much to learn about the climatic history of Antarctica.

Ice and rock, the dominating themes of Antarctica. This isolated nunatak is Oberon Peak at the head of the Uranus Glacier on Alexander Island.

Part·IV
The Antarctic atmosphere

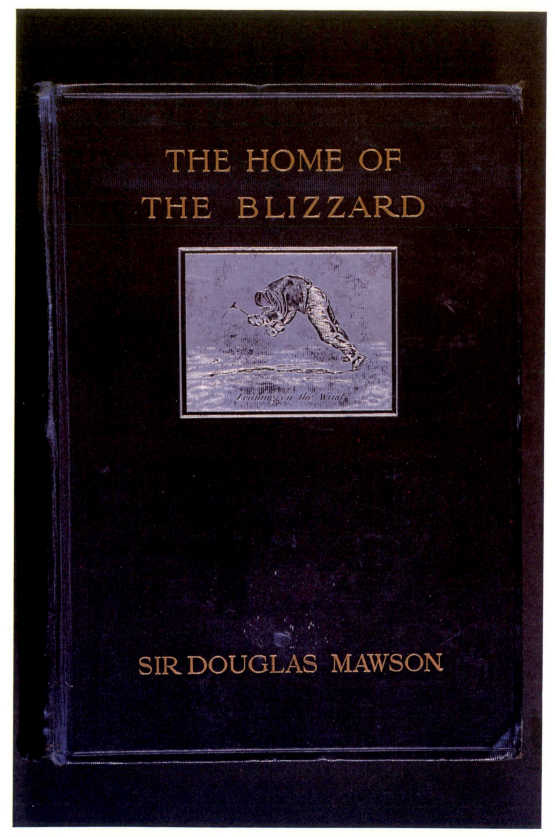

THE HOME OF
THE BLIZZARD

Leaning on the Wind

SIR DOUGLAS MAWSON

Mawson's expedition had to cope with incredible katabatic winds. '—— in good spikes, in a steady wind one had only to push hard to keep a sure footing. it would not be true to say "to keep erect" for equilibrium was maintained by leaning against the wind.

Ensconced in the lee of a substantial break-wind, one could leisurely observe the unnatural appearance of others walking about, apparently in imminent peril of falling on their faces.'

Chapter·14
Climate of extremes

Introduction

The climate of Antarctica is surely the most extreme of any on earth. It is the coldest and the most windy place on the globe and, remarkably, given the volume of ice it contains, Antarctica is also the largest desert on earth. The mean temperature is so low that fuel oil turns to jelly and boiling water thrown into the air will spontaneously 'explode' into ice crystals before reaching the ground. The wind can be so strong that the great Australian polar explorer Sir Douglas Mawson observed of the weather at Cape Denison that it 'proved to be little more than one continuous blizzard the year round; a hurricane of wind roaring for weeks together, pausing for breath only at odd hours'. With a mean annual windspeed of 50 mph (80 km h^{-1}) being recorded during 1912, and gusts in excess of 200 mph (320 km h^{-1}), he could not be accused of exaggeration! Inland, almost no snow falls, in fact for most of the polar plateau the annual rate of snowfall is below 5 cm (water equivalent) – very similar to the Sahara Desert! About the only meteorological happening one is safe from is being struck by lightning, since thunderstorms are unknown.

Geological history of the Antarctic climate

It is perhaps difficult to imagine, given these extremes of climate, that a mere 500 million years ago Antarctica was situated near the equator, and for the intervening time has probably had a mainly temperate climate supporting a rich vegetation. As Chapter 13 has shown, Antarctica was once part of the vast continental landmass known as Gondwana, and drifted through the whole range of climatic zones from the equator to the polar region as that super-continent wandered and evolved. It is now believed that Antarctica first approached the South Pole about 280 million years before present (BP), and was most probably heavily ice covered at that time since it was at the height of the Permo-Carboniferous ice age. Subsequently, conti-nental drift carried it equatorwards and then polewards again, so that it finally arrived in the vicinity of the pole about 100 million years BP. However, it only became a separate continent surrounded by the circumpolar Antarctic Ocean about 30 million years BP. It is from around then that the present climate of the continent has evolved.

It is still uncertain how the climate of the south polar zone, and indeed that of the whole globe, developed during this period. There is little direct evidence of the global variations of palaeotemperature, windspeed or precipitation, and no reliable indicators of atmospheric pressure upon which to base quantitative conclusions. Theoretical studies using computers which model possible palaeoclimates have played a part in unravelling the mysteries, but they lack sufficiently well defined boundary conditions (for instance, on the distribution of land masses and mountains) to give unequivocal conclusions.

Experimental palaeoclimatology is still largely a matter of detective work based upon the assessment of a number of indirect experimental clues. The most useful come from

Boiling water explodes into ice crystals when thrown into very cold Antarctic air.

193

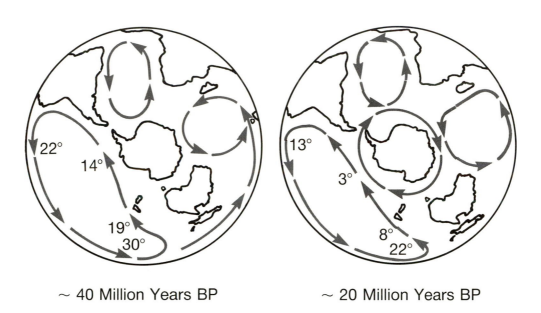

~ 40 Million Years BP   ~ 20 Million Years BP

The opening of the southern ocean, as a result of the separation of Antarctica from South America and Australia, allowed the formation of the West Wind Drift and the consequent cooling of the southern ocean and continent.

studies of the global distributions of fossils and from the geochemistry of sedimentary deposits. Both can give information on temperature and rainfall, but it is essential when interpreting these data to take account of such factors as continental drift, pole wandering and reversals of the direction of the earth's magnetic field. A major uncertainty in all palaeoclimatological work arises in the dating of the evidence.

There is general agreement amongst palaeoclimatologists that, at least qualitatively, the geological record indicates that the global climate was significantly warmer than now from the end of the Permo-Carboniferous ice age about 225 million years BP until the ice ages of the past million years. For most of this period, until about 65 million years BP, precipitation was much reduced globally. It is highly unlikely that Antarctica had a major permanent ice cap; indeed fossil evidence suggests that about 50

million years ago a cool-temperate climate prevailed which supported a vigorous vegetation, including such trees as the Monkey Puzzle (*Araucaria*) and the Southern Beech (*Nothofagus*). Thereafter, a marked increase in high-latitude precipitation occurred, for reasons that are presently obscure, heralding the start of the south polar ice build-up.

At the same time as this increase in rainfall occurred, Antarctica was separating from the continental land masses of Australia and South America. This allowed the development of the great circumpolar ocean current, the West Wind Drift, driven by the westerly circulation of the atmosphere. Ultimately this isolated the continent from warm ocean currents which had for so long transported heat from the tropical regions. The change in the oceanic circulation, and the consequent change in surface temperature, are believed to be closely related to movement in the continental positions. As the polar temperatures decreased, the temperature gradient from equator to pole increased, strengthening the westerly circulation and enhancing the cooling process.

It is likely that the formation of the West Wind Drift paved the way for the Quaternary ice ages which have periodically affected the globe in the last million years. This was of course not the only factor involved, as Chapter 11 has demonstrated. There is evidence from the Deep Sea Drilling Project sediment cores from the Southern Ocean that ice cover reached the Ross Sea coast about 25 million years BP, but then receded for reasons not yet clear. In fact, the cores suggest that the past 50 million years have been characterised by periodic changes in temperature. These may well be associated with variations in the earth's orbit around the sun which produce oscillations in the terrestrial energy budget (the Milankovitch cycles – see Chapter 11). It is probable that the formation of the present ice cap was completed about 13 million years ago. Certainly, it was at about this time that the cold Antarctic Bottom Water formed as a result of the seasonal melting of coastal ice.

Globally, the last million years have been characterised by a cyclic variation of climate, with alternating periods of glaciation and interglacial warmings. Throughout this time the Antarctic continent has remained frigid and ice covered, although at present the world as a whole is basking in a relatively warm period. Locked up in the permanent ice cap is a climatic record stretching back 100 000 years or more, covering the last ice age and the preceding interglacial warming. The main climatic parameter available is the mean surface temperature, which is derived from variations in the ratio of the abundances of the oxygen isotopes ^{18}O and ^{16}O. Other measurements related to climatic change which are used include the relative abundances of carbon dioxide (CO_2) and of atmospheric dust.

Data obtained from cores collected at Byrd Station and Dome C on the Antarctic plateau cover the past 40 000 years. The major climatic event revealed is the relatively sharp increase in temperature (estimated to be about 7°C) which occurred approximately 10 000 years ago and marked the end of the last ice age. There was a very dramatic increase in dust and decrease in CO_2 concentration associated with the peak of the glaciation. It is tempting to associate the dust with vulcanism, thereby providing evidence that screening of solar radiation by airborne volcanic dust is a major factor in ice age formation. However, analysis of the dust composition and particle size distribution suggests its presence was an effect rather than a cause of the cooling. It probably resulted from the combination of more vigorous atmospheric circulation

A frond of the tree fern Cladophlebis *preserved in the Cretaceous sandstone of Alexander Island, clear indication of a much warmer climate 100 million years ago.*

resulting from an increased temperature gradient between equator and pole, and the greatly expanded desert areas in the southern hemisphere continents which provided a source of dust at this time. The significance of the CO_2 variation is not clear; it could have been a factor in cause or effect. However, both perturbations would have contributed to the severity of the cooling at the height of the ice age through solar screening and a less efficient 'greenhouse' effect.

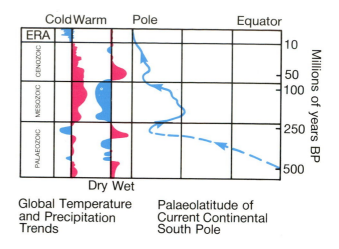

Global Temperature and Precipitation Trends

Palaeolatitude of Current Continental South Pole

The history of meteorological observations in Antarctica

The span of direct observation of the Antarctic climate is very short, just a little over 200 years. Captain James Cook was the first to bring back a reliable description of the meteorological conditions in the seas fringing the great ice continent 'near the pole which is the source of most of the ice that is spread over this vast Southern Ocean'. Forty-five years then passed before Cook's accounts of the weather near Antarctica were confirmed by the Russian explorer Bellingshausen who led the next journey of discovery into the South. The logbooks and narratives of sealing expeditions to the South American sector of the Southern Ocean give further descriptions of the weather, but up until 1839 the information available was generally descriptive and, where numerical, was of very doubtful quality. This was changed by James Clark Ross whose expedition made the first quantitative and systematic meteorological observations of lasting value near the Antarctic continent. One of the significant discoveries was that the mean surface atmospheric pressure was markedly lower in the southern hemisphere than in the northern.

The explanation for this perplexed meteorologists for some time before it was interpreted in terms of the much stronger westerly circulation prevailing in the south.

For the first 124 years of direct observations only ten expeditions penetrated south of 50°S and their observations were mostly of the ocean climate. Several of the expeditions did also collect meteorological data from some subantarctic islands. Notable amongst these were the Ross Expedition on Kerguelen, the British and German expeditions to observe the transit of Venus (1874–1875), also on Kerguelen, and the German expedition to Royal Bay, South Georgia, during the First International Polar Year (1882–1983).

At the turn of the century Antarctic meteorology underwent a revolutionary advance. The first of the wintering bases on the continent was at Cape Adare, Victoria Land, where the British Southern Cross Expedition made detailed daily observations of atmospheric pressure, temperature, humidity, windspeed and direction, cloud cover, precipitation, and sunshine from February 1899 until January 1900. These data gave the first clear indication of the weather conditions likely to confront any party exploring the interior. In all, seventeen expeditions visited the southern regions between 1897 and 1917. Of these, no less than fourteen spent a year or more there, and ten established wintering bases south of 60°S. Detailed and systematic meteorological observations were made at all these bases and on the journeys made into the interior. The Australasian Antarctic Expedition (1911–1914) to Cape Denison was notable in being the first to use radio regularly to communicate meteorological data to the outside world, a station being established on Macquarie Island for relay purposes. This expedition was also noteworthy for the

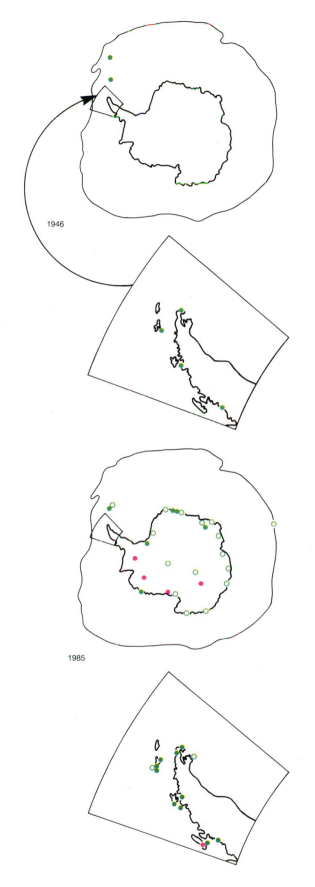

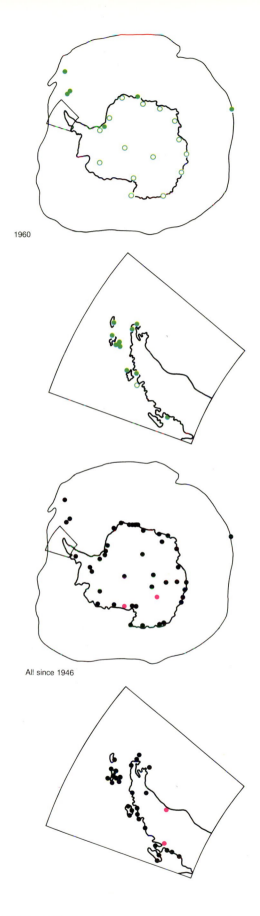

1946

1960

1985

All since 1946

The distribution of meteorological stations within the Antarctic Convergence showing the great expansion of activity resulting from the IGY, and the relatively small development since then. Stations are still far too thinly spread over the continent, though Automatic Weather Stations are starting to help.

Stations carrying out surface observations only are shown as solid green; those carrying out surface and upper air observations as green circles. Automatic weather stations are in red. All manned stations in operation for at least one winter are shown in black.

Meteorological balloon being prepared for flight during the British Antarctic Expedition (1910–13).

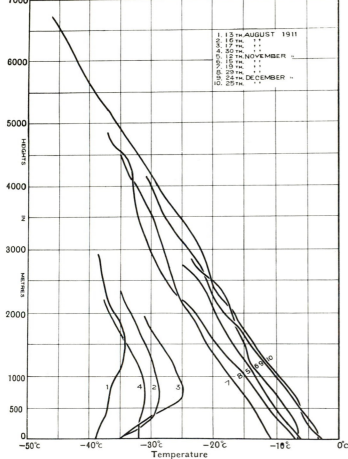

A summary of all the upper air temperatures recorded on the British Antarctic Expedition. These data provided the first systematic description of the Antarctic troposphere, including the occurrence of winter surface inversions.

incredible winds that it recorded, the normal daily condition being a full gale. The wind record was so extreme that the meteorological establishment was sceptical of its accuracy, and it was necessary to have the anemometers tested and recalibrated independently in London before the observations were accepted; 40 years later independent corroboration came from French observations made at Port Martin.

The very comprehensive meteorological programme of the British National Expedition (1910–1913) included the first measurements of the vertical profile of temperature above the continent, made using meteographs carried aloft by hydrogen-filled balloons. The meteograph recorded the temperature by marking a metal foil as the balloon ascended, making it necessary to recover the instrument. During summer this was done by taking a bearing on the package as it fell, then searching in that direction in the hope of finding it. In winter a fine silk line was attached to the package and paid out as the balloon rose; afterwards the line was followed in the polar night until the instrument was found! Unfortunately the line frequently broke half way. In all, twenty-one flights were attempted, of which ten produced good data. Rudimentary observations of the variations in lower tropospheric winds were also made by studying the behaviour of the smoke plume from Mount Erebus.

In 1903 a base was established by the Scottish National Antarctic Expedition at Laurie Island in the South Orkneys which turned out to be uniquely important for Antarctic meteorology. In 1904 this station was transferred to the Republic of Argentina which has maintained its sequence of observations ever since. The data set, though relatively short compared with those available from the northern hemisphere, forms the longest from Antarctica and is hence of particular value for studying climatic trends. A programme of meteorological observations began at the whaling station at Grytviken, South Georgia, in January 1905. This continued uninterrupted until April 1982, when it was abruptly terminated by the Argentine invasion. The data set is thus the longest unbroken run for a subantarctic island.

Admiral Byrd's expeditions during the 1930s produced important new information on the vertical structure of the polar atmosphere. Initially kites carried thermographs to determine the vertical profile of temperature, but subsequently these gave way to high-flying aircraft and an autogyro. The kites were launched from a small snow hut with a tarpaulin roof and a blubber stove for heating. Normally profiles were obtained to an altitude of about 1 km, and occasionally in excess of 2 km, using kites, and up to 11 km with the aircraft. Small hydrogen-filled balloons

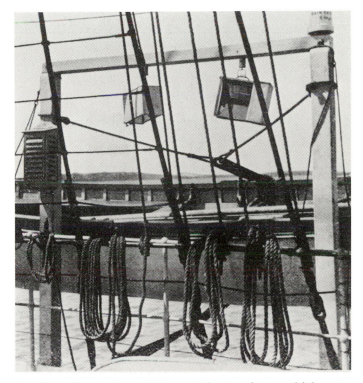

The meteorological instruments used on the Scottish National Antarctic Expedition both at the Laurie Island base and on board the Scotia.

were also routinely launched and tracked by theodolite to measure the vertical profile of wind velocity. In winter, paper lanterns containing lighted candles were suspended from the balloons to provide a target for tracking! The data provided the first seasonally representative information on tropospheric temperature and dynamics. In particular, the stable temperature inversion which occurs over the Antarctic in winter became evident for the first time.

Argentine and British expeditions which started during World War II were of great significance for Antarctic meteorology because both involved establishing more or less permanent manned stations in and around the Antarctic Peninsula. By the early 1950s there were seven British bases whilst the Argentinians operated eight. In addition, Chile had established four stations. The British bases sent synoptic weather data to Port Stanley in the Falkland Islands, from where it was rebroadcast as part of the Government-collected meteorological information broadcast known as FICOL. The Argentinians and Chilians made similar transmissions to their parent bodies. Meanwhile, the Australians had established Mawson Station

on the other side of the continent, from which synoptic surface and upper-air data were transmitted to the Australian Bureau of Meteorology.

Several scientific expeditions involving comprehensive meteorological programmes were mounted in the post-War years. The French Expedition which wintered at Port Martin during 1951 and 1952 was of particular note from a meteorological viewpoint. This site is about 60 km from Cape Denison where Mawson's expedition had recorded such extraordinary winds. Winds of similar ferocity were found to occur at Port Martin, indeed it is likely that the world record for daily average windspeed goes to the French Expedition with a figure of 48.5 m s^{-1} (108 mph). They also hold the record for the lowest sea level atmospheric pressure of 926.9 millibars.

The whaling fleets in the Southern Ocean played a major part in providing meteorological data. However, commercial pressures upon the masters of whaling vessels were such that they were most reluctant to reveal their ships' positions to competitors. To encourage them to broadcast weather information for use in forecasting it proved necessary to provide ciphers which only the Weather Bureau at the collecting centre (in South Africa) could decode. This initiative was sufficiently successful for daily weather maps to be constructed for two consecutive Antarctic summers (1955–1957) for the whole of the Southern Ocean.

Lest the impression be gained that by 1955 the meteorology of Antarctica was being widely and effectively sampled, it should be borne in mind that only twelve fixed, permanently manned weather stations were in operation south of 55°S. Most of these were located in a restricted area containing the Antarctic Peninsula and its adjacent islands, and only one continental station existed. It is also an unfortunate fact that, in general, Antarctic meteorological stations have not been located to provide the best scientific return. In the early days the expeditions were content to establish their wintering stations wherever the prevailing weather and sea-ice conditions allowed. Later, politics played (and still plays) a major role in the choice of location. This can lead to needless replication, the classic case being that of Deception Island. Here, Britain, Argentina and Chile operated meteorological stations within a few miles of each other for more than two decades. This state of affairs was abruptly terminated in 1967 by a major volcanic eruption on the island.

The International Geophysical Year (IGY) which took place in 1957/58 dramatically improved the situation. The meteorology and climatology of the world were identified as two of the primary areas of study for the IGY, and the Antarctic was recognized as a region of utmost importance for investigation. The outcome of this was an internationally coordinated programme to establish geophysical observatories in and around the continent. Synoptic surface weather observations were made at all these sites, and many also made daily upper-air measurements using balloons. A major advance resulted from the operation, through 1958, of an internationally staffed 'Weather Central' at Little America on the Antarctic continent. In addition, all the accumulated reports and data were used by South Africa to prepare a series of daily charts and grid-point data for the area, which provided the first detailed picture of the entire Antarctic meteorological environment and formed the basic material for much subsequent research. This series of analysed charts was continued by South Africa until the mid-1960s. In the meantime an International Antarctic Analysis (and later Research) Centre was established early in 1959 in Melbourne, Australia, by the cooperative efforts of several countries, acting through the International Council of Scientific Unions (ICSU), to continue on a near 'real-time' basis the work started by the Little America Weather Central. This led to the development of ongoing data analysis and research programmes during the 1960s which, in turn, enabled the World Meteorological Organisation to produce a detailed international plan in 1968 to bring the stations then in operation into the World Weather Watch.

No significant improvement in the observing network has occurred since 1968, and the spacing between observing sites still remains much larger than is desirable. Of the stations currently in operation south of 60°S, only seventeen have continuous data sets longer than 20 years. One of these is at the South Pole, six lie between 70° and 80°S, and the rest are between 60° and 70°S. This is just adequate for climatology purposes but certainly not for synoptic forecasting. In contrast, 340 stations are in operation in the USA alone, providing 50 times better spatial resolution. The virtual death of the whaling industry has left a major gap in meteorological coverage of the Southern Ocean. This is particularly true of the vast stretch of the Pacific Ocean from New Zealand to South America, where there are no islands on which to site observatories.

The impact of new technology

The IGY saw the first use of artificial satellites for scientific research. Satellites have since become indispensable for meteorological work, as they provide an unparalleled global view. Sequences of photographs taken from satellites provide information on the evolution of major weather systems, on the mean circulation of the atmosphere, and on variations in sea-ice cover. Properties of the atmosphere, such as temperature and the concentrations of important trace gases can be monitored globally by them. Communications satellites now provide a reliable means of relaying synoptic information from collection sites to regional forecasting centres in time for it to be useful. This is particularly valuable for a remote location such as Antarctica.

Observations from satellites, though critical for the development of meteorology, cannot replace fixed-point ground observations. An individual satellite may sample the whole globe each day, but the data from any specific location will necessarily be sparse, and it is very difficult to separate temporal changes from spatial changes unless ground observations are used for control. Also, techniques do not yet exist to sense remotely all the variables required, surface pressure being a prime example.

Major advances in the technology of ground observations have also occurred, culminating in the development of unmanned automatic weather stations (AWS). These consist of: sensors to measure atmospheric pressure, temperature, humidity, and windspeed and direction; a communications system, often employing satellites for relay; a microcomputer to control the operations; and some form of stored power source. Power may simply be provided by batteries, though for Antarctic use, where the AWS may be unattended for up to a year, more sophisticated supplies may be needed. Several techniques have been used with varying degrees of success; these include primary sources such as propane thermoelectric generators and radio-isotope thermoelectric generators, and wind generators for charging batteries. Radio-isotope generators have proved to be the most reliable but are also the most expensive.

The cost of establishing and maintaining a manned weather station in Antarctica is enormous. Thus the use of automatic stations makes good economic sense, and they have begun to play a major role in filling the gaps in and around Antarctica. The USA has led the field here with both sophisticated systems and more basic packages that can be dropped from aircraft, whilst both Australia and the UK have also deployed successful systems. The most extensive AWS programme in Antarctica to date has been developed by the USA with very reliable instrumentation providing temperature, pressure and wind velocity, and operating unattended for periods in excess of a year. Data is collected via the French ARGOS system which utilises American TIROS polar-orbiting satellites. Since 1980 more than twenty systems have been deployed in Antarctica, primarily in two regional networks: one on the Ross Ice Shelf aimed at studying the wind field over the shelf, and the other stretching from the French Station, Dumont d'Urville, to Dome C, for studies of katabatic winds (see p.212). The Ross Ice Shelf network also provides invaluable weather data in support of US air operations from McMurdo. A further network will become fully operational in the Antarctic Peninsula in 1986.

Weather sensors have also been incorporated into buoys deployed in the Southern Ocean, or dropped by parachute onto ice floes or icebergs. These were used to great effect during the First Global GARP Experiment (FGGE). FGGE was a period of special intensive global meteorological observation, forming part of the Global Atmospheric Research Programme (GARP) which occupied 12 months from December 1978. Over 300 buoys were released into the oceans of the southern hemisphere, providing measurements of surface temperature and pressure via ARGOS, which also tracked their positions. Throughout the winter of 1979, almost everywhere in the Southern Ocean from 20° to 65°S was within 500 km of an active buoy. This allowed a complete picture of pressure and temperature over the Southern Ocean to be available in meteorological forecasting centres in time to be used for the daily forecasts. This was a remarkable achievement of international cooperation which went largely unnoticed by the public. The data accumulated form the most complete description yet of the behaviour of the lower troposphere in the southern hemisphere, and will prove invaluable for benchmarking theoretical models of atmospheric circulation.

The global weather engine

The past and present climate of Antarctica is undoubtedly a subject of great academic interest, but who really cares if it snows tomorrow at the South Pole? Why should mankind invest so much money and skill in studying the weather of such a remote region – one which has no indigenous human population and no obvious economic benefits to offer? If the needs of the present temporary residents were the only reasons it would be very difficult to justify the resources involved. However, to devise a way of reliably forecasting weather and climate it is first necessary to understand how the atmosphere works. Fundamental to this is an appreciation of how the energy which drives the global weather systems is acquired, stored and distributed. Antarctica plays a key role in the energy balance of the globe and hence its climate affects us all in some way.

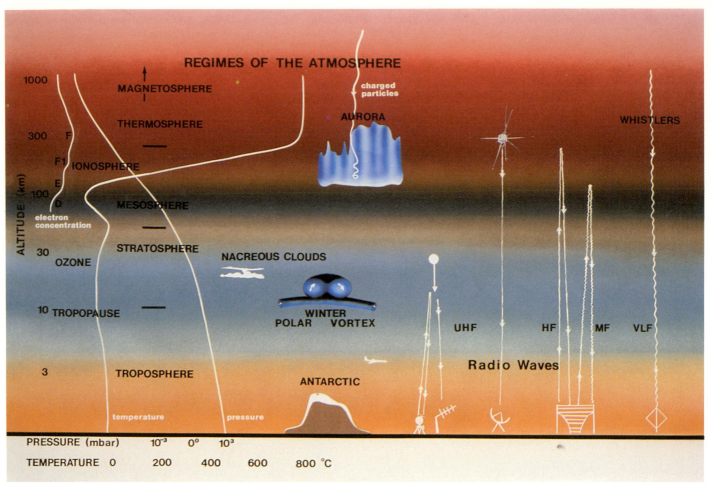

REGIMES OF THE ATMOSPHERE

MAGNETOSPHERE

THERMOSPHERE

IONOSPHERE

MESOSPHERE

electron concentration

STRATOSPHERE

OZONE

TROPOPAUSE

TROPOSPHERE

temperature   pressure

charged particles

AURORA

WHISTLERS

NACREOUS CLOUDS

WINTER POLAR VORTEX

ANTARCTIC

UHF   HF   MF   VLF

Radio Waves

ALTITUDE (km): 1000, 300, 100, 30, 10, 3

F, F1, E, D

PRESSURE (mbar)	10^{-3}	0^0	10^3		
TEMPERATURE	0	200	400	600	800 °C

The structure of the atmosphere.

The energy balance of Earth. Net input of energy over the low latitude region is exactly balanced by the net loss from the poles.

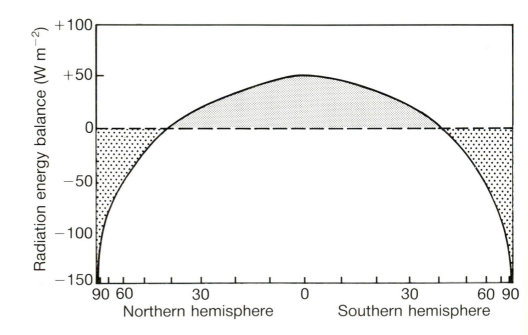

Radiation energy balance (W m^{-2})

+100, +50, 0, −50, −100, −150

90 60   30   0   30   60 90

Northern hemisphere   Southern hemisphere

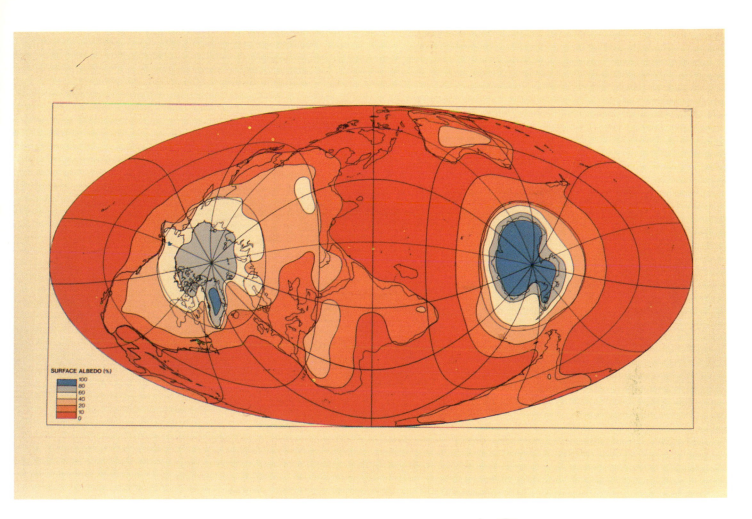

Global variations in the reflection of
radiation by the surface (albedo). Blue
areas are highly reflecting, whilst those in
red are highly absorbant. The Antarctic is a
better reflector than the Arctic, and the
spatial variations there are much simpler
and more closely meridional.

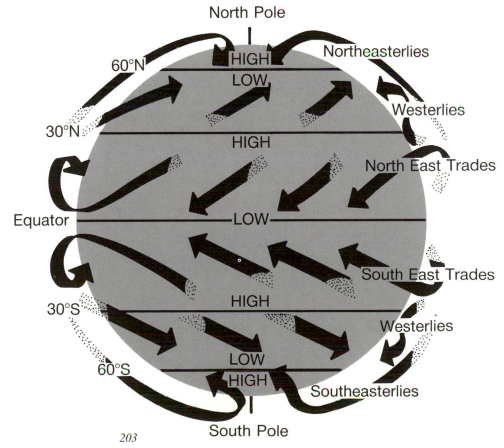

The general circulation of the atmosphere
results from the temperature gradient from
equator to pole and the rotation of the earth.

It has long been apparent to the nations of the southern hemisphere that the weather in Antarctica greatly influences their own. Meteorologists are now beginning to appreciate that accurate long-term forecasting for the northern hemisphere, and for global climate trends, requires the influence of Antarctica to be taken into account. The contrasts between Arctic and Antarctic weather also offer profound insights into the fundamental physics of the atmosphere. It is principally these factors which initiated, and have sustained, three decades of intensive meteorological research in Antarctica.

Our local energy source, the sun, emits a continuous stream of energy amounting to about 100 billion billion Megawatts (10^{20} MW). Only a small proportion falls upon the earth, arriving in two forms: electromagnetic waves (about 175 billion MW) and the solar wind (about 15 million MW). The latter consists of high-speed electrically charged subatomic particles accelerated in the sun's atmosphere. This wind is of fundamental importance for the near space environment of the earth, but electromagnetic radiation is the predominant energy source for the lower atmosphere.

The sun emits electromagnetic radiation over a very wide spectrum, but most of the output is visible light. About half of the incident energy reaches the earth's surface where it is absorbed, causing heating. The rest is either reflected back into space, from the ground, cloud tops, or by scattering from atmospheric dust, or is absorbed by various trace gases in the atmosphere and by clouds. Luckily, most harmful ultra-violet and X-radiation is absorbed by the atmosphere before it can reach the ground. The most energetic radiation is filtered out above 80 km, producing heating and ionisation in the region known as the thermosphere. Lower down, in the stratosphere, ultra-violet radiation is absorbed by ozone and nitrous oxide; whilst infra-red radiation is absorbed by water vapour and carbon dioxide.

Viewed globally and averaged over a year, the earth and its atmosphere neither warm up nor cool down because an equilibrium is established in which equal amounts of energy are received and re-radiated. Whereas most of the incident energy is concentrated in the visible part of the spectrum, that radiated is in the infra-red. The processes involved are complex but finally result in a stable temperature structure. In the troposphere, the temperature decreases with increasing altitude as little incident radiation is absorbed. A temperature minimum, the tropopause, separates the troposphere from the stratosphere. The temperature increases in the stratosphere up to the stratopause, due to absorption of radiation by trace gases, then it again decreases, in the mesosphere, as there are insufficient trace gases to absorb the incoming radiation.

The coldest temperatures in the atmosphere occur at the mesopause.

Energy input to the earth peaks around the equator and is least at the poles. The equatorial belt can be considered as the 'source' region for atmospheric energy and the poles as 'sink' regions. Heat flows from the source to the sinks, whence it is radiated to space. This flow establishes a global circulation of the atmosphere and the oceans. If the earth did not rotate on its axis, the circulation would be simply meridional, with hot air rising at the equator and, on encountering the tropopause, spreading poleward to cool and sink. Rotation of the earth introduces a sideways force on meridional motion and ultimately results in a mean westerly flow in both hemispheres. Divergence

Stratospheric temperature and wind speed vary with latitude. Near the tropopause, the atmosphere is warmest over the equator, but higher up the warmest region shifts to the summer pole. High-altitude circulation is thus different to that at low altitude, with easterly winds over the summer pole but westerlies over the winter pole.

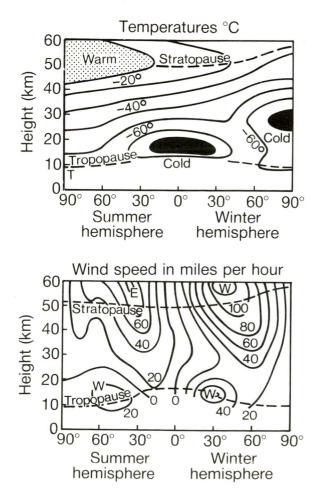

or convergence of the gas occurs locally, producing areas of low or high pressure (the familiar depressions and anti-cyclones). These develop their own local circulation systems but are entrained in the mean flow. Their development follows set patterns depending upon latitude, and the average behaviour produces the familiar tropospheric circulation systems.

Vertical motion in the troposphere, although much slower than the horizontal circulation, is nevertheless very important since it results in cooling and hence condensation to form clouds. At high latitudes the release of latent heat from this process can be a significant fraction of heat input.

Heating in the stratosphere arises from a photochemical process in which ultra-violet light energy is absorbed by the constituent molecules and subsequently used to drive chemical chain reactions. The resulting chemistry is complex and not yet fully understood but the major interaction, as far as heating is concerned, involves molecular oxygen and ozone. The heating rate is largest over the summer pole and smallest over the winter pole. This is quite different to the behaviour in the troposphere, where polar temperatures can be higher than those at the equator. The circulation system is therefore different, consisting of easterly winds in the summer hemisphere and westerlies in the winter hemisphere. The regions of strongest wind are known as jet streams.

The details of the energy flow from the equator to the poles, and the climatic consequences for different regions of the earth, is strongly influenced by the global distribution of land, sea and ice. The efficiency with which solar energy is reflected depends upon the nature of the reflecting surface. This efficiency is known as the albedo of the surface. The albedo of ice is close to unity, indicating that most incident energy is reflected; whilst that of sea water is near zero, meaning it is a good absorber. Continental land masses have albedos which vary between these two extremes. The large-scale variations in albedo are simpler in the south than in the north, and much higher values pertain to the Antarctic ice cap. Also, major mountain chains act as barriers to atmospheric circulation, and therefore introduce significant perturbations into the circulation patterns. Furthermore, the loss of energy from the circulation through surface friction varies markedly depending on the nature of the surface, and is greater over land than sea.

Arctic and Antarctic contrasts

The Arctic and the Antarctic serve the same basic thermodynamic function in acting as heat sinks. However, in many senses they are opposites and the contrasts play a key role in establishing their respective climates, and indeed that of the globe as a whole.

The most obvious difference is in the distribution of land and sea. The Arctic consists of an ocean basin surrounded by continents, whereas the Antarctic contains a pole-centred continent surrounded by ocean. There is very little land between 40° and 60°S, allowing a very

The Antarctic (right) *comprises a polar continent surrounded by oceans, whilst the Arctic* (left) *is an ocean basin surrounded by continents.*

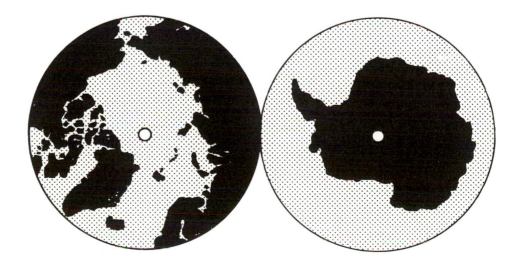

Dramatic climatic differences are shown by these contrasting photographs of the summer environment of Fairbanks, Alaska (65°N), and the British research station, Faraday, on the Argentine Islands (65°S), Antarctica. Fairbanks has a rich flora and fauna, being particularly famous for the gigantic vegetables which can be grown during the short summer season. Summertime temperature can top 32°C. The rocky Argentine Islands, in contrast, are partly covered by permanent ice caps extending down to sea level. The only successful plant life consists of lichens and mosses, and the wildlife is limited to birds and seals in the summer. The temperature never exceeds about 7°C in summer. However, the moderating influence of the southern ocean results in less extreme winters at Faraday than at Fairbanks. The diagram shows typical temperature extremes at Fairbanks (shaded) and mean monthly temperatures at Faraday.

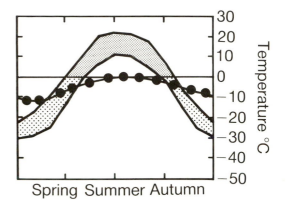

Images of microwave brightness temperature over the Arctic and Antarctic taken by the NIMBUS-5 satellite for winter days. Only the Greenland ice-cap resembles the Antarctic plateau.

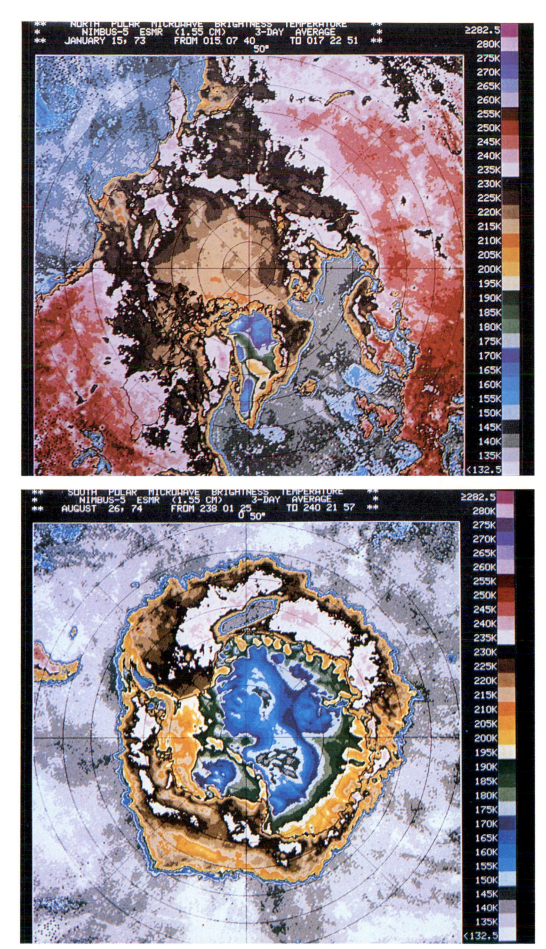

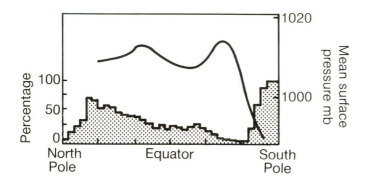

The percentage of the earth's circumference covered by land at different latitudes shows the contrast in land and sea between the two hemispheres. Mean surface pressures are lowest over the southern hemisphere where the strong westerly winds are found.

vigorous westerly circulation to develop, in contrast to the north where the continents moderate the flow. This circulation drives the West Wind Drift of the Southern Ocean and is more widely known by the evocative titles 'roaring forties' and 'howling fifties'. Averaged over the year for all latitudes, the southern circulation carries about 50% more momentum than does the northern. The boundary between the two lies roughly 3–4° north of the equator as a result of the stronger southern flows. Westerly winds imply a corresponding poleward pressure decrease, and a very pronounced hemispherical asymmetry is generally present in surface pressure.

The earth is closest to the sun during the Antarctic summer and most distant in Arctic summer. As a result about 7% more solar energy enters the Antarctic atmosphere in southern midsummer than enters the Arctic during northern midsummer. Since the Antarctic is remote from industrial activity its atmosphere contains almost no pollutants or dust to reflect, absorb or scatter incoming radiation. The Arctic suffers more in this respect since it lies within the same circulation system as the major industrial areas of the world. Furthermore, because of the high mean elevation of the Antarctic continent (about 3000 m), approximately 30% less atmospheric mass is available to attenuate the incoming radiation. The net result is that approximately 16% more energy is available to heat the surface at the South Pole in summer than is available at the North Pole in summer. Thus, other things being equal, temperatures should be higher in the Antarctic at midsummer and consequently for the rest of the year. This is demonstrably not the case. The long-term mean tempera-

ture for the southern hemisphere is about 1.6°C lower than that for the northern. This may not seem much but its manifestations are dramatic. For instance, glaciers exist down to sea level for latitudes 10° closer to the equator in the south. Also, the zone where the climate is too severe to support tree growth (i.e. where the temperature of the warmest month is less than 10°C) is three times larger in the southern hemisphere than in the northern. Even more extreme, the monthly mean temperatures on the south polar plateau range from -25° to -70°C, and even on the coastal margins are as low as -55°C, whilst those of the Arctic basin range only from 0 to -35°C. Why should this be so?

To answer this apparent paradox several interacting factors need to be taken into account. The Gulf Stream feeds warm ocean currents into the Arctic basin around Greenland and Norway, whilst no warm ocean currents penetrate the West Wind Drift into the Antarctic Ocean. Also, the strong westerly winds in the south inhibit the transfer of heat from the equator by atmospheric circulation. Thus, less heat is transferred overall to the Antarctic than to the Arctic. The Arctic Ocean, beneath its thin crust of ice, remains relatively warm (about -2°C). It therefore acts as a vast heat reservoir through the winter, so that at midwinter over five times as much heat flows into the atmosphere from the surface at the North Pole as happens in midwinter at the South Pole. Heat provided by solar radiation falling on the Southern Ocean is rapidly convected to lower levels, maintaining a fairly cool ocean surface within the Antarctic Convergence. The subantarctic atmosphere therefore remains relatively cool. The margins of the Arctic are continental land masses; heat is not convected to great depths here but is instead quickly transferred to the atmosphere.

Both the polar regions have low atmospheric vapour contents because of their low temperatures. However, as a result of the factors already identified, the Arctic is warmer, hence has more water vapour, and is thus generally more cloudy. This tends to enhance the temperature differential between north and south. Because it is warmer, there is relatively more melt in the Arctic. This tends to reduce the albedo of the surface, resulting in a typical summer value of 0.65 for Arctic ice compared with 0.90 for Antarctic ice. The northern ice is thus more efficient in absorbing solar radiation, and consequently the temperature difference is further accentuated.

This is a very simplified description of the physical processes involved. It is very difficult to trace the chain of cause and effect in atmospheric processes as the various factors all interact with each other until a state of dynamic equilibrium is achieved. However, the end result is lower temperatures in Antarctica than in the Arctic basin.

Chapter·15
The Antarctic climate today

The Antarctic troposphere

The weather of Antarctica and the surrounding subpolar ocean is dominated by a very simple tropospheric circulation system. The pressure decreases poleward from midlatitudes, producing strong westerly winds. Large temperature gradients between the cold continent and the relatively warm ocean continually create low-pressure areas (cyclones) over the ocean which travel eastward or south-eastward with the prevailing wind. Their tracks are sufficiently consistent to result in a persistent circumpolar band of low average pressure centred around 60–65°S. It is possible, though still controversial, that the mean position of this trough is influenced by the extent of sea-ice cover. The cyclones provide the mechanism for meridional exchange of cold polar air with warm moist air from lower latitudes, and thereby transport moisture into the south polar region.

The tropospheric circulation in the south can be contrasted with the north where variations in surface topography introduce considerable complications and a circumpolar trough is not apparent. The weather is frequently influenced by 'anti-cyclonic blocking', in which a well developed high-pressure region becomes stationary and consequently blocks the westerly flow. The result in summer is prolonged periods of fine weather, whilst in winter severe polar weather invades the mid-latitudes of Europe, Asia and America. Anti-cyclonic blocking is rare in the southern subpolar and temperate regions, and never persists as long as in the north. The maritime Antarctic and subpolar ocean weather thus mainly consists of a continual succession of cyclonic storms on a time scale of 2–3 days, interspersed with short periods of finer weather resulting from the intervening high-pressure ridges. This behaviour makes the circumpolar trough

The advent of satellite imagery allows a global view of the weather to be obtained. This picture shows the simple behaviour in the southern hemisphere in which cyclones just rotate around the continent.

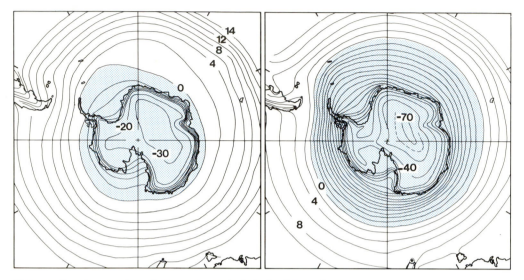

Mean surface temperatures for summer and winter in the southern hemisphere. Shaded area is below 0°C.

region one of the most cloudy areas in the world, with average cloud cover of between 6/8 and 8/8, but the climate is relatively mild; the surface temperature rarely falls below −10°C even in winter.

South of this gloomy belt the mean pressure increases, producing easterly prevailing winds at low altitudes which drive an easterly coastal current. The continental coastal zone is blessed with a higher proportion of clear days. Summertime temperatures remain relatively mild under the influence of the nearby ocean. During winter, however, the effective coastline is moved to much lower latitudes as sea ice forms, creating a much higher albedo regime. The temperature consequently falls much lower under the action of radiative cooling. This is an interactive process in which the growth of the sea ice is aided by the lower temperatures which it is helping to create. Annual sea-ice growth and decay is a very significant factor in the annual march of climate and is much more pronounced in the Antarctic than in the Arctic. Typically, temperatures reach lows of between −40° and −50°C, except around the northern end of the Antarctic Peninsula which is influenced by the maritime climate throughout the year.

Over the continental interior there is usually a high-pressure region centred over the crest of the polar plateau. However, due to the almost total absence of recording stations, the details of the pressure field are not well understood. Clear skies predominate, particularly in winter. When clouds are observed they are normally high-altitude types such as cirrus. The occasional occurrence of low cloud appears to be associated with periods of

enhanced inland transport of relatively warm maritime air. The surface temperature is basically controlled by the combination of latitude and, more particularly, altitude. The continent rises from sea level to a great plateau which reaches an altitude of over 4 km, and for which over 3.5 million km² is above 3 km altitude. For the South Pole, at an elevation of 2.8 km, the annual mean temperature is −50°C, whilst for the highest and most remote manned station, Vostok at 3.4 km, it is about 5°C colder. The latter site holds the record as the coldest place on earth with a temperature of −89.5°C.

The combination of altitude, winter darkness, weak transport of heat from lower latitudes, low average wind-speed, and intense radiation loss from the surface because of almost continual clear skies and very low humidity, produces an annual temperature variation quite unlike anything observed elsewhere on earth. Normally, the temperature of the warmest month will exceed the mean annual temperature by about the same amount as the coldest month is below it. When Paul Siple established the South Pole as a wintering station in 1956, he expected this rule to apply for the plateau. Siple determined the likely mean annual temperature from the temperature of the ice several metres below the surface and, using Amundsen's measurements of midsummer temperatures, estimated that monthly mean winter temperatures could be as low as −84°C! A year later he had discovered that the polar plateau is different, for the mean temperature at the South Pole during the coldest month of 1957 (September) was only a 'mild' −62.2°C.

The mean annual surface temperature (solid line) and altitude (dotted line) from the coast to the South Pole along 100°E longitude derived from Soviet and US data. There is one marked difference between Antarctic and high plateaux at more temperate latitudes. In Tibet and Bolivia, surface temperatures are higher than those for the free atmosphere at the same height all year round. For Tibet this difference is about 3–6°C above 3km altitude. For the Antarctic Plateau the reverse is true, underlining the significance of the high surface albedo.

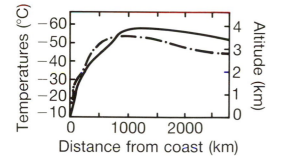

Surface temperatures at South Pole Station illustrate the occurrence of the 'pointed summer' and the 'coreless winter'. It was the rapid decline of temperature after mid-summer which caught out Captain Scott's party.

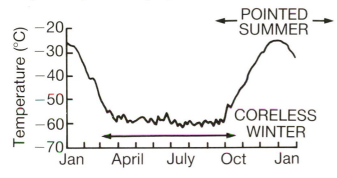

Average and extreme temperature inversion conditions over the Antarctic Plateau, illustrated with data from Vostok Station. An inversion occurs when the air temperature initially increases upwards from the ground before decreasing, rather than just decreasing upwards (lapse conditions). Inversions are normally about 500 to 1000 m thick, and the air within them is stable with little vertical transport.

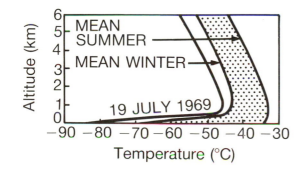

For the Antarctic Plateau there is a clear asymmetry between the durations of summer and winter. Summer is very short, only for the period from about mid-December to mid-January does the temperature exceed −30°C. This short duration, and the shape of the temperature variation, has earned the name the 'pointed summer'. It played a part in the tragic outcome of Scott's last journey. When Scott planned his expedition, only Shackleton had previously reached the plateau where, between 1 and 15 January 1909, he observed temperatures between −23° and −40°C, with a mean of −29°C. Amundsen was only on the plateau at the height of summer, but Scott was still there late into January and consequently experienced unexpectedly low temperatures which must have been greatly debilitating.

The summer warming arises from the combination of increased solar radiation (maximising at the summer solstice) and a small reduction of surface albedo for infrared radiation (resulting from slight metamorphosis of the snow surface as it ages during the spring). The first light snowfall or influx of drifted snow after midsummer restores the albedo and, with waning solar input, the temperature begins to fall rapidly. By the end of March, the sun has set for the winter and a stable situation, known as the 'coreless winter', is reached where, for the next 6 months, the temperature varies by only a few degrees. However, the extreme lows of temperature occur at the end of winter; for Vostok the minimum temperatures always occur just a day or so after the return of the sun.

A remarkable feature of the Antarctic troposphere is the presence of a very pronounced surface temperature inversion which represents the normal regime over the plateau throughout the year. Its intensity, expressed as the difference between the surface temperature and the maximum temperature above the location, varies as a function of latitude and altitude, and is much greater in winter than summer. A pronounced diurnal variation occurs in sunlight (except near the South Pole) due to radiative heating which warms the surface but not the air well above it. Inversions can be disturbed by the transport of relatively warm cloud-bearing maritime air over them, which cuts down the radiative cooling to space, whilst at the same time providing long-wave radiation input to the surface from the cloud. The inversion layer may also be influenced by increased vertical mixing of the air as a result of above-normal surface winds. Mixing is mostly caused by turbulence produced by surface irregularities such as sastrugi. Vertical mixing is important in creating surface temperature variability in the winter. Only on very rare occasions has the inversion been observed to decay completely during winter on the plateau.

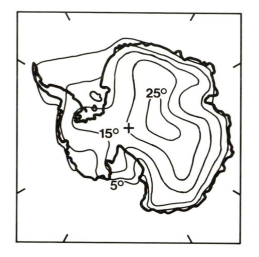

Mean surface temperature inversion conditions over Antarctica. For the plateau the contours shown represent the behaviour for all but the four months around midsummer, whilst for the coastal region they apply for the four months around midwinter. In summer lapse conditions normally apply for the coast. The mean value on the plateau is given as 25°C, although extremes in excess of 35°C have been observed.

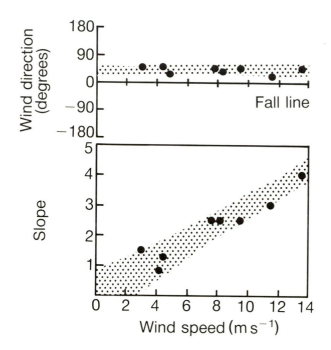

The velocity of 'inversion' winds and the slope of the plateau are related. The wind speed increases approximately in proportion to the slope, and its direction is roughly fixed with respect to the direction of maximum slope (the 'fall line'). The slopes involved are very small, typically 1 to 4 m in a kilometer. The only other place in the world where inversion winds are observed is on the Greenland ice cap.

The physics of a stable boundary layer (as the air mass within the inversion is known) is now recognized as of great importance in the general study of land–sea–atmosphere interactions. Antarctica offers a unique laboratory in which to study the phenomenon. New techniques are being developed to probe the layer with more precision. One such is the 'acoustic sounder', which utilises reflection of ultrasonic waves from turbulence within the layer to study the nature and variability of the vertical mixing. It is already clear that the dynamic behaviour in a boundary layer is much more complicated than suspected.

The behaviour of the surface winds over Antarctica is extraordinary, and the simple rules relating surface pressure variations to the resultant winds just do not apply. Instead, key factors influencing the windspeed and direction are the slope of the terrain and the strength of the temperature inversion, resulting in an 'inversion wind', which blows persistently in a direction set by the fall line of the slope, with a speed related to the magnitude of the slope. The physics is complex, involving factors such as the strength of the inversion, the velocity of the wind above the inversion layer, surface friction, Coriolis force, and gravity. It is still a subject of considerable scientific interest and uncertainty. One view, possibly oversimplified, is that the cold surface air moves down the slope under the action of gravity, although not directly down because of

the effect of Coriolis force. Strong vertical wind 'shears' (changes in speed and direction) occur through the inversion layer to maintain continuity with the winds above the layer which have unrelated velocities.

Near the base of the coastal escarpments and of the mountain ranges, two further types of wind occur, known as 'katabatic' and 'barrier' winds. Katabatic winds are associated with either a rise in temperature (Foehn winds) or a decrease (Bora winds); in either case they are severe. Barrier winds are flows moving parallel to mountain ranges. In both cases there is almost no relation between the wind and the overall pressure field. Only at some coastal sites and on the subantarctic islands are more normally behaved winds prevalent.

The katabatic winds of Greater Antarctica are extreme types of inversion winds but are still not at all well understood. The concept has been advanced whereby, at the edges of the inland escarpment where the terrain slope increases, the wind becomes more and more purely gravity-driven. Its speed increases, reducing the influence of Coriolis force, and the wind direction swings more into the fall line. Katabatics have been divided into two classes, 'ordinary' and 'extraordinary'. For ordinary katabatics the wind direction remains constant but the speed is highly variable, gusts alternating irregularly with weak winds, or periods of calm. Extraordinary katabatics are those which

A schematic representation of katabatic formation. The point at which an inversion wind changes to a katabatic wind is arbitrary, but mathematically it is defined to be when the ratio of inertial force to Coriolis force acting on the air mass (the Rossby number) exceeds unity.

The corrected (downwards by 20% for the strongest winds) maximum and minimum hourly average wind for July 13 at Cape Denison recorded by Mawson's expedition. For this month the wind exceeded gale force for at least one hour on every day, and the overall average for the month was 55mph (or force 10 on the Beaufort Scale)! A more recent reappraisal of the Cape Denison winds suggests that the correction applied was too drastic so that the actual winds were even more extreme than the expedition record indicates.

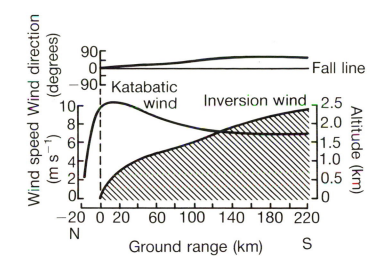

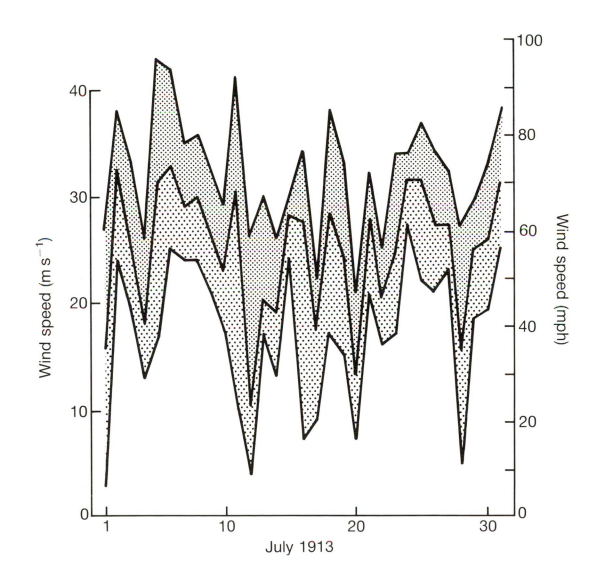

July 1913

blow uninterruptedly for days, even weeks, on end, with almost unvarying ferocity.

Extraordinary katabatic winds appear to be limited in distribution, particularly to a small sector of Greater Antarctica in the vicinity of Cape Denison and Port Martin. The power of these winds can scarcely be imagined and it is appropriate perhaps just to quote Mawson to gain an insight:

> Looking through my diary I notice that "on March 24 we experienced a rise in spirits because of the improved weather". Referring to the records I find the average velocity of the wind for that day to have been forty-five miles per hour, corresponding to a "strong gale" on the Beaufort scale. This tells its own story.

Mawson's expedition noted that high winds inhibited the formation of local sea ice. They proposed that extreme winds resulted from a strong positive feedback involving the large temperature difference between the ice-free ocean and the interior, which generated sufficient flow to keep the ocean clear of ice. However, the French found the winds at Port Martin to be equally strong whilst the surrounding ocean was continually ice covered. The idea has been advanced that the law of supply and demand operates, requiring the availability of sufficient cold air in the 'drainage area' to feed the wind. Radiative cooling in the drainage area takes time, and its strength may be quite variable because of cloud and turbulence, so that a constant supply is not to be expected, and the discontinuous nature of ordinary katabatic winds can be explained. It now seems likely that the extraordinary katabatics result from the combination of the nature of the upstream topography which produces a convergent flow, the presence of a large drainage area, and a persistent intense upstream inversion. These requirements are fulfilled inland from Cape Denison and Port Martin, and recently computer models based on them have been developed which reproduce the observed behaviour quite well. Unfortunately, however, direct observational evidence to confirm them is lacking.

Barrier winds are a manifestation of a strong surface inversion, associated with extended mountain barriers. Two such barriers exist in the Antarctic: the Transantarctic Mountains and the mountains of the Antarctic Peninsula. Both have extensive ice shelves to the east, the Ross and Filchner, respectively. South of about 65°S the wind is easterly on the shelves and a persistent temperature inversion occurs. The eastern flanks of the mountain ranges provide barriers to the wind, causing the cold inversion air to pile up, resulting in a local pressure gradient towards the mountains. The upshot is a southerly wind blowing along the eastern face of the ranges. The barrier wind on

An illustration of the effect of barrier winds using temperature data from Matienzo, an Argentinian station on the eastern side of the Antarctic Peninsula, and Faraday Station at the same latitude on the western side. The predominant weather pattern at Matienzo is of cold barrier winds with consequent low surface temperatures. The less common one is of warm (Foehn) winds which can be attributed to occasions when the circumpolar pressure trough west of the Peninsula lies well south of Matienzo. The weather at Faraday, in contrast, is largely under the influence of the major migrating cyclonic systems and is therefore generally warmer.

Ice rime (a) forms when moist air is cooled sufficiently for super-cooled water droplets to be produced. These accrete on any exposed surface to produce the characteristic milky granular deposit. If the temperature of the exposed surface is below the 'frost-point' temperature, water vapour changes state directly from the gaseous to the solid, producing hoar frost – a very light and feathery deposit (b).

(a)

(b)

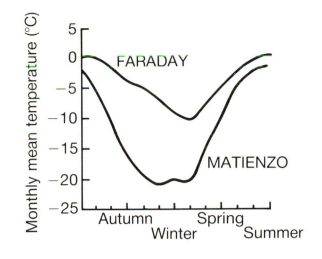

(Above, right) 'Sastrugi' is the name given to wave-like patterns carved into the snow surface by the action of the wind. It is possible to deduce the prevailing wind direction from the orientation of sastrugi.

(Below) Drifting snow at a field camp. Much of the Antarctic has very little snow fall. Most of the snow seen in blizzards is only surface drift being moved from one place to another.

the eastern side of the Antarctic Peninsula helps maintain a very harsh climate compared with that on the western side. The outflow of ice from the Weddell Sea also plays a part in this. Barrier winds are generally strong, normally in excess of 20 m s^{-1} (45 mph). It is usual for a period of barrier wind activity to last for several days but there is a relatively high incidence of calm weather in between. Some very strong gusts have been recorded, for Matienzo a gust of 86 m s^{-1} (192 mph) is claimed to have occurred on 7 August 1968.

Wind is usually accompanied by drifting or blowing snow, as loose snow on the surface becomes entrained in the air flow. The concentration of snow particles and the altitude to which they are carried depend upon the amount of loose snow available, the windspeed, and turbulence in the flow (a function of the roughness of the surface). The mass of snow picked up depends upon at least the fourth power of wind velocity, so it increases very rapidly as the wind freshens. The term 'drifting' is used to describe a layer of fine snow particles less than 2 m thick. Drifting is likely to be sustained by a wind of greater than 5 m s^{-1}. 'Blowing snow' is much more unpleasant and results from windspeeds in excess of 20 m s^{-1}. The layer can extend from 2 m to in excess of 100 m (in extreme circumstances), with visibility reduced sometimes to less than 10 m. This combination of wind and blowing snow is most unpleasant but it is sometimes possible to see blue sky and sunshine above whilst the horizontal visibility is severely reduced. However, it is normally impossible to see the sky or to decide whether precipitation is also occurring; at these times the more apt label is a blizzard.

Accumulation of snow on the continent occurs as a result of snowfall from clouds, precipitation of ice crystals from clear skies, accretion of rime or glaze ice, and deposition of hoar frost. Precipitation is greatest over the coastal zone due to cyclonic activity. It is rare inland, occurring only during an unusually strong invasion of maritime air into the region above the stable inversion. Maritime air moving inland can be cooled sufficiently for supercooled water droplets to form. When these are in contact with a surface, rime or glaze ice forms. If the surface is below the 'frost-point' temperature, direct deposition of hoar frost results. Hoar differs visually from rime in being much more feathery. Once over the plateau, the maritime air above the inversion cools until it becomes supersaturated with ice which then precipitates as ice crystals. For altitudes above 3 km, this is the predominant mechanism, accounting for up to 90% of the annual accumulation.

The question of how much accumulation actually occurs in the Antarctic is a vexed one. Direct measurements using rain/snow gauges are imprecise even at temperate latitudes; in Antarctica such measurements are almost impossible. The question is, however, hardly trivial since it addresses the long-term stability of the whole ice mass. The combination of direct measurements, with such techniques as snow stake surveys, and analysis of the annual layers of accumulation in ice cores has proved quite profitable, allowing an overall picture of the annual accumulation to be constructed. The rates over the plateau are very small; indeed it is actually a vast desert. Still, accumulation must roughly balance loss since the ice sheet is not noticeably changing in the short term. The mechanisms by which ice is lost (see Chapter 12) result overall in an annual rate of disappearance of about 2×10^{15} tonnes. The precision with which accumulation and loss can be determined is not at present sufficient to detect departures from equilibrium with any confidence. It has recently been suggested, though, that a significant increase (30% in a decade) in accumulation may have occurred in the last 20 years. If this is confirmed, and sustained, it will be of great consequence.

The Antarctic stratosphere

The circulation of the polar stratosphere exhibits two basic patterns through the year. In summer, absorption of solar ultra-violet radiation by ozone is continual, raising the temperature and resulting in weak easterly flow. For the rest of the year, heating via this process is weak or non-existent so that the stratosphere cools towards the pole. The circulation becomes westerly and intensifies to establish a stratospheric circumpolar vortex. Both polar regions follow this basic pattern but there are marked contrasts. The Arctic vortex is considerably less intense and less stable than that for the Antarctic, and it is frequently prone to major disruption by the sudden invasion of warm air from lower latitudes. This process, called a 'stratwarm', may occur at any time during the winter months, and appears to be associated with large-scale atmospheric disturbances arising from the variable surface topography and albedo in the northern hemisphere. The end of the stratospheric winter is always heralded by a stratwarm.

Winter stratwarms are almost unknown in the Antarctic. The vortex appears to be so stable and intense that it effectively seals off the Antarctic stratosphere from lower latitudes. The temperature falls steadily through the winter and the commencement of summer is marked by a single warming event. There is no 'coreless winter' or 'pointed summer' in the stratosphere. However, remote sensing of

The Dobson spectrophotometer measures the total content of ozone in a vertical column above the observing site by comparing the intensities of radiation on two wavelengths, one strongly absorbed by ozone, and the other not.

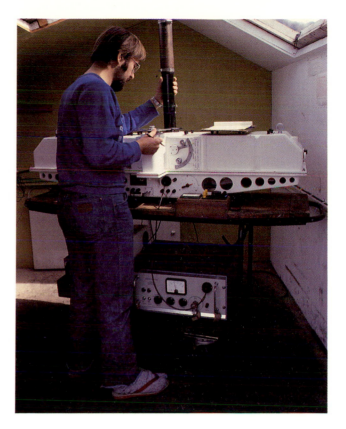

temperature from satellites indicates that wave-like perturbations occur regularly in the high stratosphere over Antarctica, producing mini-warmings. It is still not clear exactly what processes are involved in these or the main spring warming, though it seems that vertical motion driven by planetary scale atmospheric waves in the troposphere is the key.

The strength of the circulation increases markedly with altitude through the stratosphere, and is strongest at about 60°S. In the mesosphere between about 40 and 80 km, observations from satellites have shown that the pattern changes. The temperature increases towards the pole, with a temperature minimum occurring at southern mid-latitudes. This minimum does not appear to be present in the northern winter, where it is probably masked by the more complex and intense stratwarm-type behaviour.

The variations in concentration of stratospheric ozone are strongly coupled with the behaviour of the circumpolar vortex. During the winter months, ozone levels remain stable over the pole for two reasons: first, there is little or no solar ultra-violet radiation to stimulate local photochemical production; and, secondly, the vortex seals off the transport of ozone-rich air from lower latitudes. When the vortex breaks down in the spring, meridional transport takes over and the ozone mixing ratio increases steeply. Prior to the spring warming the ozone level declines poleward, whilst afterwards there is no significant latitudinal variation. The decline of ozone in summer is striking and is in marked contrast to the behaviour in temperature. Why this occurs is not yet known in detail. It is unlikely to be a result of poleward transport since temperature gradients and circulation are weak. Although the decline is fast, it is less than suggested by photochemical models. What probably occurs is that ozone is replenished from above by a slow downward motion (of the order of 10–100 m per day).

The traditional method for observing ozone in the stratosphere is spectrophotometry; it thus normally requires clear daytime conditions, though measurements can be made by the light of the full moon. For the polar regions little direct observation has therefore been made of winter behaviour. Recently chemical sensors have been used, carried by balloons, which are not limited to daytime and provide a vertical profile of ozone variation. Ground photometers are now complemented by similar instruments onboard polar-orbiting satellites, providing much finer spatial coverage than previously available, though still not of the winter pole.

There has been increasing concerning over the effects of manmade pollutants upon stratospheric ozone. This is not just an academic point because any reduction in ozone will increase the level of harmful ultra-violet radiation

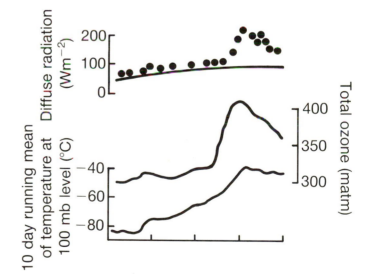

The winter vortex isolates the antarctic stratosphere from lower latitudes. Dust from the volcanic eruption in March 1963 of Mount Agung (8°S, 115°E) in Bali spread through the low- and mid-latitude stratosphere, reaching the Falklands Islands by July. However, the insertion of dust into the polar stratosphere did not occur until the spring warming. Dust in the stratosphere above Halley station was determined from the intensity of diffuse solar radiation measured at ground level (increasing diffuse radiation indicates increasing dust concentration). The spring warming was detected from the temperature recorded by radiosondes at the 100 mb level and total ozone measured from the ground by a Dobson spectrophotometer.

217

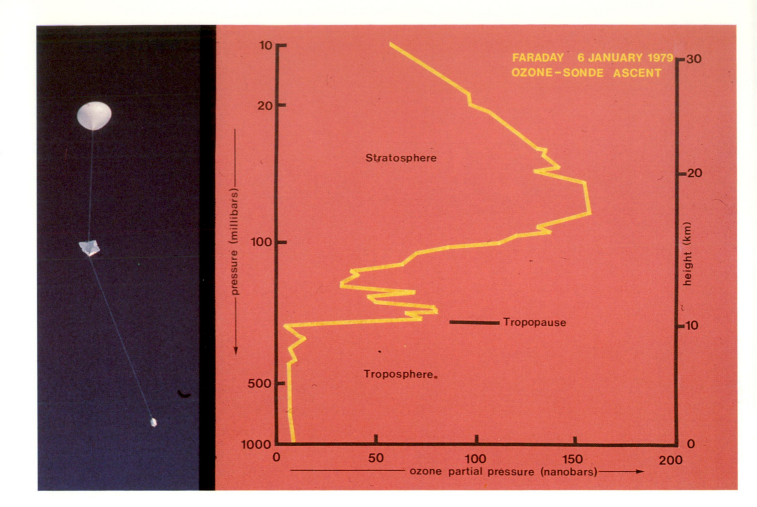

The traditional method for probing the troposphere and stratosphere uses balloon-borne instruments known as radiosondes, measuring the temperature, pressure and humidity of the air as the balloon ascends, and radioing the information back to the ground. The balloon is tracked by radar, or uses a position fixing technique such as Omega, to determine horizontal winds at various levels in the atmosphere. Normally one or two flights are done each day from participating meteorological stations. Balloons are also used to determine the vertical profile of trace gases such as ozone, as illustrated here. This traditional approach is now augmented by satellite remote sensing and measurements made from rockets and high-flying aircraft.

reaching the ground. The pollutants concerned are oxides of nitrogen released from the engines of high-flying aircraft, and chlorine from halocarbons used in refrigeration and air-conditioning systems. Both act as catalysts for destroying ozone but are not themselves dissipated by the process. Much theoretical work has been carried out around the world, without so far proving unequivocally that there is a major hazard. Studies of most long-term sets of ozone measurements have also proved inconclusive, partly because of the difficulty in maintaining a homogeneous set of photometer measurements over many years. Recent British work suggests that halocarbon effects can now be identified in the stratosphere and that these are likely to be particularly pronounced in Antarctica. Springtime ozone at Halley Station has decreased by over 30% in the past 8 years, associated with the growth in halocarbon release. This is a very major effect and appears to be a consequence of the very low temperatures maintained in the polar stratosphere even after the sun has risen at the end of winter, coupled with the fact that the catalyst–ozone mixture is cut off from lower-latitude air by the intense vortex. The spring warming produces an influx of ozone-rich air to replace most of the losses, but each year the level of catalyst is a little higher, so the minimum is deeper.

Climatic trends in Antarctica

Global climate varies year by year due to a number of natural stimuli, not all of which are understood. It does not appear, however, that such effects will produce extreme changes on an historical time scale. It may be a different story where manmade perturbations are concerned. Industrialisation has caused the release of vast quantities of carbon dioxide into the atmosphere to be added to that produced naturally by photosynthesis. Carbon dioxide is 'infra-red active', that is it absorbs infra-red radiation and thus causes local heating. The danger is

(Right) *There is considerable controversy as to whether man is damaging the ozone layer by pollution with halocarbons. The existence of a very accurate and complete set of ozone observations from Halley Station stretching back to the IGY has allowed a detailed search for such damage to be made. It is apparent that a very dramatic effect is occurring in spring where the ozone level (stipple) has fallen by more than 30% in 8 years. Halocarbon concentration is shown by the circles.*

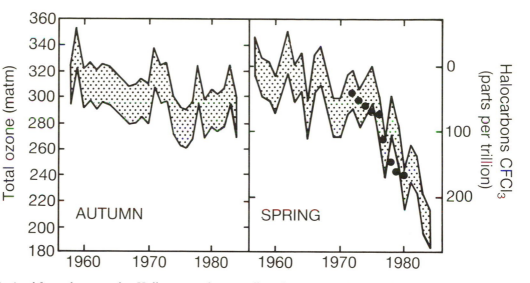

(Below) *Confirmation of the result obtained from the ground at Halley comes from satellite observations showing the appearance of a springtime 'hole' (light area in figure) in ozone over Antarctica, previously absent. The consequences of this behaviour are not yet understood, but it is clear that Antarctica offers an ideal site for further research.*

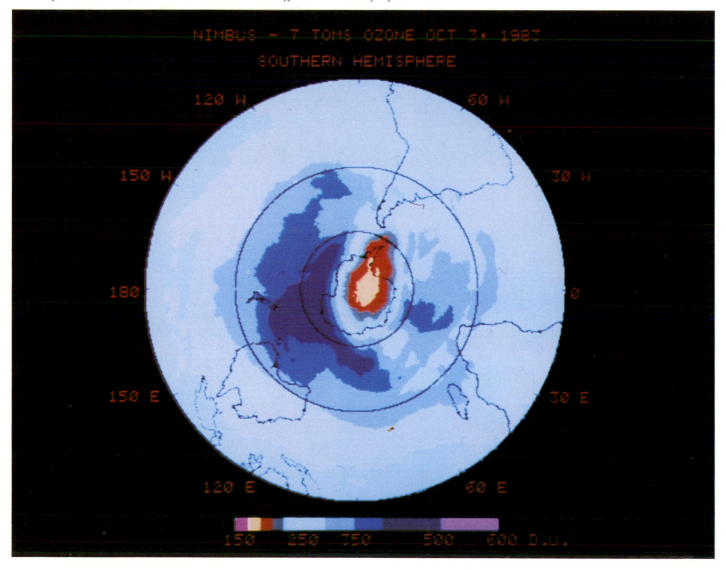

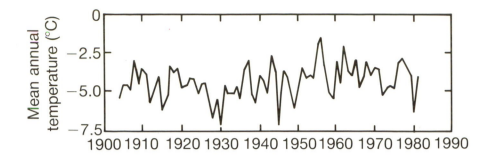

The mean annual temperature variation at Laurie Island from 1903 to the present. This is the longest uninterrupted data set from the Antarctic region. Very large changes occur from one year to the next – much larger than would be encountered at more temperate latitudes. There appear to be no statistically significant long-term trends.

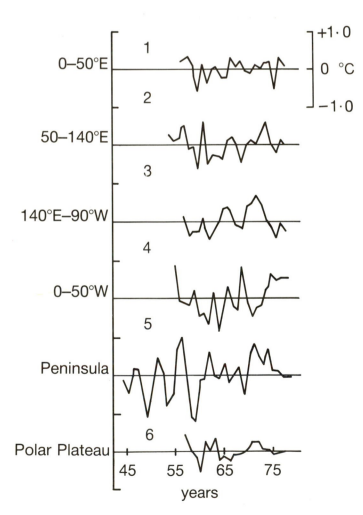

The variations in mean annual temperature in different sectors of Antarctica do not necessarily behave in the same way. This is particularly evident by comparing sectors (3) and (4). Considerable inter-annual variability is present over the whole continent but is quite clearly maximum in the Peninsula region (5).

that the increased CO_2 will intercept infra-red radiation leaving the earth, upsetting the radiation balance and consequently raising surface temperature (the 'greenhouse effect').

Atmospheric CO_2 is monitored by the USA at Maui in the Pacific and at Pole Station. Its concentration does appear to be increasing steadily by about 3% per decade, but controversy currently rages as to the significance of this for global climate. One thing is clear: CO_2-induced temperature changes are likely to be largest in Antarctica because of the close positive feedback between the extent of sea-ice cover and surface temperature. Ice cores from the Antarctic ice cap can provide baseline information on CO_2 levels for before the industrial revolution and insights into the consequences of CO_2 changes contained in the geological record. The latter reveals a very interesting paradox. The mean level, and total change in CO_2 over the past 100 years, is not significantly different from that which pertained during the 5000 years of warming marking the end of the last ice age 20 000 years ago. This appeared to have been accompanied by a mean temperature increase of about 7°C, but no such increase has occurred in the past century. It is unclear how this paradox can be resolved, though the first step must be an independent confirmation of the CO_2 and temperature data in the ice-core record.

Laurie Island provides the longest uninterrupted surface temperature record for Antarctica. This does not contain any obvious long-term trend but does show large inter-annual variability which appears highly correlated with the duration of local sea ice. The changes are larger than is normal at more temperate latitudes and may mask long-term trends. It is unlikely that a trend greater than 1°C per century is present. However, there was a significant cooling trend through the 1920s, followed by a warming up to the 1960s and a cooling trend thereafter – certainly not clear evidence of a CO_2 effect. This general pattern appears to be characteristic of the whole continent, although the span of data is shorter.

Some theoretical work has suggested that as little as 1°C increase in mean annual temperature would reduce the overall area of sea-ice cover by up to 5 million km^2 (or about 40% of the total). But the feedback mechanisms are not well understood and the effect could be much smaller. Sea-ice cover should correlate well with interannual temperature variability if there really is close coupling. Reliable sea-ice data have only been available since about 1966 when monitoring by satellites became practical. Thus any observed connection can only be tentative, and so far the data do not present a very consistent picture.

The future for Antarctic meteorology

This chapter has presented a broad picture of Antarctic weather and climate, past and present, within the global context. It should be evident that the scholarship here described is a truly international achievement. Much remains uncertain and a great deal more study is necessary before the meteorology of Antarctica is properly understood and its role in global climate defined. The first hope for the future must be that the unparalleled internationalism continues unfettered. It is crucial to note that most of what has been presented relied upon routine, perhaps mundane, synoptic observations of the weather, carefully made and documented. There is a real danger, given the high cost of Antarctic work, and the pressures to be involved in 'glamorous' experiments, that this sequence of observations will be broken. For instance, the importance of building a consistent long-term series of climate and sea-ice cover data for assessing CO_2 effects cannot be overstated. The network of observing sites is not really adequate but, fortunately, technology provides the potential to maintain, and develop, monitoring at relatively low cost through the development of automatic weather stations and through remote sensing from satellites. It is to be hoped that over the coming decade the monitoring network will be expanded, particularly inland and in the Southern Ocean using buoys, to provide coverage sufficient both for forecasting and fundamental research.

Antarctica is a unique laboratory for atmospheric research. For example, it contains an unmatched environment in which to study the physics of boundary layers, and appears to be particularly sensitive to the effects of pollutants on stratospheric ozone. The contrasts between the Arctic and the Antarctic contain important pointers to basic atmospheric processes. The current configuration of one pole with a continent surrounded by ocean and the other an ocean surrounded by continents, could not be improved on, even if the planet were specifically designed for meteorological studies. It is likely that studies of the consequences of these differences will assume greater importance in the coming decade. An important practical use of the observed contrasts should be in the testing of computerised schemes for weather forecasting and simulations of climate change.

The derivation of climatic records from the ice is a young field but it is already having a major impact on our understanding of the climatic history of the continent. It may also play a key role in identifying the principal causes of ice ages. Furthermore, the data should provide an essential benchmark against which theories predicting the temperature effects of the current manmade increase in CO_2 can be tested.

Continued monitoring of the environment should give the first warning of any major climatic change. A critical question to be resolved is that of the ice mass balance. Is this increasing or decreasing with time? So far the sign of any change is lost in the errors associated with the estimations of accumulation and loss rates. Considerable refinements in the experimental techniques are required. Satellites are likely to play a key role, by providing estimates of overall loss through calving of icebergs, and from the use of sensitive radio altimeters which will map the relief of the continent with sufficient accuracy to allow changes to be detected over a short time scale.

Chapter 16

Space research from Antarctica

Introduction

It will seem improbable to most people that the Antarctic continent should have much to offer space scientists. The purpose of this chapter is to demonstrate that for studies of that part of the solar system known as geospace, Antarctica has played a major part in the development of our understanding, and there remain rich opportunities for research resulting from the unique nature of the region.

The concept of geospace is very new and owes its development to the research opportunities provided by the space age. Whilst this concept now provides a compelling argument for upper-atmosphere research in Antarctica, the historical justifications, though pointing in the right directions, have necessarily been much less all-embracing.

The details of what is meant by the term geospace will be elucidated later, but briefly it encompasses the inter-relations between the sun's atmosphere (the heliosphere) and the earth's magnetic field and atmosphere, in a region extending from the 'surface' of the sun to about 1.5 million km outside the earth's orbit. It incorporates the sun's outer atmosphere, the local interplanetary medium with its magnetic field, and the terrestrial magnetosphere, ionosphere and thermosphere.

Oddly, the reasons why the Antarctic is regarded as a valuable base for studies of geospace have almost nothing to do with its physical surface and meteorological environment. The most significant factors are the detailed configuration of the geomagnetic field and its connections with other regions of geospace, and the availability of 'land' in the vicinity of the geographic and geomagnetic poles on which to site facilities.

Geospace

Almost all of the matter in the universe exists in a form known as a plasma. Plasma is a gas consisting of ions (atoms from which one or more electrons has been stripped thereby leaving them with a net positive electric charge), mixed with the electrons which have been removed. Since a plasma has an equal number of positive and negative electric charges, it is electrically neutral when viewed from outside, but it is capable of supporting electric currents. The physics of plasmas plays a fundamental role in many diverse areas, including such things as the development of nuclear weapons, fusion reactor development, and understanding the origins of the universe.

In Chapter 14 it was pointed out that the sun emits energy in two forms: electromagnetic radiation, and a supersonic stream of plasma known as the solar wind. The solar wind is fundamentally important to the nature of geospace. It is composed mainly of charged hydrogen (protons), with some helium, and is accelerated in the solar corona to speeds of up to 3.5 million km h^{-1} to carry mass, momentum and energy throughout the solar system. However, the wind fluctuates significantly in strength on time scales varying from seconds to decades in response to such irregular factors as solar flares and sunspots, and regular variations such as the 27-day solar rotation period and the 11-year cycle of overall solar activity. A plasma has the interesting property that under some circumstances it acts as a barrier to magnetic fields. A field applied externally cannot penetrate the plasma, whilst an internal field can become 'frozen' within it. For the solar wind, parts of the magnetic field involved in the acceleration process become entrained within the plasma as it flows through the solar system. The magnetic field which results in interplanetary space is known as the Interplanetary Magnetic Field (or IMF for short). The IMF is highly variable, in particular it often undergoes abrupt reversals in direction which can be associated with significant events in the atmosphere of the earth, such as a change in the behaviour of aurorae.

The earth possesses its own magnetic field which, in the absence of other influences, behaves roughly as though a bar magnet was situated at the earth's centre. This field approximates to a dipole field and it revolves as the earth rotates. The magnetized earth sits as a physical and magnetic obstacle in the path of the solar wind. The flow of the plasma around this obstacle generates a feature which is one of the major elements of geospace, the magnetosphere.

On the sunward side of the earth, the oncoming plasma compresses the geomagnetic field and, in the process, is decelerated until a transition region is reached where the solar wind pressure is balanced by the restoring force of the distorted dipole field. Since the wind is moving supersonically a shock wave forms at this point, known as the bow shock. Just earthward of the bow shock is a boundary region (known as the magnetosheath, or day-side boundary layer) in which decelerated solar wind plasma streams around the earth. The magnetosheath is situated at approximately 10 earth radii (R_E), about 64 000 km, from the centre of the earth in the equatorial plane, and is bounded by the magnetopause on the inside. Within this boundary there is a magnetic cavity into which direct penetration of the solar wind plasma is impossible.

As the plasma flows past the earth, a process akin to friction between it and the geomagnetic field causes the field to be stretched out into a vast tail (called the magnetotail) extending many hundreds of earth radii out into space. Another way to visualise this process is to imagine that geomagnetic field lines couple to the IMF and so are

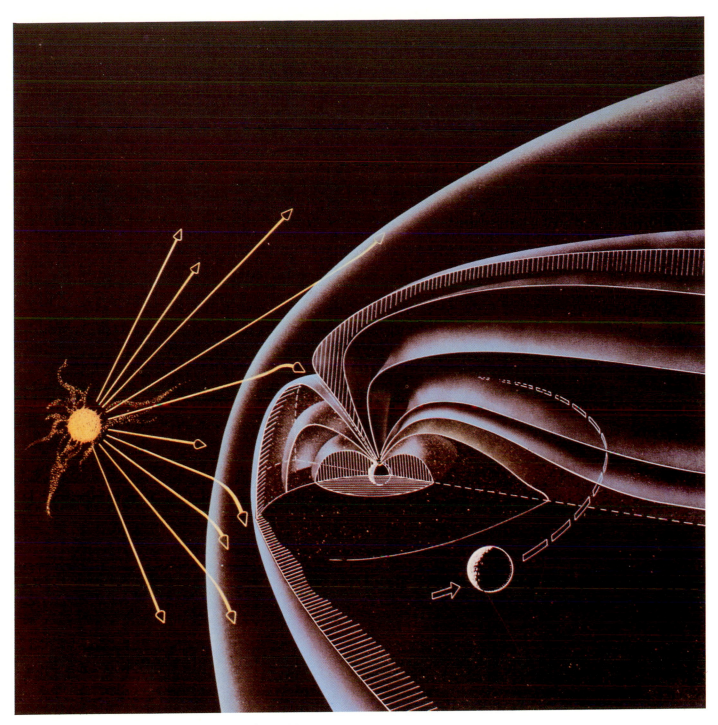

Geospace. The blue shaded contours represent the earth's magnetic field distorted by the solar wind (indicated by yellow arrows). The field line representation is to scale with the dimensions of the earth but the relative sizes and positions of the sun, earth and moon are not to scale.

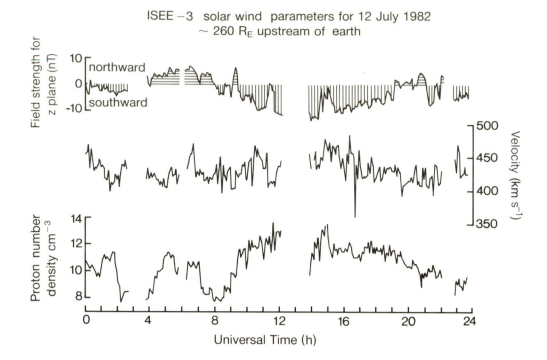

ISEE –3 solar wind parameters for 12 July 1982
~ 260 R_E upstream of earth

A typical day in the solar wind, as observed by the International Sun Earth Explorer (ISEE-3) spacecraft, approximately 260 R_E sunwards of the earth. The plasma concentration of the wind is typically about 10 particles per cm^3, the wind speed is about 450 km s^{-1}. The Interplanetary Magnetic Field (IMF) is highly variable, changing sign several times per day.

dragged away from the sun with the latter. The total extent of the magnetotail is not yet known but it appears to be in excess of 1000 R_E. The magnetosphere is thus anything but spherical, but the name has become firmly entrenched amongst the world community of space scientists.

Two quite narrowly defined polar cusps, one in each hemisphere, separate the compressed day-side magnetic field from that drawn out into the night-side tail. These provide pathways into the magnetic cavity which allow plasma originating in the solar wind and flowing tailwards in the boundary layers to penetrate deep into the polar atmosphere. Solar-wind plasma can also enter the magnetosphere through the boundaries between the magnetotail and the interplanetary medium, to form the plasma sheet, a north-south oriented reservoir of plasma extending deep into the tail.

The flow of the solar wind past the magnetosphere results in an electric field across the magnetotail, aligned from dawn to dusk, and a corresponding sunward plasma flow in the plasma sheet. It is not yet clear whether the electric field is the cause of the sunward flow or one consequence of it. The end result is the same either way, giving rise to electric fields of between 20 and 120 kV depending on the level of solar disturbance.

The sunward convection provides plasma to populate the inner and outer Van Allen radiation belts situated a few earth radii out from the earth. These radiation belt regions support an electric current (the ring current) which girdles the earth above the equator. The plasma sheet and the ring-current region are the two major 'sinks' of the magnetosphere in which plasma is stored.

The magnetosphere is constrained by the nature of its formation to always be aligned with the tail pointing away from the sun – it is said to be 'fixed in sun/earth coordinates'. Buried within it is the rotating earth with its dipole field. At some distance from the earth there is therefore a fascinating transition region between the inner co-rotating magnetic field and the outer fixed magnetospheric field. This is known as the plasmapause and is located at about 4 R_E. The doughnut-shaped volume of space within the plasmapause (the plasmasphere) contains a dense low-energy plasma, co-rotating with the earth, whose source is the ionosphere. Outside the plasmapause there is a rather sharp reduction in plasma density and a corresponding increase in particle energy.

The whole of the magnetosphere is in a constant state of disturbance because of the gustiness of the solar wind, with the various boundaries described above moving and distorting as a consequence. One important class of disturbance is known as a substorm. A substorm can be initiated by a disturbance in the solar corona which perturbs the solar wind. This may in turn compress the day-side of the magnetosphere, and both constrict and elongate the tail. The cross-tail electric field is often enhanced, driving a stronger sunward flow. Extra solar wind plasma is injected

SOLAR-TERRESTRIAL RELATIONSHIPS

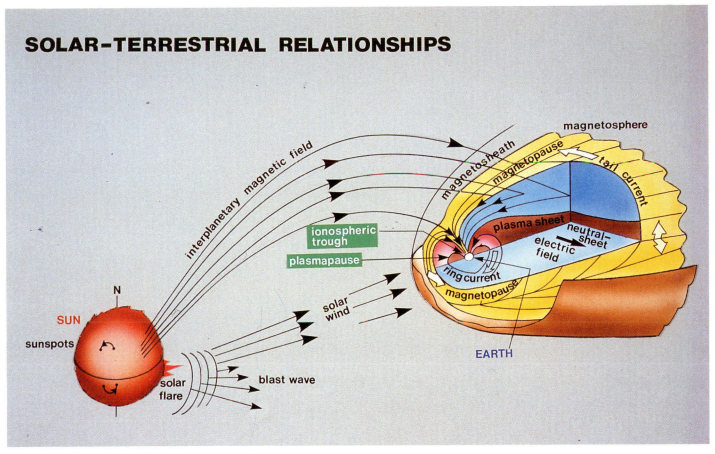

Pictorial representations of the main features of the magnetosphere.

The geospace observatories operated by the British Antarctic Survey lie on geomagnetic field lines of different lengths. Studies of very-low-frequency radio wave propagation through the magnetosphere exploit this feature. In addition, the large displacement of the geographic and geomagnetic poles in Antarctica allows critical tests to be made of the relative importance of solar radiation and charged particle effects. The magnetic field lines at Faraday thread the plasmasphere whereas those of the French station Dumont d'Urville (which lies at the same geographic latitude) are linked with the magnetotail.

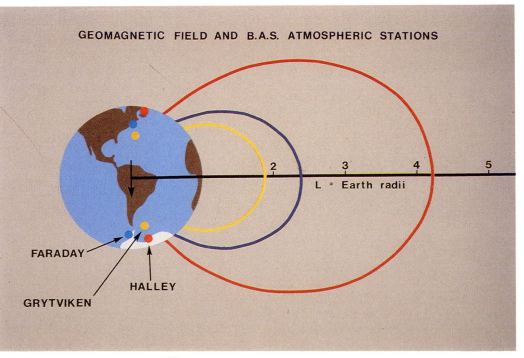

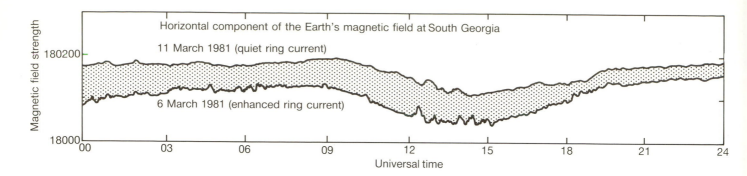

The magnetic field strength axis is labelled with values 180200, 18000. The chart title reads "Horizontal component of the Earth's magnetic field at South Georgia", with curves labelled "11 March 1981 (quiet ring current)" and "6 March 1981 (enhanced ring current)". The horizontal axis is Universal time marked 00, 03, 06, 09, 12, 15, 18, 21, 24.

The magnetic field associated with the equatorial ring current is in opposition to the north/south component of the geomagnetic field. It therefore depresses the main field. Comparison of observations of the geomagnetic field on the earth's surface for different levels of ring current activity show this effect clearly.

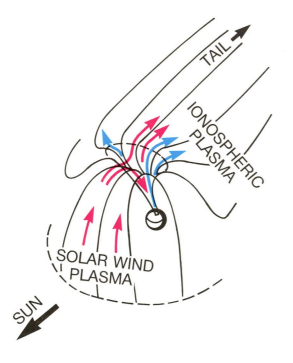

TAIL

IONOSPHERIC PLASMA

SOLAR WIND PLASMA

SUN

A three-dimensional view of one polar cusp showing how solar wind plasma can penetrate into the earth's atmosphere, and how ionospheric plasma can flow out into the plasma sheet and ring current.

into the magnetospheric sinks, and particles in the plasma sheet are accelerated earthwards to produce bright aurorae. The acceleration process is not yet properly understood but, at the risk of oversimplification can be likened, in part at least, to a 'magnetic slingshot'. Field lines are pulled out until the northern and southern hemisphere parts finally 'reconnect' in the tail. At this point the field attempts to re-establish a more dipole-like configuration by springing earthwards and, in so doing, drags particles

with it. The effect that disturbances in the solar wind have on the magnetosphere depends upon the direction of the IMF. If the IMF is southward then close coupling occurs between the geomagnetic field and the solar wind; this is called the open-magnetosphere case. If the IMF is northward the opposite situation prevails – the closed-magnetosphere case.

Major eruptions on the sun produce more dramatic disturbances in the magnetosphere, known as magnetic storms. During these the magnetosphere becomes very distorted, with the day-side very compressed. The ring current is enhanced to such an extent that the magnetic field associated with it is sufficient to produce pronounced perturbations in the geomagnetic field at the earth's surface. Auroral activity is very marked and can be observed at much lower latitudes than normal. Overall the solar wind supplies between 10 000 (quiet solar conditions) and 15 million (major disturbance) megawatts to the magnetosphere.

Since the magnetosphere is populated with both hot (energetic) and cold (thermal) plasmas embedded in magnetic fields, there are rich opportunities for the generation of electromagnetic and electrostatic waves over a broad band of wavelengths. Complex 'wave–particle' resonances occur which allow energy transfer between wave and particle. Such processes play a very important role in the energy budget of geospace as a whole. It is now known that the earth is a bright radio source, radiating about 10 MW in the kilometre waveband, as a result of wave-particle interactions on magnetic field lines associated with the auroral oval.

The magnetic field lines of the magnetosphere are, for the most part, equipotentials. That is, electrical conductivity is very high along a specific field line, but low across it, so that plasma can naturally flow in the direction of the field but must be driven across it. The effect of a disturbance in one part of the medium may therefore be propagated to a far distant part through the flow of plasma or the transmission of an electric field along the equipotential. Thus field lines act as useful tracers of the flow of energy through the magnetosphere. The field lines which traverse the most interesting regions of the medium – the tail, the cusps, the plasmapause, and the boundary layers – all have their 'feet' in the polar regions of the atmosphere. In particular they thread through the polar ionosphere, which thereby acts as one boundary of geospace, as a sink for much of the energy coupling from the solar wind into the magnetosphere, and as a source of cold plasma in the magnetosphere.

Short-wave ultra-violet radiation from the sun ionises a proportion of the upper atmosphere above an altitude of about 60 km to produce the terrestrial ionospheric plasma. For historical reasons the ionosphere is divided into several height regions. The region of greatest plasma concentration is known as the F-region and here the predominant ion is atomic oxygen, but the ionospheric plasma forms only a small part of the atmosphere at this level. Lower down, in the E-region, ions such as those of molecular oxygen, nitrogen and nitric oxide are the major species. At great altitudes, well above the level of maximum concentration, oxygen gives way to hydrogen, and the atmosphere becomes wholly ionised.

For temperate and low latitudes the concentration of the ionospheric plasma depends upon the end result of three main processes: (1) the input of solar energy, which causes the ionisation; (2) chemical reactions, which cause the ions and electrons to recombine into neutral atoms; and (3) transport processes, which move the ionisation both horizontally and vertically (the plasma may be caused to move either by imposing an electric field, or by the neutral gas pushing it).

It would be untrue to suggest that the temperate-latitude ionosphere is completely understood, but there is no doubt its main features are now clear. For the polar regions, however, the situation is much more complex. All the basic processes listed above take place there but now there is the added dimension of coupling to the rest of geospace. It is convenient to divide the polar ionosphere into three distinct zones: the polar cap, the auroral oval, and the subauroral region. The auroral oval is an annular ring girdling the polar region (north or south), within which aurorae occur. It is associated with the geomagnetic

The major structure of the polar ionosphere and its interactions with the magnetosphere.

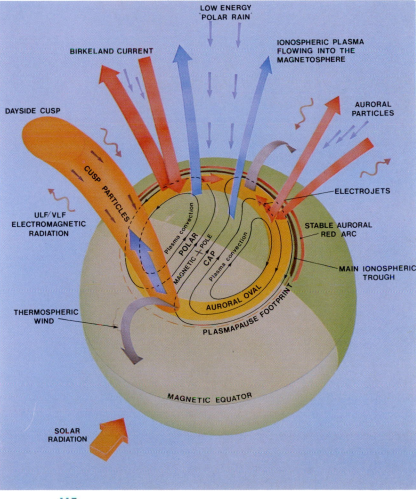

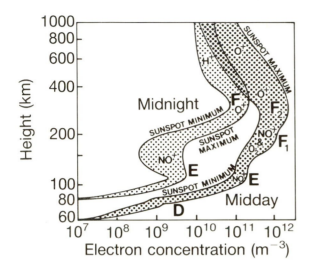

The average behaviour of the midlatitude ionosphere for daytime and night-time. The symbols D, E, F_1, F_2 identify main ionospheric 'layers', whilst the chemical symbols show which ion species predominates in each.

pole but is offset from it by about 3° towards the night-side of the earth. To a first approximation the oval is fixed with respect to the sun and the earth rotates underneath it. This localization of auroral activity arises because only on those field lines which extend out into the near tail (5–8 R_E) do the acceleration processes occur which drive particles into the atmosphere with sufficient energy to excite the neutral gas to glow. A complex electrical circuit then exists between the magnetosphere and the ionosphere, involving a magnetospheric 'generator', field-aligned flows (known as Birkeland currents), and the ionosphere acting as a resistive load. Associated with this circuit are the horizontal currents known as the electrojets, flowing towards midnight from the morning and evening in the E-region. Energy is dissipated in the ionosphere by these currents to produce heating of the neutral gas which drives a horizontal motion to lower latitudes. Thus a proportion of the incident solar-wind energy ultimately ends up in the mid-latitude atmosphere.

Near noon, direct entry of solar-wind particles is possible via the cusps. This inflow generally consists of a low-energy stream which mainly affects the F-region of the ionosphere, causing increased ionisation and heating. There is also an upward flow of plasma out through the cusps which is thought to provide the source of heavy ions in the equatorial ring current, though the process by which the particles reach there is still unknown.

The region contained within the auroral oval is known as the polar cap. Here, the magnetic field lines are open into the tail and the dominant linkage between the magnetosphere and the ionosphere is via the dawn-dusk electric field. This 'maps' down the field lines from the magnetosphere to produce an approximately uniform field directed horizontally from the dawn-side to the dusk-side of the polar cap. The field drives the ionospheric plasma across the polar cap from the sunlit side to the night-side (anti-sunward convection). During disturbed conditions plasma velocities well in excess of 1 km s^{-1} have been observed. When observations of the polar winter ionosphere were first made, it was perplexing that ionisation remained and even increased erratically although there was no sunlight. It is now known that the anti-sunward convection plays a major role by transporting plasma produced in sunlight outside the polar cap into the polar night. Normally a 'two-cell' convection pattern is established, but when the IMF is northward it is possible for more complex multicellular patterns to develop.

The return flow of the convection cells takes place in the subauroral region on the low-latitude side of the oval. Here an interesting boundary occurs, loosely associated with the magnetic field lines threading through the plasmapause, between the plasma co-rotating with the earth and that convecting. On the night-side there is normally a major depletion of the ionosphere, known as the main ionospheric trough, associated with this boundary.

The behaviour of the ionosphere is characterised scientifically using three different time bases: these are universal time (UT), local solar time (LST), and local magnetic time (LMT). By definition, universal time is the same everywhere in geospace, and by convention is taken to be the time on the Greenwich Meridian (it is equivalent to Greenwich Mean Time, GMT). Local solar time is defined with respect to the local longitude of the point in question: it is 12 LST when the sun is aligned with the local meridian, 11 LST when the sun is 15° east of the meridian, and 13 LST when it is 15° west of it. LST and UT are equivalent for the Greenwich Meridian, but are, for example, 5 h different on the eastern seaboard of the USA. Magnetic local time is defined in a similar way to LST except that it is referenced to the local magnetic meridian rather than to longitude. For most of the world the difference between LMT and LST is negligible. Near the magnetic poles, however, the discrepancy becomes very important.

The coupling between the ionosphere and magnetosphere is clearly very complex and not fully understood. The sizes and positions of the caps, ovals and troughs all change as their associated magnetospheric boundaries vary with fluctuations in the solar wind. In a sense the ionosphere can be thought of as a giant television which

Aurorae are the most obviously dramatic result of the interaction of the solar wind with the geomagnetic field. In broad terms they arise from the excitation of the atmospheric constituents at about 100km altitude as a result of collisions with energetic electrons travelling down magnetic field lines from the magnetosphere (mainly plasma sheet). As the gas atoms and molecules return to their unexcited (ground) state they emit electromagnetic radiation whose wavelength depends upon the species concerned and its level of excitation.

(a) A green auroral arc over Halley station caused by excitation of atomic oxygen to give radiation at 557.7 nm.
(b) A false colour image of the complete auroral oval over Antarctica recorded by the Dynamics Explorer (DE-1) spacecraft. The radiation, in the ultra-violet at 130.4 and 135.6 nm, is from atomic oxygen. The image confirms the reality of the oval, but also shows a cross-polar arc which is found to occur only when the IMF is northward. The combintion of arc and oval is known as a "theta" aurora.

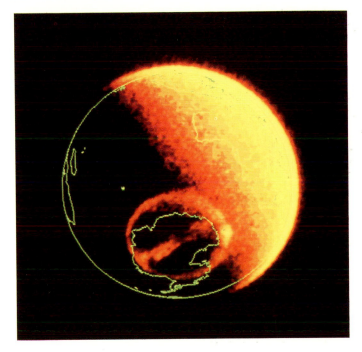

shows programmes broadcast from other regions of geospace. The most dramatic and well known of these are the aurorae which have awed and fascinated mankind from the dawn of creation. By recording the programmes with a variety of ground-based and balloon-, rocket- and satellite-borne sensors, much can be learned about the fundamental processes involved. It is this possibility which has made the polar regions such rewarding locations for geospace research.

Why Antarctica?

There remains the basic question of 'Why Antarctica?', particularly since most of the world's population, and therefore scientific resources, are concentrated in the northern hemisphere, making the Arctic more 'local'. The answer to this question is tied up with the polar contrasts, just as it was for the lower atmosphere. But now it is the details of the geomagnetic field upon which attention must be focused.

The simple approximation to the earth's magnetic field introduced earlier is simply not adequate when looked at in detail. The geomagnetic and geographic poles are not coincident, so that the 'bar magnet' really needs to be tilted with respect to the earth's rotational axis. Also, the positions of the two geomagnetic poles relative to the geographic poles are actually quite different, so that an offset and tilted magnet is required to approximate adequately the real field.

Inspection of the present configuration of the geomagnetic field reveals a number of important contrasts between the two hemispheres. First, the dip poles (the points where the field is vertical at the ground) and the invariant poles (the points were the field is strongest at the ground) are not coincident. Secondly, this discrepancy is much larger in the south. Thirdly, both the dip and the invariant poles in Antarctica are significantly further from the geographic pole than are the corresponding Arctic poles. For the southern dip pole the separation is a full 23° of latitude.

To appreciate the significance of these contrasts, it must be remembered that the ionospheric plasma is influenced both by the input of solar ultra-violet radiation (which varies as a function of LST), and by the geo-

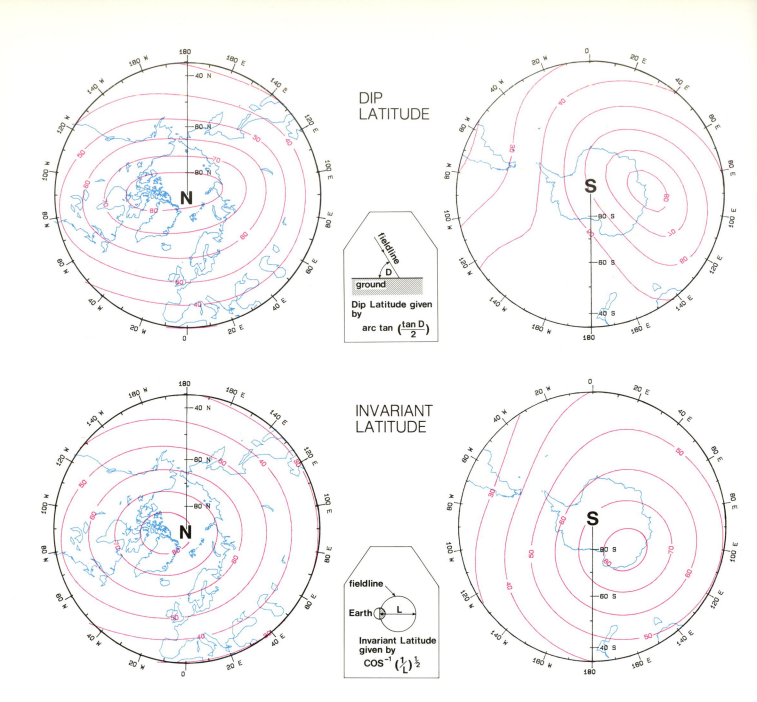

DIP LATITUDE

Dip Latitude given by

$$\arctan\left(\frac{\tan D}{2}\right)$$

INVARIANT LATITUDE

Invariant Latitude given by

$$\cos^{-1}\left(\frac{1}{L}\right)^{\frac{1}{2}}$$

Contrasts between the geomagnetic field for the Arctic and the Antarctic. The geomagnetic field is represented by two 'latitude' scales. These scales are references to the magnetic dip poles (the points where the field is vertical at the ground), and the magnetic invariant poles (the points where the magnetic field strength is greatest). They are constructed using the simple mathematical expressions shown inset.

The value of the Antarctic is well illustrated by contrasting the geophysical locations of observing sites in the two hemispheres. Here the geographic latitude of the site is plotted against dip latitude. Although there are far fewer sites in the Antarctic (open circles) their spacings provide unique combinations.

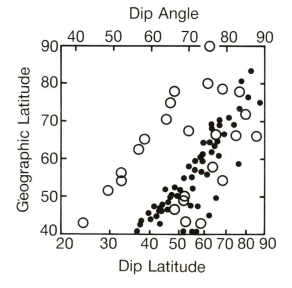

230

Part of the 21km long transmitting antenna used at the US Siple station for injecting VLF radio waves into the magnetosphere to study the interactions between the waves and energetic charged particles trapped there. This antenna has since been extended to 42km.

magnetic field (producing variations ordered in LMT). The solar input means that the ionosphere 'knows' about geographic latitude. It also 'knows' about dip latitude, because a variety of interactions between the neutral gas and plasma involve the local orientation of the field. Furthermore, it 'knows' about invariant latitude because this system identifies which field line a particular parcel of plasma is on, and therefore what magnetospheric processes it may be involved in or influenced by. An important consequence of the offset between the geographic and geomagnetic poles is that a universal-time dependence is introduced into some aspects of the behaviour of the ionosphere.

In seeking an understanding of the polar ionosphere, one very important approach is to determine which coordinate system produces the best ordering of the different types of behaviour observed. For example, electrojets tend to occur in a particular range of invariant, rather than geographic, latitudes, indicating their link with currents flowing in the magnetosphere. In contrast, the effect a neutral wind has on the plasma in the ionosphere depends more on the dip latitude, whilst the input of ultra-violet energy depends purely upon geographic latitude. It naturally follows that, in principle at least, the Antarctic will be particularly interesting because of the large separations between the coordinate systems there. Indeed, unique combinations of geographic and magnetic co-ordinates occur. It is possible, for instance, to find locations having dip latitudes ranging from under 40° (at about 60°W) to 90° (at about 140°E) at fixed geographic latitude. Having the geographic latitude constant means that the diurnal solar ultra-violet energy input does not change, so the opportunity exists for studying the influence of the geomagnetic field from temperate latitudes to the pole without any complications due to variations in this factor. Similarly, 60° dip latitude is found to occur from less than 40°S all the way to the South Pole.

The eccentricity of the south magnetic pole means that the southern auroral oval is much more displaced with respect to the geographic pole than is the case in the

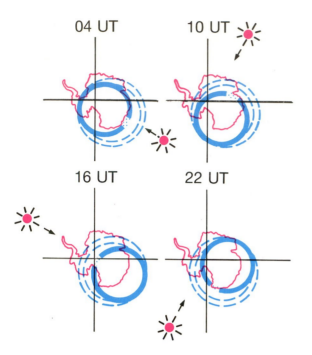

04 UT 10 UT

16 UT 22 UT

The offset between the geographic and geomagnetic poles results in significant changes in the latitudes of auroral oval and the 'footprint' of the cusp through the Universal time (UT) day. The area swept by the magnetic midnight portion of the oval as shown, is known as the auroral zone.

Around 16UT during winter, the 'footprint' of the cusp is well inside the polar night in Antarctica, but this is never the case for midwinter in the Arctic.

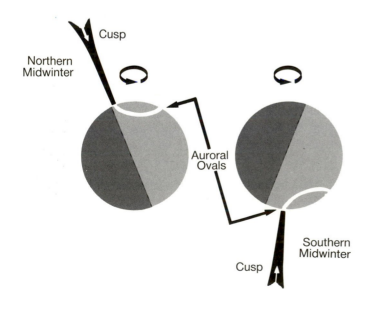

Cusp

Northern Midwinter

Auroral Ovals

Cusp

Southern Midwinter

north. One consequence of this is that the latitude at which aurora are commonly observed varies greatly in the south. It is very rare to see aurorae in the South American sector, even as far south as the Antarctic Circle, but they are commonly observed as far north as New Zealand. Another consequence is that the cusps in the two hemispheres are not symmetrical. The foot of the southern cusp varies in latitude from less than 60° up to 90°, so that during the austral winter its effects upon the upper atmosphere can be studied over a much wider range of solar zenith angle (the elevation of the sun above the horizon) than is possible in the north. In particular, at certain universal times it is buried deep in the polar night, a situation which never occurs in the north.

To capitalise fully on these unique conditions it is necessary to have a suitable environment in which to site experiments. Here the Antarctic offers both advantages and disadvantages. The continent itself provides a platform upon which facilities can be located and, in particular, allows the geographic pole to be used. However, large areas are inaccessible because of the vast Southern Ocean. This latter point makes the presence of geophysical observatories on the few subantarctic islands of particular importance. In practice the advantages have outweighed the disadvantages, for although there are many fewer sites in the south, they provide a much greater coverage of geographic/geomagnetic combinations than do those in the north.

The availability of unlimited uninhabited 'land' also has very great advantages. For instance, a group from Stanford University has utilised the combination of the unlimited space and the thick Antarctic ice cover to carry out a unique experiment using a very low frequency (VLF) radio transmitter located at Siple Station (76°S, 84°W) to investigate wave–particle interactions in the magnetosphere in the region of the plasmapause. This involves an antenna 40 km long strung from poles banged into the ice. Such an antenna is very efficient at radiating at VLF because it is supported above the electrical ground (the continental bedrock) by about 2000 m of ice.

This experiment has produced a wealth of new insights on fundamental plasma processes in the magnetosphere. One very significant outcome has been the realisation that emissions from powerful VLF transmitters, such as those used for navigation (e.g. Omega) and for communications with submerged submarines, can penetrate into the magnetosphere and there interact with electrons to 'shake' them out of the radiation belts, causing them to precipitate into the atmosphere. It also appears as though electromagnetic radiation from electricity transmission lines and major industrial activities produce similar effects. It has been suggested that the drain this causes on the Van Allen radiation belts is sufficient to alter significantly their configurations. The observed gap at about 2.5 R_E between the inner and outer belts may be almost entirely manmade.

Solar seismology

The unique geographical environment at the South Pole has also allowed Antarctica to play a very important role in the relatively new field of solar seismology. Seismic activity occurs on the sun just as it does on the earth, and measurements of this reveal much about the sun's internal structure. The experimental technique involves making careful optical observations of the solar disk at particular wavelengths, and endeavouring to detect small doppler shifts representing mechanical oscillations. Displacements of the solar diameter as small as 5 m in amplitude have been detected in this way. It has been possible to identify several characteristic modes of oscillation, with periods of around 5 minutes. It has also been suggested that a much slower oscillation, with a period of 160 minutes, may be present.

These observations have been made from mid-latitude solar observatories where they are naturally limited in duration by the daily cycle of day and night and also by atmospheric perturbations and pollution. This has posed a particular problem in establishing the reality of the longer-period oscillations. In 1979 a joint American and French team realised the great potential offered by the South Pole for such observations. During the summer the sun is continuously above the horizon, there are prolonged periods of clear weather, and the high altitude and lack of water vapour in the atmosphere make it possible to resolve astronomical features as well as at any other site in the world. A further advantage is that trends in the data resulting from the earth's rotation are absent. A solar observatory was established at the South Pole during the 1979/80 summer season and a data set continuous over 5 days was obtained. These data allowed the detailed spectra of the 5-minute oscillations to be delineated, and their persistence to be determined. Data in confirmation of the earlier observations of the 160-minute oscillation were also obtained.

Analysis of the initial data set from the South Pole continues and further campaigns have been mounted. It seems certain the South Pole will play a continuing role in solar studies. It is also possible that other astronomical observations will be made in future to take advantage of the unique geographical features there.

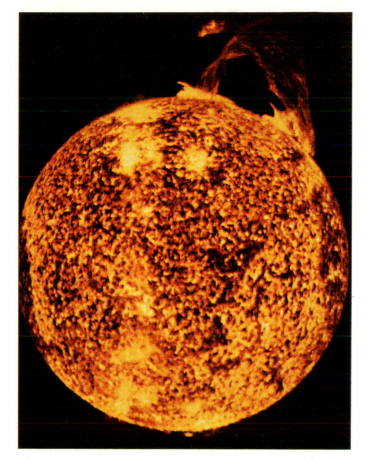

The sun, as it would look if our eyes could see far ultra-violet light. The science of solar seismology is revealing new insights into the physical behaviour of the sun – the South Pole has proved to be a valuable location for this science.

History of geospace research in Antarctica

The study of geospace from Antarctica has its earliest roots in the eighteenth-century preoccupation with investigation of terrestrial magnetism and the quest for the southern geomagnetic pole. This topic was the primary purpose of the Ross Expedition, which was charged with making magnetic observations on certain 'world term days' (days when observations would be made simultaneously around the world), with determination of the position of the south magnetic pole, and with making observations of aurorae.

Ross was not in fact the first European to see the aurora australis. This priority reportedly belongs to a Spanish mathematician and seaman Don Ulloa who 'often' observed 'a perceptible illumination', which he identified as an aurora, when rounding Cape Horn in autumn 1645. It is very questionable whether what Ulloa saw could have been aurorae because of the very low invariant latitude of Cape Horn. Only under the most extreme levels of magnetic disturbance are aurorae sighted in this region. It is now impossible to determine with any assurance what Don Ulloa actually saw, but the reflection of light from sea ice on clouds (ice blink) or from phosphorescence reflected from clouds is no more unlikely than aurorae. It

(a)

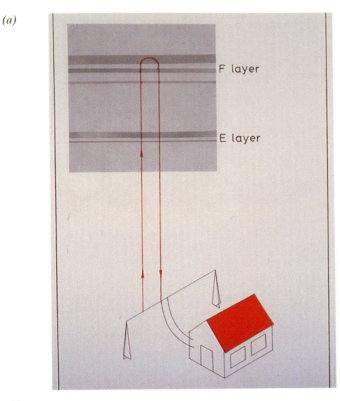

F layer

E layer

Free electrons in a plasma act as a mirror to electromagnetic waves provided their concentration (N in m^{-3}) and the frequency (f in MHz) fulfil the simple 'resonance' condition $N = 1.24 \times 10^{10} f^2$ The frequency satisfying this relation is called the plasma frequency. Thus the concentration of a plasma may be determined by illuminating it with radio waves of various frequencies until reflection occurs, giving the plasma frequency.

(a) The 'ionosonde' utilises this principle by transmitting short pulses of radio waves up to the ionosphere. The time of flight of the pulse gives an indication of the height of the reflecting layer; its frequency gives the concentration at that height.

(b) Sweeping in frequency allows a picture (known as an ionogram) of the vertical structure of the ionosphere above the ionosonde to be obtained. The height scale is distorted because radio waves are slowed down in traversing less-dense plasma

(c) a typical daytime ionogram from Scott base.

(b)

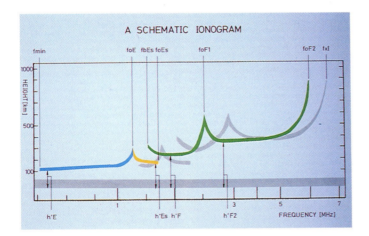

(c)

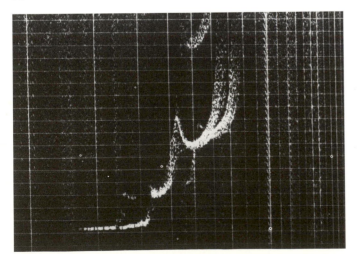

is certain, though, that Captain Cook recorded aurorae during his circumnavigation of the world in 1773, so priority probably belongs to him.

Ross would have seen several spectacular displays during his winter stay at Kerguelen in 1840 since this site lies just north of the southern auroral zone and his visit coincided with a peak in the 11-year cycle of solar activity. There would undoubtedly have been a display on the first term day (29/30 May 1840) when a major magnetic disturbance was noted.

The theme of geomagnetic observations was continued by the German Expedition to South Georgia as part of the First International Polar Year (1882/83). Regular observations of the geomagnetic field in Royal Bay were made for about a year, including manual readings made every 5 minutes on regular term days.

Apart from the Ross and German expeditions, little of relevance to geospace was done until expeditions began to establish winter camps on the continent at the turn of this century. Continuous observation of the geomagnetic field using standard instruments and standardised techniques for data analysis then became a major element of each expedition, as part of globally coordinated monitoring. These measurements were coupled to visual observations of aurorae, since it had already been noted that there appeared to be a strong link between geomagnetic disturbances and the occurrence of aurorae. Experimental verification of this theory proved to be very elusive, mainly because auroral observations were limited to periods of clear weather and no instrumentation was available, leaving only visual observations. Even so very extensive observations were made, particularly by Scott's first expedition, and by Mawson on Shackleton's 1907–1909 expedition. Mawson made studies of daily variations, monthly statistics, and of relations between auroral activity and other phenomena, such as geomagnetism and local meteorology. He suspected that aurorae were affected by

234

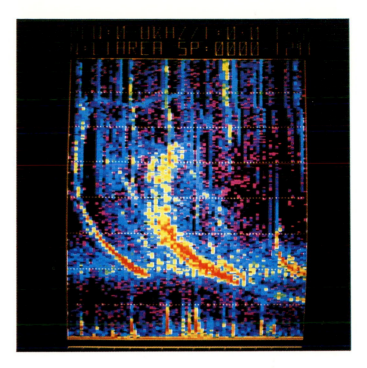

the local topography, rising higher in the sky above mountains, and also by the local weather. In neither of these suspicions was he correct. He was considerably closer to the truth, however, in being one of the first to theorise that aurorae were associated with electric currents flowing high in the atmosphere.

Several of the 'Heroic Age' explorers tried to take photographs of the aurora australis in an attempt to improve the objectivity of auroral observations and extend the data coverage, but with little success. The great Antarctic photographer Ponting failed completely on Scott's second expedition, even though he took great care to use the best lenses and photographic plates available. The first successful photograph was taken by Mawson on Shackleton's expedition, but he found it necessary to use 10-minute exposures to record anything and, as he noted, 'the curtains had altered their shape during the interval [so] the results were of little value'. By the time Mawson led his own expedition in 1911, he had much improved his equipment and was able to obtain acceptable results with exposures of as little as 10 s. After World War I photographic techniques improved sufficiently to make auroral photography routine. Even so, it took until 1939 before the rough position of the southern auroral oval was determined, 79 years after that for the north, because of the paucity of observations.

The turn of the century brought the introduction of revolutionary new physical understanding and technologies upon which the future study of geospace would be based. One key technical advance was the development of radio communications, and with it the realisation that some property of the upper atmosphere allowed radio waves to bend round the horizon, and so be used to communicate over very long distances. The exploitation of radio for communicating and for researching the nature of the upper atmosphere proceeded hand-in-hand. Mawson again played a seminal role by being the first person to introduce radio to Antarctica. He operated radio stations at both Macquarie Island and Cape Denison during 1912 and 1913, both for relaying messages and for scientific studies of the ionosphere, or 'conducting layer' as it was then known.

By today's standards radio technology in the early 1900s was incredibly crude. Transmitters consisted of mechanically driven spark generators which could only achieve radio wave frequencies up to about 500 kHz (the lower end of the medium waveband). The attainment of higher frequencies awaited the development of thermionic valves. The medium and long wavebands are now almost exclusively used for short-range broadcasting via 'ground wave' propagation. This is because the normal daytime concentration of electrons in the lower part of the iono-

Thunderstorms produce radiowave emissions over a wide range of frequencies. VLF waves can be 'ducted' along magnetic field lines, and so propagate from one hemisphere to the other, sometimes reflecting back and forth several times. The waves are slowed up by the electrons they encounter along the way, the lower frequencies more than the higher (dispersion). The result, if listened to on a radio receiver, is a characteristic whistling tone, giving the emissions the name whistlers. A study of the dispersion gives much information about the plasma environment traversed, particularly at the highest point on the field line. The photograph shows a spectrogram giving received frequency (vertical scale 0 to 8 kHz) as a function of time (horizontal range 1.5 s), with signal intensity indicated by the colour scale.

The average variations in the electron concentration of the F2 region over the South Pole observed during the IGY. The 'footprint' of the cusp passes over the South Pole at magnetic noon and enhancements resulting from the direct entry of solar wind particles stand out clearly. By convention, the South Pole keeps Universal Time.

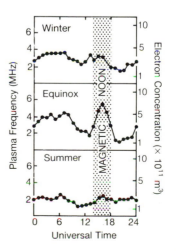

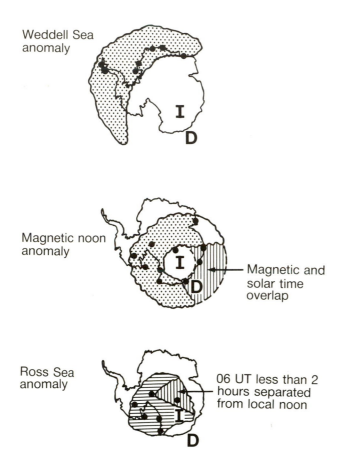

Weddell Sea
anomaly

Magnetic noon
anomaly

Magnetic and
solar time
overlap

Ross Sea
anomaly

06 UT less than 2
hours separated
from local noon

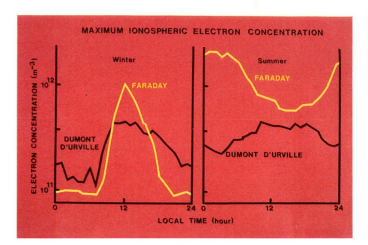

MAXIMUM IONOSPHERIC ELECTRON CONCENTRATION

A comparison of the ionosphere over Faraday Station (65°S, 65°W; dip latitude 39°S) with that over Dumont d'Urville (67°S, 140°E; dip latitude 89°S). The two sites form a unique pair as they have the same geographic latitude but differ by 50° in dip latitude. The Weddell Sea anomaly behaviour is most clearly seen for Faraday.

(Left) A schematic illustration of the various F-region anomalies. The dots locate the observing sites which contributed to identifying the anomaly, the letters 'I' and 'D' indicate the positions of the invariant and dip poles.

(Below) The amount of sunlight (and hence plasma production) incident upon the source region for plasma convection varies greatly through the UT day during winter.

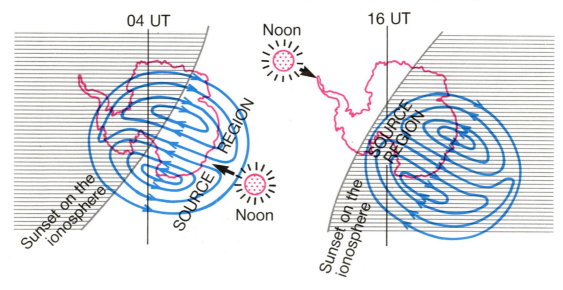

sphere is such that these wavelengths are trapped between the surface of the earth and the bottom of the ionosphere. Here they only propagate relatively short distances, unless very large powers are used. Only at night-time, when the ionisation in the normal D-region decays away, can there be any propagation via reflection from higher layers in the ionosphere, allowing much longer distances to be covered. To broadcast effectively at such low frequencies also requires very large antennae, since to be efficient radiators antennae must be about the same length as the wavelength to be broadcast (typically 1 km scale size for 300 kHz).

Mawson used 500 kHz spark transmitters giving, nominally, 1.5 kW of power. However, he was limited in the size of antennae he could build, particularly at Cape Denison where the weather was so incredibly bad. Even with these limitations the Macquarie station worked extremely well for both years and maintained regular contact with Australia. Mawson was not so lucky at Cape Denison, where a combination of poor installation and poor operating practices resulted in little or no success in the first year. The system was renovated for the second winter and thereafter, with a new operator, regular contact

was maintained with Macquarie which acted as a relay station.

The radio path from Cape Denison to Macquarie is a very interesting one since it crosses the auroral zone. It was observed that contact was only possible during the hours of darkness. Given current understanding this would be expected since the size of the transmitter/antenna in use and the long path distance ruled out successful ground wave contact. Also it was noted that contact was lost during periods of magnetic activity and when particular types of auroral activity occurred. At the time these were new and exciting findings but, sadly, their full value was never appreciated because a combination of war, the Depression, and the death of key expedition members held up publication of the research results until the 1940s, by which time they were outdated. The interpretation of the expedition's findings is now clear. During periods of increased magnetic activity, energetic electrons are precipitated into the lower ionosphere (the D-region) where they collide with neutral atoms and in so doing create sufficient new ionisation to absorb all the radio wave energy transmitted from the ground.

An early theoretical calculation demonstrating that the global thermospheric wind would tend to blow ionisation up the magnetic field lines at the same universal time for many Antarctic observing sites.

The mean summertime diurnal variations in the height of the F$_2$-region over Antarctica during the IGY. The variations match up well in universal time.

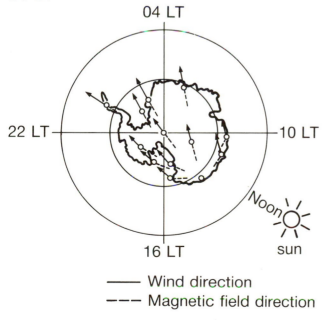

04 UT

Wind direction
Magnetic field direction

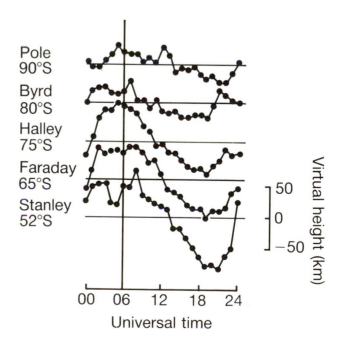

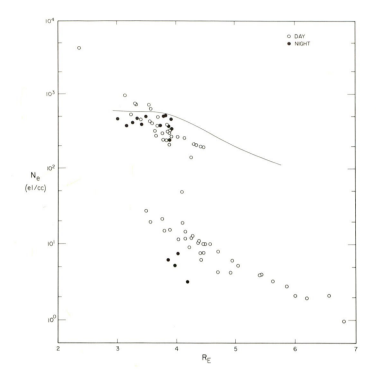

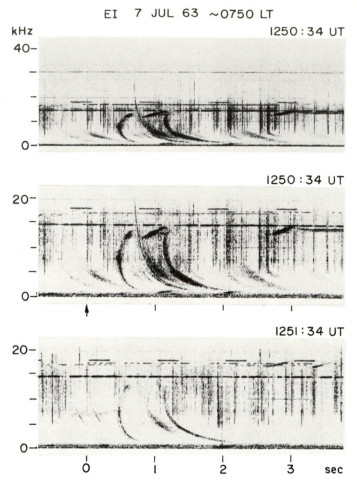

EI 7 JUL 63 ~0750 LT

The original observations from Eights Station which demonstrated the existence of the plasmapause. The left hand panel shows some of the whistler spectrograms, whilst the right hand panel gives the variation of electron concentration as a function of radial distance (expressed in units of earth radii). The abrupt step down in concentration marks the plasmapause.

Very major strides in radio technology were made during the first 30 years of this century, and one outcome was the development of an automatic instrument for probing the ionosphere, known as a Vertical Incidence Ionosonde. This instrument has played a fundamental role in studying the ionosphere, and there are currently well over 100 operating worldwide, of which twelve are in Antarctica. The earliest attempt at applying the new technology to the polar ionosphere was made on Admiral Byrd's first Antarctic expedition by M.P. Hanson in 1929 at Little America (78°34′S, 163°56′W). Hanson did not have automatic equipment but used instead the main communications transmitter of the base and a portable receiver which he sited about 15 km away in a tent. The physical hardships he endured to make his observations, in temperatures sometimes below -55°C, make sober reading but the results were fascinating.

Hanson made measurements of the virtual height of the ionosphere on several frequencies ranging from 3.5 to 11.3 MHz, obtaining complete diurnal variations for one winter day, one equinox day and a sequence of several days in summer. Solar activity was high during 1929 (a peak in the 11-year cycle having occurred in 1928), but all the observations related to magnetically quiet conditions. The outstanding discovery was that a pronounced F-region

persisted throughout the polar night, and showed a consistent diurnal variation with lowest heights occurring during local day. Unlike Mawson, Hanson very quickly analysed his data on his return home and presented his results at the spring meeting of the American Geophysical Union in 1932. These results were of great relevance to some of the questions that the Second Polar Year (1932) and, subsequently, the IGY (1957) were aimed at; yet, strangely, they were largely ignored by researchers at the time.

Little America was located at an invariant latitude of approximately 74°. With the benefit of modern understanding, it is evident that the station would have been situated under the night-time auroral oval during the UT night, moved into the polar cap in the UT day, and moved back into the daytime oval to be under the cusp at about 18 UT. Thus, quite consistent but sometimes dramatic changes would be expected through the day. In particular a strong enhancement in the amount of ionisation present would be expected at around 18 UT (equivalent to 07 LST or noon LMT) as solar-wind particles penetrate down to the ionosphere via the cusp. Unfortunately, Hanson's data are on too coarse a time scale for this effect to be readily evident.

Chapter·17

Milestones in a unique environment

Geospace studies in the IGY

Systematic study of geospace from Antarctica commenced with the IGY in 1957. At this stage, however, the concept of geospace had not been developed and almost nothing was known about the nature of the interplanetary medium or indeed about the magnetosphere. Thus the emphasis was upon exploring the polar ionosphere.

The IGY was chosen to coincide with a maximum in the solar cycle. In the event the maximum which occurred was the most intense ever recorded. It was followed in 1964 by a comparable international effort called the International Year of the Quiet Sun (IQSY) which covered the next sunspot minimum. Together these two special periods have provided a unique global data set upon which much of our current knowledge has been founded.

The IGY focused the minds of scientists and engineers the world over to develop new instrumentation and to coordinate their observations effectively. The most spectacular new tools were artificial satellites; with these it was possible to make *in situ* measurements of the polar ionosphere, as well as to start exploring the nature of geospace as a whole. Other very valuable but less eye-catching techniques for ground-based observation were also developed. These included the all-sky camera which allowed continuous monitoring of aurorae, the relative ionospheric opacity meter (riometer) with which particle precipitation into the ionosphere could be monitored, and the VLF receiver used for studying natural electromagnetic emissions.

As previous chapters have made clear, a large expansion of the manned sites took place as part of the IGY effort. The major justification for many of these installations was ionospheric research. Most of the bases were equipped with ionosondes, magnetometers, VLF receivers and all-sky cameras, and several had other sophisticated radio experiments. Riometers did not play a major role in Antarctica until just after the IGY however.

The scientific questions which were asked at the time were simple and direct: does the polar ionosphere persist during the long polar night?; does it exhibit significant diurnal variations at sites where the solar zenith angle changes negligibly through the day?; how do the north and south polar ionospheres compare?; and what effects are introduced by the very large displacement of the geographic and geomagnetic poles in the south?

The first two of these questions were quickly answered using the unique ionosonde data obtained from the South Pole station. The ionosphere did indeed persist, at a concentration and altitude inconsistent with that which could be produced by solar ultra-violet radiation alone. Furthermore, pronounced diurnal variations were evident,

The availability of virtually unlimited uninhabited 'land' allows the use of facilities such as rockets and balloons, without their usual complications such as national boundaries, commercial air traffic lanes and populated areas. Here a Super-Arcas rocket takes off from Siple Station to study particle precipitation into the D-region.

with a consistent peak occurring at 06 UT throughout the year, and another at 16 UT during the equinoxes.

Prior to the IGY, very preliminary comparisons between the northern and southern hemispheres suggested that no significant differences would be found. Only one curious feature had been noted. An ionosonde had been operated by Argentina in 1951 from Deception Island off the Antarctic Peninsula. It was found, contrary to all previous experience, that during the summer the maximum electron concentration was smallest at the middle of the day, when it should have been largest. It soon became clear from the IGY data that this result was part of a much more significant anomaly affecting all the Antarctic Peninsula and Weddell Sea sector, characterised by high concentrations at night and lower concentrations by day. During winter, more sensible variations were observed in which concentrations were low at night and high near noon. The transition between the two types of behaviour occurred quite suddenly at the equinoxes. It was appropriately labelled the Weddell Sea anomaly.

Careful study of all the ionosonde data from Antarctica revealed yet another highly puzzling anomaly. The regular variations of maximum electron concentration appeared to be a function of universal time, rather than local solar time, with a pronounced maximum at 06 UT. This was called the Ross Sea anomaly, and it was apparent that the Weddell Sea anomaly was a special case of it in which the

UT control was only evident in the electron concentration in summer. Having found such an unusual result, Arctic data were analysed in the same way and there was some suggestions that a similar but much less distinct UT effect could be identified there.

The large separation of the geographic and geomagnetic poles in the south has the consequence that for part of the continent local solar time and local magnetic time become significantly out of step. It was found that in this region there was a further anomaly in which a peak in concentration occurred at local magnetic noon. Attempts were made to verify this finding using Arctic data, but the relative configurations of geographic and geomagnetic coordinates did not allow sufficient separation between solar noon and magnetic noon for the data to be convincing.

The interpretation of all these anomalies has taken two decades, and has required both internationally coordinated field work in Antarctica and detailed observations from a variety of satellites overflying the polar regions. Considerable scientific controversy has been generated amongst theorists along the way and major advances in our under-

(a) A powerful development of the ionosonde utilises modern computer techniques to greatly expand the range of information obtained from radio waves reflected from the ionosphere. This ionosonde, one of six built by the National Oceanic and Atmospheric Administration of the USA, is located at Halley. An identical instrument has been operated concurrently at Siple.

The locations of Halley and Siple. The two 'pie' segments illustrate schematically the differences in local solar time and local magnetic time between the two places.

(a)

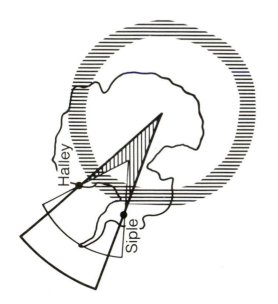

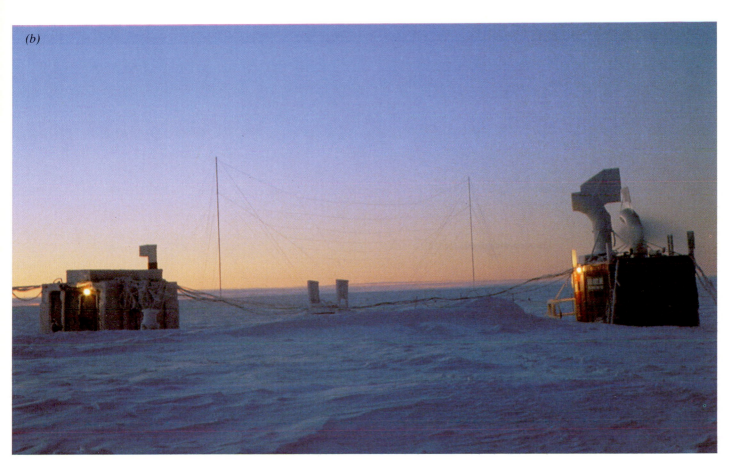

(b) The sounder is housed in a specially designed caboose (left) and provided with dedicated power supply (right). In the background is the main transmitting antenna supported by two 45 m masts.

(c) A typical digital ionogram. In this case the colour coding is used to show where the echoing region is located in the north/south plane. The region of blue originates from the poleward side of the main ionspheric trough, about 500 km south in this instance.

(d) A plot summarising a complete day of ionograms from Halley in comparison with those from Siple. The colour coding gives the plasma frequency at each height.

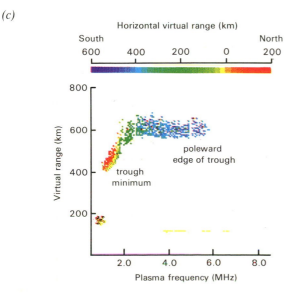

(c)

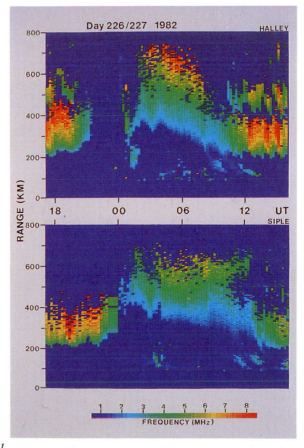

(d)

241

standing of the basic processes involved have been the end result.

It is now clear that the Antarctic anomalies result from a combination of geospace processes which are manifested particularly strongly in Antarctica because of the marked offset between geographic and magnetic poles. The processes involved are: anti-sunward plasma convection, driven by the cross-tail electric field; neutral thermospheric winds, driven both by the diurnal expansion and contraction of the atmosphere, and by momentum transfer from the convecting plasma; and charged particle precipitation into the auroral oval, cusp and polar cap.

The effect of anti-sunward convection is to move plasma generated on the day-side of the auroral zone into the polar cap and night-side auroral zone. It is thus an effective source of winter night-time ionisation provided the day-side zone is illuminated by the sun. For the southern hemisphere, there is a very dramatic change in the solar illumination through the UT day. Early in the morning the day-side zone is situated at about 60°S, and is thus receiving considerable solar input, even at midwinter, but by UT afternoon it is close to 90°S and hence receives very little solar input. The end result must therefore be a strong wintertime UT modulation in the amount of plasma convected, giving rise to enhancements in F-region concentrations in the morning and reductions in the evening, as observed for the Ross Sea anomaly. This convection effect will only be evident in winter, and only in the polar cap and auroral zone.

A horizontal motion of the neutral gas will impart momentum to the plasma by collisions, but the F-region plasma is constrained to move along the direction of the local magnetic field. It thus has a net upward or downward motion whose magnitude depends upon the wind velocity and the local dip angle. Since the density of the atmosphere falls off exponentially with increasing height, moving plasma upwards reduces its destruction through chemical processes, whilst moving it down increases destruction. Provided there is a source of plasma production (solar ultra-violet, convection or particle precipitation), the net effect of a neutral wind is thus to increase or decrease the plasma density, depending on wind direction.

Solar ultra-violet radiation heats the thermosphere, giving the greatest temperature near the subsolar point (i.e. directly under the sun) and the least at the antipodal (anti-solar) point. This heating gives rise to a predominantly horizontal wind flowing from the hot region, over the poles, to the cool region. The configuration of the southern geomagnetic field is such that this wind blows ionization upwards in the UT morning at most Antarctic stations, but downwards in the UT afternoon. This global wind will be boosted over the polar cap since the con-

vecting plasma will give momentum to the neutral gas. Given a source of ionization, the wind will therefore also generate a UT modulation of the observed F-region plasma concentrations. In summer, solar ultra-violet provides an adequate source, so that UT effects will occur then as a consequence of the wind. The effect is readily seen in the diurnal variation of the height of the F-region in summer.

The Weddell Sea sector of Antarctica does not normally come under the influence of convection or particle precipitation; thus only the global neutral wind is available to produce UT effects. In winter there is no source of ionization during the UT morning when the wind is causing an upward motion of the F-region, so no plasma enhancements are generated. In summer however, the sun illuminates the region throughout the day so the wind can do its work, giving rise to the Weddell Sea anomaly. The transition between the two types of diurnal variation occurs in the spring and autumn dependent upon the time of sunrise/sunset with respect to the time that the wind is producing upward drifts of ionisation.

Just after the IGY, the Antarctic played a seminal role in the discovery of the plasmapause. In 1963 US scientists established a station known as Eights at 75°12′S, 77°12′W where they made observations of naturally occurring VLF radio emissions known as whistlers. Whistlers originate from the electromagnetic energy released in lightning discharges. Part of this energy can become 'ducted' by the local magnetic field and constrained to travel along the field line from one hemisphere to the other, where it can be reflected back. As it travels along the field line, the plasma it encounters causes some wavelengths to travel more slowly than others, a process known as dispersion. An analysis of this dispersion allows the plasma concentration at the farthest point of the field line from earth (apogee) to be determined. Eights Station was ideally located for studies of whistlers because it sat at the foot of a magnetic field line which threads through the plasmapause (though that was not known at the time) and has its other foot in Canada, a region of unusually high thunderstorm activity. The Americans were able to measure a consistent 'knee' in the variation of plasma concentration with equatorial distance and to determine its behaviour statistically as a function of time and magnetic disturbance. The plasmapause had not at that time been postulated by theorists but the observations were quickly confirmed by *in situ* satellite observations.

Many of the facilities established in Antarctica for the IGY and IQSY were kept in operation thereafter, and new ones were added subsequently. A further major international programme known as the International Magnetospheric Study (IMS) was mounted in 1978. This involved exploration of the magnetosphere by satellites and studies of ionosphere–magnetosphere interactions using ground-based techniques in both polar regions. The Antarctic continent played a full part in this campaign. It was as a result of the IMS that the coupled nature of the various regions of geospace began to be appreciated, and the name was first coined.

Modern geospace research in Antarctica

The modern approach is to study each element of geospace in the context of its associations with the other elements. Antarctica plays its part by acting as a unique geophysical laboratory where the end results of geospace processes often stand out more clearly than elsewhere, and where theoretical interpretations can be tested effectively. There is now a very vigorous, and expanding, international programme of field work, often tied closely to satellite observations and to theoretical developments.

A very broad range of related topics is being pursued and it is impossible to detail them all here. In summary they encompass: the study of the interactions between waves and particles, with particular emphasis upon the stimulated precipitation of electrons; the nature of the coupling between the solar wind and the terrestrial atmosphere via the cusps; the exchange of plasma between the ionosphere and the magnetosphere; the coupling of the thermosphere to the solar wind via the interaction between convecting plasma and the neutral gas; and the study of the subauroral atmosphere and its associations with other regions of geospace.

Rather than present a long list of research topics covering the whole range of science going on, the value of Antarctica can be more simply illustrated by describing some of the joint Anglo-American programmes currently active which utilize two observatories, Siple Station (75°36′S, 83°36′W) and Halley (75°36′S, 26°36′W). Halley has been in continuous use for geospace research since the IGY, whilst Siple was established in 1973, primarily for studies of VLF wave phenomena. The two stations form a unique pair since they are at the same geographic latitude and therefore have the same regime of solar energy input; but they are in the sector of the continent most distant from the magnetic poles (invariant and dip), so they have the same anomalously low invariant latitude of about 60°. This puts them on the low-latitude edge of the auroral zone, at the foot of the magnetic field lines which thread through the plasmapause. The other ends of these field lines are in Newfoundland and Labrador (the so-called

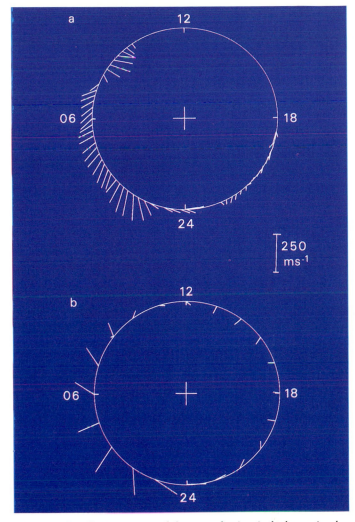

A comparison between neutral thermospheric winds determined using the Fabry–Perot interferometer at Halley and a theoretical Global Circulation model.

'conjugate points') where there is a very high incidence of thunderstorms. Halley and Siple thus experience very high whistler rates, making them ideal sites for studies of the plasmapause. A particularly interesting feature of the two sites is that they differ in local solar time by 4 h, but in local magnetic time by only 1.5 h. They are thus of great value for sorting out in which time frame (UT, LST or LMT) events are ordered.

The research work conducted at the two stations involves a loose consortium of university groups and government laboratories from the two countries. Both sites are very well instrumented and have the advantage of direct communications back to the various home institutes via geostationary satellites (ATS3 for Siple, INMARSAT for Halley), allowing ready access to experimental results. The return in terms of scientific output over the past few years has been very worthwhile, as a few examples will illustrate.

A major thrust of the research has been directed at understanding the nature of the main ionospheric trough. This feature is an important part of geospace and therefore worth studying for that reason. There is also a serious practical aspect to the work, since the trough is a major complicating factor in high-frequency (HF) radio communications. It is predominantly a night-time phenomenon, and appears to be associated with the boundary between the convecting and co-rotating plasma at about 60° invariant latitude. Halley and Siple are thus ideally located to study it, because they have the highest geographic latitude of any subauroral stations in the world and therefore provide the longest periods of winter darkness in which the trough can develop. Both stations are equipped with modern digital ionospheric radars which allow the structure and position of the trough to be monitored. One of the most interesting and unexpected findings of the research has been that trough behaviour is ordered in universal time rather than magnetic or solar time. Also, magnetospheric substorms appear to introduce significant longitudinal structure. These findings are currently provoking considerable theoretical work to produce an acceptable interpretation.

Halley and Siple are also very interesting sites from which to study wave–particle interactions. The important work being done from Siple using the VLF transmitter facility has already been mentioned, but other fascinating results on the longitudinal behaviour of the plasmapause have been obtained using naturally occurring whistlers. Studies have also been made of precipitating electrons using riometers which have revealed a further longitudinal anomaly which appears to be associated with a change in the strength of the geomagnetic field. The cause of this behaviour is not yet clear, but undoubtedly its interpretation will provide new understanding of the processes involved in particle precipitation.

At present, there is considerable interest in constructing Global Circulation Models (GCMs). These are computer simulations of the thermospheric circulation which endeavour to incorporate the most up-to-date theoretical ideas and then test them by comparing the GCM output with observations of the real world. Because of the coupling of the neutral gas and the ionospheric plasma through collisions, and the coupling of the ionospheric plasma to the rest of geospace via electric field and precipitation, GCMs need to take account of geographic, dip, and invariant latitude effects, and include behaviour ordered in UT, LST and LMT. The Antarctic is thus a very severe testing ground for GCM predictions. Recently it has become possible to measure the thermospheric wind from the ground using an optical technique which relies on making measurements of the Doppler shift of a weak airglow emission from atomic oxygen in the thermosphere. The instrument used is known as a 'Fabry Perot Interferometer' (FPI), and there are now two in operation in Antarctica. One is located at the Australian station,

Mawson, which is an auroral location where the effects of convection on the thermosphere should be strongly evident. The other is at Halley where the differences between the various coordinate systems are most marked. A GCM, which produces good results when matched against northern hemisphere measurements, has been compared with the Halley data, revealing a significant discrepancy in the morning, where the observed winds undergo a sharp shear not reproduced by the model. The cause of the shear is not yet understood but it is suspected that the discrepancy results from inadequate account of the southern polar magnetic field configuration being included in the GCM.

The future for geospace

The exploration phase in the study of geospace is now essentially complete. A good qualitative description of the overall system is available in which the main subdivisions have been delineated and the dominant processes identified. The next major challenge is to develop a quantitative understanding to the extent that the effects of a given disturbance on the sun can be accurately predicted as the energy propagates through the system and is finally dissipated in the earth's atmosphere.

This challenge can only be met by a coordinated campaign of simultaneous measurements at key locations throughout the geospace regime, using both satellites and ground-based techniques, backed up by a vigorous programme of theoretical research. The international scientific community plans to hold such a campaign in the early part of the next decade, to be called the International Solar Terrestrial Physics Programme (ISTP). At the core of the ISTP are several planned satellite missions. NASA and ISAS (the Japanese Space Agency) plan to launch four spacecraft, named WIND, POLAR, EQUATOR and GEOTAIL, to study simultaneously the two major sources (solar wind and ionosphere) and the two sinks (the ring currents and the tail) of geospace plasma. Closely coupled with this will be a programme of ground-based observations involving both polar regions, and a theory task group. They have given the whole programme the name Global Geospace Study (GGS). The European Space Agency (ESA) is planning two missions for ISTP: one, called CLUSTER, will consist of four small spacecraft flying close together in a polar orbit to study the three-dimensional microstructure of geospace; the other, known as SOHO, is designed to study the structure and behaviour of the sun. The Soviet Union will be taking part in ISTP but little has yet been revealed about their plans for space missions.

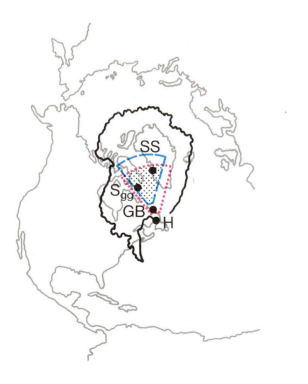

- – – – Goose Bay field-of-view'
- ·········· Halley field-of-view
- ——— Antarctic continent
- H   Halley, Antarctica
- GB   Goose Bay
- SS   Sondre Stromfjord
- S_{gg} South geographic pole

The conjugate overlap possible for backscatter radars located at Halley in Antarctica, and Goose Bay in Labrador. The maps are overlaid in invariant magnetic coordinates.

Ground-based observations from the polar regions will play a major part in ISTP, since they will be monitoring the final destination of energy flowing through geospace. However, it will not be sufficient to make observations from a few isolated locations since the aim is to achieve a quantitative assessment of energy flows. It will be necessary instead to establish networks of observing sites whose locations are chosen on scientific, rather than political, criteria.

For Antarctica, where national boundaries do not present a problem, the coordination will be undertaken by SCAR. However, it will be too expensive to increase significantly the number of permanently manned sites, particularly inland. For this reason much attention has been given to the possibility of using chains of unmanned observatories associated with key manned sites. Similar facilities are already operational for meteorological monitoring, but geospace experiments tend to be more sophisticated, requiring a more substantial housing and larger power supplies. Several attempts at developing operational automatic observatories have been made in the past decade by the Australians, Americans and British. Also, the Soviets successfully operated a chain of magnetometers along the traverse from the coast to their inland base Vostok. However, there is as yet no fully proven system. The Americans are currently evaluating an Automatic Geophysical Observatory (AGO) at the South Pole which was developed by Lockheed.

It will be important to monitor the motion of plasma over the polar cap and auroral zone. A promising technique is provided by the HF backscatter radar. This uses the doppler shift measured on HF radio waves back scattered from irregularities in the plasma to determine its velocity and hence to monitor plasma convection. The viewing area of such a radar is potentially very large.

A growing area of research which will very probably play an important role in ISTP is the general topic of conjugacy. It is well known that many phenomena, such as aurorae, particle precipitation and electromagnetic emissions, occur simultaneously in the two hemispheres, associated with the same magnetic field lines. However, little is known about the overall extent of such behaviour and, in particular, under what circumstances conjugacy ceases for field lines which go deep into the geotail. A great deal of new information concerning the dynamic topology of the magnetosphere should result from such studies. Much also remains to be learnt from investigating the perturbations of conjugacy introduced by seasonal changes in energy input and by the differences in magnetic field configuration in the two polar regions. An example here is that the electrical conductivity of the ionosphere over the summer polar cap is normally ten times greater than that in winter because of the increased solar ultraviolet radiation. Increased conductivity can effectively 'short out' the dawn/dusk electric field, so conditions may well arise where the plasma convection over the two polar caps is quite different, particularly at the solstices. The HF backscatter radar offers a very effective tool for conjugate studies since it is relatively cheap but covers a very wide range of latitudes. Suitable installations already exist in the Arctic which would be conjugate to a radar sited in Antarctica.

There can be no doubt that Antarctica has unique features which have been effectively exploited in the past for geospace research. Equally, the future for Antarctic research in the framework of ISTP looks very bright. The next decade should bring mankind a rich store of knowledge about his astronomical backyard.

The variety of satellite missions planned as part of the International Solar Terrestrial physics programme.

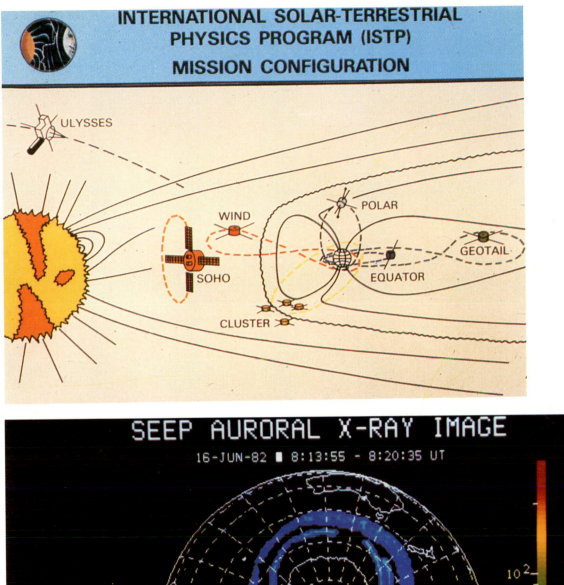

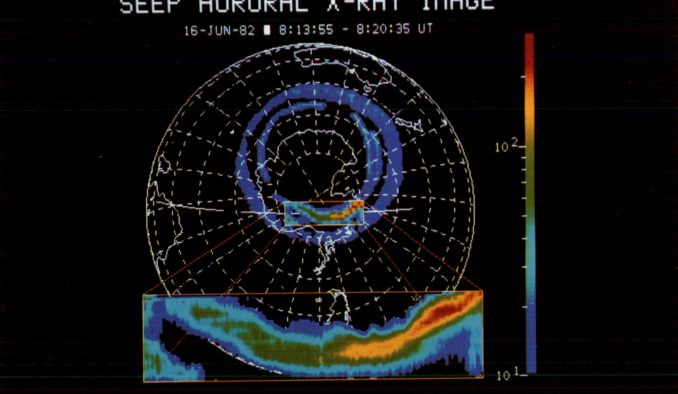

A satellite image of an 'X-ray aurora' recorded over Antarctica. X-rays are generated as energetic electrons precipitating into the atmosphere are decelerated by collisions. The emissions arise from about 80km altitude.

The Shackleton Mountains.

Part·V

Cooperation or confrontation?

Chapter·18
Science, the Treaty and the future

The role of science in the Antarctic

The enhanced scientific programmes since the 1950s are not unique to the Antarctic, but to a great extent reflect general trends of increasing diversity, specialisation, sophistication and expense that characterise world science. The past four decades have seen very significant growth and change in the nature of scientific knowledge.

In biology one thinks of population ecology and behaviour, ecological energetics, sociobiology, modelling, and above all molecular biology and its applications. Other important applied developments of ecology are conservation and pollution studies. Over the same period earth sciences saw the development of the unifying global theory of plate tectonics and sea-floor spreading, application of seismic refraction and reflection techniques, magnetometry, palaeomagnetic studies, and the possibility of recording past events from sediment cores or ice cores. In atmospheric sciences, the plasmapause was discovered only 25 years ago and the present field of solar–terrestrial physics involving the concept and structure of geospace is even more recent; automated data gathering is now commonplace, whilst super-computers contribute to global modelling of climate and weather. In short, there has been a dramatic worldwide increase in research aimed at investigating, explaining and exploiting the natural world.

An important factor contributing to these developments has been the rise of computer science, electronics, telemetry and communications to a level undreamed of 40 years ago. Linked to, and making possible, satellite technology, this has revolutionised remote sensing, data collecting and monitoring.

The Antarctic is remote, its environment is rigorous and hazardous and the logistics necessary to support science are expensive, so what has promoted the expansion of Antarctic science? Its development and role under the umbrella of the Antarctic Treaty and within the framework of the ICSU Committees, especially SCAR, can be considered in four categories: first, as a qualification for achieving consultative status in the Antarctic Treaty and in providing advice to the Treaty parties; secondly, the advancement of knowledge, academic interest and the satisfaction of intellectual curiosity; thirdly, in strategic or applied terms in relation to renewable and non-renewable resources; and fourthly, as related to natural or man-induced environmental change.

We may consider these in turn. Science is usually held to be the reason for the Antarctic Treaty – 'a continent for science' – but what real justification is there for this view? Although the original twelve signatories achieved consultative status on ratification and may keep it indefinitely, research activity is a necessary qualification for other nations to enter the Treaty as Consultative Parties and to retain that status. Article IX (see Appendix 1) states that other contracting parties have consultative status 'during such time as that Consultative Party demonstrates its interest in the Antarctic by conducting substantial scientific research activity there, such as the establishment of a scientific station or the despatch of a scientific expedition'. The preamble and Articles II and III also refer specifically to science.

National scientific activities are, however, very disparate. A recent survey analysed by country the numbers of scientific publications on the Antarctic, which may be taken as a relative measure of research activity. During a 3-year period from 1979, the exchange of information showed a more than twenty-fold spread, ranging from 29 to 626 publications!

Scientific activities are relatively non-controversial and had been demonstrated during the International Geophysical Year to defuse sovereignty issues. It seems more plausible, therefore, that science was used as a means to an end by providing an excuse to remove a potentially controversial region from international conflicts, in a unique combination of science and politics. 'It was well understood by those concerned that unless an international solution for the Antarctic could be found, a confrontation on a world wide scale might easily erupt in that area' (United Nations Study). On this argument, the primary motivation for negotiating the Treaty was a negative political one – fear of chaos at the southern ends of the earth – not the positive reason of facilitating scientific research, which seems to have been secondary. Both have, however, benefitted. The regional friction of the 1940s and 1950s has gone (although the differences between claimants and non-claimants are as deep as ever); and Antarctic scientific research has profited from its role in perpetuating this political truce, by continuing to receive financial support from governments.

The second category, intellectual curiosity, the general advancement of knowledge of a tenth of the earth's surface and contributions to the solving of global problems, has been comprehensively addressed in Chapters 5 to 17. It is undeniable that Antarctic science has made, and is making, very significant progress of this kind.

The third category, the value of strategic or applied research to the exploitation and management of renewable resources (e.g. living resources, icebergs) or non-renewable resources (hard rock minerals, oil and gas), has received relatively little attention. Strategic research is defined as research with a *possible* long-term (say 25 years) pay-off in applications. Most, if not all, of the input here has arisen from research initially planned to improve knowledge broadly.

A good example is the 10-year international BIOMASS programme, largely planned and implemented by SCAR 'to gain a deeper understanding of the structure and dynamic functioning of the Antarctic marine ecosystem as a basis for the future management of potential living resources'. The prime concern was stated to be with contributions to man's understanding of the ocean world and developing a sound ecological strategy for exploitation and conservation. The programme, which has now entered the final phase of analysis and synthesis, is widely considered to have been very succesful. It involved two international multi-ship experiments, FIBEX (1980/81) and SIBEX (1984/85), said to be the largest multi-ship operations in biological oceanography carried out anywhere in the world. As a result of BIOMASS, knowledge of the Southern Ocean has been greatly advanced in quantitative as well as qualitative senses (see Chapters 8 and 9). An international relational data base, primarily for biological data, has been established – the BIOMASS Datacentre.

The value of this non-governmental collaborative programme in providing a scientific basis for the intergovernmental Convention on the Conservation of Antarctic Marine Living Resources (CCAMLR) is unquestioned. Research on Antarctic seals, coordinated by SCAR and essentially of basic scientific interest, is related to the aims of the Convention for the Conservation of Antarctic Seals (CCAS). Uniquely for a non-governmental organization, SCAR has been formally invited, in Article 5 of that Convention, to coordinate research and provide scientific advice.

Port Martin, the first French station on the Antarctic continent.

Comparison of the production of papers by Antarctic Treaty nations.

	Biology & Medicine	Oceanography	Glaciology	Earth Sciences & cartography	Meteorology	Physics	Logistics	Other	Total	Percentage of total
Argentina	15	1	1	5		2	1	4	29	0.8
Australia	82		26	61	22	9			200	5.8
Chile	56	2	3	3	3				67	1.9
Germany (Federal Republic)	109	18	21	44	2	10	5	9	220	6.3
Germany (Democratic Republic)	15		9	31	1	6	1	8	71	2.0
France	122	4	31	31	8	29	3		228	6.6
Japan	91	4	40	201	24	83	4		447	12.9
New Zealand	58	4	24	99	4	1	10	34	234	6.7
Norway	16	5	14	7	1				43	1.2
South Africa	131	23	6	10		35			205	5.9
UK	255	8	65	113	16	80	7	44	588	16.9
Soviet Union	148	72	95	97	22	43		43	520	15.0
USA	134	53	111	157	69	35	23	45	626	18.0
Total	1232	194	446	859	172	333	54	188	3478	
Percentage of total	35.5	5.6	12.8	24.7	5.0	9.6	1.6	5.4		

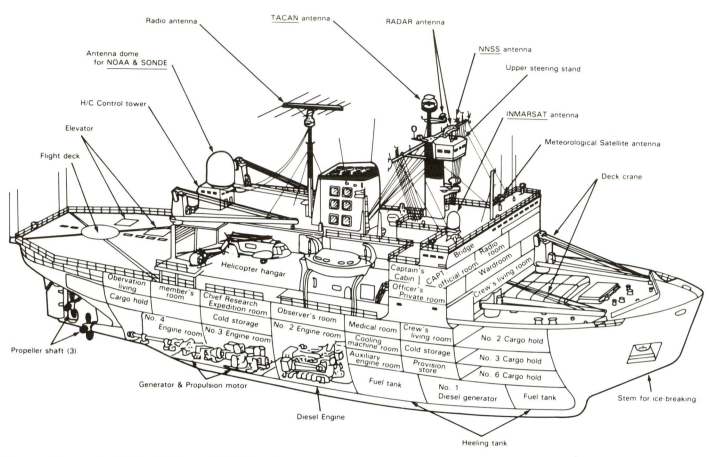

Radio antenna

TACAN antenna

RADAR antenna

NNSS antenna

Antenna dome
for NOAA & SONDE

Upper steering stand

H/C Control tower

INMARSAT antenna

Elevator

Meteorological Satellite antenna

Flight deck

Deck crane

Helicopter hangar

Bridge
Radio
room
Captain's
Cabin
CAPT.
official room
Wardroom
Officer's
Private room
Crew's living room

Obervation
living
member's
room
Chief Research
Expedition room
Observer's room
Cargo hold

No. 4
Engine room
Cold storage
No. 2 Engine room
Medical room
Crew's
living room
No. 2 Cargo hold

No. 3 Engine room
Cooling
machine room
Cold storage
No. 3 Cargo hold

Auxiliary
engine room
Provision
store
No. 6 Cargo hold

Propeller shaft (3)

Fuel tank
No. 1
Diesel generator
Fuel tank

Generator & Propulsion motor

Stem for ice-breaking

Diesel Engine

Heeling tank

The new Japanese icebreaker Shirase, *made its first voyage to Antarctica in 1983–84.*

Concerning minerals, including hydrocarbons, the basic research and surveys that have been carried out by geologists, geophysicists and glaciologists provide essential background information on likely prospective areas for the more detailed commercial exploration that would precede any exploitation. Maps have been made, the depth of ice has been contoured, and mineral occurrences (as distinct from deposits) have been recorded. Broad geophysical surveys (on land and especially at sea), coupled with ocean drilling and stratigraphic and palaeontological investigations, have pointed to the location of major sedimentary basins in Antarctica with hydrocarbon potential. Further progress will need to involve international scientific collaboration, because meeting the future research needs is probably beyond any one nation, and commercial participation could lead to suspicion about the motives. For example, plans for an overland geosciences traverse, along a line approximating 90°W, from the coast to the pole, are being discussed. A deep stratigraphic test borehole on James Ross Island, located over a major sedimentary basin in the western Weddell Sea, is another necessary

development to validate the interpretation of geophysical results. Both of these projects will be very expensive and are best achieved by international scientific collaboration, rather than by commercial interests.

It should be stressed that the consensus among scientists and industry is that commercial mineral exploration leading to exploitation is still far off, almost certainly into the next century and possibly as far into the future as three to five decades. A new technology to cope with Antarctic problems and environmental constraints has to be developed within the world economic framework. Potential hydrocarbon deposits must be viewed in the context of proven world reserves (including enhanced oil recovery from currently uneconomically extractable reserves remaining in proven oil fields, and in tar sands and oil shales). In attempting to negotiate a minerals regime, it is clear that the Treaty powers are following their earlier prudent practice of agreeing a regime in advance of a significant industry, in the knowledge that agreement is more likely than if the negotiations are left until the commercial pressures develop. There is no evidence as yet of pressure on the Treaty System from the oil industry, as some environmentalists have claimed – quite the reverse, it seems.

The fourth category is the area with potentially the most fundamental long-term import for mankind, because it is concerned with contributions to the understanding of global/geospace effects of natural or man-induced environmental change. A few examples where Antarctic studies are crucial or important will suffice: climatic change, sea-level change, ozone concentrations, levels of atmospheric gases, the record of global pollution in Antarctic ice and snow, and man-made precipitation of electrons in the magnetosphere, a newly discovered form of pollution. These have been discussed in Parts III and IV.

A major concern is the stability of the Antarctic ice sheets because if they melted completely a 60 m rise in sea level would follow. Even a small increase in their melting rate would have serious consequences for low-lying regions elsewhere. Studies of the mass balance of ice sheets and their interactions with ice shelves and the ocean are therefore important. The expansion and contraction of the Antarctic sea-ice cover is the major seasonal phenomenon in the world ocean, with enormous influence on world climate.

Understanding climate involves unravelling the complicated interactions between the atmosphere, the oceans and living organisms. For example, there is a possibility that changes in climate may be brought about by increasing levels of CO_2 in the atmosphere, due to burning of fossil fuel and cutting and burning of virgin forest. Sea water takes up much more CO_2 than fresh water and the surface layer (to 75 m) of the world's oceans can absorb up to 10% of all CO_2 produced. With winter cooling and increased salinity due to ice formation, the surface layer increases in density and sinks with the gases it is carrying; it is replaced, allowing more CO_2 to be absorbed. Biological consumption by phytoplankton also lowers the concentration of CO_2 in surface waters in summer. The major region where these processes occur is the Southern Ocean. A similar problem relates to increasing concentrations of atmospheric methane. Analysis of air bubbles in glacial ice suggests that this began a few hundred years ago.

The ozone layer shields life on earth from the adverse effects of ultra-violet radiation. In recent years a possible decrease in ozone concentration has been attributed to an increase of organic chlorine and oxides of nitrogen in the atmosphere from aerosols, refrigerator and air-conditioning systems, and stratospheric aircraft. Because of its unique properties, the Antarctic is an ideal region in which to study this problem and recent work has shown that the spring values of total ozone above the Antarctic have fallen dramatically. Predictions from Antarctic research have been confirmed by re-examination of satellite data and the implications for life on earth may be serious.

These few examples are sufficient to underline the importance of Antarctic research in such fields, and therefore the importance of negotiating a legal and political accommodation which will allow research to continue at the same or an enhanced level.

Present organization of science

The key international organization behind Antarctic science is the Scientific Committee for Antarctic Research (SCAR) of the International Council of Scientific Unions (ICSU), set up at the close of the IGY. Membership is open to countries which have a substantial continuing Antarctic research programme and a new category of associate membership, not requiring this qualification, is under discussion. In addition there are delegates representing other international scientific organizations. There is a permanent Working Group on logistics, which co-ordinates logistic activities, disseminates information and discusses developments in housing, transport, clothing, communications and other areas, and nine permanent Working Groups representing scientific disciplines. Groups of Specialists (of which there are currently five) are set up to tackle particular problems or to plan special projects. They cover Antarctic Climate Research, Environmental Impact, Sea-ice Studies, Seals, and Southern Ocean Ecosystems. Symposia and special workshop meetings are organized and the results are published (see Appendix 2). The permanent secretariat consists of a part-time Executive Secretary and an assistant.

SCAR has an advisory role in relation to the Antarctic Treaty. It has played an important part in initiating discussions which led to the Agreed Measures for the Conservation of Antarctic Flora and Fauna under the Treaty (1964), the Convention for the Conservation of Antarctic Seals (CCAS) (1972), and the Convention for the Conservation of Antarctic Marine Living Resources (CCAMLR) (1980). More recently the programme of Biological Investigations of Marine Antarctic Systems and Stocks (BIOMASS) has responded to requests from the Scientific Committee of CCAMLR by providing information, the results of research and substantial reviews of certain topics.

In addition to SCAR, a number of other international organisations are involved in Antarctic research. These include other ICSU bodies (e.g. SCOR, COSPAR, IUGS, IUBS, URSI), IUCN, United Nations agencies (IOC, FAO, UNEP, UNDP) and IWC. Scientific programmes and conferences may be co-sponsored with SCAR, but SCAR plays the leading role.

(a) Scott Base (New Zealand)
77°51'S, 166°45'E

(b) Casey (Australia)
66°17'S, 110°32'E

(c) Almirante Brown
(Argentina)
64°53'S, 62°53'W

(d) General Bernado
O'Higgins (Chile)
63°19'S, 57°54'N

Antarctic stations vary greatly in size and complexity. Those built on rock are easier to construct and maintain than those on snow or ice.

(e) McMurdo (USA)
77°51'S, 166°40'E

(f) Halley (UK)
75°36'S, 26°41'W

(g) Arctowski (Poland)
62°09'S, 58°28'W

(h) Georg von Neumayer
(West Germany)
70°37'S, 8°22'W

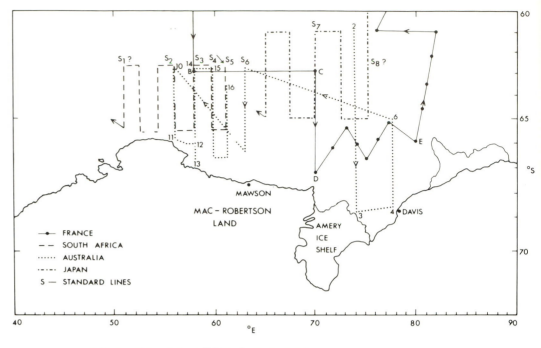

BIOMASS has produced international scientific collaboration of a new order. The two multi-ship experiments in the Southern Ocean were probably the largest ever attempted in biological oceanography. Four nations contributed to the Indian Ocean sector during SIBEX-1.

INDIAN OCEAN SECTOR SIBEX-1 CRUISE TRACKS

Possible future political arrangements

Out of an initial phase of suspicion and conflict, the scientific needs and collaboration that led to IGY brought about the creation of SCAR and its political counterpart, the Antarctic Treaty System (see Chapter 4). But the end of two decades of unquestioned international stability and largely academic science in the Antarctic was approaching in 1977 when the Antarctic Treaty first began to address the question of Antarctic mineral resources, and the developments have now come almost full circle, with political uncertainty and conflicts of interest again coming to predominate over science.

During the 1980s questions relating to Antarctic resources have emerged as a significant international pre-occupation. How else can one explain the phenomenal recent increase in membership of the Antarctic Treaty? Entering into force in 1961 with twelve members, by 1978 there were twenty members, still only the original twelve having consultative status; by the end of 1985, however, there were thirty-two members, eighteen with consultative status (see Appendix 1). It is difficult to reject a causal relation between the opening of minerals negotiations in 1977 and the sharp acceleration in the rate of accessions and applications for consultative status. Another reason may be that the magic year 1991 is approaching, when review of the Treaty is possible. These conclusions are reinforced by the armed conflict in the South Atlantic which focussed governments' attention on the potential of the Antarctic and the Southern Ocean. The provision of extra funds and an earmarked budget for BAS, which was

on a declining budget in the late 1970s, was no doubt stimulated by such considerations.

At the same time as the number of countries joining the 'club' was increasing (probably with resource-related motives), two other movements were gathering momentum. One can be summarised as the move by the so-called Third World of lesser-developed countries (LDCs) to make the Antarctic part of the 'global commons', with a moratorium on development until arrangements could be made for sharing the 'common heritage' of mankind. The other is a non-governmental movement of environmentalists and conservationists, which seeks to freeze all development unless it can be proved to have no adverse effects on the 'pristine Antarctic environment'; it clearly has some overlapping interests with the common heritage movement, although the ultimate aims are in sharp conflict. Let us examine these three main threads in the current discussions about the future legal and political arrangements for the region.

Internal accommodation within the Treaty

First we may note that the Antarctic Treaty is an excellent example of collaboration between opposing political ideologies towards solving common problems, but that various alternatives to the present arrangements, which depend on realignment within the Antarctic Treaty System, have been suggested. These are division – a reversion to the imposition of sovereignty over national

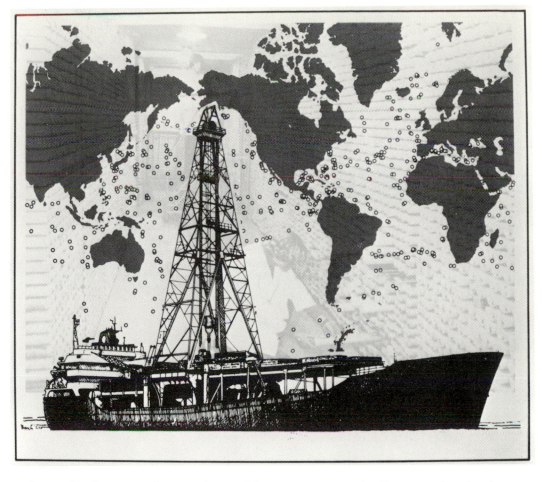

Deep drilling of ocean sediments by Glomar Challenger *has greatly contributed to our understanding of the history of Antarctica.*

claims which, as past experience shows clearly, cannot be feasible without serious international conflict; management by a consortium of active states – which would merge claims to jurisdiction over resource activities and regulate them jointly, leaving questions of sovereignty aside, would not pose legal problems but would not be acceptable on political grounds to claimant or non-claimant states; and a condominium, the joint exercise of sovereignty over a particular territory by two or more states. This has similar disadvantages and no advantages over the solution now being pursued in the negotiations on a minerals regime.

The nations involved include the two superpowers, eleven Western European countries and six Eastern European, five South American, three Far Eastern and three British Commonwealth countries. There is a wide spectrum of non-aligned countries, developed countries (DCs) and less developed countries (LDCs). The only major political groupings not represented are the Black African states and the Arab world. Far from being a small exclusive club as has been suggested, the ATCPs now represent some four-fifths of the world's population.

The Antarctic Treaty System confers no rights; it consists only of obligations and there are no sanctions between the contracting parties or between them and the rest of the world to enforce observance. In practical terms the consultative parties have incurred substantial financial costs and gained little, except to keep their options open for the future and retain a special opportunity to influence that

future. The newcomers to the Treaty undertake the same obligations as the older members. All of the original signatories would have been losers without the Treaty, and without continuing agreement to cooperate the Antarctic could yet become the scene or object of international discord. It is clear, however, that the rule of unanimity will make agreement more difficult to achieve as the group grows larger.

A United Nations takeover

Turning to the second group of proposals, an initial thought must be: if the Antarctic Treaty System is getting large for reaching agreement on issues, how much more inefficient would a yet larger grouping be, coupled with the difficulty of starting again from the beginning to negotiate a new legal regime. As one of the architects of the Treaty, Brian Roberts, has said, 'My mind boggles at the thought of 144 members [now 159] of the United Nations trying to make realistic decisions about Antarctic matters'.

November 1983 marked the first involvement of the United Nations in Antarctic matters, as a result of action by Malaysia, the Non-aligned Summit Conference, and the Caribbean Community and Common Market in that year. Agreement was reached at the UN in December

257

Mt Erebus, the largest and most active volcano in Antarctica, is the subject of research programmes by both earth scientists and biologists.

The Ross Seal, rarest of all Antarctic seals and now protected under the Convention for the Conservation of Antarctic Seals.

1983 to undertake 'a comprehensive factual study of all aspects of Antarctica' to which Antarctic Treaty nations, non-Treaty nations and non-governmental organisations have made contributions. It will no doubt be a continuing subject for further discussion during the years up to and beyond 1991. Promoters of a UN alternative which would replace the Treaty offer no practical suggestions as to where the money will come from to run the scientific stations, coordinate communications and carry on data collection such as that needed for weather forecasting.

The starting points for the 'common heritage' argument are the debate about the New International Economic Order and the conclusion, after lengthy legal wrangles, of the UN Law of the Sea Convention (UNLOSC). Signed in 1982, this provides for benefits from exploitation to be distributed to the international community, including the disadvantaged countries. In this way they seek a share in Antarctic decision making and exploitation without having to meet the high cost of participation as Consultative Parties in the Antarctic Treaty.

The parallel with UNLOSC is not close, nor is comparison with the Space Treaty approved by the UN General Assembly in 1979 (which provides that the natural resources of the moon and other celestial bodies should be regarded as the common heritage of mankind). The deep sea underlies what has always been regarded as common and no claims have been made to property in space. In contrast, Antarctica is not a no-man's land, because 85% of the continent is subject to claims of long standing, which pre-date the New International Economic Order and the North–South debate. Internationalising the Antarctic as proposed would break all precedents on the

treatment of land and the ATCPs have made it clear that they will oppose any attempt to set up an alternative to the Antarctic Treaty System. Experience elsewhere shows that the LDCs prevail only where the states with most experience and capability differ among themselves, so that some come to accept the LDC position as their own.

It is difficult to see how any country could profit from introducing instability and controversy to a region characterized by unparalleled peace and international cooperation of long standing. A way ahead may lie in the fact that the Consultative Parties have acknowledged their responsibility to the international community in some of their recommendations. A stronger endorsement of revenue sharing and global responsibility should prove to be an effective compromise and, if linked to the successful negotiation of a minerals regime, would strengthen the Antarctic Treaty System.

Environmental solutions

The third group of proposals is advanced by the non-governmental conservationist and environmentalist groups. In the 1960s and 1970s the conservation of whales was a major growth industry which, owing to its success in virtually eliminating the whaling industry, has now begun to run out of steam. Consequently, the attention of this movement has been turning towards the perceived problem of Antarctica. Whilst acknowledging the success of the 'Agreed Measures' under the Antarctic Treaty they also want large reserves in addition to the existing small SPAs

The Scott Polar Research Institute in Cambridge, UK, houses a major polar library, active glaciological research groups and the SCAR secretariat.

and SSSIs, with buffer zones around them and sanctuaries for endangered whales. The idea of designating Antarctica as a 'World Park' was put forward at an international conference in 1972, and by New Zealand at a Treaty meeting in 1975; it is now one of the solutions regularly brought up. Related ideas are that Antarctica should be designated as the last great 'Wilderness' and protected from harmful influences. It is argued that there should be a moratorium on commercial developments for, say, 30–40 years because the value of the Antarctic for global monitoring would be destroyed by industrial activities. The creation of a professional Antarctic Environmental Protection Agency is proposed to oversee all Antarctic activities. Although it is generally agreed that there should be continuing scientific cooperation in Antarctica, there is concern about the increasing level of scientific activity and its possible impacts on the environment, and it is felt to be desirable to regulate *all* activities, in a non-commercial approach, which would provide for sharing of all data and decisions.

They use the 'common heritage' argument, although it is inimical to their ultimate aims, and they do not indicate how the present funding for research could be maintained or replaced. (The annual funds involved run into hundreds of millions of pounds.) These views are actively promoted by a group of over 150 environmental organisations including the Antarctic and Southern Ocean Coalition (ASOC) from thirty-seven countries, the International Union for the Conservation of Nature and Natural Resources (IUCN) and the World Wildlife Fund.

The future of Antarctic science

The scientists have a set of truly international priorities, possibly owing to the absence of any commercial element. They are well organized, with international discussion of programmes, bilateral and multilateral cooperation and exchange of visiting scientists and observers. Almost without exception they are funded by countries that are ATCPs, because of the necessary qualifying blend of science and politics. There would be wide and general agreement in the international Antarctic scientific community that the interests of science are best served by a continuation of the present arrangements under the Antarctic Treaty System. There will need to be an accommodation between

the sharply diverging positions of claimant and non-claimant states, which success in the current negotiations on a minerals regime would secure.

Paradoxically, therefore, it appears that international science would not benefit from a wider internationalisation of Antarctica under the UN. There would no longer be a need for scientific credentials in order to qualify politically and, with the political imperatives removed, funding could well decrease. If the 'common heritage' or the 'environmental protection' movements prevailed, another level of bureaucracy and politicisation would be interposed with inevitable deterioration in organization and management of activities in the Antarctic.

One unwelcome tendency within the Treaty is that already the consultative meetings are setting up their own groups of experts, subject to political and other pressures and relying less on SCAR advice, which is separated from and largely independent of political pressures. Political and legal matters are the concern of the Treaty and so lawyers and diplomats predominate at the Consultative meetings. These are characterised by 'horse trading' and lobbying in the corridors, rather than open debate in meetings. The few scientists present have second-class status, although almost invariably they represent the only practical experience there. This applies also to the Scientific Committee of CCAMLR. A variety of environmental and conservation pressure groups are seeking official observer status at both Treaty and CCAMLR meetings in order to exert greater influence over the development of the Treaty. It is not clear which of the organisations, if any, should be treated as observers nor how representative their submissions would be of informed public opinion.

The strength of the case for Antarctic research has emerged in detail in Parts II to IV and is summarised in this chapter. There is a continuing need for academic research and, in addition, it is essential that strategic research develops and applied research begins. It would be a grave mistake for the world to ignore the contribution which Antarctic science can make towards solving or warning about global problems. All mankind, whether in DCs or LDCs, needs to be aware of the potential for future catastrophe residing in major global problems, such as climatic change, the build-up of CO_2 and the 'greenhouse effect'; the potential reduction in the shielding power of the ozone layer; the raising of sea level due to the melt of the Lesser Antarctica ice sheet; the effect of electric power line pollution in industrial regions on the magnetosphere, the Earth's protective shield from lethal ionized particles from the sun; and the build-up of 'conventional' pollutants such as heavy metals and organochlorines in our environment. While much will be possible by remote sensing from satellites and by automatic record-ing stations, ground-based observations will continue to be necessary for the foreseeable future. To be aware of, and to understand, these potential problems in quantitative terms is the first and essential step to their solution. As we have seen in Parts III and IV, the Antarctic offers particular advantages for such research.

Although Antarctic fisheries have not yet made a major contribution to solving world food problems, there is substantial future potential for krill harvesting when the economic climate is right. It could only be sustained by wise management, which depends on understanding of the biological interactions as well as on political will. Likewise, any future mineral exploitation depends on initial extensive research to provide the broad basis for intensive commercial exploration. Academic research directed to the study of plate tectonics and related areas, to mineralisation processes, and to sedimentology and stratigraphy, has strategic value and will doubtless have practical application in the future, for non-renewable resources are by definition limited and inexorably drying up. The industries that may in consequence develop in Antarctica will result in serious ecological consequences if we do not take steps to control these. Again, the key is scientific understanding of the marine, and particularly the geographically limited and fragile terrestrial and inland water ecosystems. Genetic engineering is in its infancy, but there may be future potential contributions from the Antarctic gene banks.

To a remote field party the Antarctic appears as it did to the early explorers.

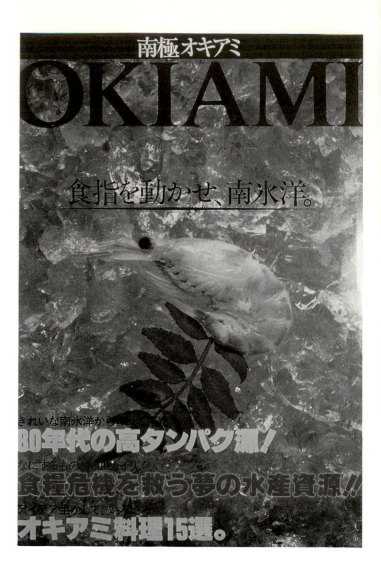

南極オキアミ

OKIAMI

食指を動かせ、南氷洋。

きれいな南氷洋から

80年代の高タンパク源！

食糧危機を救う夢の水産資源!!

オキアミ料理15選。

*Antarctic krill – the key to Antarctic food chains and any future
management of the marine resources of the Southern Ocean.*

Finally, we may ask: 'Is Antarctic science worth the money?' There is no immediate constituency in the Antarctic, unlike regions with large human populations, nor is it amenable to permanent self-sustaining settlement. But is it sensible to ignore a tenth of the earth's surface in political, military or resource terms? It is not – and certainly not if the potential future global disasters described earlier are to be prevented. For these reasons, and because the expenditure on maintaining Antarctic research is negligible in terms of the gross expenditure by the governments of the world, it should continue. But as we have seen, cost effectiveness varies widely. A recent editorial in the journal *Nature* suggested that the next step might be to devise a test of Treaty membership based on the quality of research carried out and not simply on the cost of it. Or research could be financed by a tax on commercial activities when these begin, as the 'Discovery Investigations', a cornerstone of modern oceanography, were wholly financed by a British tax on whale products in the 1920s and 1930s. What is clear is that a number of identified scientific programmes are beyond the resources of one nation acting alone, and an increasing trend towards large international projects is likely. So our thoughts naturally turn back to the IGY, which began the current expanded phase of Antarctic research, nearly three decades ago. Perhaps another burgeoning of Antarctic science can be expected in the next decade; there is no shortage of ideas, but the political arrangements must be right.

Amundsen–Scott Station at the South Pole, with the flags of all the Antarctic Treaty nations.

Appendix·1

The Antarctic Treaty

The Governments of Argentina, Australia, Belgium, Chile, the French Republic, Japan, New Zealand, Norway, the Union of South Africa, the Union of Soviet Socialist Republics, the United Kingdom of Great Britain and Northern Ireland, and the United States of America,

Recognizing that it is in the interest of all mankind that Antarctica shall continue forever to be used exclusively for peaceful purposes and shall not become the scene or object of international discord;

Acknowledging the substantial contributions to scientific knowledge resulting from international co-operation in scientific investigation in Antarctica;

Convinced that the establishment of a firm foundation for the continuation and development of such co-operation on the basis of freedom of scientific investigation in Antarctica as applied during the International Geophysical Year accords with the interests of science and the progress of all mankind;

Convinced also that a treaty ensuring the use of Antarctica for peaceful purposes only and the continuance of international harmony in Antarctica will further the purposes and principles embodied in the Charter of the United Nations;

Have agreed as follows:

Article I

1. Antarctica shall be used for peaceful purposes only. There shall be prohibited, inter alia, any measure of a military nature, such as the establishment of military bases and fortifications, the carrying out of military manoeuvres, as well as the testing of any type of weapon.

2. The present Treaty shall not prevent the use of military personnel or equipment for scientific research or for any other peaceful purpose.

Article II

Freedom of scientific investigation in Antarctica and co-operation toward that end, as applied during the International Geophysical Year, shall continue, subject to the provisions of the present Treaty.

Article III

1. In order to promote international co-operation in scientific investigation in Antarctica, as provided for in Article II of the present Treaty, the Contracting Parties agree that, to the greatest extent feasible and practicable:

(a) information regarding plans for scientific programs in Antarctica shall be exchanged to permit maximum economy of and efficiency of operations;

(b) scientific personnel shall be exchanged in Antarctica between expeditions and stations;

(c) scientific observations and results from Antarctica shall be exchanged and made freely available.

2. In implementing this Article, every encouragement shall be given to the establishment of co-operative working relations with those Specialized Agencies of the United Nations and other international organizations having a scientific or technical interest in Antarctica.

Article IV

1. Nothing contained in the present Treaty shall be interpreted as:

(a) a renunciation by any Contracting Party of previously asserted rights of or claims to territorial sovereignty in Antarctica;

(b) a renunciation or diminution by any Contracting Party of any basis of claim to territorial sovereignty in Antarctica which it may have whether as a result of its activities or those of its nationals in Antarctica, or otherwise;

(c) prejudicing the position of any Contracting Party as regards its recognition or non-recognition of any other State's rights of or claim or basis of claim to territorial sovereignty in Antarctica.

2. No acts or activities taking place while the present Treaty is in force shall constitute a basis for asserting, supporting or denying a claim to territorial sovereignty in Antarctica or create any rights of sovereignty in Antarctica. No new claim, or enlargement of an existing claim, to territorial sovereignty in Antarctica shall be asserted while the present Treaty is in force.

Article V

1. Any nuclear explosions in Antarctica and the disposal there of radioactive waste material shall be prohibited.

2. In the event of the conclusion of international agreements concerning the use of nuclear energy, including nuclear explosions and the disposal of radioactive waste material, to which all of the Contracting Parties whose representatives are entitled to participate in the meetings provided for under Article IX are parties, the rules established under such agreements shall apply in Antarctica.

Article VI

The provisions of the present Treaty shall apply to the area south of 60° South Latitude, including all ice shelves, but nothing in the present Treaty shall prejudice or in any way affect the rights, or the exercise of the rights, of any State under international law with regard to the high seas within that area.

Article VII

1. In order to promote the objectives and ensure the observance of the provisions of the present Treaty, each Contracting Party whose representatives are entitled to participate in the meetings referred to in Article IX of the Treaty shall have the right to designate observers to carry out any inspection provided for by the present Article. Observers shall be nationals of the Contracting Parties which designate them. The names of observers shall be communicated to every other Contracting Party having the right to designate observers, and like notice shall be given of the termination of their appointment.

2. Each observer designated in accordance with the provisions of paragraph 1 of this Article shall have complete freedom of access at any time to any or all areas of Antarctica.

3. All areas of Antarctica, including all stations, installations and equipment within those areas, and all ships and aircraft at points of discharging or embarking cargoes or personnel in Antarctica, shall be open at all times to inspection by any observers designated in accordance with paragraph 1 of this Article.

4. Aerial observation may be carried out at any time over any or all areas of Antarctica by any of the Contracting Parties having the right to designate observers.

5. Each Contracting Party shall, at the time when the present Treaty enters into force for it, inform the other Contracting Parties, and thereafter shall give them notice in advance, of

(a) all expeditions to and within Antarctica, on the part of its ships or nationals, and all expeditions to Antarctica organized in or proceeding from its territory.

(b) all stations in Antarctica occupied by its nationals; and

(c) any military personnel or equipment intended to be introduced by it into Antarctica subject to the conditions prescribed in paragraph 2 of Article I of the present Treaty.

Article VIII

1. In order to facilitate the exercise of their functions under the present Treaty, and without prejudice to the respective positions of the Contracting Parties relating to jurisdiction over all other persons in Antarctica, observers designated under paragraph 1 of Article VII and scientific personnel exchanged under sub-paragraph 1(b) of Article III of the Treaty, and members of the staffs accompanying any such persons, shall be subject only to the jurisdiction of the Contracting Party of which they are nationals in respect of all acts or omissions occurring while they are in Antarctica for the purpose of exercising their functions.

2. Without prejudice to the provisions of paragraph 1 of this Article, and pending the adoption of measures in pursuance of sub-paragraph 1(e) of Article IX, the Contracting Parties concerned in any case of dispute with regard to the exercise of jurisdiction in Antarctica shall immediately consult together with a view to reaching a mutually acceptable solution.

Article IX

1. Representatives of the Contracting Parties named in the preamble to the present Treaty shall meet at the City of Canberra within two months after the date of entry into force of the Treaty, and thereafter at suitable intervals and places, for the purpose of exchanging information, consulting together on matters of common interest pertaining to Antarctica, and formulating and considering, and recommending to their Governments, measures in furtherance of the principles and objectives of the Treaty, including measures regarding:-

(a) use of Antarctica for peaceful purposes only;
(b) facilitation of scientific research in Antarctica;
(c) facilitation of international scientific co-operation in Antarctica;
(d) facilitation of the exercise of the rights of inspection provided for in Article VII of the Treaty.
(e) questions relating to the exercise of jurisdiction in Antarctica;
(f) preservation and conservation of living resources in Antarctica.

2. Each Contracting Party which has become a party to the present Treaty by accession under Article XIII shall be entitled to appoint representatives to participate in the meetings referred to in paragraph 1 of the present Article, during such times as that Contracting Party demonstrates its interest in Antarctica by conducting substantial scientific research activities there, such as the establishment of a scientific station or the despatch of a scientific expedition.

3. Reports from the observers referred to in Article VII of the present Treaty shall be transmitted to the representatives of the Contracting Parties participating in the meetings referred to in paragraph 1 of the present Article.

4. The measures referred to in paragraph 1 of this Article shall become effective when approved by all the Contracting Parties whose representatives were entitled to participate in the meetings held to consider those measures.

5. Any or all of the rights established in the present Treaty may be exercised as from the date of entry into force of the Treaty whether or not any measures facilitating the exercise of such rights have been proposed, considered or approved as provided in this Article.

Article X

Each of the Contracting Parties undertakes to exert appropriate efforts, consistent with the Charter of the United Nations, to the end that no one engages in any activity in Antarctica contrary to the principles or purposes of the present Treaty.

Article XI

1. If any dispute arises between two or more of the Contracting Parties concerning the interpretation or application of the present Treaty, those Contracting Parties shall consult among themselves with a view to having the dispute resolved by negotiation, inquiry, mediation, conciliation, arbitration, judicial settlement or other peaceful means of their own choice.

2. Any dispute of this character not so resolved shall, with the consent, in each case, of all parties to the dispute, be referred to the International Court of Justice for settlement; but failure to reach agreement on reference to the International Court shall not absolve parties to the dispute from the responsibility of continuing to seek to resolve it by any of the various peaceful means referred to in paragraph 1 of this Article.

Article XII

1. (a) The present Treaty may be modified or amended at any time by unanimous agreement of the Contracting Parties whose representatives are entitled to participate in the meetings provided for under Article IX. Any such modification or amendment shall enter into force when the depositary Government has received notice from all such Contrasting Parties that they have ratified it.

(b) Such modification or amendment shall thereafter enter into force as to any other Contracting Party when notice of ratification by it has been received by the depositary Government. Any such Contracting Party from which no notice of ratification is received within a period of two years from the date of entry into force of the modification or amendment in accordance with the provision of sub-paragraph 1(a) of this Article shall be deemed to have withdrawn from the present Treaty on the date of the expiration of such period.

2. (a) If after the expiration of thirty years from the date of entry into force of the present Treaty, any of the Contracting Parties whose representatives are entitled to participate in the meetings provided for under Article XI so requests by a communication addressed to the depositary Government, a Conference of all the Contracting Parties shall be held as soon as practicable to review the operation of the Treaty.

(b) Any modification or amendment to the present Treaty which is approved at such a Conference by a majority of the Contracting Parties there represented, including a majority of those whose representatives are entitled to participate in the meetings provided for under Article IX, shall be communicated by the depositary Government to all Contracting Parties immediately after the termination of the Conference and shall enter into force in accordance with the provisions of paragraph 1 of the present Article.

(c) If any such modification or amendment has not entered into force in accordance with the provisions of sub-paragraph 1(a) of this Article within a period of two years after the date of its communication to all the Contracting Parties, any Contracting Party may at any time after the expiration of the period give notice to the depositary Government of its withdrawal from the present Treaty; and such withdrawal shall take effect two years after the receipt of the notice by the depositary Government.

Article XIII

1. The present Treaty shall be subject to ratification by the signatory States. It shall be open for accession by any State which is a Member of the United Nations, or by any other State which may be invited to accede to the Treaty with the consent of all the Contracting Parties whose representatives are entitled to participate in the meetings provided for under Article IX of the Treaty.

2. Ratification of or accession to the present Treaty shall be effected by each State in accordance with its constitutional processes.

3. Instruments of ratification and instruments of accession shall be deposited with the Government of the United States of America, hereby designated as the depositary Government.

4. The depositary Government shall inform all signatory and acceding States of the date of each deposit of an instrument of ratification or accession, and the date of entry into force of the Treaty and of any modification or amendment thereto.

5. Upon the deposit of instruments of ratification by all signatory States, the present Treaty shall enter into force for those States and for States which have deposited instruments of accession. Thereafter the Treaty shall enter into force for any acceding State upon the deposit of its instruments of accession.

6. The present Treaty shall be registered by the depositary Government pursuant to Article 102 of the Charter of the United Nations.

Article XIV

The present Treaty, done in the English, French, Russian and Spanish languages, each version being equally authentic, shall be deposited in the archives of the Government of the United States of America, which shall transmit duly certified copies thereof to the Governments of the signatory and acceding States.

Dates of ratifications and accessions

Below are listed in chronological order the dates of ratification of the Treaty by the original members, dates of accession or succession by other states, and dates of acquisition of Consultative Party status by four of these states.

United Kingdom	31 May 1960	a,b	1
South Africa	21 June 1960	a,b	2
Belgium	26 July 1960	a,b	3
Japan	4 August 1960	a,b	4
United States of America	18 August 1960	a,b	5
Norway	24 August 1960	a,b	6
France	16 September 1960	a,b	7
New Zealand	1 November 1960	a,b	8
Soviet Union	2 November 1960	a,b	9
Poland	8 June 1961	b	10
Argentina	23 June 1961	a,b	11
Australia	23 June 1961	a,b	12
Chile	23 June 1961	a,b	13
Czechoslovakia	14 June 1962		14
Denmark	20 May 1965		15
Netherlands	30 March 1967		16
Romania	15 September 1971		17
Germany, Democratic Republic	19 November 1974		18
Brazil	16 May 1975	b	19
Bulgaria	11 September 1978		20
Germany, Federal Republic	5 February 1979	b	21
Uruguay	11 January 1980		22
Papua New Guinea	16 March 1981	c	23
Italy	18 March 1981		24
Peru	10 April 1981		25
Spain	31 March 1982		26
China, People's Republic	8 June 1983		27
India	19 August 1983	b	28
Hungary	27 January 1984		29
Sweden	24 April 1984		30
Finland	15 May 1984		31
Cuba	16 August 1984		32

a Twelve original member States initialled the Treaty on 1 December 1959; dates given are those of the deposition of the ratification of the Treaty.

b Sixteen States (12 original members and 4 others) have Consultative Party status. These acceding States became Consultative Parties on the following dates; Poland, 17 September 1977; Federal Republic of Germany, 23 June 1981; Brazil and India, 12 September 1983.

c Papua New Guinea succeeded to the Treaty after becoming independent of Australia.

Appendix·2

Major Symposia and Conferences with which SCAR is associated

	Place	Year
Antarctic Meteorology – SCAR/WMO	Melbourne	1959
Antarctic Glaciology – IASH/SCAR	Helsinki	1960
Logistics Symposium – SCAR	Boulder	1962
Antarctic Biology – SCAR/IUBS	Paris	1962
Antarctic Geology – SCAR/IUGS	Cape Town	1963
Antarctic Oceanography – SCAR/SCOR/IAPO/IUBS	Santiago	1966
Polar Meteorology – ICPM/WMO/SCAR	Geneva	1966
Antarctic Ecology – SCAR/IUBS/SCIBP	Cambridge	1968
International Symposium on Antarctic Glaciological Exploration – SCAR/IASH	Hanover	1968
Antarctic Quaternary Studies – SCAR	Cambridge	1968
Antarctic Geology and Solid Earth Geophysics – SCAR/IUGS	Oslo	1970
Antarctic Ice and Water Masses – SCAR	Tokyo	1970
Energy fluxes over Polar Surfaces – SCAR/ICPM/WMO	Moscow	1971
Technical & Scientific Problems Affecting Antarctic Telecommunications – SCAR	Sandefjord	1972
Human Biology & Medicine in the Antarctic – SCAR/IUBS/IUPS	Cambridge	1972
Antarctic Quaternary Studies – SCAR	Canberra	1972
Polar Oceans – SCOR/SCAR	Montreal	1974
Adaptations within Antarctic Ecosystems – SCAR/IUBS	Washington	1974
Living Resources of the Southern Ocean – SCAR/SCOR	Woods Hole	1976
Circum-Antarctic Marine Geology – CMG/SCAR	Sydney	1976
Antarctic Geology & Geophysics – SCAR/IUGS/ICG	Madison	1977
Antarctic Glacial History and World Palaeo-environment – SCAR	Birmingham	1977
Antarctic International Magnetospheric Study (IMS) – IAGA/SCOSTEP/SCAR	Melbourne	1979
Ross Sea – SCAR	Queenstown	1980
Antarctic Glaciology – SCAR/IGS	Columbus	1981
Comparison of Late-Miocene and Plio-Pleistocene Coolings of the Southern Ocean and their Influence on World Palaeoenvironments – SCAR/INQUA	Moscow	1982
Antarctic Earth Science – SCAR/IUGS/IUGG	Adelaide	1982
Antarctic Logistics – SCAR	Leningrad	1982
Polar Meteorology and Climate – ICPM/SCAR	Hamburg	1983
Nutrient Cycles and Food Webs in the Antarctic – SCAR/IUBS	Wilderness	1983
International Biomedical Expedition to the Antarctic – SCAR	Anchorage	1984
Space observations for Climate Studies – COSPAR/SCAR	Grazu	1984
Biology of Fur Seal – SCAR/US Marine Mammal Commission	Cambridge	1984
Scientific Requirements for Antarctic Conservation – IUCN/SCAR	Bonn	1985
Polar Meteorology – ICPM/SCAR	Honolulu	1985
Nagata Symposium on Geomagnetic Conjugate Studies – SCAR/IAGA	San Diego	1986
Antarctic Glaciology – SCAR/IGC	Bremerhaven	1987
Antarctic Earth Sciences – SCAR/IUGG	Cambridge	1987
Antarctic Biology	(Australia)	1988

Abbreviations

CMG	Commission on Marine Geology
COSPAR	Committee on Space Research
IAGA	International Association of Geomagnetism and Aeronomy
IASH	International Association of Scientific Hydrology
ICG	Inter-Union Commission on Geodynamics
IAPO	International Association of Physical Oceanography
ICPM	International Commission on Polar Meteorology
IGS	International Glaciological Society
INQUA	International Association on Quaternary Research
IUBS	International Union of Biological Sciences
IUCN	International Union for the Conservation of Nature and Natural Resources
IUGS	International Union of Geological Sciences
IUPS	International Union of Physiological Sciences
SCIBP	Special Committee for the International Biological Programme
SCOR	Scientific Committee on Oceanic Research
SCOSTEP	Scientific Committee on Solar–Terrestrial Physics
WMO	World Meteorological Organisation

Appendix·3
Further information on Antarctic science

More detailed information on Antarctic activities can be obtained from:
The Executive Secretary, SCAR, Scott Polar Research Institute, Lensfield Road, Cambridge CB2 1ER, UK, or from national bodies at the following addresses:

Argentina Instituto Antártico Argentina, Cerrito 1248, Buenos Aires.

Australia National Committee for Antarctic Research, Australian Academy of Science, P.O. Box 783, Canberra, ACT 2601
Antarctic Division, Channel Highway, Kingston, Tasmania 7150

Belgium Comité national belge pour les Recherches dans l'Antarctique, Institut royal des sciences naturelles de Belgique, rue Vautier 29, B-1040 Bruxelles

Brazil Comissao Nacional de Pesquisas Antarcticas, Av. W3 Norte, Quadra 511, Bloco 'A', Edificio Bittar II, 3a Adar, 70750 Brasilia.
Instituto Brasileiro de Estudos Antarcticos, Av. Rio Branco 124, 22 Pav., Rio de Janeiro

Chile Comité Nacional de Investigaciónes Antárcticas, Avenue Luis Thayer Ojedo 814, Santiago

China, People's Republic National Committee for Antarctic Research, China Association for Science and Technology, Beijing

France Comité National Français des Recherches Antarctiques, 39ter rue Gay-Lussac, 75005 Paris

Germany, Democratic Republic National Committee on Antarctic Research, Telegrafenberg, DDR-1500 Potsdam

Germany, Federal Republic SCAR National Committee, Deutsche Forschungsgemeinshaft, Kennedyalle 40, 5300 Bonn – Bad Godesburg 1
Alfred Wegener Institut für Polarforschung, Columbus Center, D-2850 Bremerhaven

India Department of Ocean Development, South Block, New Delhi 110001
National Committee for Antarctic Research, Indian National Science Academy, Bahadur Shah Zafar Marg, New Delhi 110002

Japan National Antarctic Committee, Science Council of Japan, 22–34 Roppongi 7, Minato-ku, Tokyo
National Institute for Polar Research, 9–10 Kaga 1-chome, Itabashi-ku, Tokyo 173

New Zealand National Committee on Antarctic Research, PO Box 13247, Armagh Post Office, Christchurch
Antarctic Division, DSIR, PO Box 13247, Armagh Post Office, Christchurch

Norway Norwegian National Committee on Polar Research, Norsk Polarinstitutet, Rolfstangveien 12, Postboks 158, 1330 Oslo Lufthavn

Poland Komitet badan Polarnych PAN, PKiN, pok 2100, 00-901 Warszawa

South Africa South African Scientific Committee for Antarctic Research, CSIR, PO Box 395, Pretoria 0001

Soviet Union Soviet Committee on Antarctic Research, Academy of Sciences for the USSR, U1 Vavilova 44, Building 2, Moscow B-333
Arctic and Antarctic Institute, Fontanka 34, Leningrad 192104

United Kingdom British National Committee on Antarctic Research, Royal Society, 6 Carlton House Terrace, London SW1Y 5AG
Scott Polar Research Institute, Lensfield Road, Cambridge CB2 1ER
British Antarctic Survey, Madingley Road, Cambridge CB3 OET

United States of America Polar Research Board, National Research Council, Commission on Physical Sciences, Mathematics and Resources, 2101 Constitution Avenue, Washington DC 20418

Uruguay Instituto Antártico Uruguayo, Casilla Correo 10, Montevideo

Acknowledgements

The contributors wish to acknowledge first the support and assistance of their wives and families during the long gestation period of this volume.

We wish to thank the following organisations for the use of material included in this volume:

British Antarctic Survey, Scott Polar Research Institute, SCAR, Alfred Wegener Institute, Antarctic Division (New Zealand), Antarctic Division (Australia), NASA, NOAA, Trans Antarctic Association, Mitchell Library, National Science Foundation (Division of Polar Programs), US Navy, Scripps Institution of Oceanography, University of Alaska, University of Iowa, University of Delaware.

Diagrammatic material has been redrawn from journals and books published by Academic Press, Macmillan, American Geophysical Union, Pergamon Press, Cambridge University Press, Elsevier.

Photographers contributing to the volume were:

D. G. Allen, W. Block, W. N. Bonner, S. Bowling, D. Carpenter, G. C. S. Claridge, J. G. Cogley, J. C. Ellis-Evans, I. Everson, C. J. Gilbert, A. J. Gow, T. Guilfoyle (IBEA), D. Hamer, L. D. B. Herrod, T. Hoshiai, R. M. Laws, R. Ledingham, E. C. G. Lemon, I. W. Lovegrove, T. S. McCann, J. G. Paren, D. A. Peel, M. A. Pomerantz, R. A. Price, P. A. Prince, R. G. B. Renner, A. S. Rodger, M. Sanders, C. Scott, J. Siren, I. Somerton, C. W. M. Swithinbank, B. Thomas, W. Vaughan, R. Vondrak, D. W. H. Walton, M. G. White, D. D. Wynn-Williams.

British Antarctic Survey provided the resources for the preparation of the text and diagrams. We wish to thank Miss S. Norris and Mrs S. Murray for all their efforts in the preparation of the volume.

Select bibliography

Antarctic literature now consists of a large number of books and articles published in many languages. Details of the majority of these, both general and scientific, can be found in a specialist bibliography of 15 volumes (see below). In addition, many of the scientific and technical papers are available in an on-line data base. An important source of information are the symposia sponsored by SCAR (Appendix 2) and details of the most recent of these are listed below.

This bibliography aims to introduce the interested reader to some key publications within each scientific field, providing a gateway to more detailed information available from specialist libraries.

The two largest libraries in the world for Antarctic literature are the Scott Polar Research Institute, Lensfield Road, Cambridge, UK, and Cold Regions Bibliography Project, Science and Technology Division, Library of Congress, Washington DC 20540, USA.

Bibliographies and recent SCAR symposia

[Roscoe J] (1968) *Antarctic Bibliography*. Greenwood Press, New York. 147 p. Covers period up to 1951.

[Thuronyi G] (1970 – current) *Antarctic Bibliography*. Library of Congress, Washington DC. 14 volumes + indices, covering 1951 to present.

Cold Regions Database (access through 'ORBIT'). File covers period 1962 to present and contains scientific and technical publications pertaining to snow, ice, permafrost and frozen ground.

Oliver RL, James PR and Jago JB (eds) (1983) *Antarctic Earth Science. Proceedings of the Fourth International Symposium on Antarctic Earth Sciences, held at the University of Adelaide, South Australia, 16–20 August 1982*. Australian Academy of Sciences, Canberra. 697 p.

Siegfried WR, Condy PR and Laws RM (eds) (1985) *Antarctic Nutrient Cycles and Food Webs. Fourth SCAR Symposium on Antarctic Biology, Wilderness, South Africa, 12–16 September 1983*. Springer Verlag, New York. 700 p.

[Swithinbank CWM *et al.*] (eds) (1982) *Proceedings of the Third International Symposium on Antarctic Glaciology, Ohio State University, Columbus, Ohio, 7–12 September 1981*. International Glaciological Society, Cambridge. 361 p.

Part I

American Geographical Society (1975) *History of Antarctic Exploration and Scientific Investigation*. Antarctic Map Folio Series, Folio 19.

Auburn FM (1982) *Antarctic Law and Politics*. Hurst, London. 361 p.

Beck P (1986) *The International Politics of Antarctica*. Croom Helm, London.

Bertrand KJ (1971) *Americans in Antarctica 1775–1948*. American Geographical Society, New York. 834 p.

Fuchs VE (1982) *Of Ice and Men – the story of the British Antarctic Survey 1943–73*. Anthony Nelson, Oswestry. 383 p.

Fuchs VE and Laws RM (eds) (1977) *Scientific Research in Antarctica*. The Royal Society, London. 288 p.

Gould LM *et al.* (1967) Antarctic. *Annals of the International Geophysical Year* 44, 1–201.

Hardy A (1967) *Great Waters*. Collins, London. 542 p.

Headland RK (1986) *Chronological List of Antarctic Expeditions and Related Historical Events*. Cambridge University Press, Cambridge.

King HGR (1969) *The Antarctic*. Blandford Press, London. 276 p.

Lovering JF and Prescott JRV (1979) *Last of Lands – Antarctica*. Melbourne University Press, Carlton. 212 p.

McWhinnie MA (ed) (1978) *Polar Research – To the Present and the Future*. AAAS Selected Symposium 7. Westview Press, Boulder. 309 p.

Orrego Vicuna F (ed) (1983) *Antarctic Resources Policy – scientific, legal and political issues*. Cambridge University Press, Cambridge. 335 p.

Orrego Vicuna F and Salinas Araya, A. (1978) *El Desarrolo de la Antartica*. Editorial Universitaria, Santiago. 374 p.

Priestley RE, Adie RJ and Robin G de Q (eds) (1964) *Antarctic Research. A Review of British Scientific Achievement in Antarctica*. Butterworth, London. 360 p.

Quartermain LB (1967) *South to the Pole: the early history of the Ross Sea Sector, Antarctica*. Oxford University Press, Oxford.

Quigg PW (1983) *A Pole Apart – the emerging issue of Antarctica*. McGraw Hill, New York. 299 p.

Sullivan W (1957) *Quest for a Continent*. McGraw Hill, New York. 372 p.

Sullivan W (1961) *Assault on the Unknown – the International Geophysical Year*. McGraw Hill, New York. 460 p.

Tonnessen JN and Johnsen AO (1982) *The History of Modern Whaling*. Hurst, London.

Van Mieghem J and Van Oye P (eds) (1965) *Biogeography and Ecology in Antarctica*. Junk, The Hague. 762 p.

Part II

Bonner WN (1980) *Whales*. Blandford Press, Poole. 278 p.

Bonner WN (1982) *Seals and Man. A Study of Interactions*. University of Washington Press, Seattle. 170 p.

Bonner WN and Berry RJ (eds) (1980) *Ecology in the Antarctic*. Academic Press, London. 150 p.

Bonner WN and Walton DWH (eds) (1985) *Key Environments – Antarctica*. Pergamon Press, Oxford. 381 p.

Clarke A (1983) Life in cold water: the physiological ecology of polar marine ectotherms. *Oceanography and Marine Biology Annual Review*, 21, 341–453.

Everson I (1977) *The Living Resources of the Southern Ocean*. Food and Agriculture Organisation, Rome. 156 p.

Holdgate MW (ed) (1970) *Antarctic Ecology*. 2 vols. Academic Press, London. 998 p.

Kock K-H, Duhamel G and Hureau J-C (1985) Biology and status of exploited Antarctic fish stocks: a review. *BIOMASS Scientific Series* No. 6, 1–143.

Laws RM (ed) (1984) *Antarctic Ecology*. 2 vols. Academic Press, London. 850 p.

Llano GA (ed) (1977) *Adaptations within Antarctic Ecosystems. Proceedings of the Third SCAR Symposium on Antarctic Biology.* Smithsonian Institution, Washington DC. 1252 p.

Smith JE (ed) (1967) A discussion on the terrestrial Antarctic ecosystem. *Philosophical Transactions of the Royal Society, Series B*, 252, 167–392.

Stonehouse B (1972) *Animals of the Antarctic: the ecology of the far south.* Peter Lowe, London. 171 p.

Part III

Adie RJ (ed) (1972) *Symposium on Antarctic Geology and Solid Earth Geophysics. Oslo, 1970.* Universitetsforlaget, Oslo. 875 p.

Behrendt JE (ed) (1983) Petroleum and mineral resources of Antarctica. *United States Geological Survey Circular* No. 909.

Craddock C (ed) (1982) *Antarctic Geoscience. Symposium on Antarctic Geology and Geophysics, Madison, Wisconsin, 22–27 August, 1977.* University of Wisconsin Press, Madison. 1172 p.

Drewry DJ (ed) (1983) *Antarctica: glaciological and geophysical folio.* Scott Polar Research Institute, Cambridge.

Husseiny AA (ed) (1978) *Iceberg Utilization.* Pergamon Press, New York. 760 p.

Imbrie J and Imbrie IP (1979) *Ice Ages.* Macmillan, London. 224 p.

Kerr RA (1984) Icecap of 30 million years ago detected. *Science*, 224, 141–142.

Lorius C *et al.* (1985) A 150 000 year climate record from Antarctic ice. *Nature*, 416, 591–596.

McGinnis LD (ed) (1981) *Dry Valley Drilling Project.* Antarctic Research Series No. 33. American Geophysical Union, Washington DC. 465 p.

Paterson WSB (1981) *The Physics of Glaciers.* Pergamon Press, Oxford. 380 p.

Peel DA (1983) Antarctic ice: the frozen time capsule. *New Scientist*, 98, 476–479.

[Polar Research Board] (1985) *Glaciers, Ice Sheets and Sea Level: effect of a CO_2-induced climatic change.* Report of a workshop held in Seattle, Washington, 13–15 September 1984. National Technical Information Service, Springfield. 320 p.

Pritchard RS (ed) (1980) *Sea Ice Processes and Models.* University of Washington Press, Seattle. 474 p.

Robin G de Q (ed) (1983) *The Climatic Record in Polar Ice Sheets.* Cambridge University Press, Cambridge. 212 p.

Swithinbank CWS, McClain P and Little P (1977) Drift tracks of Antarctic icebergs. *Polar Record*, 18, 495–501.

Wolff EW and Peel DA (1985) The record of global pollution in polar snow and ice. *Nature*, 313, 535–540.

Zumberge JH (ed) *Possible Environmental Effects of Mineral Exploration and Exploitation in Antarctica.* SCAR, Cambridge. 59 p.

Zwally HJ (1984) Observing polar ice variability. *Annals of Glaciology*, 5, 191–198.

Part IV

Dudeney JR (1981) The ionosphere, a view from the Pole. *New Scientist*, 91, 714–717.

Eather RH (1980) *Majestic Heights: the aurora in science, history and the arts.* American Geophysical Union, Washington DC. 323 p.

Farman JC, Gardiner BG and Shanklin JD (1985) Large losses of total ozone in Antarctica reveal seasonal ClO_x/NO_x interactions. *Nature*, 315, 207–210.

Frakes LA (1979) *Climate through Geological Time.* Elsevier, Amsterdam. 310 p.

Hargreaves JK (1979) *The Upper Atmosphere and Solar Terrestrial Relations, an Introduction to the Geospace Environment.* Van Nostrand Reinhold, London. 298 p.

Lamb HH (1972) *Climate: Present, Past and Future. Vol. 1. Fundamentals and climate Now.* Methuen, London. 613 p.

Lamb HH (1977) *Climate: Present, Past and Future. Vol. 2. Climate History and the Future.* Methuen, London. 835 p.

Lanzerotti LJ and Park CG (eds) (1978) *Upper Atmosphere Research in Antarctica.* Antarctic Research Series No. 29. American Geophysical Union, Washington DC. 264 p.

Ratcliffe JA (1970) *Sun, Earth and Radio: an introduction to the ionosphere and magnetosphere.* Weidenfeld and Nicolson, London. 256 p.

Rubin MJ (1962) The Antarctic and the weather. *Scientific American*, 207, 84–94.

Rycroft MJ (1985) A view of the upper atmosphere from Antarctica. *New Scientist*, 108, 44–51.

Schwerdtfeger W (1984) *Weather and Climate of the Antarctic.* Developments in Atmospheric Science No. 15. Elsevier, Amsterdam. 261 p.

Index

Numbers in **bold type** refer to illustrations